False Consciousness

EXPLORATIONS IN
INTERPRETATIVE SOCIOLOGY

GENERAL EDITORS

PHILIP RIEFF

Benjamin Franklin Professor of Sociology
University of Pennsylvania

BRYAN R. WILSON

Reader in Sociology, University of Oxford
Fellow of All Souls College

Also in this series

THE SOCIAL FRAMEWORKS OF KNOWLEDGE

Georges Gurvitch
Translated by M. A. and K. A. Thompson

FROM SYMBOLISM TO STRUCTURALISM:

Lévi-Strauss in a Literary Tradition
James A. Boon

LUCIEN LÉVY-BRUHL

Jean Cazeneuve
Translated by Peter Rivière

IDEOLOGY AND THE IDEOLOGISTS

Lewis S. Feuer

GURVITCH

Georges Balandier
Translated by M. A. and K. A. Thompson

CARNETS

Lucien Lévy-Bruhl
Translated by Peter Rivière

False Consciousness

An Essay on Reification

JOSEPH GABEL

Translated from the French by
MARGARET A. THOMPSON
With the assistance of
KENNETH A. THOMPSON

Introduction by
KENNETH A. THOMPSON

Harper & Row Publishers
New York, Evanston, San Francisco

LIBRARY OF CONGRESS CATALOG CARD NUMBER: 75-9377

STANDARD BOOK NUMBER: 0-06-136177-1

First published in French as *La fausse conscience*
copyright © Editions de Minuit, Paris, 1962, and
translated by arrangement.

PRINTED IN GREAT BRITAIN

Contents

Contents

Introduction

In this study of false consciousness Joseph Gabel sets out to give a new cutting-edge to a concept that has been badly blunted by constant misuse. At the same time he is offering a contribution to the development of a general psycho-sociological theory of consciousness and of the conditions of dialectical thought in particular. To this end he uses a method of 'socio-pathological parallelism', drawing parallels between a reified, non-dialectical perception in the socio-political sphere (false consciousness) and in the clinical-psychiatric sphere (schizophrenia). The key similarities are in the basic orientations to space and time in each case. To put it crudely: false consciousness and schizophrenia tend to over-spatialize and under-temporalize.

Whether Gabel's attempt to rejuvenate the concept of false consciousness is likely to be successful must be left for the reader to judge. What is certain is that, in making the attempt, he provides a fascinating demonstration of the possibilities for cross-fertilization between Marxist social theory, existential psychiatry and phenomenological sociology. Each of these perspectives has its own insights to offer on false consciousness and to some extent they are complementary and convergent.

The contributions of Marxist theory to the topic are perhaps sufficiently well known to obviate the need for any introduction here. Gabel surveys them in some detail. He regrets the polemical usage of the concept by those so-called orthodox Marxists who strive to preserve a closed, dogmatic system from internal deviation or external contamination. He states his preference for a more open Marxism which is not afraid of embracing within itself varieties and disagreements and adopting new insights from outside. It is not surprising, therefore, that he focuses mainly on the unorthodox Marxism of Georg Lukács's *History and Class Consciousness* when searching for a Marxist theory of consciousness that can integrate the key concepts of false consciousness, alienation and ideology. The common denominator for these concepts is *reification*, and this is the main ingredient of that particular sub-dialectical rationality which Gabel claims is common to both false consciousness and schizophrenia.

The aspects of Lukács's discussion of reification which are most useful for drawing parallels with findings on schizophrenia are those concerning the effect of rationalization of labour under capitalism in transforming 'the basic categories of man's immediate attitude to the world: it reduces space and time to a common denominator and degrades time to the dimension of space'.[1] The connections between this process of transformation of basic categories of orientation (spatialization of time) and the conditions of alienation and false consciousness are spelled out in an illuminating passage. Having quoted Marx's description of the way in which, through the subordination of man to the machine, men are effaced by their labour, 'in which the pendulum of the clock has become as accurate a measure of the relative activity of two workers as it is of the speed of two locomotives', Lukács comments:

> Thus time sheds its qualitative, variable, flowing nature; it freezes into an exactly delimited, quantifiable continuum filled with quantifiable 'things' (the reified, mechanically objectified 'performance' of the worker, wholly separated from his total personality): in short, it becomes space. In this environment where time is transformed into abstract, exactly measurable, physical space, an environment at once the cause and effect of the scientifically and mechanically fragmented and specialized production of the object of labour, the subjects

[1] Georg Lukács, *History and Class Consciousness*, trs. Rodney Livingstone, London, Merlin Press, 1971, p. 89. It is worth noting here the parallel between Lukács's phrase 'the basic categories of man's immediate attitude to the world' and the term 'mode of being-in-the-world' which is used by existential psychiatrists and phenomenological sociologists.

of labour must likewise be rationally fragmented. On the one hand, the objectification of their labour-power into something opposed to their total personality (a process already accomplished with the sale of that labour-power as a commodity) is now made into the permanent ineluctable reality of their daily life. Here, too, the personality can do no more than look on helplessly while its own existence is reduced to an isolated particle and fed into an alien system. On the other hand, the mechanical disintegration of the process of production into its components also destroys those bonds that had bound individuals to a community in the days when production was still 'organic'. In this respect, too, mechanisation makes of them isolated abstract atoms whose work no longer brings them together directly and organically; it becomes mediated to an increasing extent exclusively by the abstract laws of the mechanism which imprisons them.[2]

Gabel points out in some detail the parallels between this mode of being-in-the-world and the findings of psychiatrists about schizophrenia. More specifically, he discusses the findings of 'existential psychiatrists' about the constituents of the mode of being-in-the-world of schizophrenics. Phenomenological and existential psychiatry began in the work of Minkowski and Binswanger in the inter-war period, and it shares with the more recent tradition dating from Dilthey, the conviction that the humanistic disciplines should employ a humanistic conception of 'understanding'. Thus, the delusions of the schizophrenic do not require us to instantly search for a causal explanation in terms of 'outside' physiological or Unconscious facts. We should first of all seek to understand them as organized systems of meaning produced by the subject to balance and disguise the disorder of his being-in-the world and the disintegration of his personality.[3] The first task, therefore, is to decipher the 'internal' rationality of the system of meaning; and, in the terms of what became known as *Daseinsanalyse*, to analyse the individual's particular mode of being-in-the-world.

---

[2] Ibid., p. 90.
[3] Maurice Roche, *Phenomenology, Language and the Social Sciences*, London, Routledge and Kegan Paul, 1973, p. 211.

We will not embark on a history of the existential movement in psychology; that has already been provided by Rollo May and his associates in their famous volume *Existence: A New Dimension in Psychiatry and Psychology* (1958). However, as Gabel makes frequent references to the work of members of that movement, without always explaining the general character of the movement and the derivation of its key concepts and methods, it might be worth sketching out its main features.

The movement sprang up spontaneously in different parts of Europe in the 1920s. The chief figures were Eugene Minkowski in Paris, Erwin Strauss in Germany and then America, and V. E. von Gebsattel in Germany, who represented the first, or pheno-menological, stage of the movement. The second stage, which Rollo May has termed the existential stage, was represented by Ludwig Binswanger, A. Storch, M. Boss, G. Bally, Roland Kuhn in Switzerland, and J. H. Van Den Berg and F. J. Buytendijk in Holland, followed by numerous 'practitioners' in America. The major philosophical influences were Husserl in phenomenology and Heidegger in existentialism, but there is no real break between the two. In fact, of course, Heidegger was a pupil of Husserl, and Heidegger's philosophy has been described as a phenomenology of human *Dasein*: it is based on the contrast between existence as *Vorhandensein* (characteristic of things) and as *Dasein* (for human beings). *Dasein* is a difficult word to trans-late, but as Binswanger and others designate their school as *Daseinsanalyse* it is obviously crucial. Its significance is revealed if we keep in mind that it is made out of a combination of *sein* (being) and *da* (there); the emphasis is on the fact that 'man is the being who *is there* and implies also that he *has* a "there" in the sense that he can know he is there and can take a stand with reference to that fact'.[4] In English the term 'being' tends to have a rather static and passive connotation when used as a general noun, in contrast to the meaning of *Sein*, which suggests an active *becoming*. It is this latter aspect of being—its potenti-ality and the possibility of choice and active design—which is stressed by existentialism.

The main emphasis of psychiatric phenomenology has been

[4] Rollo May, op. cit., p. 41.

on investigation of the patient's subjective states of consciousness. It does not oppose other approaches, such as endocrinological and chemico-biological psychiatry or psychoanalysis, but rather insists on the need to also try to understand what the psychotic individual really experiences. Phenomenological psychiatry has adopted a 'categorical' frame of reference as a method of investigating the structure of states of consciousness, attempting to reconstruct the inner world of patients through an analysis of basic categories of inner experiences such as time, space, causality and materiality. The two basic categories of inner experience, time and space, are examined in great detail.

To the phenomenologist the category of time is of crucial importance and it featured prominently in the works of Husserl and Heidegger. Especially strong in its influence on Minkowski was Bergson's contrast between experienced 'duration', the subjective time of inner experience, and 'homogeneous time', the quantified, spatialized time of the clock and the calendar. The capacity to transcend the immediate boundaries of time, to see one's experience self-consciously in terms of the past and the future, is the unique quality of human existence. Human existence is always in a state of becoming. The first major work by Minkowski was concerned with interpreting a case of schizophrenia in terms of this Bergsonian view of the time dimension.

In this essay of 1923,[5] Minkowski discussed the case of a depressed schizophrenic who possessed extremely strong guilt feelings and delusions of persecution. The patient's most terrifying delusion was his feeling each morning that he was going to be tortured to death that evening, the certainty of which was never shaken by its failure to happen the previous day. As far as the patient was concerned each day was a separate island with no past and no future. His experience of time was completely fragmented, rather than flowing; the future was 'blocked'. Traditionally, and in Freudian psychiatry, the distortion of experienced time would be explained by some cause located in a

[5] E. Minkowski, 'Etude psychologique et analyse phénoménologique d'un cas de mélancolie schizophrénique' in *Journal de Psychologie normale et pathologique*, vol. 20, 1923, pp. 543–58.

physiological abnormality or in the patient's sexual Unconscious. But Minkowski saw no need to 'reduce' matters in this way. He proposed that the distorted attitude towards time should itself be taken as the basic disorder. This thought 'disorder' was part of the organized system of meaning produced by the patient to balance and disguise the disorder of his being-in-the-world, and the disintegration of his personality. Thus thought disorders are reflections of down to earth existential disorders. What Minkowski did not throw much new light on was why a person's mode of existence, or mode of being-in-the-world, should have become so disturbed. Why should the patient think his future is blocked?

It is here that Binswanger and existential analysis went beyond Minkowski. Binswanger was one of Freud's earliest followers and remained a close friend even after he gave up Freud's theories. Although he was one of the first proponents of phenomenological psychiatry alongside Minkowski in the early 1920s, he later shifted towards existential analysis. His new system was expounded in his major work of 1942,[6] and later illustrated in several famous case studies of schizophrenics: Ilse, Ellen West, Jürg Zünd, Lola Voss, and Suzanne Urban.[7]

The few differences between phenomenology and existential analysis have been summarized as follows:

1. Existential analysis does not restrict itself to the investigation of states of *consciousness*, but takes into account the entire structure of *existence* of the individual.

2. Whereas phenomenology had emphasized the unity of the individual's inner world of experience, existential analysis emphasizes that one individual may live in two or more, sometimes conflicting, 'worlds'.

3. Phenomenology takes into account only immediate subjective worlds of experience. Existential analysis strives to reconstruct the development and transformations of the individual's 'world' or conflicting 'worlds'. Binswanger stressed the fact that

[6] *Grundformen und Erkenntnis menschlichen Daseins* (Basic Forms and Cognition of Human Existence), Zurich, 1942.

[7] *Schizophrenie*, Pfullingen, 1957.

this study implies a biographic investigation conducted according to psychoanalytic methods.[8]

Binswanger stated that existential analysis took as its philosophical foundation Heidegger's account of the fundamental structure of existence and his description of it as *being-in-the-world*. The formulation *being-in-the-world* as used by Heidegger, is, therefore, in the nature of an ontological statement, a thesis about an essential condition that determines human existence in general. In particular it identifies being-in-the-world with the notion of transcendence or transcending (*Ueberstieg*)—the unique capacity of human beings for transcending the immediate situation, which in turn depends upon man's self-awareness. This is man's essential freedom: to reflect on past and future, to symbolize, to take responsibility for designing one's own world. Binswanger insisted that existential analysis was not itself a philosophy, although it built on Heidegger's philosophy: it was intended to be an empirical science, and its *ontic statements* would be statements of factual findings about actually appearing forms and configurations of existence. Thus it would study different models of being-in-the-world, different types of 'world-formation' or 'world-design' as these could be discerned in the life-history of patients.

The essential human freedom of taking responsibility for one's own 'world-formation' or 'world-design' is lost when the individual is overwhelmed by a single 'world-design' (*mundanization*). This can occur for many reasons, but it is characterized, according to Gabel, by the common denominator of loss of a sense of dialectical flux and by a process of reification of the world-design. The chief symptom of this common denominator is the spatialization of time in the structure of the mode of being-in-the-world of the schizophrenic and in the state of false consciousness in the socio-political sphere. Binswanger stated that time is the central problem for existential analysis because 'transcendence is rooted in the very nature of time, in its unfolding into future, "having been" (*Gewesenheit*), and present'.[9] And Gabel notes that time is a dialectical dimension not only because, contrary to

[8] Henri F. Ellenberger in May, op. cit., p. 121.
[9] Binswanger in May, op. cit., p. 194.

space, it is impossible to conceive of it in a state of rest, but also because its progression effects a dialectical synthesis, which is constantly being recreated, from its three dimensions of present, past and future. It is a totality which can be dissociated by reification of the past or the future, and examples of this can be found in ideological thought (reification of the past), utopian thought (reification of the future) and in schizophrenia. Such dissociation in all cases produces a perception which is out of touch with reality—a false consciousness.

The emphasis by existential psychiatry on the concept of *being-in-the-world*, with its implicit inclusion of social relationships, brings this school close to humanistic and phenomenological sociology. Heidegger's ontology distinguishes three modes of world, or three simultaneous aspects of our being-in-the-world: *Umwelt*, literally meaning 'world around', includes biological needs, drives and instincts; *Mitwelt*, literally the 'with-world', is the world of interrelationships with other human beings; *Eigenwelt*, the 'own-world', is the mode of relationship to one's self. Binswanger held that classical psychoanalysis dealt only with the *Umwelt*, the mode of instincts, drives, contingency, biological determinism; and the *Mitwelt* of social relationships is treated as an epiphenomenon of *Umwelt*. Classical sociology, of a positivist or over-determinist kind, was likewise tempted to emphasize the *Mitwelt* to the exclusion of the *Eigenwelt*, taking an over-socialized view of man, so that he was regarded simply as the sum of the roles he is required to play. Humanistic sociology, like existential psychiatry, has constantly sought to regain a balanced view of human existence, which gives due weight to the *Eigenwelt* aspect. From Max Weber and George Herbert Mead onwards it has called attention to the need to take account of 'the self in relation to itself'.

Recent humanistic sociology of a phenomenological kind has drawn even closer to existential psychiatry in its ontological commitments, its descriptivist method, and its anti-reductionism. These shared characteristics are illustrated by the attention paid to understanding modes of being-in-the-world in terms of the person's own terms and concepts rather than externally imposed or derived ones. As Binswanger puts it for existential analysis:

It can let existence actually speak up about itself—let it have its say. In other words, the phenomena to be interpreted are largely language phenomena. We know that the content of existence can nowhere be more clearly seen or more securely interpreted than through language; because it is in language that our world-designs actually ensconce and articulate themselves and where, therefore, they can be ascertained and communicated.[10]

The main contribution of these phenomenological approaches to elucidating the nature of false consciousness is that they take seriously the task of discovering how people actually 'do' their thinking and their being. The existence of social structures such as classes, capitalism, families, nations, and bureaucracies, is not called into question by insisting that when it comes to explaining how they determine action we need to understand how they are present in people's experiences. And there is no substitute here for studying the formulations and rationalities of the people concerned, for this reveals how they experience the structures.

Gabel began his study by asking the question: Why is it that the concept of false consciousness has not become as popular as other Marxist concepts in bourgeois academic circles, part of the general *embourgeoisment* of Marxist ideas? His answer was that the problem of securing agreement on the criterion of authenticity or falsity of consciousness had seemed insoluble. At the very least, this book throws new light on the issue and, more ambitiously, it makes a substantial contribution to the development of a general psycho-sociological theory of consciousness.

Kenneth A. Thompson
The Open University

---

[10] Binswanger in May, op. cit., p. 200.

I dedicate this book, which is written to oppose fanaticism of all kinds, to the memory of my mother who disappeared at Auschwitz in 1945 and my father who died unconsoled in New York in 1968.

Preface

Recent history has witnessed two major explosions of false consciousness: racism and Stalinist ideology. They belong to the past, but their passing has provided invaluable evidence that false consciousness—treated by traditional Marxism as a rather academic concept—is ever present in our daily life and can have tragic consequences.

Marxist literature includes relatively few works devoted exclusively to false consciousness. Apart from a forgotten essay by P. Szende[1] it is particularly worth mentioning in this context, Mannheim's *Ideologie und Utopie* and Lukács's *Histoire et Conscience de Classe*. Mannheim's work has exercised no mean influence on Anglo-Saxon intellectual life; Lukács's work—aided by enthusiastic disciples and a belated, but quite first-class, translation[2]—left its mark on a whole area of French thought.[3] It had even more success abroad than in his own country and the 'Lukács case', which was the main talking point in philosophical circles round about 1951, is still widely remembered. I shall avoid reopening this case which is, fortunately, now closed. One fact, however, deserves to be emphasized, for it throws crucial light on the central problem of my study: it was not as an idealist that Lukács became the object of censure—but mainly as a *dialectical theorist of false consciousness*, who was involved in a political system which could not admit the legitimacy of the

[1] I am thinking of P. Szende's *Verhüllung und Enthüllung* (439) which appeared in 1922.
[2] *Histoire et Conscience de Classe*. French translation by K. Axelos and J. Bois, preface by K. Axelos, Paris, Edition de Minuit, 1960.
[3] Cf. *Aventures de la Dialectique* by M. Merleau-Ponty.

problem of false consciousness without its undermining the ideological foundations of its own existence.[4]

This is perhaps the crux of the problem. Theoretical Marxism is essentially critical of false consciousness, but political Marxism *is* false consciousness. It is not an appendage to Marxist politics; in the form of *ideology* or *utopia*, false consciousness is a corollary of concrete political action.[5] *Praxis* is dereifying and dialecticizing; effective political practice is forced to use techniques of collective persuasion which reify and de-dialecticize thought.

'The drama of alienation is dialectical' said H. Lefebvre.[6] An excellent observation, but one which requires concrete content. I have turned to psychopathology for this 'concrete content' convinced that a Marxist theory of consciousness, whose absence Merleau-Ponty noted,[7] is to be found at the intersection of findings from the study of pathological consciousness and false consciousness. *Schizophrenia*—described by one psychiatrist[8] as *Nature's great experiment*—in fact clearly represents a form of reified consciousness, characterized on the existential level by a deterioration of dialectical *praxis*, and on the intellectual level by a de-dialecticization of cognitive functions, a phenomenon described long ago by E. Minkowski as *morbid rationalism*.[9]

---

[4] Cf. in this connection my article (170). The curious thing was that these criticisms and Lukács's own self-criticism at the time were essentially concerned with the aesthetician and the literary theorist, though it was mainly on the practical level that the diffusion of the ideas in *Histoire et Conscience de Classe* needed to be prevented. The discussion of the 'Lukács case' took place in an atmosphere that was typical of *Verhüllung*; a climate of false consciousness.

[5] It would be interesting to study the *utopian* climate which was prevalent in France at the time of the fall of the Fourth Republic and the inception of the Fifth.

[6] H. Lefebvre (299), p. 111.

[7] Merleau-Ponty (328), p. 58, '. . . Marxism needs a theory of consciousness'.

[8] This is the Viennese psychiatrist, Josef Berze, author of a brilliant (but forgotten) work on schizophrenia (51).

[9] The idea of the loss of dialectical *praxis* among schizophrenics is one of the central ideas of L. Binswanger's pathographies which appeared in the *Archives Suisses de Psychiatrie* between 1944 and

The appropriate rationality of false consciousness, characterized by a loss of the dialectical quality of thought[10] is therefore clearly a social form of morbid rationalism; inversely, I consider the onset of schizophrenia as an individual form of false consciousness. This mental state therefore constitutes a real bridge between the areas of social and clinical alienation; it is a form of alienation both in the Marxist sense and in the psychiatric meaning of the term. It is significant in this regard that the writings of the young Marx devoted to the alienation of human work, anticipated certain mechanisms that psychiatrists discovered only much later in their own research.[11] This is a phenomenon that—to borrow H. Aubin's expression—could be described as *socio-pathological parallelism.*[12]

Examples in psychopathology of this parallelism will be brought out in the second part of this study. Defined as an *individual form of false consciousness,* schizophrenia finds a new nosological unity centred on the concept of morbid rationalism within the framework of a unitary conception ('total concept') of alienation, capable of embracing both its social forms and its clinical aspects. As far as the problem of false consciousness is

1954. The hypothesis of a de-dialecticization of the cognitive functions is also implicit in Minkowski's theory (cf. the notion of 'morbid rationalism'). Since 1946 I have emphasized the importance of anti-dialectical identification in the morbid epistemology of the mentally sick (171 and 183) and in 1951 I attempted a Marxist reinterpretation of E. Minkowski's ideas in my article: *La Réification, Essai d'une psychopathologie de la pensée dialectique* (177).

Dr. Jacques Lacan, in his paper at the Congress of Rome in 1953 (275), spoke of the unusual make-up of a *madness which objectifies the subject in a language without dialectics* (cf. the account of J. Lacroix in *Le Monde* of the 19 July 1956). Given the dates, I formally reserve my rights of scientific priority as far as this interpretation is concerned.

[10] This is translated among other things, into the preponderance of the *spatial* element in relation to the temporal element in the perception of the world by false consciousness.

[11] Cf. my article 'Le concept de l'aliénation politique' (*Revue Française de Sociologie,* 1960, I, pp. 457–8) where I tried to demonstrate certain analogies between the concept of alienation as used by the young Marx and the Swiss psychiatrist Jacob Wyrsch (475).

[12] H. Aubin (21), p. 71.

concerned, my conception allows for the delimitation of its scope and the protection of its autonomy against encroachment from both sides.

In fact, non-Marxist thought risks seeing the theory of false consciousness as nothing more than a recasting of crowd psychology. Without going so far as to deny the importance of the constants of collective psychology in the process of de-realization of consciousness, my analysis, by showing that *individual* forms of false consciousness exist, constitutes a warning against this simplistic interpretation.

On the other hand, certain theorists influenced by dogmatic or official Marxism would want to reduce false consciousness to a system of errors issuing from class interest. From this viewpoint the theory of false consciousness would tend to be confused with a sort of sociology of knowledge of wishful thinking. This interpretation is eminently dangerous; in fact, by including too great a variety of forms of de-realist thought, it provides an obstacle to an over-all structural description; furthermore, it leads rather paradoxically to the dismissal of certain *legitimate* forms of false consciousness.[13] False consciousness thus defined runs the risk of degenerating into a catch-all concept, of weak explanatory value for actual events, of scanty speculative interest for the thinker desirous of achieving a synthesis.

This is a dilemma for which the use of the socio-pathological parallelism might offer a possible solution. Seen from the viewpoint of this parallelism, false consciousness, like mental disorder, involves a rationality of a particular type—a sub-dialectical rationality in my terms—*related to the person* by mechanisms

[13] The type of *self-interested illusion* is that of perpetual exiles who believe systematically that the regime that they are fighting is close to its downfall. The recent adventures of Cuban exiles graphically illustrate this form of illusion which, however, does not constitute an authentic form of false consciousness; it does not enter into any general interpretation of the phenomenon, be it Luckács's or Mannheim's or my own.

Inversely national-socialist ideology was the crystallization of an *authentic* form of false consciousness. Now, it could not be described as 'a system of errors issuing from class interest'; it was a genuine case of the development of collective mental disorder.

whose 'interest factor' is neither the exclusive driving force nor even the main driving force. It is not to be confused with collective psychology, nor with the effects of 'mass persuasion', even though it is partially dependent on both of these. Its most valid area of application is without doubt the elucidation of the problem of the totalitarian mentality.

To publish a work on false consciousness is always something of a gamble. Such a work risks offending prejudices and susceptibilities in a period of intense ideologizing and awakening only little interest during periods that are indifferent to ideology. There are intermediary periods—'twilight' times to borrow Karl Mannheim's expression[14]—which are conducive to the discussion of the problems of false consciousness, such as the latter years of the Weimar Republic or the end of the Fourth Republic in France. We are currently witnessing a certain decline in ideologies,[15] a phenomenon due to the importance attached to technology in East-West competition, and also, doubtless, to the sudden historical promotion of a Third World only moderately interested in ideological debates.

Must we conclude that there is a lessening of false consciousness in the world? This is by no means certain, even though this question has been raised, notably by Mannheim.[16] In the socialist camp of the future 'interpretative scholarship remains absolutely necessary; it need not permanently foster a kind of logical disorder'.[17] Written in 1955 by Raymond Aron, these lines are still relevant. Perhaps we are witnessing a decline in false consciousness in the East, a decline which could be due to the progress of socialist enlightenment; this is more or less I. Deutscher's

[14] Cf. the whole of this remarkable passage in *Ideologie und Utopie*, German edition, pp. 40–1.

[15] The term 'ideology' is used here in its Marxist sense: system of ideas subject to the charge of false consciousness. Cf. p. 14, Engels's definition and his discussion.

[16] Cf. in this connection an interesting passage in *Ideologie und Utopie* where Mannheim evokes the perspective of a 'total coincidence between existence and consciousness in a universe which has ceased being in a state of becoming' (German edition, p. 243).

[17] R. Aron, 'Idéologie communiste et religion', *La Revue de Paris*, May 1955.

interpretation. But one can just as validly diagnose it as an effect of the focusing of interest on the Third World which is more easily captivated by brilliant achievements in space than by the best of books on dialectical materialism. It is possible that we have witnessed a shifting of false consciousness to sectors of world opinion temporarily hostile to ideologies. Now if ideology is an expression of false consciousness, it is not false consciousness itself. We must avoid sharing the illusion of the sick person who believes that he is cured of his fever when he has broken his thermometer.

Royaumont, September 1961

Preface to the Third Edition

Since 1962 this thesis has been published in German and Italian; it has also stimulated rather a large number of reviews in the press. When a work is so well received at its publication, it is a gratifying outcome. It is not due—I hasten to add—to its 'merits' but mainly to the strong topicality of its subject-matter. The German minister for foreign affairs Willy Brandt warned some time ago of the danger of an 'outbreak of irrationality in the political sphere'. Sixteen years after the ideological phenomenon of Stalinism, the problem of false consciousness still remains.

At the same time one can see beginnings of the penetration of this concept into so-called 'bourgeois' university circles. This 'enbourgeoisement' of ideas of Marxist origin is characteristic of advanced industrial societies, which on the economic level have not hesitated in profiting from certain teachings from Marxist economics.[1] In the same way, these same ideas lose some of their potency in officially Marxist social contexts, hence a certain ideological levelling. It is actually easier—or, if you like, less risky—to support a Marxist thesis at the Sorbonne than in Moscow, not to mention Peking.

The concept of reification has been adopted in scientific circles which no longer remember many of its Marxist-Lukácsian origins. Amongst the numerous articles which attest to this fact I shall confine myself to quoting 'Langue et réification' by P. Souyris[2] and 'La Notion de réification dans la mythologie

---

[1] Cf. in this connection K. Mannheim's work: *Freedom, Power and Democratic Planning*, New York, Oxford University Press, 1950.

[2] *Esprit*, February 1967.

primitive' by L. Krader.[3] The 'Ethnologie générale' in the Pléiade Collection includes no less than eight references for the term 'reification'. As for the somewhat 'inflated' fortune of the theory of alienation, it is too well known to require lengthy consideration.

The concept of false consciousness has been somewhat slow to follow this course. Neglected on the 'left' as a possible instrument of an undesired demystification, suspected on the right for its Marxist origins, it has led a marginal existence for a long time. This ostracism is coming to an end. Certainly the number of publications devoted to the problem of false consciousness remains infinitesimal compared to the enormous amount of literature on alienation or reification. Nevertheless, one now has a choice, though not exactly an embarrassment of choices.

It would be as well to mention first the publications of R. Ruyer[4] who points out—as I do—an *individual* dimension to false consciousness. In an earlier work,[5] this author—referring to E. Minkowski's work—considered the schizophrenic character as well as the a-dialectical and anti-historical structure of *utopian* consciousness. If one accepts, as Mannheim does, that utopian consciousness is one aspect of false consciousness, then this tends to support my own interpretation. P. Ricoeur is also interested in this problem; one of his students has written a thesis on false consciousness in Nietzsche's work. A. Touraine seems to have discovered an interest in it during the recent student disputes.[6] In a work inspired by Lukács, Jean Ziegler[7] warns of the danger of false consciousness in the Third World. Finally, I shall quote an article by Paul Mattick on Karl Korsch; it is evident that Korsch, somewhat of an 'unattached intellectual' in the latter

[3] *Diogène*, October–December 1966 (56).

[4] R. Ruyer, 'L'Inconscience, la fausse conscience et l'inconscient', *Journal de psychologie normale et pathologique*, July–September 1966.

[5] R. Ruyer, *L'Utopie, les utopies*, Paris, P.U.F., 1950, pp. 70, 98, 107, 111, 120, 276 and *passim*.

[6] Cf. A. Touraine, *Le Mouvement de mai ou le communisme utopique*, Paris, Seuil, 1968, p. 75.

[7] Jean Ziegler, *Sociologie de la nouvelle Afrique*, Paris, Gallimard, 1964.

half of his career, used this category more deliberately than Lukács, who was very involved at that time in making a political choice.[8] Andreani, professor at the faculty of Nanterre, organized a seminar on the problem of false consciousness in 1968–9. Last but not least, a recent book of R. Aron's[9] gives the impression that the author now recognizes the importance of this problem for Marxist thought if not for political studies in general. Doubtless the next step will be the integration of false consciousness into the conceptual framework of political science, in the same way that reification is integrated into ethnology and psychology. It seems that this process is with us here and now.

A few remarks about certain criticisms. In an article where the present work is not explicitly quoted but which concerns it indirectly,[10] Raymond Ruyer observes that 'Marxism, like psychoanalysis, seeks to be a therapy, by means of true consciousness, for false consciousness caused by social existence or subconscious censorship'.[11] But these 'absolute theories' mutually expose each other, whence Ruyer's paradoxical conclusion that a psychiatrist or a psychoanalyst '. . . who is also a Marxist . . . seems

---

[8] Cf. P. Mattick, 'Karl Korsch', in *Les Cahiers de l'institut de science écononique appliquée*, August 1963, Suppl. no 140, pp. 159–180. Mattick particularly emphasizes the role of the category of false consciousness in his critical review of Korsch. Cf. quoted article, p. 167 and *passim*.

For his part, Lukács describes as false consciousness the illusion that economic life can be controlled within the frameworks of the capitalist system (*Geschichte u. Klassenbewusstsein*, p. 76). It is evident that too marked a polemical intention drains the category of false consciousness of all specific content. At best one could accuse him in 1923 of a *theoretical error*. In fact, the later evolution of capitalism shows that Lukács was quite mistaken.

[9] R. Aron, *D'une sainte famille à l'autre. Essai sur les marxismes imaginaires*, Paris, Gallimard, 1969.

[10] R. Ruyer, 'La Conscience et les théories des théories', *Revue de métaphysique et morale*, October–December 1967, pp. 406–13. Passage about the problem of false consciousness, p. 409.

[11] R. Ruyer, loc. cit., who repeats an old observation made by N. Berdiaeff. Cf. *Les Sources et le sens du communisme russe*, Paris, Gallimard, 1938, p. 131.

cruelly condemned to silence. Experience shows, however, that he produces work after work.'[12]

It would be easy for me to be ironical too. I prefer to take the objection seriously. Plain common sense—in complete harmony with 'experience'—suggests that the convergence of two doctrines on a specific question makes the position of those who hold both of them *more tenable*. Because all Christians believe in God, is it therefore reasonable to 'condemn to silence' all supporters of ecumenism? With Ruyer's logic one can prove anything. It is easy to 'functionalize' Christopher Columbus's discovery; to demonstrate—with S. Madariaga—the influence of Jewish psychology or of the Castilian political context. Must one conclude that America does not exist? Likewise, by exposing the psychological underpinnings of Marxist options, psychoanalysis *does not refute Marxism*; it confirms and implicitly extends the validity of a Marxist category. Convergence and concurrence should not be confused.

Robert Vander Gucht formulated some important epistemological observations concerning the limits of the normal and the pathological in terms of reification, relationships between science and ideology, etc. These same criticisms have been expressed by L. Goldmann but only during oral discussions. I have tried to reply to them.[13] I wish to thank Vander Gucht and the *Revue philosophique de Louvain* for their courtesy.

The main epistemological question which is raised here is certainly that of the *criterion* of authenticity or falsity of political consciousness; it is in short the problem of the normal and the pathological in sociology, a problem which was one of Durkheim's preoccupations. It is a singularly difficult problem, for the 'falseness' of a form of consciousness (its 'ideological' or 'utopian' character) is often revealed *post festum*; the Lukácsian text to which I referred earlier, constitutes a warning against the temptation to consider as 'false' *a priori* all manifestations of the adversary's consciousness. By emphasizing the existence of analogies

[12] Ruyer, loc. cit.

[13] Cf. *Revue philosophique de Louvain*, February 1964, pp. 189–192 and November 1964, pp. 97–105 (response to Vander Gucht). This later article appears in the appendix of this book.

in structure between social alienation and clinical alienation—
the problem of normality being practically if not theoretically
resolved for the latter—I believe that I have got somewhat
closer to solving this problem.[14]

Finally, Robert Paris reproaches me for 'using such an impre-
cise and unscientific category . . . as totalitarianism. . . . One might
wonder in fact if the subsumption under this term of such
different historical phenomena as Nazism or Stalinism is not
rather dependent on this type of false identification . . . that the
author puts at the centre of false consciousness.'[15] Certainly, no
one would dream of 'equating' Nazism, Fascism and Stalinism.
But neither could one prevent a historically oriented sociology
from observing the existence of certain analogies and from
questioning their meaning. The construction of 'ideal types' such
as *totalitarianism* or *totalitarian mentality* is part of the methodology of this interrogation; it is therefore a legitimate step if one
succeeds in avoiding the trap of ontologizing working hypotheses.[16] In the eyes of the contemporaries of Assurbanipal, there
was a huge chasm between the war methods of the Assyrians
and the Egyptians. 2,500 years later, however, the historical concept of 'oriental despotism' is still operational.

I would not want to end this preface without mentioning
some friends: Kostas Axelos who included this work in his
prestigious collection 'Arguments', Georges Lapassade who,

[14] This problem is central to Mannheim, but the solution that he
proposes is exclusively sociological and therefore insufficient. Mannheim considers the *intelligentsia* as a social stratum inclining towards
authentic consciousness; he tells us nothing about the criteria for this
authenticity. Now, in psychopathology and generally in medicine,
the discussion about criteria and limits of normality is theoretical; in
practice, no one considers schizophrenia or pneumonia as 'normal'
states. Consequently, the use of the schizophrenic nature of false consciousness as evidence may be considered as a step forward in the
search for an 'objective criterion'.

[15] R. Paris, 'La fausse conscience est-elle un concept opératoire?',
Annales E.S.C., May–June 1963, p. 599.

[16] This is precisely what Stalinism from 1950 onwards could not,
or would not, avoid. During that time it essentially equated Nazism
and American capitalism, postulating an uninterrupted continuity
between Hitler and Truman.

during long and passionate discussions, allowed me to clarify certain points in my own thinking, and Dr. George Torris who willingly read the proofs. This book is an expression of my loyal friendship.

September 1969

Part One

The Problem of Alienation

'I am therefore concerned with the establishment of peace inasmuch as it relates to the intellect and things of the intellect. This point of view is false since it separates the mind from all the rest of its activities, but this abstract operation and this falsification are inevitable: every point of view is false.'

(Valéry: Variétés I/22)

'I am not a Marxist.'

(Marx)

I

False Consciousness and Ideology

Observations about the schizophrenic nature of political ideologies arise periodically in polemical discussions.[1] The presence of these de-realist structures appears on analysis as one aspect of a more general phenomenon whose role in Marxist philosophy has often—and unjustly—been neglected. The 'obscuration' by Marxian orthodoxy of the importance of the *ideological phenomenon* is itself one aspect of the ideologization of Marxism. In other words, it is one aspect of its transformation into a political doctrine, forced to reify its goals by the play of the underlying social psychological structures, and thus testifying to the generality of the phenomenon of false consciousness.

By emphasizing the importance of this phenomenon (the question as to whether and to what extent he was the first to describe it is beyond my scope), Marx was not only one of the founders of political psychology, but a forerunner in another field: the study of 'de-realist' thought. 'Mental derangement' in psychopathology is one aspect of this general phenomenon. There certainly exists an animal psychiatry; but man alone is capable of having states of delirium, just as he is the only being for whom authentic consciousness—which is the result of a dialectical transcendence over false consciousness—is not (whatever Bergson may say) an *immediate given*, but a *conquest*, achieved only gradually in the process of individual maturation.

The problem of false consciousness is not merely central to Marxian doctrine, it constitutes its entire framework; a great many—if not all—of the problems that Marxist thought poses

[1] Cf. note 11, p. 81.

B

are, in the last analysis, problems of false consciousness.[2] A Marxist theory of mental derangement is not therefore an 'external' application of Marxism to a scientific problem (e.g. 'dialectical materialism and mathematics') but rather a kind of quintessential explanation: as a dialectical criticism of ideology, Marxism is already in fact a theory of mental derangement. The rise of totalitarian thought confirms the validity and even the actuality of this part of Marxist theory, whereas there remains so little of real value in Marx's economic thought, once considered central to his system.

B. Croce entitled one of his books: *Ce qui est vivant et ce qui est mort dans la philosophie de Hegel* (*The Living and the Dead in Hegel's Philosophy*). If one were to raise the same question about Marx, the response would undoubtedly be that the doctrine of alienation is clearly the *living part* of his whole system: the fact of totalitarianism on the one hand, and the actuality of the problem of schizophrenia on the other, confirm the validity of this part of Marxist theory.

However, the conceptual framework of the theory of alienation is not free from equivocation. This seems to be the current fate of doctrines that combine reflection and militant politics. It is perhaps stating the obvious to point out as Jacubowski[3] did that the 'social existence' (*Soziales Sein*) of the Marxists is not synonymous with *infrastructure*; without stating this explicitly, certain parts of Marxist orthodoxy postulate this synonymy. It is obvious that the fact of belonging to a national group in 1789 constituted for the French working class one element of its 'social existence' which determined to a large extent the forms of action it took; it would clearly be wrong to talk about infrastructure in this connection. In theory the terms 'ideology' and 'false consciousness' are corollaries ('ideology is a process that the so-called thinker accomplishes doubtless consciously, but with a false consciousness', wrote Engels).[4] But here again—apart from

[2] For example when L. Goldmann studies the way in which the 'noblesse de robe' projected its class position on the religious level (Goldmann (196) *passim*) he is in fact analysing a form of false consciousness.

[3] Jacubowski (238), p. 33. [4] Engels, *Lettre à Mehring* (34), p. 139.

the imprecision of the statement—this is only a relative truth. If ideology is by definition dependent on false consciousness, the inverse is not always true: racist consciousness, the height of false consciousness, existed as such before finding ideological expression. The ideological character of scientific theories also raises a particular problem. By emphasizing the social determinism (*Seinsgebundenheit*) of science, the sociology of knowledge[5] allows the elements of a false consciousness to be discerned (the scientist's work 'objectively' expresses his social equation when subjectively he may believe himself to be in the service of truth alone), but this result would be attained at the price of calling into question the very 'notion of truth',[6] and the victory of the sociology of knowledge would appear from then on as a dangerous Pyrrhic victory.

A similar difficulty arises in connection with the ideological nature of economic representations. Like all forms of consciousness, these representations are 'determined by existence'. The data that they reflect (capital, salaried work, private property, etc. . . .) are no less realities and not simply products of the mind; consciousness of their existence and their role could not therefore —according to G. Salomon[7]—be rightfully described as *false consciousness*. Thus the unity of the Marxist notion of superstructure tends to disintegrate or threatens to become a mere verbalism. A thinker who was very close to Marxism (F. Tönnies) proposed introducing an intermediary category between infrastructure and superstructure composed of law and politics.[8] The semantic evolution of the term 'ideologie', which was always used pejoratively by Marx and Engels, but which tends to have lost this characteristic since Lenin[9] and the dual utilization (philoso-

---

[5] To translate '*Wissenssoziologie*' the following French expressions can be used: '*Sociologie de la connaissance*', '*Sociologie du savoir*' (R. Aron) or '*Gnoséo-sociologie*' (G. Degré). Cf. J. Maquet (317), p. 20, where the question is dealt with in depth. I use the term '*Sociologie de la connaissance*', except in contexts requiring the use of an adjectival form where only the term '*gnoséo-sociologie*' can be used.

[6] R. Aron (18), p. 75.   [7] G. Salomon (410), p. 410.

[8] Tönnies, quoted by G. Salomon (410), p. 409.

[9] Cf. Chambre (100), p. 44 and *passim*. Since Lenin, one talks of proletarian *ideology*; the recognition of ideologization is obvious.

phical and psychiatric) of the concept of alienation, serves to create an atmosphere in this area which is not always that of clarity.

Now, a coherent concept of alienation underlies *Histoire et Conscience de Classe*; it provides a common denominator for different 'ideologies'; furthermore, it encompasses a sector of clinical alienation, thus making a coherent interpretation of schizophrenia possible. This will be the main subject of a subsequent chapter. Two facts characterized Lukács's position in 1923 (they are to be found in an esoteric form in his self-criticism):[10] the importance given to reification in the process of alienation

[10] Cf. G. Lukács's letter (*Arguments*, December 1957, no. 5, pp. 31–2).

'For 20 years I have on several occasions publicly declared that I consider my book *Histoire et Conscience de Classe*, published in 1923, excessive and in many respects, erroneous. Here are the main reasons for my position: the theory of knowledge which is expressed in this book, oscillates between the materialist theory of reflection, and the Hegelian conception of the identity of subject and object, which implies the negation of the dialectic in nature; in the statement about alienation, I repeated the Hegelian error which consists of identifying alienation with objectivity in general.' I shall try to show later that this 'Hegelian error' is particularly fruitful in the interpretation of schizophrenia. As for the subject-object dialectic, there exists in *Histoire et Conscience de Classe*, a certain terminological hesitancy; sometimes Lukács uses the term 'Einheit' (=dialectical unity) and sometimes the term 'Identität'. For example, here is a typical quotation: 'Contrary to the dogmatic meaning of a given reality totally foreign to the subject, the need arises to consider from this Subject-Object identity all data as a product of this Subject-Object identity; each duality as a special case of this primitive unity (*Ureinheit*). But this unity (*Einheit*) is action.' (*Histoire et Conscience de Classe*, p. 136.) Despite a certain terminological confusion, it is clear that this is not a question of the Subject-Object identity (which idealism often attains through absorption of the Object by the Subject), but of the *dialectical unity* of the acting subject and the 'acted upon' world, a unity which makes a sort of dialectical personalization of the historical subject possible, through the expedient of the active knowledge of the world and the self-knowledge of the possibilities of action proper.

The study of schizophrenics' manner of being-in-the-world is significant in this respect: on the one hand the rupture of the acted upon dialectical unity, Self-World, is translated in Binswanger's observations into a collapse of the *Dasein* (*Verweltlichung*); and

and the demonstration of the links which unite this to a personal conception of the dialectic (a conception which owes as much to Hegel and even to Bergson as to Marx) and whose central element is neither the famous transformation of quantity into quality nor even the establishment of the 'moving' character of reality, but the *category of the concrete totality* on the one hand, and the *Subject-Object* dialectic and the reificational deterioration[11] of this dialectic on the other. In other words,

on the other hand the abstract devaluing, depersonalizing anti-dialectical identification with surrounding people or objects (Roheim (405) p. 117) and the processes of abstraction in general (Binswanger (60) p. 28), constitute techniques of integration in this dialectical-axiological failure.

I shall return to these questions; let me say for now that in the light of information from *clinical* alienation, Lukács's conception does not appear at all idealist.

[11] The term '*Verdinglichung*' has two possible French translations and moreover, equivalent ones: *réification* and *chosification*. The term 'objectivation' should be reserved for '*Vergegenständlichung*'.

The combined psychological and sociological nature of the present study obliged me to employ a personal terminology for which I alone am responsible. By 'reification' I mean an existential entity involving mainly phenomena of spatialization and devaluation, an entity whose clinical expression is schizophrenia. I use 'chosification' (objectification) to designate the state of mind of the sick person who experiences himself as a thing. When Binswanger's patient Jürg Sünd experiences the decline of 'the free self into an unfree object' (*aus freiem Selbst zu unfreiem Objekt* (60), p. 22) this is an experience of 'chosification' (objectification) which is set in a *reificational* context represented in such circumstances by the characteristic loss of temporalization referred to by Binswanger.

Despite certain difficulties, Lukács's ideas as presented in *Histoire et Conscience de Classe* are now well known. Since Kostas Axelos's translation appeared while my study was in the process of publication, I was not able to make use of it; the references always refer to the German edition. Besides the extracts from the book which appear in *Arguments* (no. 3, 1957; no. 5, 1957; no. 11, 1958) and publications by L. Goldmann [(200) and (199 *bis*), pp. 64–106], I have taken the liberty to refer to my own two publications [(177), 1951 and (173), 1952], where the Lukácsian point of view is summarized from the viewpoint of its relevance for psychopathology. A detailed study of Lukács's conception will follow later, pp. 145 ff.; the reader who is unfamiliar with the problem is advised to turn to it straight away.

from this viewpoint one can not separate (except artificially) the question of the dialectical or non-dialectical structure of existence and thought, from the general problem of alienation; one is 'alienated' to the extent that one leaves the field of the dialectic. A descriptive outline of the spatio-temporal structure of reified existence is to be found in Lukács; this description is certainly dependent on the influence of Bergsonism which, at the time of writing of *Histoire et Conscience de Classe*, played an important and (a significant and relatively unknown fact) progressivist role in Hungary.[12] The world of reification in Lukács is a spatializing, anaxiological world; its dialectical transcendence ('disalienation') is therefore essentially an act of temporalization and valuation.[13] Lukács's thought thus contains not only (as has rightly been said) 'the elements of a real existential philosophy',[14] but also an axiology of the historical action of the working class; alienation is also—and for Lukács almost by definition—an axiological crisis.

The question of knowing to what extent such a conception of alienation (the aim of which is to find an anti-dialectical reificational core beneath various manifestations of alienated existence) is consistent with Marx's thought, is marginal to my subject.[15] In

[12] The 'obscuration' of the obvious dialectical value of Bergsonism constitutes one of the most astonishing ideological exploits of Marxian orthodoxy. Cf. Jankélevitch (240), first chapter, on the role of totality in Bergson's thought, and Joussain (246), p. 52, who, by denouncing 'the possible dangers of a philosophy of becoming' from the conservative side, *a contrario*, confirms its dialectical value. Here I want to strongly emphasize a point which will be developed elsewhere: *the world of reification is the centre of a decline of dialectical temporalization with a compensating prevalence of spatial functions.* This is the link with the psychiatric conceptions of Minkowski and Binswanger.

[13] Cf. in this connection, G. Pankow's work (376).

[14] Berdiaeff (47), p. 133.

[15] In his very clear article, A. Cornu (115) arrives at a conception which is fairly close to *Histoire et Conscience de Classe.* 'Alienated work, which separates man from the fruit of his activity, in effect transforms the relationships between men and objects. By this process of 'chosification' (objectification) where the human element is transformed into a material object foreign to man, into merchandise, all relationships between men become a function of money' [(115), p. 74]. 'Through the abolition of private property and profit, com-

short this is the problem of Marxist orthodoxy in *Histoire et Conscience de Classe* (or, if you like, the problem of the legitimacy of a 'Western Marxism'); this problem has been extensively discussed elsewhere.[16] Lukács's work offers us a coherent conception of alienation, and this coherence is not challenged by psychopathology, which acts rather as its touch-stone; furthermore, the common denominator that it provides for the various aspects of the ideological phenomenon is not only intellectually satisfying, but also conforms to the facts (including, at times, experimental facts). If, despite G. Salomon's objection, the economic representations clearly have an *ideological* character this is not therefore only because they are explained by the material conditions of existence (Salomon observes, not without reason, that this *'Seinsgebundenheit'* does not detract from the objective, practical nature of economic facts), but because from the viewpoint of non-transcended reification, they appear to be extra-temporalized and de-dialecticized.[17] If—to take as an example a quite different superstructure—racist consciousness is a typical form of false consciousness (and consequently racist

munism suppresses the alienation of human work and the 'chosification' (objectification) of social relationships' (ibid.). The Hegelian origins of the reificational concept are likewise emphasized [(115), p. 73]. But Cornu also insists on another principle idea: alienation has a positive value for Hegel; a negative value for Feuerbach and *a fortiori* for Marx [(115), p. 68 and p. 72]. Naturally the same applies to Lukács's reification and this observation is sufficient to disparage the criticism of idealism brought against *Histoire et Conscience de Classe.*

[16] Cf. Merleau-Ponty (328) and Garaudy et al. (185).

[17] Jean Lacroix characteristically described Marx as the 'brilliant introducer of the notion of time into political economy'. (Cf. in this connection Calvez (85), p. 451 ff.) Now, according to Lukács, reified economic representations have a spatializing structure (cf. (309) p. 101), and are consequently atemporal. These representations can therefore have an ideological and even a schizophrenic nature while directed at concrete realities and not products of the mind. It was not only as a theorist of the transcendence of reification that Marx anticipated existential philosophy; he also anticipated it as the 'brilliant introducer of time', which amounts to the same thing. These considerations seem to have escaped G. Salomon's attention.

ideology a true ideology), this is not only because it 'takes as natural' an originally social, therefore, historical and transitory racial condition, but also because it practises a reifying vision (an actual *delirious perception*) of the racial enemy, as is shown by experimental research. One can demonstrate the reificational structure of religious alienation (if religion is an ideology, it is as reification and not as mystification, as we shall see later on) from morals or the juridical *apparatus*; the forms of reification (schizophrenization) of political ideologies constitute a special problem. Lukács's theory of alienation entails therefore at least this methodological advantage of safeguarding the uniqueness of the concept of ideology as a geometric locus of the manifestations, no doubt varied in their nature, of the non-dialectical perception of dialectical realities. One important sector of the field of clinical alienation responds to this definition. The integration of the theory of false consciousness into a dialectical context is not therefore, a contingent fact; a *consistent* theory of false consciousness could only be dialectic (the inconsistencies of Pareto's conception which tried to build a theory of false consciousness on the non-dialectical postulate of the constancy of human nature, are an example of this);[18] on the other hand, a consistent dialectic ('idealist' or 'materialist') ends up by rediscovering, in one way or another, the problem of ideology. The history of ideas offers a few suggestive examples: the 'Ruse de la Raison' in the frameworks of Hegel's thought, the 'Universe of Discourse' in L. Brunschwicg's system, the notion of cociocentrism[19] in Piaget. Bergsonism is no exception and the possibility of an ideological critique with Bergsonian foundations is doubtless one dimension of the dialectical value of this doctrine.[20] 'Bergson'—writes V.

[18] Cf. further, criticism of Pareto's ideas, pp. 56–9.

[19] Sociocentrism is a form of collective egocentrism; a system of thought involving a favoured element and consequently, without possible reciprocity in the various stages. Cf. Piaget (388), 1951. I have used the term collective egocentrism [(179), 1949]; the expression 'sociocentrism' is more concrete.

Ethnocentrism is sociocentrism with an ethnic base. I shall show later that non-dialectical (reified) perception of reality is common to them both.

[20] The possibility of a Bergsonian interpretation of schizophrenia (Minkowski) is another.

Jankélévitch—'emphasized very carefully the variety of ideo-logical phantoms which perpetually insinuate themselves between thought and facts, and mediate knowledge.'[21]

One point thus appears established: the problem of dialectical thought is inseparable from that of alienation; 'the drama of alienation is dialectical'.[22] As an expression of a form of non-dialectical existence the concept of reification is, for its part, consubstantial with the processes of alienation. Lukács criticized the importance that he had given to this concept in *Histoire et Conscience de Classe*: we have no reason to do likewise.

I propose—without any concern for orthodoxy—the following definitions for the concepts in question. False consciousness and ideology are two forms of non-dialectical (reified) perception of dialectical realities, in other words, two aspects (or better: two degrees) of the rejection of the dialectic. Anticipating the subse-quent demonstration of the anti-dialectical structure of schizo-phrenia, I may say that these are two phenomena of a *schizo-phrenic* nature.

False consciousness is a *diffused state of mind*; ideology is a *theoretical crystallization*. The objective, scientific value of such theoretical crystallizations is naturally subject to caution; it is not *ipso facto* worthless. In fact, just as in psychopathology, one distinguishes between error and delirium, it is essential to dis-tinguish between false consciousness and scientific error. Having said this, it is plausible to postulate that a consciousness that 'corresponds with what exists' (*Seinsadäquat*) also possesses a superior 'epistemological fate' in relation to a non-correspond-ing consciousness, but this postulate has no absolute value.

Let us take an example. The German biologist Ernest Haeckel brought out a book *Die Welträtsel* in 1899, proposing a 'defini-tive' solution to the enigmas of the Universe. This state of mind was present in a whole sector of German scientific life at that time. On reading the works of certain biologists (e.g. Wilhelm Bölsche), one gets the impression that for these scientists the

[21] Cf. Jankélévitch (240), p. 1.
[22] H. Lefebvre (299), p. 111. But this is merely a more striking formulation of the philosophical conception which underlies *Histoire et Conscience de Classe*.

Darwinian discovery, along with certain others such as Lyell's geological discoveries, was the last word in science. Such a conception was of social origin (*'Seinsgebunden'*) due to the way German science had developed and especially to the apparently timeless solidity of the German establishment in that period. The consciousness of these scientists was therefore false in two respects: they were for a large part unconscious of the sociological conditioning of their views; they had (like certain thinkers in the age of enlightenment) a reified conception of scientific truth.[23] Haeckel's discoveries are nevertheless of prime importance from the scientific point of view. Similarly, an economist who considered the historically valid laws of the capitalist system to be eternal, would be acting out of false consciousness in that respect.[24] Nevertheless, within the frameworks of this false consciousness, valid discoveries can be made concerning the laws of the crises of capitalism.

Anti-semitic consciousness (and racist consciousness generally) is doubly false. It reifies the image of the racial enemy, and it considers as ahistorical and 'natural' racial peculiarities of historical origin; this is one important aspect of the definition of reification in Lukács.[25] The keenness of Jews for money is

[23] Jeanne Hersch (222) talks of 'enlightened optimism' for which 'reality is transparent to science'; one can, therefore, by separating the causes of error, arrive at practically definitive truths: the conception of scientific truth is extra-historical and therefore, anti-dialectical. This conception is pretty well common to the enlightenment thinkers, the German scientific life of the Wilhelmian period, and the epistemology of contemporary Maxian orthodoxy; R. Garaudy's work (184) is highly instructive on this point.

[24] Like, for example, Jevons (244) and (245) who offers what is no doubt a valuable study of the decennial periodicity of crises, explaining it by means of the action of sun spots(!). This is a remarkable example of the reified conception of economic facts.

[25] Remember that economic reification in Lukács consists of considering as natural, therefore extra-historical, the laws of the capitalist system based in reality on historical and relative interpersonal relationships. The supposed intellectual inferiority of Blacks is—to the extent that it exists—a historical and social product; ethnocentrism sees in it a natural law, or even the expression of divine will (the 'curse of Ham').

This is, therefore, a reificational phenomenon. It is essential,

indisputably an historical phenomenon; being the result of conditions of life in the ghetto, it disappears in the assimilated intellectual. By considering reificationally these historical products as the expression of a natural law, racist *false consciousness* denies history: racist *ideology* tends to build on false consciousness a pseudo-history which, instead of explaining the Jew through history, claims to explain History through the Jew.

Another idea occurs at this point, attributable to J. Paulhan: the *illusion of totality*.[26] One can enlarge it and speak of the *illusion of encounter*, *illusion of dereification*,[27] *illusion of temporalization* (illusion of History) and generally the *illusion of the dialectic*. The usefulness of this notion—notably in the psychopathology of deranged experience and sexual perversions—will become apparent later.[28] For the moment I will suggest a new point of reference for defining the relationships between false consciousness and ideology: if the first is always a dialectical deterioration, the second often crystallizes an *illusion of the dialectic* (illusion of totality) which sometimes appears—especially in psychopathology —as an *illusion of value*.[29] By definition there can be no ideology without a foundation of false consciousness, but there can be bouts of false consciousness without a true ideological development; the most typical example in recent history is certainly American McCarthyism[30] that can rightfully be described as a

however, to emphasize that throughout this study, the author works with a very broad extrapolation from the conceptual apparatus of *Histoire et Conscience de Classe*.

[26] J. Paulhan (382), p. 27.

[27] The desire for speed related to sexual frenzy in certain milieux is doubtless a form of the illusion of disalienation: *speed alone* corresponds to a false existential dialectic.

[28] Cf. the notion of 'delirious neostructuration' discussed by Hesnard which is a delirious illusion of totality in sexual pathology (sexual reification), the illusion of *pars pro toto* of the fetishist. Cf. Von Gebsattel (191) and below, pp. 175 ff.

[29] For example, in fetishism, the illusion of encounter which is also an illusion of totality and illusion of value; the clinical example of fetishism is the experimental proof of the correlativity of these philosophical concepts.

[30] At a conference in Paris (March 1959) Herbert Marcuse pointed out that the technical impregnation of American life (the

growth of false consciousness practically bereft of ideology, even in the pejorative sense of this latter term. Other movements distinguish themselves on the other hand, by extraordinary ideological developments. The merit of experimental research such as Adorno's[31] is precisely to have succeeded in perceiving the reificational structure of false consciousness at the pre-ideological level. To talk of false consciousness without ideology is certainly a useful abstraction, but all the same it is an abstraction. In fact—as Pareto said—'. . . men want to reason; it is unimportant whether it is good or bad'. It is rare that a group can express its false consciousness without some kind of a justificatory rationalization (often of a moral nature) and this often fulfils the functions of a real ideology in miniature. In relation to false consciousness ideologies often play the same role as derivations in relation to residues in Pareto's system.[32] Finally, one can usefully compare false consciousness to the diffused delirious state of mind,[33] and ideology to

'refrigerator civilisation') rendered ideologies useless. This is true, but this civilization is a long way from excluding false consciousness. McCarthyism is one of the rare examples of *pure false consciousness* in modern history.

Permit me to refer to my study on McCarthyism [(180), 1954], to my knowledge the only one to have seen this movement as a form of false consciousness. The loss of historical temporalization in McCarthyism—a phenomenon typical of schizophrenization in the sense given to it in Binswanger's studies—is pointed out among other things, by O. Lattimore [(189), p. 58], who speaks of 'mastery of timing'.

Obviously, this is still the same question: is it a matter of a conscious 'mastery' or, on the contrary, a structural transformation of the spatio-temporal frameworks of political thought? This question, which will reappear in various contexts, is the criterion of the partial or total character of the concept of ideology.

[31] Adorno (7), an exhaustive analysis of whom will be carried out later. This is a microsociological study of the pre-fascist personality; it emerges from his study that this personality possesses a schizoid vision of the foreign world. Cf. further, pp. 119–36.

[32] For Pareto, 'derivations' are intellectual systems of justification for the deep tendencies that are 'residues', such as the desire for domination, etc. Cf. the critical review of Pareto's ideas (Aron (17) and Ziegler (477), and later, pp. 56–9).

[33] The *Wahnstimmung* of the Germans. The most suggestive

the delirious system, this latter often being an illusory neostructuration (Hesnard), therefore an illusion of totality.[34]

The expression 'bout of false consciousness' was used earlier; this medical analogy corresponds in the circumstances to a sociological reality, whatever may be the justified reservations that the use of such parallels may deserve elsewhere. A permanent fund of false consciousness exists in collective psychology: every collectivity is egocentric, though to various degrees; furthermore, every collectivity through the single fact that it transcends its members, tends to spatialize duration. But this permanent fund from time to time experiences exacerbations which demonstrate—though without creating—its illusory structure. Certain theories about great historical oscillations can thus be interpreted as *oscillations in false consciousness.* Szende (whose book *Verhüllung und Enthüllung* was one of the first studies of political alienation seen in the light of the general character of false consciousness) distinguishes between 'historical periods of alienation' and 'periods of disalienation'; certainly the idea is right, though one might dispute the details. V. Zoltowski refers to an empirical basis to distinguish between spatializing periods in which analytical functions are prevalent and temporalizing periods which are mainly synthetic. The results of a non-Marxist research inquiry thus reveal certain themes of overt Marxism for—precisely because of the theory of the schizophrenic nature of false

literary description of 'Wahnstimmung' is the atmosphere of Kafka's *The Trial* and *The Castle.*

[34] An important comment should be made here. I have tried to define the concepts of false consciousness and ideology with the aid of the conceptual framework from the study of mental derangement and by taking into account their relationship as postulated by Marx. But (and I cannot over-emphasize this), there is no absolute opposition. There is no ideology without false consciousness. An atmosphere of false consciousness tends to secrete almost fatally an ideology, however primitive. On the other hand, 'false consciousness' has no adjectival form. The terms 'ideological' and 'ideologization' have no homologue for 'false consciousness'. Taking into consideration these particulars and stylistic requirements, I shall often use from now on 'ideological' for 'in relation to false consciousness' and 'ideologization' for 'process of formation of false consciousness'; the context will allow us to avoid any confusion.

consciousness—spatializing periods can be likened to the *Verhüllungsperioden* (periods of alienation) of Szende.[35] Wars (hot and

[35] G. Rattray-Taylor (395) based on the hypothesis of an alternation of *patristic and matristic* periods in history a theory which, contrary to the title of his work, is not a 'sexual interpretation of History', but is a theoretical conception very close to that of the 'Sex Pol' school (Viennese Marxist-psychoanalysts among whom W. Reich, who died tragically a short time ago, occupied a preeminent position at one point). Reproduced here according to G. Rattray-Taylor [(395), p.96], are the essential characteristics of these two types of periods:

Patristic	*Matristic*
1 Intolerance in matters of sexuality.	1 Liberal attitude towards sexual questions.
2 Limitation of the freedom of women.	2 Freedom of women.
3 Women considered as inferior and source of sin.	3 Women enjoying a privileged situation.
4 Chastity more appreciated than fulfilment.	4 Fulfilment more appreciated than chastity.
5 On the political level, authoritarianism.	5 On the political level, democracy.
6 Conservatism.	6 Progressivism.
7 Mistrust of research.	7 No mistrust of research.
8 Inhibition, fear of spontaneity.	8 Spontaneity.
9 Obsessive fear of homosexuality.	9 Obsessive fear of incest.
10 Accentuation of the differences between the sexes (particularly in dress).	10 Few differences between the sexes.
11 Ascetism, fear of pleasure.	11 Hedonism.
12 Religion of the father.	12 Religion of the mother.

It might be maintained that, during patristic periods, identification taking place between people *of the same sex* would tend to become absolute, which would mechanize and spatialize the collective experience of lived time, while in a matristic period, identification taking place *between different sexes* (the leader is still a man, but his identification is feminine), would leave more room for intuition about various things, and therefore, for the spirit of synthesis and a dialectical attitude.

V. Zoltowski bases his work on the statistics of works of history and geography published during a given period to distinguish between spatializing–analytical and temporalizing–synthetic periods following in succession according to regular rhythms (478) and (479).

cold) exacerbate false consciousness by means of a dual mechanism: accentuation of sociocentrism and the increasing role of the convenient political lie, both being factors of de-dialectization of consciousness. Doubtless it is due to reaction to this that periods immediately after wars are sometimes marked by the appearance, or blossoming, of intellectual movements of dereification such as

Now, it follows from the role of the loss of temporalization in alienation (false consciousness and schizophrenia), that the spatializing periods of V. Zoltowski may constitute in theory the equivalent of the reificational periods, periods of alienation (*'Verhüllungsperioden'*) of P. Szende (439), p. 85, and perhaps, to a certain extent, correspond to the 'patristic' periods of Rattray-Taylor. Temporalizing periods correspond to the periods of disalienation (*'Enthüllungsperioden'*) or matristic periods. The notion of schizophrenization corresponds to the extreme degree attained by spatialization; 'patristic' impregnation is translated politically into the 'principle of the leader' which is integrated into the total context of the phenomenon of false consciousness.

On the other hand, by making the fundamental structure of scientific progress depend on the general spirit of the time, Zoltowski is very close to the theory of the sociology of knowledge. I consider this research as an experimental confirmation of Lukács's ideas, particularly with regard to the opposition between 'concrete totality', the dialectical principle of temporalizing periods ('spirit of synthesis') and spatialization (reification) with an analytical emphasis in science.

H. Stolze [(434), p. 94] discussed the masculinization of modern life, due—paradoxically—to the economic conditions which force women to undertake masculine tasks. Now, man represents a spatializing principle (cf. Andrieux (10) which is an experimental study of feminine spatial inadequacy). In this same context one might recall the involved theory of the Hungarian architect P. Ligeti (305) who diagnoses a regular alternation between periods with either an architectural, plastic or pictorial dominance, in which there is a structure corresponding to the collective life, pictorial periods representing the dominance of the individual, chance and liberty; by contrast those which are predominantly architectural, signifying an increasing role of the mass, law and order(!!) (Reification and totalitarian existence.)

To synchronize these different theories (taken somewhat at random) would require a separate work. Furthermore, it is possible to make criticisms of details; for example, Szende (in 1922) believed himself to be living in the middle of a period of disalienation —which is very debatable. Contrary to V. Zoltowski, I think that a

surrealism after the First World War and existentialism after the Second.[36] Small countries, situated from an intellectual point of view, at the crossroads of the great international intellectual movements—in a place therefore, where the powerful influences of sociocentrism are neutralized—constitute (aided also by the decentralizing effect of the intellectuals' polyglottism) a favourable ground for dialectical thought and, consequently, dereification;[37] on the other hand, ethnic groups appear to encourage to a

kind of entropic law dictates these alternations: technical progress (and progress in city life) introduces an irreversible and cumulative spatializing factor (schizophrenization). For me, this is a matter of oscillations of false consciousness in its various manifestations: style of life, style of research, forms of sexuality, artistic expressions; these oscillations are dependent in the last analysis on the objective evolution of the infrastructure.

[36] Cf. later in connection with 'Psychiatric criticism of existentialism' (139) my point, pp. 246 ff. Calvez thinks that existentialism 'is an attempt to save the subject, not from his enslavement to a subjective world, but from his enslavement to an objective world, the tyranny of technical civilization. There would not be too much subjectivity, there would not be a lack of objectivation, on the contrary there would be too much objectivation' [(85), p. 50]. This is a complicated way of saying that existentialism is a doctrine of dereification. As for the relationships between surrealist and existentialist humanism, cf. Alquié (9), p. 144: 'Breton's materialism emanates from a well understood Marxism, a rare thing today. His point of departure is not the material-object but a particular relationship between man and the object.' It would be interesting to know Lukács's relationship to surrealism; we have no documents on this subject.

For the history of the relationship between surrealism and Marxist orthodoxy, see M. Nadeau (364), R. Vailland (452), T. Tzara (451), etc. In the first edition of *Critique de la vie quotidienne* [(299), p. 20], we read the following judgement: 'Literary and political reaction and pseudo-revolution come together.' Lefebvre reproaches surrealism for 'undervaluing reality to the benefit of the magical and the supernatural'. What emerges from many accounts of this work is that, despite the originality of his thought, Lefebvre, a prisoner of the reification of the Marxian orthodoxy of the period, confuses surrealist *disalienation* (a disalienation whose preference for the supernatural is merely an instrument) with a sort of derealism. Their 'derealism' did not prevent the surrealists from being, from 1926, the first 'realist' critics of Russian reality.

[37] Mannheim believes that the *unattached intelligentsia* has a

certain extent anti-dialectical, defocalized thought. But the most favoured ground for non-dialectical thought is the totalitarian state: false consciousness is the normal atmosphere of totalitarian states and parties.[38] Conversely, in the field of facts, not ideas, parliamentary democracy appears, for want of better, to be the regime allowing the maximum of disalienation (or if you like, the minimum of alienation) compatible with collective existence: decentration of opinion due to the play of the plurality of parties; attenuation of judicial reification through the institution of the courts and through respect for the rights of defence. This is not the place to go further into this subject. The theory of alienation, inseparable from dialectical philosophy, seems also to constitute a chapter in the general doctrine of democracy when seen from this viewpoint.

Utopian thought is one of the forms of crystallization of the false consciousness of social classes interested in change; it is a reification of the future ('future-thing' according to S. de Beauvoir).[39] The existence of utopian consciousness teaches us an important lesson. Marx could never completely free himself from a

special gnoseo-sociological potentiality. My observation is in fact an application of this postulate; there are also 'unattached' countries whose intellectual climate favours the adoption of a dialectical consciousness. As an example on might quote Hungary where the Marxist effort has always been oriented towards the dialectic (Lukács, Fogarasi and several less well known theoreticians), and Austria. The problem of alienation and related questions have always been central in Hungarian Marxism (even after 1945!). But other facts can be added to this geographical factor: periods of crisis or great national transition bring these problems into the foreground of actuality, for example, in Germany in about 1930 or in France between 1956 and 1958. Szende writes [(440), p. 427] that the approach of social change is marked by a hecatomb of political abstractions; the consciousness of their abstract–reified character would indicate the imminence of social convulsions.

[38] For this whole question W. Daim's book (120) is worth consulting, especially the chapter on Nazism. Cf. also the decline in a totalitarian regime of the function of the legal advocate, the official agent of decentration and de-reification in the face of the State *apparatus*; totalitarian justice does not allow an interlocutor.

[39] S. de Beauvoir (37), p. 165.

psychology of interests, inherited from the philosophy of the enlightenment: the possessing classes would obscure the dialectical aspect of things, for the dialectic is incompatible with their interest in self-preservation. Reification of the future in utopian consciousness shows that social strata wholly 'interested in change' can, however, undergo the de-dialecticization of historical temporality: the roots of the phenomenon are therefore deeper than the Marxist conception implicitly supposes. (Marx also overestimated the importance of mystification in religious alienation.) Despite the traditional terminology, it is above all a crisis in *temporalization* which makes utopian thought illusory: utopia is above all a uchrony. In fact the temporality of utopian consciousness involves three elements incompatible with a real temporalization: a *bifurcation of historical time* which follows on the one hand a causal sequence and on the other affective dynamics; a hiatus between present and future; and, thirdly an *end to historical time* once the utopian moment is achieved.[40] Despite the psychology of interests factor pointed out by Marx, a social stratum interested in change can undergo the de-dialecticization of its perception of reality in at least two ways: the irrational involvement in a world of utopian structure, and a reification of its instruments of combat which 'create state reasons for their

[40] The theory of the '*Vorgeschichte*' in Marx (the realization of socialism is the beginning of real human history) [cf. (321), p. 74] is the point of impact of the subsequent eruption of utopian consciousness. But nearly all the theorists of the bourgeois revolution in France, including Condorcet, the most dialectic of them all, were influenced to a certain extent by an unformulated theory of '*Vorgeschichte*' during the bourgeois revolution: the beginning of the reign of reason and virtue ...

It would be interesting to study systematically the '*aufkläristes*' survivals in Marx; the Rousseauist belief in human kindness represented by the working class (Salomon (410), p. 415); the element of mystification in religious alienation (it is not as mystification but as non-dialectical consciousness that religion is ideology); the psychology of interests in the gnoseo-sociology of dialectical thought. From this point of view Marx was perhaps the last great thinker of the 'enlightenment'. Marxist orthodoxy faithfully appropriated all the '*aufkläristes*' elements in Marx's doctrine (Korsch (264), p. 23, note), i.e. the least dialectical components.

advantage',[41] or, in other words, cause it to be surrounded with an atmosphere of anti-dialectical false consciousness.

EXPERIENCE OF VALUES AND FALSE CONSCIOUSNESS

The doctrine of false consciousness involves an implicit axiology based on the devaluing nature of the reificational process with the value-giving (axiogenic) quality of the concrete totality as a corollary; and it concludes with the principle of axio-dialectical equivalence (value as subjective experience of the dialectical quality and formal coherence of reality). It is as an extreme case of this process of devaluation that the universe of concentration is situated within the ambit of the alienation of human work as described and denounced by Marx. By basing his theory of *economic* value on the depersonalizing identificatory, anti-dialectical, abstract principle,[42] Marx made clear the reifying and depersonalizing character of the capitalist economy; but, at the same time, he blocked the properly axiological effort of his successors who thought that with the theory of value in *Capital*, the first and last word of Marxist axiology had been written. A pseudo-axiology of immediate usefulness was insinuated into the void thus created: the famous objective moral science, a real case of infantile regression—and no one, not even Lukács, thought it possible to produce a Marxist integration (*Umstülpung*) of the dialectical theories of a Dupréel or a Köhler. We shall return to this question of the axiological aspect of reification, whose major importance and experimental justification lie in the field of psychopathology.

[41] R. Aron (18), p. 67.
[42] Cf. this passage: 'The act of exchange in its formal generality (the fundamental act for the theory of "marginal utility") suppresses the usage value as such; it creates this relationship of abstract equality between concretely unequal, or even, incomparable data ... *The subject of exchange is thus just as abstract, formal and reified as its object.*' (So ist das Subjekt des Tausches genau so abstrakt, formell und verdinglicht wie sein Objekt.) Lukács (309), p. 116.

In summary, the conception that I suggest is as follows: false consciousness and ideology are two aspects of the reificational rejection of the dialectic: false consciousness as a diffused state of mind (*Wahnstimmung* type), ideology as its theoretical crystallization of a generally justificatory nature (derivation). These are *schizophrenic* phenomena to the extent that this state of mind can be defined as having a reificational structure. The spatio-temporal structure of false consciousness is characterized by the preponderance of static, anti-dialectical spatial experience; it is related to the structures described in Minkowski's *La Schizophrénie*. The result (logical and empirical) is a crisis in temporalization, which in its turn relates back to L. Binswanger's psychopathological conceptions. As a form of depersonalizing[43] and dissociative existence, reification is a process of devaluing; this observation constitutes the possible point of departure for a Marxist axiology. It is as a crisis in dialectical temporalization—at the level of the dimension of the historical future—that utopian consciousness joins this combination.

TOTAL AND PARTIAL CONCEPT OF IDEOLOGY

This important distinction comes from Mannheim.[44] The author of *Ideologie und Utopie* established three essential differences between the partial and total concept of ideology: (1) the partial concept relates only to a part of the convictions of the adversary, whereas the total concept relates to his whole view of the world (*Weltanschauung*); (2) the partial concept analyses the opposing ideology at the psychological level, the total concept at the theoretical or nosological level; (3) the partial concept is dependent on a psychology of interests, the total concept operates with

[43] I shall return later to this depersonalizing characteristic of reification, an important element in its integration in psychopathology (cf. Balvet's thesis (29) and further p. 145). I should point out that the English translators of *Ideologie und Utopie* [(316), p. 249] translate *Verdinglichung* with a disarming and significant naivety as 'Impersonalization'(!).

[44] Cf. Mannheim (315), pp. 9–10 (German edition).

the help of a functional analysis (in my terms *structural* is prefer-able). Consequently, the total concept of ideology is the only corollary of false consciousness; the utilitarian political lie, the 'mass persuasion' by propaganda is substituted for false con-sciousness in the partial concept. Only the total concept seems to be entirely compatible with the theory of historical materialism; the partial concept, by reducing the process of ideologization to an act of decision, thereby leaves the field of Marxism proper. It is curious to note that ideological criticism in Marx quite often operates with the aid of the partial concept. Mannheim was right to quote such a passage from *Misère de la Philosophie*[45] as an example of the application of the total concept, but in his criticism of religious alienation ('the opium of the people'), the analysis of the sociological conditions of the development of dialectical thought, the partial concept of ideology reappears at the same time as that of voluntary mystification. The 'Formes élémentaires de la vie religieuse' are closer to the total concept of ideology—and also to historical materialism—than Marx's criti-cism of religious alienation.

Finally utopian consciousness often co-exists with a partial view of ideological criticism. In fact, the structural criticism of opposing ideologies is often, if not always, a dialectical criticism. The utopian view which excludes the dialectic for the future, could not utilize it as a critical weapon in the present; it willingly seeks refuge in partial ideological criticism which exempts it from any deep examination of the dialectical value of opposing thought as well as from any analysis of the mechanisms of its dependence on the conditions of existence. The typical thinker of the age of enlightenment accepted the possibility that historical evolution would cease after the victory of Reason and Virtue. From then on, its ideological criticism was confined to the level of denouncing mystification or stupidity; it was disinterested in any

---

[45] [(316), p. 51](pp. 44–5 of the French edition). The quotation is suggestive. But the Marxian explanation of the rejection of the dialectic through conservative interest typically depends on the *partial* concept of ideology. The two forms of ideological criticism therefore co-exist in Marx's thought, which allows Marxist ortho-doxy—whose ideological criticism most often operates at the partial level—to use genuine texts from Marx to support its point of view.

structural criticism (dialectical and sociological) which exceeded both its possibilities and its needs. Among the thinkers of the enlightenment, as in Stalinism, the utopian structure of consciousness and the partial conception of ideological criticism characteristically developed together.

Let me say finally that having defined schizophrenia as an attack of a reificational and hence anti-dialectical nature, my view of the schizophrenic character of false consciousness is a continuation of Lukács's thought, but also Mannheim's. The Marxist orthodoxy of such a view is certainly open to question. I confess to being personally insensitive to the importance of problems of '*appellation contrôlée*'; the possible reproach of injured-Marxism about the value of introducing the Bergsonian dialectic in this context is immaterial. The problem is not the quest for a correct exegesis of texts, however venerable they may be, but for a way of defining alienation capable of: (a) serving as a common denominator for the different forms of ideology; (b) allowing a precise definition and delimitation of the concepts of ideology and false consciousness, and (c) defining a sector common to individual alienation (clinical) and social alienation. If the suggested conception meets these three demands the question of its conformity to the texts becomes of secondary importance.[46]

THE PROBLEM OF THE IDEOLOGICAL NATURE OF SCIENCE

I shall briefly touch on this problem, which is slightly outside my subject, but Lukács's concept of alienation suggests a possible

---

[46] Cf. Lefort [(300), p. 46]: 'the enquiry about the terms on which the idea of alienation is admissible (i.e. discerning what Marxists currently make of this term), can be eliminated as purely metaphysical. What is needed is a sociological description.' This is exactly my goal except that I want to make use of a psychopathological phenomenon (schizophrenia). Cl. Lefort's article constitutes a remarkable attempt at a completely undogmatic application of the concept of alienation to a problem of ethnology (the 'cattle world' of an African people); his positions are close to those of Lukács, though he does not quote him.

solution to a difficulty with regard to the coherence of the Marxist notion of superstructure.

The problem was clearly posed by R. Aron in an early work.[47] To confer an absolute value 'on the theory of a correspondence between ideas and classes' is tantamount to undermining 'the notion of truth' which is essential to any science, natural or human. E. Grünwald who regarded the sociology of knowledge not as a science, but as 'a schema of possible interpretations'[48] suggested that it could become a science by renouncing all sociological pretensions;[49] this is a bit like the American general who considered that there was only one kind of good Indian: a dead Indian. If one removes from the sociology of knowledge the scientific and the sociological element, one wonders what remains.

A loop-hole exists: to admit the existence of privileged 'points of view' (*Standorte*) for consciousness and knowledge. This question of the *privileged point of view* is central to Marxism, for the theory of *Vorgeschichte* is one of the touchstones for the process of ideologization in orthodox Marxism, as I shall show later. In fact, the Marxists have always considered that the proletarian perspective favoured the dialectical perception of reality; Mannheim maintains that the *unattached intelligentsia*[50] are in a privileged position for realizing the totality of perspectives. The dialectic is therefore at the centre of the two conceptions,[51] but the analogy stops there, and it would be folly

[47] R. Aron (18), p. 75.
[48] Cf. Grünwald (205), p. 66. Mannheim (316), pp. 276–7 went further: he distinguished two kinds of gnoseo-sociological interpretation: 'Sinngemässe Zurechnung' which corresponds to Grünwald's 'schemas of possible interpretations', and 'Faktizitäts-zurechnung' which, while considering the results of the first as necessary working hypotheses, tries to establish effective causal relationships and individual analyses. Grünwald's mistake was clearly that of considering the first step to be the whole of the sociology of knowledge. [49] Grünwald (205), p. 234.
[50] R. Aron (16), p. 88, translates 'freischwebende Intelligenz' as unrooted intelligentsia. I prefer the English translation of Wirth and Shils who speak of 'socially unattached intelligentsia' (English edition, p. 137).
[51] 'Totality' as used by Mannheim is a synthesis of perspectives; it is none the less a dialectical category, though in a different sense to Lukács's.

to search for the Marxism of a non-existent intellectual class as Robert K. Merton[52] does in Mannheimism. The gnoseo-sociological value-coefficient of 'praxis' is the stumbling-block in this problem; for the Marxists (Lukács and orthodoxy are in agreement on this point), this coefficient goes unchallenged: Mannheim shows the limits of this positivism.[53] Marx refers to a psychology of interests on the collective scale; Mannheim takes the elements of an egocentric psychology to be the agent of de-dialecticization of consciousness; the degree of 'determination by the conditions of existence' (*Seinsgebundenheit*) would be in inverse proportion to authentic consciousness; this is to denounce *a priori*, though not without justification, collective socio-centrism or egocentrism which, by making consciousness dependent on a privileged system, produces phenomena of false consciousness through destructuration and distortion of the conceptual apparatus of thought. (Formation of egocentric concepts.)[54] Each of these two conceptions thus sets the limits of the other. The psychology of interests that Marx invokes is valid only in certain demonstrated cases. In other cases, the *obscuration* of the dialectical aspect of things produces, on the contrary, autistic and maladapted collective behaviour;[55] on the other hand, the appearance

[52] Robert K. Merton, quoted by J. Maquet (317), p. 104.

[53] Marx's biography would tend to suggest that Mannheim is right; it is not 'through interest' that Marx becomes a dialectician, but as a result of his 'unattached' position between two forms of religious alienation; he was no longer a Jew and had not become Christian. But Marx is but an individual case and one of the valid criticisms to be made of Mannheim is that he wanted to make sociology out of concepts of individual validity.

[54] Cf. my study (179), p. 470.

[55] For example, McCarthyism, which is a phenomenon of anti-dialectical false consciousness and is characterized by ineffectual behaviour cf. (180). In another area of ideas, American racism, the reified, anti-dialectical perception of supposedly 'inferior' racial groups, is a tragic error which can transform a powerful, loyal and socially useful minority into an insoluble problem, and in the long run make a revolutionary factor of it. The French point of view—because of the Algerian war—is a singularly well situated gnoseo-sociological *Standorte* for understanding the scope of the American racist error which does not correspond to any interest, however poorly or well perceived. The point of view of the *more dialectic*

of utopian consciousness, which reifies duration by reifying the future, constitutes a powerful part of the de-dialecticization of the consciousness of social strata interested in change. It is not therefore so much the concern for change which is important in this context as the degree of reification of consciousness. As for Mannheim, his conception is more valid for the *intellectual* than for the *intelligentsia*; furthermore, he underestimates the variety of social context that can mould thought. Pareto says that most doctrines are right in what they denounce, and wrong in what they affirm: the discussions in the sociology of knowledge illustrate this adage well. The Marxists are completely within their rights to assert that, as knowledge is an active process, it is paradoxical to attribute a privileged gnoseo-sociological *Standorte* to a social strata which is scarcely involved in 'praxis'. A Mannheimian may retort that the ideologization of official Marxism (not only an indisputable fact, but almost an *undisputed* fact in the period between 1947 and 1953) removed for all time the postulate of the immunity of proletarian consciousness in the face of ideological danger. The problem is still the following: to maintain the ideological character of science (i.e. its determination by the conditions of its existence, *Seinsgebundenheit*) while respecting the evidence of its objective value. The hypothesis of privileged *Standorte* for knowledge —from a Marxist or Mannheimian viewpoint—does not resolve this problem. At its extreme I have seen it end in a dichotomization without a dialectic ('true proletarian science—false bourgeois science') which does not constitute a transcendence of false consciousness, but is its realization in an extreme form.

Certainly the problem is simplified if only one agrees to reduce the scope of the concept of superstructure. Sociologists influenced by Alfred Weber[56] tend to isolate three fundamental totalities in

Federal authority (since it permits the progressive integration of Blacks into the fullness of citizens' rights and refuses to consider their present inferiority as the expression of natural law or divine will) is at the same time more consistent with the interests of the dominant social strata in America. It can be seen that it is impossible to relate the gnoseo-sociological problem of the dialectic to a problem of interests.

[56] Von Schelting for example (415).

social processes: the social process (*Gesellschaftsprozess*), the world of culture (*Kulturkosmos*) and the process of civilization (*Zivilisationsprozess*), this latter being characterized by the cumulative nature of its results. In the same order of ideas, Mannheim[57] distinguishes three superstructural spheres each with specific dynamics: the sphere of cultural structuration bound up with states of mind (art),[58] the sphere of dialectical rationality (metaphysics, philosophy of history, human sciences) and, lastly, the sphere of progressive rationality (natural sciences, economics, law). This is a somewhat questionable classification: the medieval economy did not in all respects constitute progress in comparison with the Ancient economy, and law in the twentieth century, tainted with totalitarianism, marks a certain regression compared to nineteenth-century law. Having made these reservations, it is indeed tempting to limit the validity of the theory of historical materialism to the cultural and moral area, and then the theory of 'progressive rationality' would be simultaneously dependent on two factors: the social position of the scholar, and the whole context of ideas in which these problems appear, and which is subject to dynamics of a more or less *idealist* nature. But by accepting such a limitation on its validity, historical materialism would undermine its own foundations, for, as a scientific doctrine it is itself part of the 'progressive rationality'. Marxism can certainly not explain Marx, an individual phenomenon. But Marxism cannot be allowed to fail to explain itself.

For Marxism, this is an important, even vital, problem. By proclaiming the social determinism of science, the sociology of knowledge tends to keep it in the category of ideology, but can a 'scientific ideology' be dependent on false consciousness and at the same time correspond to the facts? Where must the notions of ideology and false consciousness be separated? The Marxist concept of superstructure is not sufficiently solid to support such an operation. Must one deny the objective value of science? This would be going against the evidence; it is by no means certain that twentieth-century law is better than nineteenth-century law, but what is certain is that the sick are cared for

[57] Mannheim (314), p. 30.
[58] Seelengebundene, gestalthaft-kulturelle Sphere.

better in 1959 than in 1856. Must we accept, as Grünwald does, the failure of the sociology of knowledge as a science or, with Von Schelting, its failure only in the scientific area? Historical materialism seems to me to be incapable of accounting for the fact that Marx became a revolutionary and a dialectician not because he 'belonged' to the working class, but, on the contrary, by virtue of his 'unattached' position at the intersection of different religious, and even national, alienations. It now risks seeming incapable of giving an account of Marxism itself which would be less 'determined by the conditions of existence' than dependent on ideic (not to say 'idealist') dynamics appropriate to the field of 'progressive rationality'. Must one be resigned in that case to reducing it to the dimensions of an economic theory which to a large extent has been superseded? It is, therefore, the very coherence of Marxism as a world view (*Weltanschauung*) which challenges the validity of gnoseo-sociological theory. By abandoning the theory of social determinism of scientific knowledge (just as in another area, it abandons the idea of the social determinism of mental derangement),[59] orthodox Marxism in fact records the failure of Marxist sociology.

It is here that Lukács's conception of alienation supplies a precision which facilitates the solution of the problem. By virtue

[59] Permit me to refer to my contribution [cf. (107)] in which I analyse the very special gnoseo-sociological position of psychiatry, accounting for the fact that this discipline revealed the extreme degree of the dialectical decadence of orthodox Marxism between 1947 and 1953. In point of fact Pavlovian psychiatry is almost totally abstracted from the social context; this abstraction is *legitimate* in a certain perspective; as such it does not become a dialectical step. In Russian psychiatry, deranged thought is not 'seinsgebunden', it is an epiphenomenon of physiological data. I shall return to these questions later, pp. 229 ff. to show particularly how the conception of *Daseinsanalyse* is both more dialectic and more concretely materialistic, despite an apparently idealising terminology. In the sociology of knowledge, the situation is analogous; the dialectical and materialist theory of determination by the conditions of existence is rejected. Cf. the severe criticisms of Mannheimism, Lukács (310), p. 506 *et passim*; Fogarasi (159), appendix, and the Russian contributions (156).

of the necessary differentiation between false consciousness and objective error, a scientific statement can keep its value while objectively belonging to a reified context.[60] In dialectical terms this means—this is elementary, but it is necessary to say it— that the *dialectical nature* and *scientific validity* of a theory are not necessarily interdependent. Not only can a dialectical theory be false (which goes without saying), but—something that is less obvious—a profoundly anti-dialectical theory can be valid if only one does not ask the scientist for definitive truths but only the maximum *historically possible* congruence with the facts. The anti-dialectical abstraction thus apears as a legitimate dimension of the research in a given gnoseo-sociological context, a context which includes among other things the state of laboratory techniques. Newton's mechanics today appear as an anti-dialectical abstraction in relation to relativity: in the seventeenth century *that* was objective science; statements like Einstein's would have *justly* been accused of being metaphysical dreams by contemporaries. To raise the problem of catatonia as a function of an isolated toxic action is less dialectical than to raise it as a function of a form of integration of the sick person into social reality; it is perfectly possible, however, that this syndrome is actually due to an isolated toxic action.[61] One can suggest, even

---

[60] Ethnocentrism always provides good examples. It is well known that Israelis have a high incidence of certain arterial disorders (Bürger's sickness) and mental disorders (schizophrenia). The reason for this is once again *social*: smoking and sedentary habits for the former; the 'castrative' structure of the Jewish family, and the alienated position of the Jewish collectivity as a whole, for the latter. To consider them as natural (biological) laws is *false consciousness* (reificational projection into nature of a social, therefore, historically relative, law); to build on it a justificatory theory of inferiority is to create an *ideology*. From the statistical and medical point of view the facts are none the less accurate.

[61] Obviously, even if a definite toxic mechanism was discovered, catatonia would depend no less causally on the social context but in a more complicated way, which the legitimate abstraction could not afford to ignore.

Here is a straightforward example. A woman dies from poisoning. A toxicologist states that she *died from the effects of arsenic*. A

without raising the postulate (or rather: the problem) of the natural dialectic, that some sciences are more dialectical than others; anatomy is less dialectic than physiology; but it is neither less useful nor less scientific.

Now, dogmatic Marxism tends to confuse the validity of a theory and its dialectical nature. It is the methodological aspect of the theory of reflection: since Nature is dialectical, any method which gives tangible results is *ipso facto* described as dialectical. One forgets that if Nature is perhaps dialectical, the human spirit has a dialectical capacity that is limited by its historical horizon and also by its natural limits (by the 'creatural state' according to one Catholic thinker). In certain cases, the abstraction is therefore *legitimate* (Aristotle's *physics* was *for his time* more scientific than the atomism of Democritus, whose intuition was inspired and uncontrollable in the gnoseo-sociological context of the time); but it does not become *dialectic* for all that. R. Garaudy clearly exposed the elements of a Marxist epistemology; the role of abstraction and its dangers are emphasized, but one looks in vain for the elementary observation that the dissociative abstraction of totalities is not a *dialectical moment* of knowledge but an *anti-dialectical technique* legitimized by the fact that in a given historical context (the state of laboratory techniques being part and parcel of this context) the human mind can not embrace the totality of the dialectical interrelations which underlie reality. When Marx 'quite consciously uses the static, fictitious (!!) means of abstraction taken from economic theory' (G. Salomon),[62] he is not proceeding in a dialectical way; he is using an anti-dialectical technique of abstraction legitimate for his time. To put forward the dialectical characteristic as the only criterion of validity is the same as making the dialectical capacity of the

social inquiry reveals that she killed herself because her home was hell; *it was her family life that killed her.*

In comparison with the second, the first opinion rests on an anti-dialectical abstraction; the toxicologist has no means of including the totality of the situation. Within the frameworks of this legitimate abstraction, however, his diagnosis is scientifically impeccable.

[62] '. . . so dürfen wir nicht vergessen, dass Marx die *statisch-fiktiven* Abstraktionsmittel der ökonomischen Theorie ganz bewusst gebraucht.' (Salomon (410), p. 405.)

human mind ahistorical; Claude Bernard in his laboratory could not (I would almost say: *did not have the right to*) think as dialectically as Lapicque in his. The scientific perception of reality therefore involves almost inevitably a non-dialectical dimension which marks the gnoseo-sociological limits of knowledge; while being *less dialectical* the theories in this dimension *are no less valid* than the others. E. Meyerson's epistemology reflects—better than R. Garaudy's—the inevitable ambiguity of the act of knowing: on the one hand there is identification, an anti-dialectical, spatializing step, the expression of the inevitable element of reification in the social act of knowing; on the other hand, there is intuition of various matters relating to the concrete specificity of reality as totality.

Another problem arises: is the social conditioning of ideologies *constitutive* or *selective*? E. Grünwald (one of the rare theorists to be interested in the problem of the 'intermediary mechanism' in the relationships between infrastructure and superstructure) concludes that the action of society is constitutive with regard to the object of knowledge (*Erkenntnisobjekt*) and selective with regard to the object of experience (*Erfahrungsobjekt*).[63] It seems more simply that the action of society is constitutive when—consistent with the state of its techniques and needs—it raises problems, and selective *vis-à-vis* given responses. One of the criteria of this social selection in the scientific area is precisely the dialectical criterion. The *problem* of relativity could be posed *constitutively* only in technical conditions making Michelson's experience possible, and Einstein's dialectical *response* could be accepted *selectively* only in a receptive social context; the fate of relativity in reified gnoseo-sociological milieux illustrates this thesis. The social context acts selectively by suggesting a choice of orientation determined by the options which stand out in research[64] by automatically favouring (by social promotion and

[63] Grünwald (205), p. 85.
[64] A researcher interested in the problem of schizophrenia (and doubtful about finding an audience) will direct himself towards organic theories in the U.S.S.R., solutions of existential anthropology in West Germany, and analytical research in Argentina; now each of these orientations can produce valid contributions. In France

even more by public reception) work consistent with the intellectual orientation of the moment, through the state organization of intellectual life: creation or suppression of professorial chairs, organization of academic programmes, etc. As an example of this selective dependence of individual effort on the social context let me cite the great name of Hughlings Jackson, an inspired dialectical thinker, who went completely unnoticed in a period with an anti-dialectical orientation, but an era which was none the less a brilliant time for science. *Direct State pressure* on intellectual life is properly part of the sociology of knowledge, but its study does not raise any particular scientific problems.

So, the Marxist response to the dilemma of the sociology of knowledge is outlined. The implicit epistemology of Marxian orthodoxy blocked all progress in this area: as one identifies (whether consciously or implicitly, it makes no difference) the dialectical validity and character of a doctrine, one is at the same time obliged to describe as 'dialectical' any method which leads to a tangible result, and this description becomes at best a generalization devoid of meaning, and, at its worst, the expression of a sociocentric dichotomization. Orthodox Marxism is thus led to a double paradoxical conclusion: on the one hand to reject the sociology of knowledge and, along with it, to eliminate science (Marxism included!) from the superstructure and, on the other hand, by pronouncing a global condemnation (and apt to be unjust) of the adverse scientific superstructure, to rediscover the notion *of Seinsgebundenheit* at an infinitely more primary level: that of polemics.

In my terms, the ideological character of a scientific theory resides, just like that of the other elements of the superstructure, in the anti-dialectical elements that it can involve, for that is the

at the present time each of these orientations may have an audience, but this fortunate opening up of scientific life is itself a gnoseo-sociological fact and dependent on the post-war political and social context (cf. in this connection Percival Bailey's interesting analysis in his article on Janet and Freud (25); the details of this analysis are outside my subject). It is still the case that, in a different gnoseo-sociological context, *Le Temps Vécu* would have had a relatively restricted audience despite the already established notoriety of its author.

selective element of its 'dependence on the conditions of existence';[65] it is also through this that it distances itself abstractly from reality, to the extent that it is supposed to involve a dialectical structure.[66] However, anti-dialectical periods are far from being scientifically sterile; the results of the deliberate practice of abstraction accumulate and are used in later syntheses. Without the contribution of the experimental apparatus of a Jacques Loeb or a Georges Bohn, the dialectical neo-vitalism of a Von Bertalanffy or a Driesch (or even the dialectical-materialist biology of Marcel Prenant) could not have been what it is. Dialectical results, having once been arrived at, remain established: having overcome certain well-known obstacles—the existence of which is anticipated by the sociology of knowledge—the dialectical theory of the evolution of species will no longer be questioned.[67] This is not the place to go deeper into this problem. My aim was merely to show that, precisely because it considers reification, an anti-dialectical theory, as a non-contingent constitutive element of the processes of alienation, Lukács's conception is capable of contributing to the solution of the dilemma of the sociology of knowledge—which is akin to a question of confidence in Marxism—without sacrificing either the postulate of the social conditioning of knowledge or that of the obvious objective and cumulative value of science. A coherent conception of alienation is thus offered, somewhat far from Marxist texts perhaps, but one which permits the safeguarding of the unity of the concept of superstructure and gives a precise meaning to the fundamental notion of the social determination of consciousness. Finally it allows us to relate the problem of alienation in psychiatry to a Marxist foundation—or at least a dialectical one.

From one of the best present-day interpreters of Marxism

[65] Selective in Grünwald's sense.

[66] I shall not go into the question of the dialectic of Nature. Lukács, who did not admit its existence at the time of the appearance of *Histoire et Conscience de Classe*, revised this opinion, justly perhaps.

[67] However, there is little chance of a return to the rehabilitation of relativity in the U.S.S.R., condemned earlier in the climate of extreme reification in the period before 1953.

comes this unequivocal statement: 'Certain interpreters venture to put forward the word "alienation" in connection with this phenomenon. This goes beyond Marx's thinking. *It is advisable not to confuse objectivation and alienation*, even if the objectivation appropriate to the world of commodities is the field in which historical economic alienations will germinate. Also I have preferred to speak here only of an illusion, which results from the objectivation of work into a thing-value', and Calvez adds: 'the illusion nevertheless is tenacious because the objectivation it reflects is fundamental'.[68] This is clear: from the point of view of the orthodoxy of *Histoire et Conscience de Classe* (Calvez does not quote Lukács, but the allusion is obvious), Father Calvez places himself on the same ground as the critics of the Lukácsian work. It is not impossible to find quotations from Marx likely to invalidate this point of view, but that is not the essential problem. The question of consistency with Marx's thought is important for the scholar who is trying to fix the exact limits of Marx's thought; it is essential for the committed philosopher who is defending the orthodoxy of a political position; for other points of view it can be completely a matter of indifference. My aim has been—all questions of orthodoxy aside—simply to find a formula for *social* alienation which might concretely encompass a sector of *psychiatric* alienation, that is to say for which the clinical and phenomenological study of schizophrenia 'madness par excellence' (M. Blanchot), might provide experimental support. Lukács's view which involves elements as 'psychopathological' as the category of totality, reification or anti-dialectical false identification, seems to be able to offer such a formula.[69]

Even from the orthodox Marxist point of view, the conception of alienation in *Histoire et Conscience de Classe* is defensible if only one is careful to distinguish between textual orthodoxy and spiritual orthodoxy; it is clearly the latter that Lukács is referring to when he observes that real Marxian orthodoxy is essentially

[68] Calvez (85), pp. 228–9 and *passim*.
[69] Cf. my publications (183), 1949; (177), 1951 and (173), 1952 where the psychopathological use of data in *Histoire et Conscience de Classe* (the idea of 'reified consciousness' in psychopathology) is developed in a naturally more summary fashion than in the second part of the present work, but with the aid of clinical material.

C

an orthodoxy of method.[70] Lukácsism does better than remain faithful to the texts: in certain questions he literally rescues the reality of Marxism, mainly by emphasizing the precursory role of Marx in the current discussion of problems of structure[71] as well as in the field of rational thought.[72] Without the Lukácsian contribution Marxism risks finding itself sooner or later faced with the option of appearing either as an ideological justification of a historical enterprise, or an outmoded economic theory.

RELIGIOUS ALIENATION IN DURKHEIMIANISM

It is curious to observe that in the question of religious alienation, Lukács's view is related perhaps as much to Durkheim's as to Marx's. The transcendence of religious alienation was one of the major internal events of Marx's life, but at the same time—it is

[70] 'Orthodox Marxism has nothing to do with the uncritical acknowledgement of the results of Marx's research, nor with a "belief" in such or such thesis, nor with the interpretation of a sacred work.' Marxian orthodoxy is essentially an orthodoxy of method (Orthodoxie in Fragen des Marxismus bezieht sich vielmehr ausschliesslich auf die Methode), Lukács (309), p. 13.

[71] Cf. in this connection an (unpublished) contribution by Merleau-Ponty at the Colloquium on the problem of structure (Fondation Nationale des Sciences Politiques, December 1957).

It is through Lukácsian categories that A. Hesnard's work seems to be in point of fact a Marxist psychopathological doctrine. It is the same with Minkowski's ideas except that it is the concept of spatialization that Lukács's theory of alienation places in a Marxist perspective while in Hesnard it is the idea of structure (totality). But in *Histoire et Conscience de Classe*, these notions are complementary (reification is destructuration *and* spatialization). Lukács's work, therefore, constitutes a possible link between Minkowski and Hesnard.

[72] Reification is a form of substantivation of relationships; it is in this respect that egocentrism is a reifying condition. There exists a curious analogy between Lukács's thought and that of Brunschwicg: the transcendence of the Universe of Discourse by that of reason in French philosophy corresponds to the victory of class consciousness over the reified world in the Hungarian Marxist (cf. my work (179), p. 486, note).

appropriate to call upon Calvez's authoritative commentary on this point—he was not a sociologist of religion and actually one 'often had the impression that apart from peripheral work the religious problem was absent' from his work.[73] Just as his idea of the sociological conditions of dialectical thought is tainted with an element of the psychology of interests which brings it to a more primary level of the concept of ideology than that which underlies his whole system, so also his religious criticism (the opium of the people!) suffers from the effects of the influence of the theory of 'the priests' deception' (*Priestertrug*), an essential element in the ideological criticism of the Age of Enlightenment.[74] This is perhaps the key to the 'apparent insignificance of the criticism of religion in Marx's work',[75] whose thinking on this point is a compromise between the polemist's and the scholar's point of view. One could maintain that primitive religion is *false consciousness* (this comes from Durkheimian ideas); it is hard to see how one could describe it as justificatory ideology, or even interest-derived mystification.

This is not the place to go deeper into the question of the relationships between Marx and Durkheim's thought.[76] As a thinker about religious alienation, the author of *The Elementary Forms of the Religious Life* is aided by his knowledge of primitive religions that are devoid of any conscious mystification, and by the absence of any partisan point of view. Durkheim maintains that collective existence '. . . augments our strength by all that we derive from it, and raises us above ourselves'.[77] In moments of

[73] Calvez (85), p. 73.

[74] The French bourgeoisie from before 1789 exercised a considerable economic power before seizing the political power that it was to exercise unchallenged under the *Directoire*. Its ideological criticism sought therefore, to denounce one form of reification while justifying another. It thus saw itself condemned to never transcending the partial concept of ideology (Mannheim); the denunciation of a utilitarian mystification whose transcendence was to open up the Age of Reason, the reificational hypostasis of the reign of the bourgeois class being thus placed under the protection of natural law. The implicit religious sociology of Marx never completely freed itself from this tradition.

[75] Calvez (85), p. 93.

[76] Cf. Cuvillier (118), whose point of view I share.

[77] Halbwachs (212), p. 85.

collective exaltation '. . . he feels that he is raised above himself and that he lives a life different from that which he ordinarily leads'.[78] In short, primitive society is an 'axiogenic' totality whose formal quality is translated subjectively into an impression of increased strength or value ('mana' is both); the primitive projects into nature in a reificational fashion a source of values which is in reality only super-individual, i.e. social, a superhuman principle. The analyses of the French School of sociology therefore demonstrate a real process of reification at the basis of primitive religious phenomena without any factor of conscious, organized mystification intervening; primitive religion appears in the view of Durkheimianism as an almost pure form of false consciousness. But since there is religious alienation without mystification among primitives, this may also be so for religions higher up the scale; mystification is not, therefore, consubstantial with the religious phenomenon in general. On the other hand, the Durkheimian definition of the religious phenomenon—a definition which involves the reificational element—allows for an account of the structure of 'secular religions' (Monnerot)[79] whose explanation escapes—and with good reason—dogmatic Marxism. For a general sociological theory of false consciousness, the Durkheimian notion about the religious phenomenon offers a contribution whose value should not be underestimated.

RELIGIOUS TEMPORALITY ACCORDING TO M. ELIADE

The study of certain aspects of religious temporality offers an interesting confirmation here. Mircea Eliade's ideas belong in a framework which has only an indirect relationship with my subject. But in a study centred on the notion of reificational deterioration of temporalization as a common denominator in the social and individual forms of alienation, a convergence of this order can not be ignored.

Eliade shows that most religious rites are *repetitions* of archetypal acts. Thus 'matrimonial rites also have a divine model,

[78] Halbwachs (212), p. 88.   [79] J. Monnerot (353), p. 277.

and human marriage reproduces hierogamy, particularly the union between Heaven and Earth'.[80] 'The Indian ceremony of the coronation of a King, *râjasûya*, is merely the earthly reproduction of the ancient consecration that Varuna the first sovereign carried out for his own benefit; this is what the *Brâhmana* repeat endlessly ... Ritual explanations, which are fastidious but instructive, come back to the statement that, if the King performs such or such an act, it is because at the beginning of time, on the day of his consecration, Varuna performed this act.'[81] The archetypal acts are meant to have taken place at the 'beginning of time' (*in illo tempore*); in reality they are extratemporal. In a general way, 'each of the examples ... reveals to us the same "primitive" ontological notion: an object or an action becomes real only to the extent that it *imitates* or *repeats* an archetype. Thus reality is acquired exclusively through *repetition* or *participation* ...' and Eliade adds that 'men would therefore tend to become archetypal and paradigmatic. This tendency may seem paradoxical, in the sense that man in traditional cultures recognizes himself as real only to the extent that he ceases to be himself ... and is content with *imitating* or *repeating* the acts of *another*. In other words, he does not recognize himself as *real*, i.e. as "really himself", except to the extent that he ceases precisely to be real.'[82]

Now the predominance of repetition involves the *abolition of time*. 'A sacrifice, for example, not only exactly reproduces the initial sacrifice revealed by God *ab origine*, at the beginning of time, but it still takes place in this same primordial mythical moment; in other words any sacrifice repeats the initial sacrifice and *coincides* with it. All sacrifices are carried out at the same mythical moment of the Beginning; through the paradox of the rite, profane time and duration are suspended.'[83] 'We perceive therefore a second aspect of primitive ontology: to the extent that an action (or an object) acquires a certain *reality* through the repetition of paradigmatic acts and through that alone, there is an implicit abolition of profane time, duration, history; he who

---

[80] (141), p. 47.
[81] (141), p. 55.
[82] (141), p. 63.
[83] (141), p. 65.

reproduces the exemplary act is thus transported into the mythical period where the revelation of this exemplary act takes place.'[84]

The result is a certain degree of depersonalization of individuals and situations with the transformation of man into an archetype through repetition.[85] 'Popular memory has difficulty in retaining "individual" events and "authentic" figures. It functions in the midst of different structures; categories instead of events, *archetypes* instead of historical people.'[86] Finally, 'this eternal return' translates an *ontology uncontaminated by time and the future.* Just as the Greeks, in the myth of the eternal return sought to satisfy their metaphysical thirst for the ontic and the *static . . .*[87] so the 'primitive' by conferring a cyclical direction on time, annuls its irreversibility.[88]

Obviously Eliade's thought opens up more perspectives than I can embrace here. It is risky to approach a problem of religious philosophy and sociology in the frameworks of a study which is interested in the problem of religion only by virtue of religious *alienation*; whatever Marx may say about it, religion is not just that. Furthermore, a Lukács-Eliade rapprochement might seem shocking to many readers, as the two thinkers are far from being on the same side. But the relationship of ideas involves more than that of ideologies. I have decided not to reproduce very fully these texts (well known in other contexts) although they offer to the central idea of my study a confirmation and a caution: it is as an expression of a non-dialectical consciousness (expressing itself on the level of spatio-temporal structures through a loss of temporalization) that certain aspects of the religious phenomenon belong to the realm of false consciousness. This same notion of loss of temporalization appears in a central place in the study of clinical alienation—of schizophrenia—with Minkowski and Binswanger; this will be discussed later. Is the Buddha who is 'not only capable of abolishing Time, but also of travelling backwards through it',[89] not also the image of catatonia?

[84] (141), p. 65.　　　　　　　　　[85] (141), p. 67.
[86] (141), p. 75.　　　　[87] My italics.　　　[88] (141), p. 134.
[89] Cf. also, further to the work cited, Eliade's article 'Symbolisme indien de l'abolition du temps' (*Journal de Psychologie*, October–December, 1952, no. 4). 'For the Buddha, *time is reversible . . .* the

Buddha not only becomes capable of abolishing Time, but he can also travel backwards through it . . .' (ibid., p. 433). For the Buddha *'all temporal movements are rendered present,* that is to say that the irreversibility of time is abolished' (ibid., p. 434).

The schizophrenic significance of Buddhism has often been apparent. Klineberg [(259), p. 509] points out that in an asylum in Peking there are schizophrenics who have found stability in the study of Buddhism. Cf. also Alexander (8). What is important for us is that religious sociology shows a relationship between a form of sub-temporalization and a catatonic image; without committing oneself, one can say that this is a sufficiently serious argument against toxic explanations of this syndrome.

II

Ideology and Dialectics

'Natural History, otherwise known as natural science, need not interest us here; but we ought to be concerned with the history of men, since almost the whole of ideology is reduced, either to an erroneous conception of this history, or to a *complete abstraction of this history.*'

Marx: *Oeuvres philosophiques* VI, pp. 153–4.

False consciousness and ideology can therefore be defined as forms of sub-dialectical perception of social reality. This definition is for the time being a working hypothesis intended to draw out a common denominator for the very varied concrete forms that false consciousness has taken throughout history. This is not a superfluous step. 'Without being able to go into the details of a systematic typology of these possible different positions', writes Lukács,[1] 'it should be established straightaway . . . that the different forms of "false" consciousness represent qualitative "structural" differences and these differences influence in a decisive way the forms taken by the social action of the classes concerned.' This statement is crucial. The constitution of false consciousness as a univocal sociological concept is thus held in abeyance and in any case it is subordinate to the immense task of writing a 'universal history of false consciousness'. Lukács, nevertheless, continues to use the concept of false consciousness, although, curiously enough, often between inverted commas. Here there is a contradiction, or at least a definite imprecision. While ignoring purely and simply the problem of false con-

[1] Lukács (309), p. 66.

sciousness (which it has transformed into a polemical criticism of the irrationality of opposing thought),[2] orthodox Marxism for its part has resolved the problem by suppressing it; the result is that, separated from the notion of false consciousness, the concept of ideology automatically rediscovers its non-pejorative pre-Marxist meaning (one speaks of *proletarian ideology*) and the whole of its ideological criticism moves towards the partial conception.

By defining ideology and false consciousness as a function of the dialectical quality of consciousness and thought, an effort is made to separate out this common denominator, the lack of which forces one either to work with ill-defined concepts or to obscure real problems. G. Salomon uses a typical expression: ideologies are derivations or reflections (*Derivate*) and at the same time products of derivation (*Depravat*).[3] My definition is centred on the notion of '*Depravat*' interpreted as a schizophrenic loss of dialectical perception of reality, that is to say, as a manifestation of reified consciousness. It is not sufficient that a product of the mind be a 'reflection of the conditions of existence' (*Derivat*) in order to figure as ideology; it must also signify a dialectical loss. In fact, these two processes often go hand in hand, since the influence of collectivities tends to de-dialecticize thought by making it egocentric. This distinction runs the risk of remaining theoretical in many cases (although not always); it is mainly a statement of principles. Let us take, with some reservations, an instructive example: the thought of the child, which is less socialized than that of the adult, is *less dependent on the conditions of existence*; at the same time, since it is less dialectic, it is curiously *closer* to ideology.

[2] 'La Destruction de la Raison' (310) is a curious compromise between these two tendencies.
[3] G. Salomon (410), p. 420. Salomon does not talk about dialectical deterioration associated with ideological perception of the world, but neither does he specify the exact nature of what he calls the 'depravat'.

SOCIOLOGY OF KNOWLEDGE AND IDEOLOGY

On this basis let us take up again the problem of the sociology of knowledge and ideology. Reference is made to scientific ideologies ('psychoanalysis is part of the ideology of American capitalism'). Can the single fact of 'depending on the conditions of existence' reduce a theory to the level of ideology? In this case, we are faced with the following dilemma: either to separate the concept of ideology from that of false consciousness and speak of ideology as a synonym for 'superstructure' or to admit that the sociology of knowledge is in effect a part of the general theory of false consciousness, which is equivalent to recognizing its implicit—and dangerous—interdependence with a sceptical view of truth. It is important, therefore, to show that in the sociology of knowledge, as elsewhere, the word 'ideology' has meaning only as a corollary to a sub-dialectical perception of social reality. One specification is essential at the outset. Certain theorists—Kautsky among others—have a tendency to consider historical materialism as a doctrine in which the dialectical element must be 'brought from the outside'; from the exclusive perspective of a dialectic of the future this view is correct. In the perspective of a dialectic of the totality, historical materialism—just like Durkheimianism—is, in the final analysis, only the sociological formulation of a dialectical principle: the validity of the category of concrete totality in the field of the social sciences.[4] Historical materialism, therefore, does not need to be 'dialecticized' externally. We shall see later that the single fact of being a dialectical conception consistent with psychiatric facts leads

[4] Cf. from among so many other possible ones, this quotation from *Histoire et Conscience de Classe*: 'Bourgeois historical science is also interested in concrete investigations, so much so that it criticizes historical materialism for violating the concretely unique character of historical processes ... And yet, where it believes that it has found the concrete, it by-passes [the concrete] in the most total way: *society as a concrete totality* (Lukács's italics); the system of production at a given level of social evolution, with the class divisions which result from it.' [(309), p. 61.] Cf. also this other passage where it is a question of 'knowledge of society as a historical totality' (309), p. 186.

Daseinsanalyse towards a real sociologism whose formulations actually agree with those of Marxist philosophy.

Marxism considers that consciousness is determined by the conditions of existence. Applied to the problem of the origin of scientific theories, this statement forms the basis of the sociology of knowledge. Classical Marxism neglected the problem which arises here: that of the intermediary mechanism. This problem has already been raised with regard to collective superstructures such as religion or ethics. It becomes acute when one approaches the problem of the scientific superstructures which are so largely dependent on individual inspiration. The problem of the intermediary mechanism here becomes that of the passing of the contents of collective consciousness to individual forms of consciousness. I propose to show: (a) that the dialectic plays an important role in intermediary mechanism, and (b) that it is useless to speak in terms of *ideologies* unless the notion of de-dialecticization is introduced in one form or another. In other words, the sociology of knowledge in its entirety is not a chapter in the theory of false consciousness, but the *sociology of knowledge of dialectical thought* (in other words, the study of conditions favouring or restraining the dialectical position of scientific problems) is certainly one.

THE MEDIATING ROLE OF THE DIALECTIC IN THE SOCIOLOGY OF KNOWLEDGE

According to Ernst Grünwald's view, the action of the social context on the superstructures is constitutive or selective. Selective action is differentiated for its part into selective action as a function of collective needs, and selective action as a function of the dominant ideas. It is convenient, in view of later developments, to designate as mechanism 'A' the constitutive element, as mechanism 'B' the selective mechanism as a function of needs, and as mechanism 'C' the selective mechanism as a function of dominant ideas.

In a letter to Engels,[5] Marx—who did not use the term 'sociology of knowledge', but constantly practised it—pointed out that

[5] Marx, *Lettre à Engels*, 18 June 1862.

Darwin's theory (of which, it is important to remember, he was a fervent supporter[6] reflected on the biological level the forms of existence in English society at that time. From the point of view of the sociology of knowledge, this is constitutive action 'A'. When, in a given society, under the influence of economic necessities, or even military necessities, the majority of young physicians opt for a certain branch of research to the detriment of others, we have an example of selective mechanism type 'B'. When a certain conception of sexuality is badly received in a conservative milieu this is a selective mechanism of type 'C'. The sanction of selection (like all social sanctions) can be either organized or diffuse, and I have emphasized earlier that authoritarian state selection (censure, etc.) is quite properly one of the mechanisms studied by the sociology of knowledge. Whether young mathematicians opt for the study of tensorial calculus in the hope of finding a job more easily or simply on orders from a superior, makes a considerable difference from the point of view of political sociology. From the point of view of the sociology of knowledge it is rather a matter of indifference.

Such a classification is certainly schematic and takes account only very incompletely of the complexity of gnoseo-sociological facts. Factor 'A' embraces a wide variety of data: the action of work techniques and work patterns; the gnoseo-sociological role of primitive religious experience, as Durkheim showed in his study of the social genesis of categories etc. . . . Furthermore, there is an interaction or, more precisely, an intervention of factors, particularly between selective factor 'B' and selective factor 'C', which complicates the problem. Politics intervenes other than in the form of open constraint by the State, and its action constitutes what one would describe as the 'gnoseo-political factor'. Finally, the action of the present context is superimposed on that residual action of the past context, without this superimposition obeying any criteria of coherence. The result is that the data is so complex

---

[6] An important reminder for it shows that for Marx the single fact of being *determined by the conditions of existence* was hardly synonymous with being of doubtful scientific value. Marx thought of dedicating *Capital* to Darwin: the latter declined this honour. Engels, in his discourse at Marx's grave, compared Marx to Darwin.

that my classification could not hope to reflect it.[7] As it is not my intention to write a textbook on the sociology of knowledge, but simply to examine the relationships of this discipline with the theory of false consciousness, my classification may suffice as a working hypothesis.

[7] Here is a (very schematic) example from psychoanalysis.

I start from the postulate that Freudian doctrine is, as a whole, 'a dialectical reaction against reification in psychology' (Caruso (91), p. 779); the role of the sexual element is well known.

The difficulties of Freudianism's beginnings (especially in university milieux) are in the realm of factor 'C', as was its disgrace in orthodox Marxist circles between 1947 and 1953, a disgrace that it shared with numerous other dialectical theories.

The present development in the United States dates, partly, from the Roosevelt period, an intellectually tormented 'dialectical' period and of revolutionary historical significance, which saw also a growing interest in Marxism, the sociology of knowledge, etc. At the present time, a more conservative context, the development of psychoanalysis persists as a consequence of its acquired dynamism, thanks to a social need due to the multiplication of neuroses (factor 'B'), but also due to the action of a *gnoseo*-political factor: as psychoanalysis is censored in Russia, it benefits from a favourable prejudice in the U.S.A., by virtue of the great antagonisms in world politics. It can be seen that the sedimentation of different gnoseo-sociological mechanisms does not follow any criteria of close coherence: the intellectual of the 'New Deal' was interested in psychoanalysis because he believed it to be close to Marxism; the intellectual with conservative tendencies in 1961 might have adhered to it for diametrically opposite reasons.

As for the role of factor 'A' (constitutive), I refer to Percival Bailey's article (25) which shows the differences between Freud's social milieu and that of his contemporary Janet. The spectacle of Jewish family life in Central Europe must have played the same gnoseo-sociological role for Freud as did the spectacle of English life for Darwin.

Official Marxist criticism between 1946 and 1953 for its part presented the role of psychoanalysis as a conscious instrument of social and racial oppression (cf. 'La Psychanalyse contre le people noir', *La Raison*, no. 3, pp. 88–95), and even as preparation for war!

This is an example of a partial (and biased) ideological criticism, which offers condemnation of a conscious desire for mystification instead of concretely analysing the social context involved. The fact that Marxian orthodoxy has itself abandoned this form of criticism, proves its weakness in a striking way.

It is clear, in fact, that the validity of factors 'A' and 'B' in the sociology of knowledge does not involve *ipso facto* the appearance of phenomena of false consciousness. To say that Claude Bernard's work presupposed the existence of certain techniques, that Darwinian theory reflects life in a certain society or that Mitchourine's research was favoured by the needs of Russian agriculture, is to assert the validity of the postulate of the sociology of knowledge on the constitutive or selective level. This is not a sufficient reason to speak of false consciousness in connection with these theories and still less to question the scientific validity of their results. Marx observes that Darwinism 'depended on the conditions of existence': at the same time he hails it as an immense step forward for science and the dialectic. Moreover, what Marx observed in connection with Darwin he could have observed about his own work: *Capital* would not have been conceived, at that time, anywhere other than in London. It is appropriate to emphasize that the criterion of validity of a theory falls within the scope of epistemology; the sociology of knowledge claims no competence in this area.[8] Consequently, to speak of 'scientific ideologies' with a basis solely determined by the infrastructure is not only (let me say this for the sake of the orthodox reader) to deviate from Engels's terminological usage, but also (and this is far more serious) to make of the concept of ideology a catch-all concept of little operational value.[9] It is better in this case to say 'superstructure' and 'superstructural' (which, at least, does not involve any value judgement) and to reserve 'ideology'

[8] J. Maquet [(317), p. 107 ff.] reproaches Mannheim for not distinguishing between gnoseology (*Erkenntnislehre*), the study of the ontological significance of knowledge, and epistemology (*Wissenschaftslehre*), a sort of 'border territory between science and philosophy' [(317), p. 108]. The examination of the value of experimental criteria depends on this latter discipline; it is totally foreign to the sociology of knowledge.

[9] If we do not define ideology as a 'Depravat' (sub-dialectical perception) it must be defined in another way. One is tempted to define it as 'Derivat' ('situational dependence'); it is a bit like asking a neurologist to work with the concept 'everything that depends on the nervous system' (delirious and normal thought, sleep, thermo-regulation, etc.). This is not a false concept. It is a concept without operational value.

for *Depravat*, i.e. to the forms of theoretical crystallization of a sub-dialectical perception of reality. The fact that these two forms often go hand in hand ('superstructure' is often at the same time 'ideology', the *Derivat* often also the *Depravat*) is another matter; what is important is that they are not necessarily corollaries. Finally, the problems of scientific validity would benefit if they were radically separated from this context and left to experimentation, or, on the reflexive level, to epistemology. A serious source of confusion might thus be eliminated.

On the other hand, according to classical definitions, false consciousness is a consciousness *inadequate to the situation* (*Seinsinadäquat*). It is possible to show—by taking up a position in the realm of a dialectic of totality—that it is still a sub-dialectical perception of social reality which presides over this 'inadequacy to the situation' in the sociology of knowledge, and this concerns the action of factor 'A' as much as it does factor 'B'. If it is true that the genesis of Darwin's work was constitutively influenced by the spectacle of English life, this fact of '*Seinsgebundenheit*' is not sufficient to give us the right to talk about scientific false consciousness, and consequently, ideology. This latter appears only to the extent that there is obscuration of the effect of the social situation of the scholar, i.e. that when there is a failure to appreciate the 'scholar-society' totality which is in fact an aspect of historical materialism formulated in dialectical terms. In other words, it is not the *validity* of the historical materialist principle which is responsible for the existence of false consciousness—in this case, Marxist sociology would actually be the sociology of the Cretan liar—but the *misunderstanding of this validity*, and it is the misunderstanding of a dialectical structure.

The third mechanism (factor 'C') remains: social selection as a function of dominant ideas, of the *Zeitgeist*. Now, the history of ideas shows that society or collectivities (classes) fairly often adopt or reject theories according to the extent to which they are dialectical in nature. In fact, on the one hand, at the centre of the more or less conscious preoccupations of collectivities, are collective egocentrism and its excesses, social and economic reification and dereification, the absolute or historically relative (dialectical) character of a social system or its ethnic basis; on the other hand, certain of the great choices in scientific work (between identification or intuition of various things, levels of abstraction, analysis or synthesis), if seen in the perspective of a dialectic of totality, can be interpreted in terms of a more or less dialectical perception of reality. (Leaving aside any question of validity). The result is that the criterion of the social acceptance or elimination of doctrines (that of selective *Seinsgebundenheit*) is often the dialectical criterion. The early difficulties of Freudianism, relativity,[10] the fate of Darwinism, the debate surrounding the heredity of acquired characteristics and many other examples in the history of ideas, attest to the importance of the dialectical criterion in the selective mechanisms of the sociology of knowledge. Was not the trial of Galileo to a certain extent that of the dialectic against reification?[11]

François Simiand warned against accepting any commonly used definition as a preliminary to the empirical approach to problems. Whatever may be the value of such a warning, it is difficult to apply it here, because, placed as it is at the intersection of intellectual thought and politics, the conceptual framework of the theory of alienation has frequently been used in advance of any precise definition. My definition of ideology and false consciousness aims to reduce this impression by utilizing information from the psychopathology of madness. The value of this definition will depend on its usefulness, but if this definition meets objections, then another must be found and this is not easy. I have depended on the notion of 'Depravat'. One might just as well base it on the notion of 'Derivat', and define ideology

---

[10] Cf. Szende (439), pp. 68–9, who devoted a study (untraceable at the present time) to sociological factors and the gnoseo-sociological fate of Einstein's theory, whose short-lived disgrace under Stalinism constitutes a characteristic action of false consciousness.

[11] Aristarque of Samos stated the heliocentric hypothesis in the third century B.C.; he was accused of impiety. His example proves that the state of Greek thinking would very soon have permitted the transcendence of geocentrism and, if this transcendence did not take place, the reasons for it were gnoseo-sociological: the Ptolemaic system corresponded scientifically to Greek ethnocentrism. There is no necessity to go further into the question of whether this problem of collective egocentrism is at the same time a problem of the dialectic.

as a *situationally determined intellectual structure (Seinsgebundenes Geistesgebilde)*. Obviously, this covers science as well as religion or law, but this is a statement which does not state very much. It has real significance only from the standpoint of a theory of unilateral determinism of ideology by economics (in other words, from the viewpoint of popular Marxism); this notion, which was challenged by Engels, no longer has any defenders. One may—more validly—define ideology as a system of ideas that has become a weapon. In doing this one excludes at least religion (unless one reduces criticism of religious alienation to its most elementary level: the criticism of the 'priests' deceit' or the 'opium of the people') without departing too far from the dialectical criterion of ideologization, because the ideas that have become weapons must, in order to be effective, adapt themselves to the sub-dialectical structure of crowd psychology, and thus undergo a utilitarian reification. The same applies to the definition of ideology as *theory having a function of social masking (Verhüllungstheorie)*; this applies to the theory of law but not to juridical action itself;[12] it has difficulty in encompassing primitive religion. One can, finally, define ideology traditionally as all the theories of political movements; this definition, which rides rough-shod over all the experience of Marxism, is a facile solution. On the other hand, by defining ideology as the theoretical systematization of a de-dialecticized (reified) vision, a valid common denominator is suggested for *superstructures* as different as morals, religion, or the whole juridical phenomenon, as well as for

---

[12] Kelsen [(256), p. 458] strongly emphasized the importance of this distinction precisely from the point of view of the theory of ideologies. Obviously, the 'Rechtstheorie' can be understood as a theory intended to conceal the true nature of social reality; law itself is a social fact, the expression of a power relationship certainly, but far removed from any function of dissimulation. Now, the trouble is that at the same time law is a superstructure (and even the epitome of superstructure) and, furthermore, a characteristic reificational product. The same applies to primitive religion, which is certainly a reificational superstructure, but in no way *ideology* in the sense of *Verhüllungstheorie*; it is certainly the only way that the primitive man has to express his sociality. One can see the point at which it becomes difficult to avoid confusion in defining ideology as a function of its single role as a factor of social dissimulation.

the various aspects of political alienation, one of which, *ethno-centrist ideology*, will be the subject of a special chapter.

MECHANISMS OF DE-DIALECTIZATION

It seems likely that this de-dialecticization is *sometimes* dependent on a conservative interest psychology (*Konservative Interessen-psychologie*), as Marxism implies. Scheler's formula is striking: 'the lower classes prefer future considerations, the upper classes present considerations'.[13] G. Salomon was therefore, in a sense right to define Marxism as the synthesis of a psychology of interests and a sensualist philosophy,[14] but the main lesson from the study of utopian consciousness is that de-dialecticization (spatialization) of historical time can be independent of any conservative interest, conscious or not. By reifying the future, proletarian consciousness arrives at the same schizophrenic structure of historical time[15] as the bourgeoisie arrives at by reifying the past; the process of ideologization of orthodox Marxism bears witness to this. Lukács could reproach bourgeois consciousness for being a '*post festum* consciousness',[16] but one is

[13] 'Die Unterklassen stets zur Werdensbetrachtung, die Ober-klassen zur Seinsbetrachtung neigen.' M. Scheler (414), p. 207.

[14] G. Salomon emphasizes the Marx-Bacon relationship. Ideology for Marx is essentially dependent on *idola fori* and *idola tribus*. A critique of language would have been close to Marx's preoccupa-tions. Briefly, the theory of ideology in Marx would be a mixture of nominalism, empirico-sensualism and psychology of interests ('Nominalismus und Empirio-Sensualismus in Verbindung mit Inter-essenpsychologie' (Salomon (410), p. 395); this striking phrase is worth remembering. P. Szende, for his part, in his various writings, strongly emphasized the progressivist nature of sense experience which he inadvisedly likens to the dialectical perception of reality.

[15] Schizophrenic in Minkowski's sense (spatialization of duration in morbid rationalism).

[16] Lukács (309), p. 255. 'The past which dominates the present, the *post festum* consciousness (das *post festum Bewusstsein*) in which this domination is expressed, are only the expression (*der gedank-liche Ausdruck*) of a fundamental economic fact in a capitalist regime (and only in a capitalist regime): reified expression (der verdinglichte Ausdruck) of the inherent possibility in capitalist

tempted to reply that utopian consciousness for its part is an 'ante festum consciousness' in the literal sense of the term; consciousness of the celebration constantly promised for tomorrow. By placing the criticism of reification in the centre of his conception of dialectical philosophy, Lukács limits the importance of the 'psychology of interests' factor; from this point of view, his thinking marks a step forward in relation to Marx's.

Furthermore, it provides the main bridge, by means of reification of the future (utopian consciousness), to total relationism. Since Marxian orthodoxy, for its part, is involved on the diametrically opposite side (dogmatic epistemology of definitive truths, denunciation of conscious mystification in the adversary, sociocentric dichotomization), this is, incidentally, one of the aspects of the 'Lukács problem' over which so much ink has been used. In fact, because official Marxism challenges—with good reason! —any criticism of utopian consciousness, it is doomed never to go beyond the stage of the partial concept of ideology. Inversely, the importance given to reification allows the withdrawal of the processes of de-dialecticization of consciousness from the exclusive hold of the psychology of interests, and here again the fate (or if you like: the 'vicissitudes') of the dialectic in the frameworks of orthodoxy provides the possibility for experimental verification.

PSYCHOLOGY OF CROWDS AND FALSE CONSCIOUSNESS

Consequently, it is possible to go a little further and to look for the causes of de-dialecticization beyond the level of conservative or progressivist political involvement, i.e. beyond the interest factor, but also beyond the reificational factor. Ziegler (who was influenced more by Pareto than by Marx)[17] is one of the few to point out the importance of the constants in crowd psychology in the process of ideologization. It is almost a common-place

relationships to be renewed and to extend themselves due to incessant contacts with living work.' A marvellous passage, but when Lukács discussed, in 1923, the socialist system where the *present* was to dominate the past, one can afford to be sceptical in 1961.

[17] Ziegler (477).

however; but most of the theorists of false consciousness (except Pareto) retain from their Marxist heritage a respect for the mass and a mistrust of all that may seem to be a criticism, even indirectly, of collective action. It is not surprising that a study like G. Le Bon's involving, along with remarkable intuitions, disillusioned judgements about the future of socialism,[18] did not stimulate any interest in Marxist circles. As for Freud's study,[19] it divided the Marxist criticisms of psychoanalysis by channelling the most severe ones.

Now, in a general way, crowd psychology is pre-dialectical; it provides fertile ground for the de-dialecticizing action of reification, and also propaganda. This is without doubt an important moment of the process of ideologization, when, faced with the demands of immediate efficiency, propaganda ceases to depend on a dialectical vision of the world.[20] Freud emphasized the importance of identification with the leader; now the identificatory function is, in epistemology, a de-dialecticizing, spatializing function. To say that the 'extreme father' complex (of which the 'leader theory' is only the extreme case) belongs to an anti-dialectical pattern of false consciousness, is *a priori* a statement devoid of meaning; seen in the dual sense (psychoanalytical and epistemological) of the concept of identification, it assumes, by contrast, a precise meaning. Crowd psychology is anti-dialectical

[18] Cf. this passage: 'let us not forget that with the present day power of crowds, if a single opinion could acquire enough prestige to compel recognition, it would soon assume such a tyrannical power that everything would immediately have to yield to it. The age of free discussion would then be ended for a long time . . .'
We leave it to the reader to decide if this passage depends on 'remarkable intuitions', 'disillusioned judgements', or both.

[19] Freud (166).

[20] Obviously here again there are two levels, the level of false consciousness which corresponds to the anti-dialectical structure of the vision of the world of crowds as such, and the ideological level which gives to these structures an appearance of system with—sometimes—a dialectical pretension (illusion of dialectic).

Marxism was from this point of view a gamble: that it is possible to make efficient propaganda with dialectical data, i.e. offering no economy of intellectual effort. This gamble is paid for by a failure and this failure is one (rather misunderstood) dimension of the historical significance of orthodox Marxism.

because of its tendency towards schematization, its aversion to novelty,[21] its incapacity for structuration (time in crowds, a non-structured succession of present moments, is analogous to the temporality of the 'flight of ideas' studied by Binswanger), and lastly because of its dichotomizing (Manichean) tendency. It is understandable that its eruption into political consciousness by means of strong collective emotions might have parallel effects on the two factors already considered: conservative psychology and reification of consciousness.

G. Vedel's study[22] significantly illustrates this convergence. Under the title *Le rôle des croyances économiques dans la vie politique*, this article is in reality an analysis of one aspect of economic false consciousness, but—and this point is important—the mechanism of de-dialecticization, independent of any psychology of interests, depends here essentially on the incapacity for synthesis (a dialectical incapacity) of crowd psychology. This approach produces results that are very close to those of Marxist analyses—certain of Vedel's formulae closely resemble Marx's[23]—but without being forced to call upon the notion of class consciousness. For example, there is the question of contradiction 'resolved by a synthesis of a magical nature';[24] we have seen elsewhere the analogous role of the *illusion of totality* in the processes of ideologization. Now, between the mechanism described by the Marxists ('obscuration of a dialectic of the future due to conservative interests') and that described by Vedel ('incomprehension of concrete structures as a consequence of the synthesising incapacity of crowd psychology'), there is no incompatibility of theory: they are two

---

[21] Le Bon (290), p. 38. Cf. the familiar misoneism of schizophrenics, 'paleologic thinking tends to perpetuate existing conditions' [Arieti (12)].

[22] G. Vedel (457).

[23] 'False opinion does not become real by being generalised, but it transforms reality' (Vedel (457), p. 47). 'Ideology becomes a material power by taking possession of the masses' (Marx, *Critique de la philosophie du droit de Hegel*).

[24] Vedel (457), p. 46. The term 'magical' is dominant in Vedel's study; one might note that schizophrenia has been described as the *magical psychosis* par excellence. Cf. Roheim (405).

different aspects of sub-dialectical, and consequently ideological, perception of social reality.

The variations in the dialectical quality of consciousness therefore play a primordial role in the processes of sociological alienation; its importance in clinical alienation will be brought out later. These variations are a function of various factors: conservative psychology tending to deny the dialectical nature of the economic categories of a given economic system; reification of the consciousness factor of spatialization of duration; eruption of pre-dialectical archaic elements; the action of propaganda which pays for its efficiency by dispensing with the effort that the dialectical situation of the problems requires; defocalization of thought due to the appearance on the scene of privileged systems (collective egocentrism) with regression to a pre-dialectical stage similar to child thought, involving a prevalence of spatial functions with a loss of dialectical temporalization. A hierarchy of these factors is so much more difficult to establish since their respective importance varies from case to case. It is probable that Marxism overestimated the role of the conservative interest as a factor of de-dialecticization; it totally ignored the role of constant effects in collective psychology. The same applies to the question of relationships between egocentrism and dialectics (the de-dialecticizing action of individual and collective egocentrism) which has never been systematically examined from the Marxist viewpoint.[25]

VILFREDO PARETO'S POINT OF VIEW

It is interesting to examine how the dialectical character of the drama of alienation is reflected in V. Pareto's thought. The author of the *Traité de Sociologie* is one of the main theoreticians

[25] Permit me to refer to my two studies [(176), 1948 and (179), 1949] which contain the outline of a theory of collective egocentrism as a sub-dialectical and spatializing (schizophrenic) perception of social reality. However, there is no systematic elaboration of these contributions.

of false consciousness, certainly the only one to approach the problem from a conservative point of view (the 'Karl Marx of the bourgeois class').[26] It is not the intention here to take up this involved and notorious theory. Pareto sees history as a circulation of elites; he distinguishes, not without some arbitrariness, between logical acts and non-logical acts and admits the predominant historical role of the latter.[27] 'The chief factor in the evolution of peoples has never been truth, but error,' Le Bon states.[28] Man acts according to certain constants in his 'nature' known as 'residues'; he later explains his action with the aid of justificatory systems called 'derivations'.[29] The details of this view, which has been criticized at times, lie outside our subject. His central idea is attractive: we have seen that in its relationship to false consciousness, ideology can be defined as a derivation in relation to a residue.[30] Pareto has been compared with Marx, though a comparison with Mannheim is certainly more fruitful. By linking his theory of the circulation of elites to a critique of false consciousness, Pareto is in fact denouncing utopian thought (his anticipatory critique of Stalinism is still valid); but by postulating the extra-historical constancy of human nature in his actual analysis of the majority of residues, he himself falls into ideology. It is therefore a critique of utopia without being a critique of ideology (Marxian orthodoxy represents the opposite case), which explains its potentialities for acceptance by conservatives.

Now, there could not be a consistent critique of the one without the other, and the dialectical criterion of ideologization provides

[26] This phrase is from the Italian socialist journal *Avanti*, in its obituary article, 1923. Cf. Bousquet (77), p. 23.

[27] Cf. Bousquet (77), Ziegler (477) and the very critical discussions of R. Aron (17) and (18). The developments which follow are very largely dependent on these two latter contributions.

[28] Le Bon (290), pp. 73–4.

[29] The terminological coincidence with G. Salomon's notion of *Derivat* is fortuitous. Ideology is, according to my definition, a *derivation* of false consciousness in Pareto's sense, but a *Depravat* (=subdialectical perception) in Salomon's sense.

[30] In psychopathology, the delirious system is a derivation, but the determination of the 'residue' poses the delicate problem concerning the original cause of the trouble, which will be discussed later.

the stumbling block in such circumstances.[31] This criterion in fact reappeared in Pareto, but he 'turned it on its head'. The circulation of elites would create—if we are to believe this author—an illusion of progress; the elites which take over power really are worthy of it. Political movements are obliged to appear as if they believe in the possibility of real progress; but in relation to the desire for power acting as residue,[32] this postulate of possible progress is a derivation, or in other words, in Marxist language, a phenomenon of false consciousness. 'Only he who is content with derivations and transforms them into fetishes of an absolute nature can believe in the existence of an evolution'(!) writes O. Ziegler, critically interpreting this thesis of Pareto's.[33]

In summary, it is straightforward: for Pareto, History is antidialectical: it is the belief in the dialectic which, by reifying itself, becomes false consciousness. The only ideology is utopianism. The man who believes in progress is merely a fool; only the Calliclès and their followers are in the right. To be fair to Pareto: the fundamental ahistoricism of social conservatism here appears undisguised. However, progress does exist; utopian character does not therefore reside in the belief in progress, but either in the illusion of its end at the utopian moment, or in a non-dialectical conception of the relationships between past and present which, seen from a utopian viewpoint, cease to be moments of a totality.[34]

[31] Laswell defined utopia as a 'systematic counter ideology' [(287), p. 14, note]. He does not see at all the common element: the rejection of historical duration of which only the occasion of its eruption varies—the present for ideology and the future ('future thing') for utopia. Stalinism was both ideological and utopian; the *temporal* hiatus between present and future grew after the ascendancy of the *spatial* hiatus between a privileged system and a non-privileged residue (sociocentrism). 'Utopias are realisable,' said Berdiaeff.

[32] Ziegler emphasizes the intellectual relationship between Nietzsche and Pareto; the circulation of elites is somewhat the sociology of the eternal return. The author of *Volonté de puissance* would to a certain extent have been the Hegel of the 'bourgeois Karl Marx'.

[33] Ziegler (477), p. 681.

[34] Plato's Republic is a utopia because (a) its foundation was supposed to end History and (b) the state of Athens in Plato's time and its state at the utopian moment are considered as two fixed points that no concrete history is supposed to bring together in 'good

It is not *too dialectical a conception of the* present, but an *insuffi-ciently dialectical conception of the future* which marks the utopian nature of a consciousness. If it is permissible to speak of a utopian consciousness in certain thinkers of the Enlightenment, it is not because they believed themselves to be promoters of progress —this claim was justified—but to the extent that they considered it definitive and postulated its subsequent end; like other forms of false consciousness, utopian consciousness is inseparable from an ahistorical view. The same applies to Marxism whose utopian potentiality is at the level of the theory of the *Vorgeschichte*,[35] i.e. at the level where *the dialectic ceases.* Pareto's conceptions thus do not hold up very well against factual evidence. It is necessary to discuss him, however, for two reasons. First, his importance is such that a study of false consciousness could not have claimed to be complete if he had been ignored; second, because a criticism of Pareto's ideas is singularly instructive regarding the role of the dialectic in the mechanisms of false consciousness. It shows—in a distorting mirror if you like—how the drama of alienation could not be anything but dialectical.

form'. Utopian thought is not therefore too dialectical, but the opposite; it is in this respect that it resembles the other forms of false consciousness.

[35] Cf. (321), p. 74. 'The relationships of bourgeois production are the last contradictory form of the process of social production ... With this social formation the prehistory (*Vorgeschichte*) of human society is therefore achieved.' Sentences heavy with meaning. Marx does not especially stipulate the arrest of the historical dialectic, but implicitly he admits its possibility. In fact, for many Marxists, the conquest of Nature at this point had to replace the historical self-conquest of man: a spatial struggle takes the place of the temporal struggle. It is impossible to resist citing here the extraordinary Soviet epic of the conquest of space. On the other hand, by using the word 'prehistory' Marx forcefully separates socialism from all the other earlier social forms, which are lumped together as a virtually homogeneous whole. Once socialism is realized (or believed so to be) this line of temporal demarcation becomes rigid separation in space and the foundations of an evolution towards sociocentric dichotomization are laid.

DIALECTIC OF THE TOTALITY AND
DIALECTIC OF THE FUTURE

This dialectical view of alienation arises mainly from *Histoire et Conscience de Classe*. In the process of ideologization, the fate—and the decline—of the dialectic of the totality and that of the dialectic of the future are often interdependent. Thus, ethnocentrism appears as the reificational neglect of a dialectic of the totality at its 'false consciousness' level (Adorno) and as the rejection of a dialectic of history at the ideological level. The dialectic of totality and the dialectic of the future have found, in the course of the history of ideas, almost pure expressions. Gestaltism is the form *par excellence* of a dialectic of pure totality without genetic sub-structure. This circumstance has not escaped orthodox Marxist theoreticians who have centred their criticism on this point;[36] it is well justified, except that because of the 'all or nothing' ('black' or 'white') approach of orthodoxy, these authors confuse the notion of 'insufficiently dialectical theory' with that of 'non-dialectical theory'. Certain writings of Engels[37] and Plechanov[38] are, by contrast, examples of an almost pure dialectic of the future, to a large extent neglectful of problems of structure. Now, these two aspects of the dialectic are inseparable[39] and one is quite tempted to republish the famous words of Kant about them. A dialectic of the single future is blind, for the historical future presupposes an axiology, and value is inseparable from structure, unless one does not stop at the solution of a heteronomic valorization, which gives merely an illusion of historicity, as we shall see later.[40] For its part a dialectic of pure

[36] Notably R. Garaudy (184) and also the journal *La Raison*, *passim*.

[37] For example, L. Feuerbach.

[38] For example, the otherwise admirable (and forgotten) essay of Plechanov, *Beiträge zur Geschichte des Materialismus: Holbach, Helvetius, Marx*.

[39] The famous 'change of quantity into quality' is the dynamic aspect of the principle of totality as I shall show later.

[40] Cf. Lukács (309), p. 196 ff., a remarkable criticism of what I call a 'dialectic of the pure future'. 'The dialectic of the Eleates

structure (like Gestaltism) is actually suspended in a void[41] and the temptation arises to look for the explanation that one did not wish to seek in the field of genetics in the domain of essences. One can see that these two broad aspects taken *separately* do not easily withstand the idealist temptation.

One of the essential meanings of *Histoire et Conscience de Classe* consists precisely in that it does not separate these two aspects of the dialectic; this fact—which some people might be tempted to see as a sign of undifferentiation in the conceptual apparatus of a relatively young thinker[42]—constitutes to my mind the dimension of Lukács's thought which enables this work to provide a geometric locus for the different forms of alienation, *clinical alienation included.* Accused of idealism, Lukács here seems to be the most materialist of thinkers, for the synthesis of these various aspects of the dialectic implicitly contains the principle of historical materialism as a dialectical and historical sociology of the concrete totality. But this observation is perhaps a warning; it is not a proof, for *Histoire et Conscience de Classe*—like most other works—is not a sacred text. By contrast, the information gained from a study of schizophrenia possesses an experimental value for a sociological theory of alienation. In fact it confirms Lukács's conception: in the clinical accounts of schizophrenia, deterioration of the dialectic of the totality (with dissociation as the extreme form) and deterioration of the dialectic of the future (with catatonia as the extreme form) seem quite

clearly shows the contradictions inherent in the movement in general; the moving object remains unchanged. Whether the moveable arrow is moving or resting matters little—it remains in the dialectical turbulance unchanged in its objectivity (*Gegenständlichkeit*) as an arrow, as a thing . . . In Marx, by contrast, the dialectical process transforms the objective forms of objects (*die Gegenständlichkeitsformen der Gegenstände*) into a process, into a flux.'

[41] Cf. Garaudy (184), whose criticism is correct except that genetic colour blindness is specific to certain *Gestaltists* and so not consubstantial with *Gestaltism.*

[42] Cf. K. Axelos's criticism [(309), French edition, preface, p. 8 and *passim*], which does not seem to me to have any foundation: the undifferentiated terminology of Lukács expresses a profoundly concrete perception of the real which has certainly benefited from the great lesson of Bergsonism.

interdependent. Joseph Berze defined schizophrenia as a great experiment of Nature (*grosses Naturexperiment*).[43] Anticipating some subsequent conclusions we can from now on describe it as the great experimental datum in both dialectical thought and the sociological problem of alienation. In fact, if it is true that the notion of non-dialectical or sub-dialectical perception of reality possesses in the realm of facts as tangible an expression as a mental disorder, that proves—and the demonstration is doubtless not unnecessary—that the notion of 'dialectical thought' is neither a polemical concept of doubtful objective validity nor, on the contrary, an independent 'essence' and anterior to all psychology (in Brentano's or Husserl's sense), but the expression of something real; the dialectic 'exists' to the extent that schizophrenia exists.[44] In this order of ideas the possible 'deduction' from schizophrenia in my initial hypothesis (reificational syndrome) has the significance of an experimental test for the conception of alienation, which is the basis of my study. The phenomenology of a mental disorder can thus virtually assume experimental significance in relation to social alienation.

This methodological verification is capable of being extended. In fact, one can object to my study for failing to have an experimental basis and to its results for being without any practical value: to define false consciousness as a schizophrenic structure and schizophrenia as an individual form of false consciousness would be to go round in circles, to indulge in a sterile game with concepts, in a word, to practise metaphysics. Now, nothing is more foreign to my intentions than to wish to engage in metaphysics. But the quantitative evaluation of experimental results is

[43] J. Berze (51) p. 55.

[44] Since a psychiatrist asked me to define the dialectic, I thought I might give the following definition: 'The dialectic is the opposite of the way schizophrenics live and think.' I shall do my best to establish later that this is not a whim. The result is that the very concept of dialectical thought (which has only just begun to penetrate into non-Marxist circles) finds its justification there. Schizophrenia existed in the world before Hegel. On the other hand, this definition (supported by the symptomatological deduction that I shall attempt) also supports the arguments in favour of schizophrenia as a unitary nosological concept. Two debatable notions confirm each other.

not the only form of legitimate empirical approach in sociology. The critical study of ideologies (such as appear in journalism for example) is one legitimate approach, empirical if not experimental, particularly when its results converge with those from experimental research.

H. Aubin is the first to my knowledge to use the term 'socio-pathological parallelism'.[45] The observation that different concrete manifestations of sociological alienation have the common denominator of lacking the dialectic, and that, on the other hand, one sector of clinical alienation combines pathological forms of existence and non-dialectical (reified) consciousness, corresponds to one aspect of this parallelism. Now, in the latter framework, the terms *sociological* and *clinical* reciprocally perform the function of experimental data, and the fact that this may be a question of 'spontaneous' experimental data does not constitute a perceptible difference. False consciousness is 'experimental' in relation to the clinical phenomenon, for it eliminates one section of individual factors (C. Schneider's 'tertiary factor') which are an obstacle to conceptualization in psychopathology.[46] In this category of ideas, it is permissible to say without too much of a paradox that 'derealist thought' in social psychology not only possesses a schizophrenic character, but that it constitutes in a certain sense a *purer* form of schizophrenia than the mental disorder of the same name. Inversely, in relation to the concept of false consciousness, which is after all an abstraction, schizophrenia constitutes a living tangible reality. These considerations explain the fact that, despite its apparently tautological character, the statement of the schizophrenic nature of false consciousness might enrich our knowledge and contribute towards clarification of the concepts involved in the two cases. The socio-pathological discussion thus ends by confirming the (disputed) nosological unity

[45] H. Aubin (21), p. 71. But my earlier studies on reification in psychopathology are, in fact, applications of this parallelism.

[46] C. Schneider distinguishes beyond the primary and secondary symptoms of schizophrenia, tertiary symptoms, dependent on the individual personality: a professor raves differently from a farmer [(422, p. 96]. As for the difference between primary and secondary syndromes, see below pp. 222 ff.

of schizophrenia; by adopting the total (structural) concept of ideology (Mannheim), and the unitary theory ('total concept') of alienation that can encompass both forms of social and clinical alienation.

III

Outline of an Axiology of Alienation

'. . . the meaning and consciousness of class are the same thing.'

Calvez: La pensée de Karl Marx, p. 206.

'Form is the highest judge of life. A directing force, an ethical element, is contained in the structuring capacity; the single fact of being structured entails an implicit value judgement.'[1]

Lukács: Die Seele und die Formen, p. 370.

Marxian orthodoxy has always been sterile in the area of axiology. Ruyer, in his short book, devoted only two pages—very much in the Lukácsian vein in any case—to the implicit axiology of historical materialism.[2] But he cites no work on Marxist axiology, and with good reason.

---

[1] Die Form ist die höchste Richterin des Lebens. Eine richtende Kraft, ein Ethisches ist das Gestaltenkönnen und ein Werturteil ist in jedem Gestaltsein enthalten.

[2] 'There is in philosophical Marxism, a therapy through consciousness which reminds one of Freudian therapy, but which also recalls the Spinozism of the later books of the *Éthique*. *It invokes, not the idea of the Infinite or of naturing Nature, but the idea of Totality, borrowed from Hegel.* The fully conscious man is no longer an economic man, trapped by his own works; he is free, for he has appropriated his "total essence", he no longer allows his will to be transformed into social nature; he transforms nature into will. *He is both subject and object of the future; he is disalienated.* It would perhaps therefore be more exact to say that the axiological naturalism of Marxism has a tendency to lead on, not to objective, mystical idealism as in Spinoza, but to the idealism of Freedom.' (*Philosophie de la Valeur*, p. 138.) My italics.

This sterility is one of the many consequences of the ideologization of official Marxism which, by bringing Marxist thinking to the pre-dialectical level, has by the same token brought it to a pre-axiological level. In his treatise on historical materialism, Bakharin formulated an instrumental theory of ethics; this view outlived its author. Moreover, the existence of a *theory of* (economic) *value* in *Capital* created the illusion that there would be a Marxist axiology.

Now, if Marx's theory of economic value is not an axiology, neither is it its negation. It is its *negative* in the photographic sense. Marxian analysis is the phenomenology of a process of reificational devaluation which shows how, in the capitalist economy, commodity becomes value and man becomes commodity. The result is that a Marxist axiology which had wanted to go beyond economic theory has its route marked out: negative extrapolation from the analyses of *Capital*. This route necessarily leads towards a materialist re-evaluation of certain non-Marxist dialectical axiologies: among others, the Lukács-Dupréel convergence is significant. As a matter of fact, *Histoire et Conscience de Classe*, a real axiology of proletarian historical action, contains implicitly all the elements of a Marxist theory of higher values. These are the elements that I shall try to bring out.

The following items will be studied in turn:

(1) the relationships between totality and value;
(2) the spatio-temporal structure of the process of reificational devaluation;
(3) reified value, otherwise known as social sacredness.

TOTALITY AND VALUE[3]

According to Ruyer, 'any form can be considered as a capitalised value, and any capital can be considered basically as mnemic,

[3] I am using the terms 'Gestalt' and 'concrete totality' as synonymous expressions; the problem of their mutual relationships will be considered elsewhere. On the other hand, in the texts quoted (notably Ruyer), the word 'form' is obviously used in its Gestaltist meaning without any connection with Aristotelian 'form'.

since all form subsists mnemically'.[4] Negative values are often bad
or weak forms, 'current language often characterises a person or
an unsuccessful work by reducing it *to its material constituents*; a
bad speech is only *verba and voces*; bad music is only noise;
an unartistic picture a daub; an inefficient machine a piece of
scrap-iron . . .'.[5]

There is nothing surprising in the fact that the main contemporary theorist of the theory of form, W. Köhler, promotes a
Gestaltist view in axiology. For Köhler[6] the essential characteristic
of value is its requiredness; now, this requiredness is difficult to
separate from a certain formal context. 'In summary,' writes
Ruyer, 'for Köhler, dynamic form and *requiredness* or value,
having exactly the same properties, are *one and the same thing*.'[7]

The point of view that Lalo defends in *l'Art et la Morale* is
wholly analogous. For Lalo, value is above all an *energizing* concept, in some way the moral equivalent of the notion of physical
energy. 'Since Nietzsche borrowed it from the economists and
transmitted it to contemporary pragmatists, the notion of *value*
plays a role in philosophical speculation similar to that which
energy or force has in modern science. Force or energy are at the
origin of all phenomena: in the beginning was force. But one can
only define or even establish their existence through their effects,
which are precisely these phenomena. For example, in order to
explain mechanical movements or chemical combinations, one
must suppose that what has caused them is a modification of
interatomic or electrical energies, that we do not know in any
way except by other, qualitatively very diverse, effects, although
they are not without a quantitative common measure. Our thinking thus isolates hypothetical, abstract notions, which are alone
capable of explaining concrete relations.'[8]

A second fact which catches Lalo's attention is that axiological
existence has support from elements which, taken by themselves,
are devoid of value. 'Every conscious imperative is the reconstruction of a concrete action by separate elements each one of
which taken alone has no value, or at least has no value of the

[4] R. Ruyer (409), p. 25.   [5] Ibid., p. 32 (my italics).
[6] W. Köhler (261), pp. 63–102.
[7] R. Ruyer (409), p. 145 (my italics).   [8] Lalo (285), pp. 125–6.
D

same order; but whose assemblage or *synthesis* has to acquire precisely this value as an essential characteristic.'[9] 'All values being essentially concrete are in theory also as complex as one another. We approach each one mindful, as Plato said, of the one value, truth . . . However, taken alone, each one is anaesthetic, as in the isolated state, the conditions prior to truth are alogical, or, like the elements of life, inanimate.'[10] 'For reasons of the same order, it must be said that the foundations of all morals are amoral. *The synthesis of amoral elements* becomes morality.

'In theory therefore, the genesis of values is the same in the area of knowledge or truth, or beauty, serious activity or morality: *each value is always the synthesis of elements without value*, and they differ among themselves through the particular form that this group assumes.'[11] Value is in short an indivisible whole; it is destroyed by analysis which leaves intact only the bricks, but dislodges the axiological edifice. Lalo uses the word 'synthesis'. We can substitute in its place the word 'form' (Gestalt). One thus ends up with this formula: *value is a formal quality*, *Gestalt-qualität*.

Finally, 'all conscious imperatives and values can be reduced to a few applications of this very general formula: premeditated or spontaneous organization of life, physical or moral life, unconscious or conscious, individual or collective'.[12] 'Everywhere that some living synthesis occurs, *the whole acquires a value that its elements do not possess*; or else, they possess another value, of an inferior order . . . To say that in art, erotic acts can be the condition or the element of a superior morality, although at first sight any attempt to relate these two partial concepts seems to reveal a reciprocal hostility, is not more contradictory than establishing and demonstrating that the number 12, even and compound, is the sum of two numbers 5 and 7, odd and prime. So many elementary properties are, in effect, irreconcilable as long as their whole is not totalized by this "synthetic judgement" as Kant calls it.'[13]

[9] (285), p. 127. [10] (285), p. 154.
[11] (285), p. 161. [12] (285), p. 127.
[13] (285), p. 178. The relationship that Lalo establishes between axiological experience and synthetic judgement corresponds to the

In short, the three main ideas of Lalo are: the energizing nature of value ('value is the pyschological form of universal energy'); its synthetic essence (I call it: formal quality); finally, vital organization as an axogenous factor; the creative life of values. On this last point, Lalo's thesis joins with that of supporters of a moral vitalism such as that discussed by the author of 'Morale sans obligations ni sanctions', or, closer to us, Dominique Parodi.

E. Dupréel has shown that every value possesses two essential characteristics: consistence and precariousness. Now, these two characteristics are found in the world of form: consistence corresponds to the autoconservative tendency of forms, the intensity of which acts as a measure of the difference between weak and strong forms; on the other hand, we know that forms disappear once the boundary that holds the elements together has disappeared (precariousness). The classical example of the gestaltists for temporal form is melody; now, nothing is more consistent and at the same time more precarious than a melody. Life, too, being essentially a formal organization of inorganic elements, participates in this axiological bipolarity: its consistency is seen in its tendency towards autoconservatism and assimilation, unknown in the world of raw elements, its precariousness in the fact that often a minimal cause is enough to destroy it; life—at least in its essential organs—does not admit the notion of spare parts.

The result is that value is essentially a corollary of *dereification*; for its part, reification also entails a devaluation. In fact, a 'thing' is both *less precarious* and less *consistent* than an organized being or a conscious being. Less precarious because its existence depends less on accidents (one can replace the works, even the essential ones, of a watch), less consistent, because, in theory, the pieces of machinery do not possess this faculty of assimilating the environment which characterizes the most modest of living beings.

relationship which exists between reified thought and analytical judgement; it is the same observation made from two different viewpoints. Cf. Szende's ideas on the significance of apriorism in authoritarian ideologies (*Verhüllung und Enthüllung*, p. 69 and *passim*), and those of G. Marcel who sees in the spirit of abstraction 'a transposition of imperialism into the mental world'. (G. Marcel (319), p. 116.)

Likewise, undifferentiated matter is both less precarious and less consistent than pieces of machinery. Pure axiological thought here converges with Lukács's views; totality, the central category of working-class consciousness is the principle par excellence of dereification in history. Axiological thought, however little it may make an effort to reflect the structure of reality, seems almost fated to rediscover dialectical themes.

One can go further. What characterizes value above all is a sort of autotranscendence; value is a perpetual transcendence of self. Likewise, reality organized into form is in a constant state of autotranscendence; a totality is more than the sum of its parts. The result is a sort of pre-dynamism (the dynamism of a coiled spring) as characteristic of formal existence as of axiological existence. We saw earlier how the Dupréelian criteria of consistency and precariousness were found in the world of forms. Lastly, formal organization always contains a hint of finality; now, all finality, even unconscious, involves an idea of value. 'In the living world, the object of all concrete action which authorises the hypothesis of a finality or, as Bergson said, of a "vital impulse", represents a value for the person who accomplishes this action.'[14]

Pierre Janet described as 'suspensive' the tendencies which can be arrested at different moments of their activation and which can remain for some time in some way suspended without immediately ending in complete consummation. We are all familiar with the role attributed by the famous author of 'Débuts de L'Intelligence' to suspension in the genesis of memory: 'memory is suspended action'. Taken in its widest sense, suspension is an important differential element between organized matter and crude matter, and, on the psychological and moral level, one of the factors of humanization. With the exception of the highest and the lowest—the immediately physiological values and ideal values— our values are *values of suspension*; the most characteristic of them is money which is stored up, suspended enjoyment. One can even extend this notion to ideal values as well as to immediate values; in the first case, by moving back the limits of suspension beyond individual existence, in the second by recogniz-

[14] (285), p. 126.

ing that it is the organism itself which brings about the suspension, as shown by the numerous 'reserving' functions, such as the glycogenic function of the liver. Suspension therefore appears to be a constant axiological existence. Now, this is also an essential element in formal organization. Musical enjoyment is not the fact of a current impression, but the memory of the preceding one and the hope of the following; it is therefore essentially the result of a suspension. The notion of suspension is therefore a further element of affinity between the notions of value and form.

Finally, the implicit axiology of Durkheimianism can be formulated in Gestaltist terms. Axiological action is of collective origin. Society is in relation to its members an autonomous totality: to belong to it signifies consequently 'to be more than oneself', an auto-transcendence, an increase in strength, since the social being is superadded to the individual; the primitive being translates this ill-defined intuition of social energy by means of a mysterious principle—the 'mana' of the Polynesians—the role of which is familiar from the theories of the French sociological school. 'Mana' is both strength and value; on this point, the Polynesians are completely in agreement with Lalo. In 'Gestaltist' terms, this fact can be defined in the following manner: society, being a form, the subjective experience of its formal qualities, is translated to the individual scale by an experience of values which is both the first religious experience of man and at the same time a process of alienation[15] in the Marxist sense of this term.

The convergence of these doctrines cannot be fortuitous. It would be exaggerating to say that Gestaltist theory resolves all problems of axiology—(as Köhler seems to believe)—but at least it resolves some of them. In fact—at the risk of being somewhat schematic—one can conceive of two possible origins of the existence of value in the world: an extrinsic origin or an intrinsic

---

[15] Cf. *Formes élémentaires de la vie religieuse*; the process which personalizes the actual experience of the structural value of the collectivity is without doubt a process of reification (the 'infrasocial' value—expression of the fact that 'I am not alone'—is alienated in extra-social and extra-temporal (i.e. divine) personages.) This convergence is to be counted among the similarities between Marxism and Durkheimianism. Cf. Cuvillier (118).

origin (*Strahlwert* or *Eigenwert* according to W. Stern's termin-ology). The first hypothesis barely escapes the temptation of a theological explanation, a temptation made stronger because this latter offers an easy solution to reflection: things have a value because they reflect a superior value: this latter 'immediate datum', does not need to be explained. The second barely conveys the transcendence of the value which adds something to reality: its explanation thus risks remaining blocked at the level of imme-diate values. Herein lies a curious dilemma for axiology.

Being *more than the sum of its parts*, by making possible a finality and a transcendence, without leaving the area of the auto-nomy of values and their rational explanation, the dialectical category of totality (form) manages to help get over this dilemma. [It is] an eminently dialectical synthesis since it is based on a dynamic and energizing concept of value. It is therefore diffi-cult to separate axiology and dialectic since they are two different expressions of the same fact: the dynamic and organized charac-ter of reality. The dialectic of consistency and precariousness in Dupréel's axiology is one aspect of this axio-dialectical equiva-lence.

TEMPORALIZATION AND VALUATION

Consequently, irreversibility is a condition of all valuation: a value situated on a reversible continuum is not a true value. The 'axiogeneous' role of temporal irreversibility was pointed out a long time ago by Ostwald; it is a corollary of a dialectical theory of value. 'In the world of classical mechanics one could commit the greatest of follies and infamies without any loss. Since every event is reversible, one can repair all the consequences of any action by restoring the initial state. Thus, all possibility of a valuation disappears. There would not even be any means of complaining about lost time, the temporal flow itself being reversible in an absolute manner ... The inexorable sentence "facta infecta fieri nequeunt" would have no validity, life would be delivered from all tragedy ... In a reversible world, there would therefore be no means of distinguishing between positive or negative value—or between various degrees of values. The notion of value would therefore be theoretically impossible.'[16]

Space thus appears as the anaxiological dimension of the spatio-temporal continuum; the psychopathology of schizophrenic states will not contradict this thesis. Complex interrelationships exist between the notions of *space, aggressiveness* and *devaluation*. Space predisposes to *aggressiveness*.[17] For its part, aggressiveness spatializes its object mainly by favouring anti-dialectical identification.[18] V. Zoltowski, whose works I have referred to many times,[19] observes that 'international aggressive acts are more frequent in spatializing times', pacifist contacts (international congresses) being more numerous during 'temporalizing' periods. Aggressiveness ahistorizes and devalues its object; for its part, the absence of controllable history in a person channels aggressiveness.[20] Schilder described curious phenomena of spatial distortion through aggressiveness: contraction of space, loss of perspective, sadistic annihilation of space,[21] the space of unity and identification,[22] and magical space, the closest to the spatio-temporal structure of mescalinic intoxication as described by Beringer and Mayer-Gross. Without wanting to go into critical details here, let me say that for me this particular distortion of space through the effects of aggressiveness is mainly an over-spatialization; it is only when purged of its axiogeneous temporal-dialectical elements that space, deprived of all consistent structure, lends itself to distortion,[23] as we have seen in another context

[16] Ostwald, quoted by Stern (433), volume 2, p. 9.
[17] Cf. Minkowski (337), p. 183.
[18] Cf. further the relationship between the aggressive content of the conceptual framework and the number of egocentric, 'identificatory' expressions, p. 92.
[19] V. Zoltowski summarized above, p. 16 (note).
[20] The stranger is a person without a temporal dimension—'pure space'; cf. below, pp. 271 ff.
[21] Schilder (418), p. 283.
[22] Schilder (418), p. 277.
[23] Likewise in relation to the sadistic annihilation of space (Schilder (418), p. 283), it should be remembered that 'negation is the negation of space, that is to say it is itself spatial' (Hegel, *Encycl*, 143); a total absence of space is equivalent to an invasion by space ['Raumlosigkeit ist Allraum', Wolff (473)]. The reifying-spatializing action of

apropos the sociocentric (identificatory) formation of political concepts.

REIFIED VALUE AND SOCIAL SACREDNESS

The notion of social sacredness can be defined as a consistent, but not precarious value; from Dupréel's viewpoint of axiology, it is a non-dialectical pseudo-value. It embraces an extreme variety of phenomena: the extra-temporal, *a priori*, consistent, but not precarious, racial 'value' is a sociocentric sacredness. It is in the cult of a non-precarious sacredness that, seen from the axiological perspective, the essence of religious alienation resides;[24] the question as to what extent the great contemporary religions still remain dependent on this axiological form of alienation is beyond the scope of my subject. As for a possible psychopathological exploitation of the notion of sacredness as a 'reified value', we shall return to Binswanger's case of Suzanne Urban; the general tenor of this observation strangely resembles that of the famous work of R. Otto.[25]

As a reified value, sacredness lives under the sign of identity ('Ehje aser ehje'—'*I am the one who is*', said Jahweh)[26] whereas for a dialectical conception of value, identification, respectful of the consistency of values, but not of their precariousness, is a devaluing function,[27] just as it is a depersonalizing function in psychiatry,[28] and a de-dialecticizing one in logic. Certain axio-

---

aggressiveness has been shown in sexual pathology in Boss's comments on sadism (74), p. 75, and in sociology in the experimental study of ethnocentrism.

[24] That is to say in the reificational projection of human values.

[25] R. Otto (374).

[26] Textually: *I am identical to myself*. Cf. in this context Binswanger (62) and my review of the French translation (169 *bis*).

[27] Cf. Polin (390), p. 114 and *passim*; identity is the expression of immanence; to compare values is to operate a transcendence, i.e. to transcend dialectically the relationships of identity through the invention of a new value. This 'non-identifiable' quality of values has inspired many sayings of the kind: 'Love is much more than love', or 'A polytechnician is a man who knows everything, but nothing more.'   [28] Cf. C. Thompson (446).

logical dilemmas of medieval thought are in reality *problems of precariousness* which are difficult to resolve in the frameworks of the fundamental postulate of an extratemporal value-giving value.[29] Reified value is its own justification; it is *a priori* and not *a posteriori*, analytical and not synthetic. Szende has often emphasized the role of the *a priori* and the *analytical element* in authoritarian thought. Without automatically accepting certain of these peremptory formulae,[30] it is certain that authoritarian value is an *a priori*, analytical and identificatory value; with this threefold condition, it is not a value, but 'value'. Szende also emphasizes the 'plebeian nature of sense experience' contrasting with a certain aristocratism of the rationalist attitude; these theoretical conceptions contain a certain degree of truth, especially in axiology. The axiology of racial 'value' is an example of it; lacking any precariousness it is totally independent of experience, it is its own justification, it is explained analytically by itself; it is an autistic, anti-dialectical identificatory value. The racist considers himself to be superior because he is superior; the idea that a black student who exposes himself to maltreatment in order to be able to follow a university course, represents a far more authentic human value than his own, is beyond the understanding of his autism. Nothing shows better the coherence of the notions of devaluation, alienation, reification and schizophrenization than the study of racist consciousness. The value judgement

[29] For example the problem of evil and the axiological problem of creation. Divine values supposedly being non-precarious, one can not see why God created the world (God has no need of 'praxis' to be valued). The only form of axiologically coherent divine existence is that naive and moving one of 'Verts Pâturages': a powerful being but not all powerful. Omnipotence is devaluing (inversely, existence in a devalued, reified world is translated by a subjective impression of omnipotence). This is without doubt the axiological significance of the doctrine of the Trinity: the earthly mortality of Jesus carries the element of precariousness without which there is no true value. 'He whose death (precariousness) conquered death (devaluation).' As for deciding whether there is a contradiction—even from the axiological point of view—between this image and that of the Father, this is a problem which is not for us to resolve, nor even to pose.

[30] Such as 'Das Bestehende ist *a priori*, das Werdende *a posteriori*' [(440), p. 461], which is the same as equating rather hastily '*a posteriori*' and 'dialectical'.

that it entails sanctifies the dissociation from reality which loses its own axiological quality. The axiological step is reversed, 'turned on its head', not in the idealist sense, but in an anti-dialectical, anaxiological sense. The alterocentric (dialectical) value judgement judges the subject as a concrete totality: it evaluates the different moments on an equal basis and thus forms an overall judgement aiming to reflect the concrete richness of this totality as a dialectical unity of opposites. Egocentric judgement on the other hand operates on two levels: it dissociates this axiological totality in consistent and non-consistent moments from the postulates of the privileged system: the non-consistent moments are the object of obscuration and devaluation.[31] This demand for homogeneity of value judgement recalls the mechanism of paranoid, deranged perception.[32] Consequently, the autonomous axiological character of reality is atrophied; it becomes a question of illumination. We can speak of axiological alienation when the value ceases to be a matter of personal achievement and becomes dependent on 'participation' in a valuing factor 'external to the person', such as the racial factor.

I have tried to show the axio-dialectical parallelism on three levels: that of concrete totality, central in axiology and dialectics;

[31] The ethnocentrist does not perceive the personality of his racial adversary as a concrete totality, a dialectical synthesis of qualities and faults, but as a homogeneous juxtaposition of elements of a negative valuation. The devaluing homogeneity is in itself the single factor of spatialization; furthermore the benefit of a possible evolution is refused to the *outgroup* member: whatever his efforts may be 'a Negro will remain a Negro'. There is therefore double obscuration of the dialectical quality of reality: as totality and as future.

It is convenient to distinguish between dialectical synthesis of opposites and mechanical juxtaposition of irreconcilables. To say that Jews are gifted in music and not in painting is to construct a concrete portrait, true or false, it matters little. To say that they have at the same time a tendency to separate themselves from others and a tendency to insinuate themselves [cf. Adorno (7), p. 75] is to bring together in an impossible, therefore an illusory, totality, irreconcilable characteristics whose negative egocentric valuation constitutes the only link.

[32] Cf. the works of P. Matussek (322) and (323); their application in sociocentric psychology (172) and pp. 124 ff.

that of value-giving temporalization with the devaluing role of space as a corollary; and that of the axiological dialectic of 'consistency' and 'precariousness'. As a factor of dissociation in totalities, depersonalization and de-dialecticization, economic re-ification is at the same time a factor of devaluation. In this order of ideas, it is permissible to observe that *Histoire et Conscience de Classe* is actually a study of Marxist axiology and probably the only one.

The notion of a 'reified consciousness' independent of economic reification permits the enlargement of this conception. Collective egocentrism, by dichotomizing the human universe, also dissoci-ates the axiological totality 'consistency—precariousness'; the result is a general reduction in the axiological contents of exis-tence, a little—I apologize for this banal image—like when one cuts a bank-note in two. The privileged system is established as an exclusive value without precariousness; the non-privileged residue is down-graded to a value without consistency: these then are 'values'. Likewise the logic of alienation—the logic of 'false identities'—is heteronomic, the axiology of collective egocentrism is an axiology of alienation,[33] the valuing criterion being *external to the person*.[34] It is therefore to the extent that alienated axio-logical consciousness fails to appreciate or obscures the autono-mous axio-dialectical quality of reality that it can be described as *false consciousness* and this is in accordance with the definitions given above.

[33] Cf. further C. Lefort's study (300) which shows the alienation of a South African tribe in terms of the *cow*, its principal wealth. There exists a 'cow world' among the Nuiras similar to what we refer to as a *mechanistic world*.

But any form of alienation (without making an exception of clinical alienation) involves an axiological crisis by virtue of the postulate of axio-dialectical parallelism.

[34] The value 'external to the person' in relation to this latter, in a spatial situation; the intrinsic value, by contrast, is in the dialectical-temporal trajectory of the personality understood as a process of dialectical personalization.

IV

Schizophrenic Structure of
Ideological Thought
Political Alienation

No part of Marxist philosophy has more contemporary relevance than that of *political alienation*; and none has more need of being given a modern interpretation. Do the forms of political alienation that preoccupied Marx really hold any interest other than a historical one for our contemporaries who have gone through the nightmare of a 'German Ideology' far more formidable than that which Marx knew, and who have witnessed the birth of false consciousness of an intensity that was unheard of a century ago?

The theory of the schizophrenic nature of ideologies fits into three different contexts. Mannheim's total concept of ideology postulates that ideologization is not the consequence of a spontaneous mystification, but the corollary of a radical transformation of the conceptual apparatus of political thought. I accept this theory but would add that this transformation is of the same order as that describing schizophrenics. My view is, therefore, the total view of ideology taken to its ultimate conclusions. In the second place it can be integrated into the context of a critical analysis of schizophrenization, a cultural phenomenon.[1] Finally, it is dependent on the interpretation of schizophrenia as a reificational syndrome. The result is that certain connections can be made only later, and mainly in note form. The aim of the present chapter is to define the concepts being used and to sketch out the integration of this phenomenon into a general theory—clinical and sociological—of alienation.

[1] H. Ey (148), p. 22.

The term 'schizophrenia' is used here provisionally in Minkowski's sense,[2] that is to say, as a synonym for geometrism and morbid rationalism. A subsequent extension of this nosological concept will be attempted: its sociological integration is one stage in this extension. By showing the schizophrenic nature of false consciousness one provides a necessary basis for dialectically integrating with morbid rationalism certain other clinical data which 'co-exist' with spatialization, but which can only be properly related to the latter by means of this preliminary sociologization. The need for this sociologization simply expresses the fact that mental illness is (more than other ailments) a *social fact*.

An example from *medical pathology* will illustrate what we have just said and *a priori* may seem more clear. Retinitis is a dreaded complication in diabetes; however not all diabetics are candidates for retinitis. An individual factor intervenes which is mainly responsible for the existence of variants; nevertheless, our physiopathological knowledge is sufficient in this area for the nosological unity of diabetes to withstand the existence of clinical forms. In the psychopathology of schizophrenia, this physiopathological knowledge is lacking—though perhaps only temporarily: as a result, since the common denominator of different forms is not evident, the very unity of this mental condition has been disputed. Cautious authors speak of *schizophrenias* in the plural,[3] but I feel—the term is Müller-Suur's—that we should talk about *schizophrenia* in the singular.

The introduction of the concept of reification into the psychopathology of schizophrenia is an effort to provide this common denominator. According to my hypothesis morbid rationalism is the expression par excellence of reification in psychopathology, the other symptoms of schizophrenia being more or less direct expressions of it. I advanced this hypothesis in 1951: later work seems to have justified this view.[4]

Now, two facts should be noted here. Reification, the unifying

[2] In his book (340), 1927 and his earlier writings. The *Temps Vécu* marks a certain trend towards *Daseinsanalyse*.

[3] Kretschmer is one of them (266).

[4] Cf. my two publications (177) and (173).

concept in schizophrenia, is a concept which is *sociological* in origin. The sociological forms of reification constitute, in comparison with clinical data, a coherent whole in which the different parts co-exist not only empirically, but can be deduced from each other. The dialectical course which I follow is therefore the following: we start with the concept of morbid rationalism: this is displayed in ideologies; from these we no longer find morbid rationalism but the *phenomenon of a schizophrenic attack*, which, as a reificational syndrome, keeps the structural coherence of the ideological phenomenon. The sociological incorporation of Minkowski's doctrine thus provides the factor of nosological unification for the results of physiological research, which until now has been sought in vain.

It is hardly necessary to summarize here E. Minkowski's widely known concept. Minkowski emphasizes the importance of the 'loss of vital contact' which, from the Bergsonian perspective of his work, is essentially a loss of contact with duration. The schizophrenic is a person dominated by spatiality. This is therefore one[5] of the great dialectical concepts of psychopathological phenomena, a concept whose dialectical element comes neither from Hegel nor Marx, but from Bergson, an equally legitimate source. I have demonstrated elsewhere[6] the existence of a certain intellectual kinship between Minkowski and Lukács, the latter anyway having been subtly influenced by Bergson, in a way which he never took advantage of. For Minkowski, the loss of vital contact is represented by spatialization; the loss of concrete 'praxis' in the world of reification ends in a similar result.[7] This observation opens up several possibilities in sociology as well as in psychopathology: the 'materialist-sociologizing' re-evaluation of Minkowski's concepts is one of these possibilities. It involves several stages.

At first I tried to show that morbid rationalism involved a pathological preponderance of the function of identification in

---

[5] I say 'one' of the possible dialectical concepts because, contrary to the dogmatic point of view, there is no special dialectical solution to the problems of science; there are only perspectives which are more or less dialectical.

[6] Cf. (173), 1951 and (177), 1952.

[7] Cf. Lukács (309), p. 101.

the sense of M. E. Meyerson's epistemology.[8] An element of non-dialectical logic is thus displayed in morbid rationalism, allowing the sociological incorporation of this theory and its subsequent utilization in the critique of ideologies. The logic of ideological thought has in fact an identical basis as I shall take the opportunity of showing.

Secondly, morbid rationalism is interpreted as a 'reificational syndrome',[9] that is to say, as the clinical form of a reified existence and logic that is non-dialectical. A concept from dialectical sociology—the loss of 'praxis'—is thus substituted for the 'loss of vital contact' which, for Minkowski, belongs to a purely natural dialectic without any sociological implication. Furthermore, the category of dialectical thought as a critical instrument for mental derangement is of the same order as when it functions as a Marxist instrument for the critique of ideology. We, thus arrive at the theory of the structural identity of ideology and schizophrenia.[10] The expression 'political schizophrenia' regarding contemporary polemics[11] corresponds to the ideological reproach of earlier political discussions: thought enclosed within itself, dogmatic, detached from reality, unchanged by experience.

[8] Cf. my work (171), Madrid, 1946 (181) and (183). My concept is close to S. Arieti's (cf. below, pp. 224 ff.); I outlined mine independently of him at approximately the same time.

[9] I alone am responsible for this rather bold neologism having used it in 1952 [(173), p. 323, note]. It refers to a pathological form of 'reified consciousness' corresponding, from the essentially (but not exclusively) nosological point of view, to morbid rationalism.

[10] Cf. Campbell (quoted by Kaufmann (254), p. 363): 'The delusions of the unbalanced and the belief of the orthodox are more closely akin than is usually recognised.'

[11] I think I was the first to describe false consciousness as 'schizophrenic thought' (cf. my contributions (176), 1948 and (179), 1949). This diagnosis reappeared in discussions in the press between 1955 and 1958. These were years of questioning, slightly similar to the later Weimar years; such an atmosphere favours the discussion of problems of ideology. In speaking of 'political schizophrenia' (M. Duverger, *Le Monde*, 14 February 1957) one is really entering the field of the total conception of ideology. In addition to this article, I would quote from the same author's 'La Politique de Pirandello' (*L'Express*, 13 February 1958) ('One should not compare the acts of a schizophrenic with the reasoning of normal people'); Albert Camus

Analysis of the mechanism of formation of political concepts and spatio-temporal frameworks of thought shows that over and above its shock value this statement corresponds to a real analogy, scientifically demonstrable and based on a loss of the dialectical quality of thought.

The concepts 'space' and 'time' correspond here to the common-sense definition. Certainly it is an abstraction, but an abstraction well used by a millennial 'praxis'; it is neither more nor less legitimate than any other abstraction, for example, that which separates near space from distant space. Nothing forbids the use of common-sense concepts if their usage allows one to arrive at a coherent description. Thus, the possibility of 'reviewing the course of time' or more simply of re-evaluating *ex-post facto* past events (to rewrite history) is a sign of the spatialization of time—itself a function of the criterion making possible the separation of time and space; it is from the very possibility of such steps that one can take advantage of common sense to separate artificially these two theoretically inseparable aspects of the continuum of social and individual life. If there exists in mental pathology a certain complementarity between space and time it is not therefore the expression of a law, but a question of perspectives: the same phenomenon will appear, depending upon the perspective adopted, as loss of temporalization or as spatial dominance. In other perspectives it may appear in the form of destructuration, devaluation or de-dialecticization. To speak of spatialization at the root of false consciousness is tantamount to simply saying that the hypothesis of a preponderance of the reversible element of the spatio-temporal continuum at the expense of its irreversible element makes it easier to describe the combination of behaviour and collective value judgements for which it provides a common denominator. The hypothesis of a schizophrenic spatio-temporal structure of ideological thought must be understood in

('Le Socialisme des Potences', *Demain*, 21–27 February 1956, pp. 10–11: schizophrenic nature of leftist thought); E. Morin in *France Observateur*, 25 October 1956 ('Univers schizophrénique delirant', p. 19), etc. It is remarkable that these quotations relate to very different political movements, which corresponds closely to the generality of the ideological facts.

this sense, which—if I have properly understood his thinking—
is the same as that of J. Piaget's research; it has nothing in
common with a metaphysical explanation.

'REWRITTEN HISTORY' AND
FALSE CONSCIOUSNESS

It might be a good idea to make a digression at this point. From
Orwell onwards reference has been made to what has come to be
known as 'rewritten History'; it is one aspect of the ideologization
of historical sensitivity of the same order as the obsession with
repetition in the interpretation of reality. However, two radically
different forms of re-evaluation of historical action need to be
distinguished. It is possible to change what have previously been
accepted as the facts about whole entities that have gone
through a process of expansion over time: the coronation of
Charlemagne in 800 possesses a much more concretely rich
significance for us than for its contemporaries who might have
seen it as an act of courtesy without real historical significance.
But it is equally possible to modify *ex-post facto* the historical
factitiousness of the past as a function of the sociocentric
exigencies of the present. Despite a superficial similarity these
two steps belong to radically different mental universes.[12]

Let's take an example. The American general, Benedict Arnold,
covered himself with glory on Washington's side in the first phase
of the War of Independence. Subsequently, he reneged; but his
memory is still honoured in the U.S.A. There is nothing in
common between the approach of the historian who states the
facts while emphasizing that this general could not remain worthy
of his earlier glory, and the one who in the first place says 'the
traitor of 1781 could not be the hero of 1775', but asserts later:
'therefore he was not'. The first step is realistic, the second is
de-realistic. The first postulates the possibility of a personal
dialectic (a 'mélodie vitale'); the second denies this possibility. The
first considers historical value as both *consistent* and *precarious*;

---

[12] Cf. Henri Gouhier's article (204).

the second only as precarious.[13] The first step is the assertion of the dialectical nature of historical fact; the second is its negation.[14]

This second approach implies a schizophrenic structure of historical time. Roheim spoke of 'identification with the past'. An article by the South American psychiatrist Honorio Delgado is doubly significant in this respect: it concerns the reification of time among schizophrenics; furthermore the author describes on a clinical scale the phenomenon typical of false consciousness: *ex-post facto* re-evaluation (or annihilation).[15] The methodological usefulness of the notion of schizophrenization is evident here. For Lukács, reification is a phenomenon with an economic basis which has real meaning only in the context of a capitalist economy. But in *Histoire et Conscience de Classe*, it also appears as a phenomenon of schizophrenic structure; some of Lukács's descriptions anticipate Minkowski's and Binswanger's. Consequently it becomes possible—at the risk of leaving the field of historical materialism[16] to a certain extent—to consider the notion of *reified consciousness* as an autonomous object of investigation, without

---

[13] Considering the privileged system as a uniquely consistent value, without precariousness (the sacred).

[14] To summarize, the first approach is temporalizing and the second is spatializing. The first integrates the action in wider significant totalities, in an ever increasingly concrete time proportionate to its axiological enrichment. Arnold's betrayal assumes a particular significance with Washington's victory (his defeat would have conferred on him a different one), a new significance with American economic growth in the nineteenth century, still another with its present day scientific growth. The opposite approach (the traitor of 1781 was never the hero of 1775; he has always been *what he is now*) obscures concrete duration by retroactive identification (Roheim speaks of identification with the past); historical duration thus mutilated, tends towards a spatial form. This is a fundamental phenomenon of the process of ideologization.

[15] Honorio Delgado (123), p. 17. *Reificacion del tiempo y doble cronologia.* Ibid., p. 14 'frustracion del presente e invalidacion de lo acaecido'. This is exactly the *ex-post facto* temporality of ideology.

[16] L. Goldmann [(199 *bis*), p. 86] considers some of my publications to be dependent on Bergsonian tradition rather than Marxist tradition. I believe that the two are not contradictory and that, furthermore, questions of orthodoxy, be they Lukácsian, are of secondary importance.

necessarily seeking to discover an economic context acting as a causal factor in the background. In other words, the notion of schizophrenization confers an autonomy on the phenomenon of reification of consciousness in relation to its economic basis and, among other things, this autonomy permits its utilization in the criticism of *utopian* consciousness.

Let us return to the example of schizophrenia. I have tried to show[17] (this is the central idea of this study) that this was a clinical form of reified consciousness with an anti-dialectical logic and an identificatory basis as a corollary. This hypothesis does not rule out *a priori* organic pathogeny; dialectical thought being a 'costly' intellectual technique, it is possible to suggest that an individual weakened by an *organic* cause might appeal in his *psychological* perception of reality to the comfort of non-dialectical thought.[18] There can therefore be phenomena of reification of consciousness outside a capitalist context, independent even of any economic context whatsoever. To the extent that the view expressed in *Histoire et Conscience de Classe* considers reification as a phenomenon strictly bound to the capitalist economy, this concept must be dialectically transcended.

One could go further. By abandoning the organicist hypothesis —I am still taking the clinical example—schizophrenia may be interpreted as a function of the sick person's 'manner of being in the world' (In-der-Welt-Sein). L. Binswanger is the nearest of all psychopathologists to an open Marxist (Lukácsian) view of psychopathology. One finds in his work both elements of a dialectical critique of delirious action as an expression of reified thinking and—this coincidence is not a chance one—elements of a concrete sociological interpretation of madness. However, it would be wrong to draw from this dual observation the conclusion that schizophrenia is a reflection of social reification; this would be too simple. A failure[19] wants to begin his life again, to arrest time and later make it flow back; it ends in a delirious blockage of

[17] Cf. my contributions (171) 1946; (183) 1949; (177) 1951; (173) 1952, and the second part of this study.
[18] Cf. in this connection, the eclectic conception of the American psychiatrist, L. Bellak (41, 42, 43).
[19] This is L. Binswanger's 'Jürg Zünd' case.

temporalization (*Zeitigung*) with all its consequences; the crushing of *Dasein* by the world (*mundanization*) is the end of this process. Obviously there is a causal link between the social factor (failure) and the reificational syndrome; in no way an individual *reflection* of social reification. Reification is a phenomenon with many facets: devaluation in one perspective, de-dialecticization from another, loss of temporalization or the subject-object dialectic from yet other perspectives. But it is also a homogeneous whole whose aspects are naturally interdependent: any factor (organic or psychical) which forms part of it may set in motion a decline of the whole, and this is a form whose specificity is not a 'reflection' of the social context, but an expression of the individual historical specificity of the sick person. The extreme variety of valid psychodynamic mechanisms from the standpoint of a particular therapeutic impact, like the persistent parallelism of the organicist and psychogenetic interpretation, becomes clear in the perspective of this interpretation.

It also offers a means of understanding the notion of political alienation as schizophrenization. Classically, reified consciousness would be a reflection of capitalist economic reification; if proletarian consciousness is reified, this would be to the extent that it remained prisoner of this capitalistic reification. In opposing it, the working class would come to realize the identity of the historical subject and object in a general context of dereification, which, from the point of view of the sociology of knowledge, is the best combination of historical conditions for the stimulation of dialectical thinking. In its broad outline this is Lukács's view. A very recent development, however, shows irrefutably that working-class consciousness can undergo a process of de-dialecticization for which it would be singularly unjust to hold capitalist economic reification responsible—however indirectly. I analysed the mechanisms for it earlier: irruption of utopian consciousness (prepared by Marxist theory of *Vorgeschichte*), appearance of sociocentrism, permanence of the influence of the constants of crowd psychology. In summary: just as in psychopathology there can be a form of 'reified consciousness' unrelated to economic reification (schizophrenia), so also in sociology there can be (and indeed there are) forms of 'reified consciousness' which are linked to the conditions of existence so to speak[20] without being in any way a reflection of a form of economic reification. The term *political alienation* would gain in clarity by being reserved for them. It is a general phenomenon which has preferred places and periods of exacerbation, but from which no ideology is completely exempt.

Now this form of alienation is of a *schizophrenic* structure. This is first and foremost an empirical observation: it follows from the critical analysis of ideologies as they arise in the political life of different countries. But it also follows from the analysis of the mechanisms for egocentric formation of political concepts and from the description of the spatio-temporal structure of the world of false consciousness. These two problems are nevertheless connected. The conceptual apparatus of ideologies is formed in an egocentric way: the presence of a privileged system in the field of consciousness encourages anti-dialectical identification at the expense of intuition about differences, and this by virtue of a mechanism close to the logic of schizophrenics.[21] On the other hand, egocentrism spatializes duration; in fact an extratemporal privileged system structures time as a function of its demands and not according to objective criteria. Such a continuum where the notions of 'before' and 'after' have no more absolute value and which as a result permits going back into the past, beginning again at 'zero hour', *ex-post facto* manipulations, is functionally an equivalent of space. The existence of this non-structured (or egocentrically structured, which amounts to the same thing) continuum is the common denominator of various manifestations of political false consciousness; the world of economic reification is

[20] It is useful here to delimit very exactly 'social being' (*soziales Sein*) and 'infrastructure'. Cf. Jacubowski (238) p. 33, and above, p. 4.

[21] Arieti says that the schizophrenic 'identifies' on the basis of the identity of *predicates*, a subjective and therefore egocentrizable element (cf. below, pp. 224 ff, for a summary of his concepts). The formation of sociocentric concepts such as 'anti-communist' or 'unAmerican' is dependent on the same kind of process: one conceptualizes as a function of a privileged system and the concept implies a false identification: one can be 'unAmerican' as an anarchist, a Communist or even as a National Socialist.

of a spatializing structure according to Lukács. It is on the basis of this parallelism that one can speak of reified consciousness outside any economic context.

COLLECTIVE EGOCENTRISM IN THE EGOCENTRIC FORMATION OF POLITICAL CONCEPTS

Egocentrism is a kind of perception of reality involving a privileged system which by definition cannot enter into reversible relationships. The classic example is from child psychology, but there exist collective forms of egocentric psychology that one can call collective egocentrism, sociocentrism or ethnocentrism. Between these different forms there is naturally no clear boundary.

Collective egocentrism plays an important role in the process of ideologization. In fact, if the transcending of egocentrism can be relatively complete in the mature individual, collectivities are rarely exempt from a certain degree of egocentrism, though the intensity of it is naturally dependent on a complex play of factors. This applies to large collectivities (races, classes), but also to those of lesser importance such as political parties, which tend to surround themselves with an atmosphere of *'raison d'Etat'* in miniature. It is in this context that the study of *esprit de corps* as a form of false consciousness arises.[22]

[22] The *esprit de corps* is based on the *illusion of totality*; the *'corps'* in question is taken for the legitimate expression of a wider totality. It is therefore a form of false consciousness by reason of the displacement of the centre of gravity of thought of a superior totality towards an inferior totality; a devaluation with *axiological illusion*, for the restricted values of a restricted group tend to be hypostatized and to acquire a pseudo-universality. Furthermore, the *esprit de corps* is *egocentric, autistic* and inclined to identification and repetition: intellectual traditionalism, following the father's profession without a true vocation. It is, in certain cases (e.g. officers), the depository of great values. In the intellectual professions it can be, like all forms of reification, a factor of sclerosis. Furthermore when the 'illusion of totality' takes the upper hand (in other words, when ideology surpasses false consciousness), it can become a source of grave dangers. It can be seen that the nostalgia for historical repeti-

To say that, all in all, the child thinks less dialectically than the adult appears to be a summary observation and indeed is one. It is dangerous to claim to reduce to a concise formula such a vast field of investigation. Certain well-known data in child psychology are far from confirming such an interpretation: the importance of the identificatory function (particularly in play), the late assimilation of structures (totalities), and the belated acquisition of the notion of moral intent and non-utilitarian values. Seen in a certain light, it would follow from this that the integration of the child into the world of 'praxis' would be a process of dialecticization, in other words, a sort of individual disalienation.[23] This is an hypothesis. On the other hand, the de-dialecticizing action of collective egocentrism is experimental data.[24] One aspect of the importance for Marxism of Adorno's research is, as we have seen, to have perceived experimentally a phenomenon of false consciousness at the pre-ideological level. Two other dimensions have shown the possible use of the concept of reification outside its relationship with the economy and have brought out implicitly the axio-dialectical correlativity in ethnocentrism.

Let us imagine three systems 'A', 'B', 'C'. Between these systems there exists a network of dialectical interrelationships whose hierarchized continuation constitutes what one might call their 'personality'. L. Brunschwicg writes, 'we are fooled by a childish, inexact language when we say of a body that it has weight and it breathes; the weight and the respiration are something quite other than the predicates of a subject; it is the consequence of the proximity of terrestrial mass, it is a function of chemical exchange with the environment. Briefly, from the point of view of real

tion characteristic of certain of its aspects (the call to the States General), which is a form of elimination of historical duration, has no contingent occurrence.

[23] I cannot here go into in any detail the relationship between Piaget's thought and Marxism. Cf. on this subject the two contributions of L. Goldmann (197 and 198).

[24] This is certainly one significance of the privileged gnoseo-sociological situation of the intelligentsia for Mannheim: a state of non-participation which protects the consciousness from the de-dialecticizing effects of sociocentrism.

reason, which is the antipodes of scholastic reason, the being does not consist of a single abstraction but in the fact that each part of the whole reacts on the whole'.[25] What exists really is the cluster of intellectual relationships which allow the individual to be placed in universal space with its dimensions certain and which dominate the circumstances of his history.[26] The problem of the hierarchy of these relationships is both important and delicate. If 'A' is a person, 'B' a chess club and 'C' the Palais-Bourbon, it is clear that the relationship between A and C is more important than the relationship between A and B, but if 'A' turns out to be the world chess champion, this fact naturally creates a radically different 'hierarchical' situation.

One of the main attractions of sociocentrism certainly consists of the fact that it brings a convenient solution to these problems of hierarchy. In fact if one of the systems at issue is established in a privileged system the relationships which unite both to the others become in their turn *privileged relationships*; they will surpass the others in the processes of identification which preside over the formation of concepts. The result is an economy of effort in practical collective psychology. But at the same time it results in a loss of the dialectical quality of the perception of reality and this by means of two convergent biases. The presence of the 'privileged relationship' appears as a foreign body in the concrete totality of relationships whose combination constitutes the object; it fixes the intellectual process at the analytical level and thereby blocks the dialectic of analysis and synthesis, the importance of which was rightly emphasized by R. Garaudy. Furthermore, the artificial (heteronomic) primacy of the relationship necessarily involves an obscuration of the non-privileged relationships and also historical data; this results in a preponderance of non-dialectical identificatory functions with dissociation from totalities and an ahistorical spatializing perception of reality.

To quote a concrete example, the precise determination of notions of left and right constitutes an important and difficult problem in political sociology. Certainly one can dispose of

---

[25] L. Brunschwicg (79), p. 133 (the last sentence is a quotation from J. Lagneau).
[26] Ibid., pp. 132–3.

traditional criteria; present day problems continually reveal their insufficiency. It is accepted that a fixed (extra-temporal) privileged system in relation to which the concepts of 'left' and 'right' can be defined, literally plays the role of a compass. But it is a dangerous facility which demands in exchange the sacrifice of the dialectical quality of the perception of reality, since the presence of a privileged system dissociates the totalities of collective perception.[27] It therefore favours ideologization.

R. Garaudy writes: 'The concept, when it is real, i.e. when it correctly reflects external reality, does not remove us from the concrete, it brings us closer to it.' And later: 'Abstraction is both analysis and synthesis: by creating the concept "dog", we extract from a complex of properties a small number of these properties, common to all dogs. We select a few properties and hierarchize them, retaining only the essential ones. This is an analysis. But at the same time we bring together and organize in a unique concept what is inherent in all dogs examined separately. This is a synthesis.'[28]

This is correct as far as dogs are concerned: the importance of the category of the totality which here carries the name of 'synthesis' will be retained. However, it is justifiable to ask if the term 'hierarchy' does not invite the danger of egocentric distortion: it is not sufficient that a hierarchy exists, it is also necessary for it to be recognized or, more exactly, *it exists only when recognized*. The differences which exist between Garaudy's dog and a wolf have quite a different hierarchical place in the mental universe of a professor and a shepherd. A professor of comparative anatomy in his dissecting room can substitute a wolf for a dog, and explain to his pupils the rather minimal anatomical difference between the two animals; in an analogous situation the differences would be most crucial for the shepherd.

[27] This is the mechanism of deranged perception according to P. Matussek.

[28] R. Garaudy (184), p. 211.

IDENTIFICATORY EXPRESSIONS
(EGOCENTRIC CONCEPTS)

Political conceptualization is to a large extent of the 'shepherd type', i.e. more pragmatic than scientific, and provides evidence of the possibility of distortion that could be described as hierarchical, heteronomic or egocentric (sociocentric). There results a phenomenon whose role in ideologies was carefully studied after 1945 by Hungarian Marxists, B. Fogarasi and G. Nador: false identification.[29] False identification is the identification of two different data after dissociation from their respective totalities and obscuration of the non-identifiable residue as a function of a privileged criterion whose hierarchical primacy is externally assured. The history of the data at issue is, in its turn, obscured or even transformed *ex-post facto* to conform to the exigencies of the moment. The identificatory act can allude either to an absolute identity or to a relative identity in the form of a conspiracy.[30] The limits of the two are never well defined. A zoologist who, having been successively bitten by a dog and a cat, used as a scientific concept 'the animal species which bites zoologists' would be guilty of false egocentric identification. Political conceptualization is not always at a superior logical level. False identification is an important aspect of the anti-dialectical structure of ideologies and, at the same time, a valued technique of economy of effort for propaganda.

[29] Cf. Fogarasi (160), pp. 71–5, summarized by me in (179) p. 481. Nador (365) talks about *false identification* and *false differentiation*, which corresponds to the same distortion of the conceptual framework in the 'field of gravitation' of a powerful source of socio-(ethno)centrism.

[30] Absolute identity: when a national socialist maintains that every Jew (or Negro) is a communist. Relative identity ('conspiracy' level) when without postulating this total identity, he considers that Judaism and Communism are necessarily partly linked. The interest of these rather elementary considerations lies in demonstrating the anti-dialectical component of the notion of conspiracy; a bond of comprehension is thus established between the rationalist forms and the paranoid forms of the schizophrenic attack.

The rapprochement with Meyerson's epistemology demands recognition and it is certainly welcome. I really believe that Meyerson's identification corresponds to the social-reificational constituent of the act of knowing, and at the same time marks the historical and individual limits of the possibility of a dialectical concrete perception of reality as a totality. It is by means of this expedient that the thinking of the author of *Identité et Réalité* can be integrated into a systematic sociology of knowledge. But between Meyerson's identification and that of ideological thought there is this major difference, that the first is exempt from egocentrism (or at least tends to be free from it), and it is a lucid scientific act which knows its limits. Having said this it is permissible to observe that the 'human spirit's appetite for identity' has given birth to two offspring of unequal merit: scientific effort and ideology. In certain circumstances this allows strongly ideologized political thinking to appear in the guise of uncompromising rationalism.

The most numerous examples of *false identities* are to be found in official Marxist publications between 1947 and 1953, a period which saw the culmination of the ideologization of Marxist orthodoxy. Their number has diminished since and, in a general way, the evolution of orthodoxy has marked, from 1953, a discreet return to the dialectic, and a discernible change in its attitude towards scientific theories.

This type of false identification is the sort that asserts that 'Les mains sales' is the 'Juif Suss' of 1951.[31]

[31] This assimilation of Sartre's play into the Nazi film was done in *L'Ecran Français*, in 1951. A certain number of other examples appear in my articles in 1947 (176) and 1949 (179). Cf. Sartre 'Operation Kanapa' (*Les Temps Modernes*, March 1954, p. 1723) who criticizes this phenomenon on the level of the partial concept of ideology, i.e. as a polemical technique, and not as a structural element of a logic. Cf. also the very fertile article of I. Silone (428). False identification is a nosological prolongation of the party-class identification; it is a sociocentric, schizophrenic, spatializing element.

Certain 'identifications' are madly absurd such as that which claims to link pyschosurgery with the criminal experimentation in concentration camps (*La Raison*, no. 5, p. 7 editorial) or the comparisons between mental hospitals in France and concentration camps.

These false identities are crystallized in identificatory expressions (egocentric concepts) of which some are newly formed ('deviationist'), and some are born from the subsequent egocentrization of pre-existing concepts. The term 'fascism' at a certain point was defined as a function of that particular anti-communism which in 'the network of intellectual relationships' characteristic of fascism was only one of them and not necessarily the most important. Other identificatory expressions have encroached upon the scientific area such as the term 'Weismanno-Morganism' (two doctrines denying the heredity of acquired characteristics and differing on all other points), the term 'Machism', etc. . . .[32] These expressions have gradually left the scene because of the détente and also because of the unquestionable intellectual disalienation which characterizes new developments.[33]

Another example—a more topical one—is that the state of Israel is currently described as *imperialist*. From all the evidence the concept is defined egocentrically as a synonym for *anti-arab*. From the English viewpoint (which is neither more or less valid as a viewpoint) Israel seems more like the first anti-imperialist country in the Middle East. This example clearly shows the stages of egocentric logic: (1) egocentric definition; (2) false identification (Israel would be a state of the same type as Japan was in the past!); (3) false differentiation—by virtue of the same egocentric

The sudden decrease in the number of these false identifications in 1953, and their temporary reappearance in 1956, poses a curious problem in the sociology of knowledge. They are in fact dependent on the degree of accumulated aggression; aggression de-dialecticizes and spatializes. But they also depend on the degree of sociocentrism. The détente on the one hand, the increasing importance of China on the other by the same token could have contributed to this de-ideologization of the superstructures of Marxist orthodoxy, the first by lessening the aggressive burden on the conceptual framework of political thought, the second by undermining the situation of the U.S.S.R.'s 'privileged system', and by diminishing the intensity of sociocentrism.

[32] Einstein was described as a 'Machist' (*Questions Scientifiques*, p. 158): this is worse than simplistic.

[33] They reappeared during the Hungarian uprising in 1956, which was compared to the Chouans and to the White Terror of 1929; value judgements aside, the wheel of History had turned between 1920 and 1956.

distortion of the conceptual framework, since German politics under Hitler were not directed against Arabs, they were not considered imperialist!; (4) obscuration of historical data that do not conform with the sociocentric point of view: in these circumstances, data concerning the very 'anti-imperialist' origins of the State of Israel. Thus Israel appears as a purely spatial entity without a historical dimension. Furthermore, it ceases to be seen as a totality; the 'relationships' likely to give a positive judgement are obscured[34] and the whole presented as a mechanical juxtaposition of elements of an exclusively negative value.

This combination clearly illustrates the logical structure of false identification in general. No ideology has introduced so many false identities as Marxian orthodoxy between 1947 and 1953, but I should add, however, that none is completely exempt. At the time of the 'witch-hunts', the egocentrically defined concept 'red' ('unAmercan!') described liberals as anarchists, passing over the different forms of Marxist Thought.[35] The Southern racist convinced that the emancipation of Blacks serves the interests of communism; the ghetto Jew who forms the concept of 'Goim' (Gentile) to unite all non-Jews under the sign of a supposed common hostility; the Ghibelline for whom the 'enemies of the monarch, whoever they were',[36] are Guelphs; the anti-parliamentarian who disapproves of all 'parties', these are all guilty of false sociocentric identification based on the postulate of the fundamental homogeneity of the enemy world.

THE PRINCIPLE OF ANALOGY IN LAW

One form of sociocentric identification is the *principle of analogy* which has been the object of passionate arguments in juridical

[34] That is to say its role in 1947 (its 'negative relationship with imperialism') which was objectively the true precursor of anti-imperialism in the Middle East. This example shows that collective egocentrism selects *ex-post facto* the historical factitiousness which inevitably involves a dissociation of the concrete totality of the network of intellectual relationships of the entity in question.

[35] Cf. on this subject O. Lattimore (289).

[36] Zeigler, *Vie de l'Empereur Frédéric II*, p. 138.

circles in the U.S.S.R.[37] An example of judgement by analogy is given by Schlesinger: sentence of death for counterfeiting a passport *by analogy* with the law against the production of false money.[38] Unquestionably it is a false identification; it can be clearly seen that there is a common element in the two offences (counterfeit of a document printed by the State), but their moral and intentional context cannot be measured in the same way. Normally, law is a reificational phenomenon; there do exist false consciousness and juridical ideologies.[39] Like Meyerson's *Cheminement de la Pensée*, the juridical act involves a sociocentric, identificatory element and an 'intuition about differences', intended to temper the action of the former. It is significant that at the Assizes, extenuating circumstances must concern the criminal, and not the crime.[40] In fact, since the crime is defined in a sociocentric way (as a function of the society which does not tolerate it and not as a function of the criminal who commits it) it could not be 'extenuated'. The record of the criminal's personal history, his social circumstances, his intentions, can in retrospect extenuate the effects of the legal 'clause', the result of an abstract, identificatory, ahistorizing, anti-dialectical, depersonalizing act.

[37] Cf. Schlesinger (420), pp. 225–6, and Chambre (100).

[38] Ibid. (420), p. 226, note.

[39] G. Lukács (309), p. 118 (*Arguments*, December 1958, p. 28), which emphasizes the 'more conscious reification' of the positions of juridical science. Cf. also my study of *Kafka, romancier de l'aliénation* (175): *The Trial* is the portrayal of judicial reification. The ideology-type in juridical matters is the theory of natural law (Lukács, ibid.): the bourgeoisie opposed this theory in the multiplicity of 'franchises' of medieval origin and also in the extra-legal position of the prince, but it refused to see it as the expression of a relationship of strength ('facticiousness, foundation of validity') and believed that it could base both form and content of law on eternal reason. Here again, ideology is a sub-dialectical perception supported by a theoretical derivation. Cf. also the conceptions of Paschukanis who deduced 'the fetishism of law' from that of commodities [Chambre (100), p. 220] which is, however, debatable.

[40] A famous trial nearly went to Appeal because the jury accepted extenuating circumstances for certain misdeeds attributed to the accused and refused them for others. Now, extenuating circumstances relate to the criminal; in theory, a crime cannot be extenuated; it is the criminal who can be totally or partially excused.

One of the functions of the Assizes institution is without doubt to attenuate judicial reification; this is a dialectical, personalizing work of 'de-identification', structurally close to that of the psycho-analyst. The 'principle of analogy' is of a contrary inspiration. It translates a more intense sociocentrism and therefore a stronger reification, with a consequent promotion of the importance of the identificatory constituent of the judicial act. It is furthermore a general characteristic of totalitarian justice which tends, independently of the degree of reification of its economic foundations, to emphasize judicial reification.[41]

The importance of anti-dialectical identification in the process of ideologization should not be underestimated: it is a turn-table between the different aspects of false consciousness. It is the atom of non-dialectical logic, the factor of dissociation of concrete totalities, and it is also an agent of spatialization, for space alone lends itself to total identification; objective or subjective time, filled with irreversible events is by definition refractory. It constitutes a link with schizophrenia both through the intermediary of the phenomenon of spatialization and through the role that it plays in the logic of schizophrenics (Arieti). It is the expression of the dichotomous structure of different forms of sociocentrism as well as of another fundamental fact of political thought: the tendency to 'think against', to push to the extreme—even to the absurd—the saying 'Omnis determinatio est negatio'.[42]

---

[41] It should be noted, however, that the principle of analogy has never been an undisputed principle of Soviet law. The discussions that it has generated are unrelated to this subject; for the details, cf. Schlesinger (420) and Chambre (100). Against A. Vichinsky, Tavgasov was able to uphold the incompatibility of this principle with the 1937 constitution [Schlesinger (420), p. 225].

[42] By virtue of this implicit Manichean postulate of ideological thought, the enemies of enemies so often enjoy an undeserved favourable prejudice; for the political Manichean one is either 'imperialist' or 'anti-imperialist'; the dialectical reasoning which stipulates that one can be against one imperialism and for another is beyond his comprehension. One can see the egocentric structure of this reasoning. The child says 'I am the only one in my family to have a brother.' The word 'brother' does not involve a reversible relationship; *his* brother is essentially brother. The same applies to the political Manichean: to be 'anti-imperialist' is not a relationship

Egocentric concepts tend to crystallize a real or supposed hostility concerning the *outgroup*, generally real in what concerns the group proper. The corresponding words are often 'anti . . .', or, at least, imply a definition in terms of supposed aggressive negation. They constitute an extremely effective instrument of propaganda. In fact, egocentric concepts pander to 'the appetite for identity of the human spirit;[43] furthermore, a propaganda directed 'against' is always more efficacious than a propaganda 'for'. A clever technique of persuasion must benefit its public with the comfort of pre-dialectical thought,[44] while giving it the illusion of arriving

---

but the attribute of a substance; further, it is set in a 'black-white' context, which knows no third term, or, in other words, which ignores synthesis in all the accepted meanings of this term. I do not want to engage in polemics, but I should give an example: it is in this perspective that the infatuation of certain left-wing groups for Nasserism and the F.L.N. appears as an *act of false consciousness*.

[43] Calvez (85), p. 100. From all evidence it is more convenient and more efficacious to say 'Roosevelt's America is the Jews' (thunder of applause) than to lead an over-excited audience (and including a percentage of unemployed) to study dialectically the sociography of the Jewish minority in the United States.

An example: Adlai Stevenson's campaign in 1952 was almost totally lacking in concern for crowd psychology. The result is well known.

[44] In his pamphlet on political propaganda, J. M. Domenach writes of the 'law of simplification and the single enemy' [(131), p. 49]; he emphasizes the necessity for asserting the invariability from the appropriate point of view [(131), p. 77]. Cf. also in this connection N. Leites's study: *The Third Internationale on its changes of policy*, Laswell (287), pp. 298–333. The ontologization of these anti-dialectical structures of propaganda is an essential factor in the de-realization of collective consciousness; as to knowing if their de-realizing is primary or secondary, this is the problem of the partial or total characteristic of the concept of ideology which is discussed elsewhere. Cf. the very elaborate argument of N. Leites: and particularly the chapter 'Denials of Change', ibid., p. 300. One can see here very clearly how the hypothesis of infallibility (socio-centric postulate in my terminology) results in a negation or mini-mization of the importance of changes. For me, this is one aspect of the loss of dialectical temporalization in the world of false consciousness and, consequently, one aspect of the schizophrenic structure of the process of ideologization. But this phenomenon assumes all its significance only in a total context.

at a scientific understanding of reality. The danger of false consciousness appears at the same time as the temptation to ontologize[45] these utilitarian pre-dialectical structures: it is even more difficult to withstand them when they are shown to be more useful in practice.

A reading of the daily press shows that a relatively important sector of political discussions consists of establishing false identities on the one hand and their polemical denunciation on the other. All egocentric concepts can be established in a private language which measure the cohesion of a group, but at the same time the intensity of its false consciousness.[46] 'A common language is indicative of the solidarity of a group; many oppositions between "in-group" and "out-group" are explained by the fact that the groups are incapable of communicating.'[47] This is accurate only to a certain extent; these private languages are both cause and effect of the hostility of groups and rather more effect than cause.

Words constituted thus acquire a commensurate power, they become depositories of a sometimes magical power. This aspect of false consciousness (the over-reification of the word which is already reificational in its essence) was analysed in a book with the revealing title: *The Tyranny of Words*, by Stuart Chase. In reality, every word rests on an anti-dialectical 'false identification' ('the expressed thought is a lie', said the Russian poet,

[45] Cf. the notion of antithetic and heterothetic dialectic of Kranold (265) and that of the ontologization of negativity in my contribution (170) which also contains a summary of Kranold's unavailable work. Propaganda is based on violent, concrete negation and on utopian affirmation: a concrete 'against' and an extra-temporal 'for'. The action of the two converges towards a de-dialecticization and, consequently, towards ideologization: a dialectic of pure antithesis is an illusion of dialectic.

[46] More exactly: the number of private expressions measures the cohesion of a group and its identificatory words the degree of its false consciousness; the latter is therefore indicative of collective autism. A stranger wishing to enter a group begins by making its private vocabulary his own. Laswell [(287), p. 321] points out that in 1918, the German soldiers began to use the particular vocabulary of allied propaganda; the German Services judged it to be a serious phenomenon; and so it was.

[47] Sapir, quoted by Klineberg (259), pp. 49–50.

E

Tchouchev):[48] the conceptual apparatus of strong sociocentrism only serves to exalt this anti-dialectical structure by blocking the dialectical function of secondary synthesis whose importance Garaudy rightly emphasized.[49]

These observations which go back to Bacon's theory of idols are certainly not original. What is important to emphasize is that these structures are currently described in publications about schizophrenia: we have seen the role of the identificatory function in ideologization and in the logic of schizophrenics. Schilder[50] pointed out the distortion of space under the effects of aggression; the distortion of the conceptual framework in the field of sociocentrism is a similar phenomenon.[51] The 'tyranny of words' that have become independently powerful has been analysed in schizophrenics by Katan, Roheim[52] and other writers.

IDEO-AFFECTIVE INDIFFERENTIATION AND IDENTIFICATORY FUNCTION IN IDEOLOGY AND SCHIZOPHRENIA

Sociocentric identification is basically affective; it approves of a non-differentiation between the intellect and the emotions in the operations of thought. J. Monnerot quite rightly defined ideology as 'thought charged with feeling where each of these two elements

[48] J. Stuart Chase says concisely: '. . . most languages . . . with their equating verb "to be", their *false identifications*, spurious substantives, confused levels of abstractions, and *one-valued judgements* are structurally dissimilar to our nervous system and our environment.' Sullivan says that language is always magical to a certain extent [(438), p. 7].

[49] M. Garaudy (194), p. 211.

[50] P. Schilder (418), pp. 279–81 and *passim*.

[51] Cf. on the relationships between aggression and sociocentrism, this pleasing comment of Huxley and Haddon: 'One can define a nation, cynically but not falsely, as a society united by a common mistake as to its origins and a common aversion for its neighbours' (quoted by Klineberg (259), English edition, p. 378).

[52] Cf. also Dr. Logre's article: 'Les mots magiques', *Le Monde*, 10 May 1957.

corrupts the other'.[53] This state of non-differentiation explains the genesis of the false identities of sociocentrism; it is the identity of the subjective reaction which is unduly noologized.[54]

The same phenomenon has been described and confirmed experimentally in schizophrenia. Berze and Schilder pointed out, quite a long time ago,[55] the importance of a process of affective neo-structuration of the foundation of the conceptual apparatus of thought; it is at least as valid for ideology as for schizophrenia. The same authors also speak of 'paralogical identifications'[56] (I would say: anti-dialectical). As in ideology, this identificatory preponderance has an affective foundation: the experiences of schizophrenics involve 'an inextricable mixture of perception, thoughts and feelings'.[57] H. L. Raush proposed studying this mixture experimentally.[58] Neutral objects and objects that have an affective connotation are presented to schizophrenics and control subjects and they are asked to evaluate their dimensions. In comparison with normal subjects, the schizophrenics tend to overestimate the dimensions of the symbolic objects compared to the neutral objects. Raush draws two conclusions from this: 1. that the distortion of objects depends as much on the nature of the stimulus as the changes in the self, and 2.—more significantly —that the paranoid defence mechanisms are linked to the projection of an 'artificial stability' on to the external world. What also happens is that the ideo-affective confusion stimulates in the mentally ill a deterioration in the sense of perspective. Now, perspective is the dialectical part of the experience of space: it is a partially temporalized spatial dimension. Certain forms of reified consciousness are accompanied in psychopathology by the loss of the notion of depth.[59] Without wishing to draw too

[53] J. Monnerot (353), p. 297, but it is not here so much a question of *ideology* as *false consciousness*.

[54] Cf. Ribot: 'Affective reasoning expresses the state of the subject and nothing more.'

[55] *Affektive Umgestaltung der Begriffsgrundlagen*, Berze (51), p. 61.

[56] Berze (51), p. 62.   [57] Berze (51), p. 54.   [58] H. L. Raush (396).

[59] Cf. Tellenbach's works on the space of melancholics (442); Tellenbach expressly uses the term reification in connection with the melancholic consciousness.

hasty conclusions from an isolated experience, let me point out that among schizophrenics, as in ideology, logico-affective undifferentiation is a corollary of the appearance of phenomena of reification.

DICHOTOMIZATION AND SCHIZOPHRENIA

The dichotomizing Manichean perception of reality (the 'black-white' view) is characteristic of the collective and individual forms of egocentrism. It exists in the child. In a study devoted to youth 'gangs', Redl observes that when a person belongs to a *code dangerous outgroup*, he is no longer considered as a person but as the depersonalized symbol of the system of hostile values.[60] According to Laswell, political symbolization is inseparable from dichotomization.[61] It is perhaps not quite that simple. In theory there can be a political symbolism without any Manichean vision. But two phenomena appear independent: the confusion of the symbol and the symbolized and dichotomization without nuances, are two manifestations of the sub-dialectical structure of the psychology of crowds. The result is that *effective* political symbolism is really the dichotomous symbolism one can observe daily.

Each of these two phenomena is currently observed in schizophrenics. The first ('symbolism of identity') is classic. The rigid dichotomization into 'good' and 'bad' has often been observed. The 'precocious paranoid position' of M. Klein involves a division of the object into a subsequently introjected 'good' part and a 'bad' part. A paranoid creator of a delirious theocratic system, rigidly divides humanity into Catholics and heretics, this second category covering all nonconformists.[62] Similar descriptions are to be found in publications by Berze, Pankow, Abadi, A. Modell and others.[63]

---

[60] Redl (397), pp. 373–4.
[61] Laswell (288), p. 189: 'Symbolization necessitates dichotomization.'
[62] I published this observation in 1952 (173).
[63] Minkowski [(340), p. 109] talks of 'antithetic attitudes' among

It would be pointless to continue to enumerate these analogies. A whole group of intellectual structures is to be found in schizophrenia, in different aspects of political alienation and (to a certain extent) in the psychological development of the child. These are exteriorized according to the individual case (and also according to the observer's viewpoint) as dissociation from totalities, as devaluation, as predominance of the identificatory function in relation to intuition of diversity, or as predominance of the spatial function in relation to the temporal function. The notion of 'reified consciousness' corresponds to this whole group; Lukács's reification with an economic basis is a special case. Lukács was not familiar with the problem of schizophrenia; in 1923 he did not foresee the problem of utopian consciousness. The result was that his doctrine of alienation also sprang from a 'partial concept' which needs to be broadened.

This conception of ideology enters into the wider context of what a psychiatrist called the 'schizophrenic tenor of our civilization'.[64] It is an old theme. The criticisms of machinism, which was very fashionable before the war,[65] are in fact the ones with this 'schizophrenic tenor'. P. Borensztàjn, in 1947, observed that the transformation of clinical categories of psychoses in the direction of a schizophrenization[66] corresponded to a similar transfor-

these people (who are not always 'sick' in the clinical sense of the word) for whom 'every act of life is seen from the point of view of the rational antithesis of the yes or the no or, rather, of the good or the bad, or the permitted or the forbidden, or the useful or the harmful'. These antithetic (dichotomizing) attitudes are currently observed among schizophrenics. Cf. for example, Pankow (376), p. 67 ('the path of sin', 'the path of holiness'); Berze (51), p. 62; Abadi (1) (antithetic attitude in a sick person blind from birth); Modell (351), etc.

[64] H. Ey (148), p. 22. But Dr. Ey considers surrealism as the expression of this *schizophrenic tenor*; I think that it is a defensive reaction: an aggressive return to the concrete in the face of the threat of false consciousness. The same dualism of possible interpretations exists on the subject of existentialism. Cf. the 'psychiatric critique' of this school by L. Duss (139) and further, pp. 189 ff.

[65] The works of Carrel, Gina Lombroso and others. Cf. the still relevant book of G. Friedmann (168).

[66] P. Borensztajn (73).

mation in the whole literary and cultural scene.[67] N. Berdiaeff devoted eloquent pages to denouncing dissociation in culture.[68] I could cite still more names.[69] The schizophrenic structure of ideologies is manifested above all in their autistic nature, that is to say, their estrangement from reality, in their impermeability to experience, whilst it was mainly the dissociation which attracted the attention of philosophers of culture. The American sociologist Read Bain published under the title *Our Schizoid Culture*[70] an interesting study (though somewhat brief) centred on the different aspects of 'dual morality' which is in effect a schizophrenic phenomenon of false consciousness.[71] The importance of projective

[67] This is a huge subject. I hope I may be permitted to refer to my own publications on the significance of Kafka's work—the 'novelist of alienation' (175 and 179 *bis*)—as well as to an article devoted to Camus's *L'Etranger* (174). L. Goldmann [(200) and (199 *bis*), p. 92], considers the work of Robbe-Grillet to be the reflection of reification; it has been described elsewhere as *schizophrenic* with reference to Minkowski's theory (cf. *France-Observateur*, 5 December 1957, p. 20). Another successful work, Beckett's play *Waiting for Godot*, is, in our terms, a parody of utopian consciousness. There is a whole field of socio-literary research which could at the same time be an experimental study of social psychology: it would show the reflection of reification in literature and seek to establish to what extent this reflection possesses a schizophrenic nature and, more particularly, a morbid rationalist one.

[68] Cf. (48), p. 123. Berdiaeff was one of the first non-Marxist writers to recognize the importance of Lukács. Cf. (47), p. 142.

[69] Gilbert Robin (194), p. 17, also evokes a 'collective schizophrenia' whose effects can have repercussions on the maturation of children.   [70] Bain, *Our Schizoid Culture* (26).

[71] 'We praise free competition and we practise the system of capitalist monopolies; we advocate organization of business and claim to forbid the organization of labour etc....' (Read-Bain's article dates from 1935: there have been changes since.) Cf. also L. Goldmann [(200), pp. 98–9] '... the dualism of capitalist reification becomes—in Hitlerism—that of the head of a concentration camp or the torturer who, at home, was incapable of killing a fly, liked the music of Bach and was a good father'. But reification is not only dissociation; it is also spatialization, therefore morbid rationalism. One of the merits of V. Zoltowski's research (cf. pp. 16–17, note) is certainly that it in fact centred on the spatializing aspect of schizophrenization, though Zoltowski, a disciple of Simiand, does not use the conceptual framework either of the Marxists or of psychiatrists.

and 'morbid rationalist' (spatializing) aspects of superstructures, due in large part to the ontologization of the world by propaganda, seems to have escaped him. They are however probably two aspects of the same fundamental datum.

The schizophrenic structure of ideologies has also often been pointed out, but in the majority of cases they have been isolated comments which are not part of a coherent theory of alienation. Kelsen[72] observes that ideologies are contradictory—or dissociated perhaps—for they mask reality while partially reflecting it. P. Szende considers that the technical principles of ideological masking (*Verhüllung*) are abstraction, mechanization and hypostasis.[73] J. Monnerot compared the impermeability to experience of ideologies to that of delirious states.[74] The role of mental stereotypes in false consciousness is well known.[75] Koestler talks of political neuroses.[76] The conception of the schizophrenic nature of false consciousness is therefore the convergence point of a cluster of data translating from various angles the permanence of an axiological and dialectical crisis in social consciousness. In certain contexts, this crisis is seen mainly as a crisis of values, in others essentially as a crisis of truth.

SPATIO-TEMPORAL STRUCTURE OF FALSE CONSCIOUSNESS

'Class consciousness', writes J. Domarchi, 'is first and foremost consciousness of time. The manner in which an individual apprehends the three temporal dimensions (past, present, future)

[72] Kelsen (256), p. 450.

[73] P. Szende (439), p. 77. Szende does not use the term schizophrenia, but the analogy is clear.

[74] Monnerot (353), p. 277.

[75] Cf. Walter Lippmann, *Public Opinion*. J. Moffatt-Mecklin carried out an interesting study on the psychology of the Ku-Klux-Klan [(352), pp. 103–14] based in large part on the omnipotence of stereotypes.

[76] Cf. Koestler (262), an article very rich in ideas which shows numerous reificational structures ('political fetishism', p. 9, 'fixation' on utopia, p. 11, etc.), but the term 'neurosis' must not be taken too seriously.

is closely conditioned by his situation and his role within society.'[77] The reification of the past in the consciousness of conservatives has often been commented upon; at this extreme it ends in the homogenization of time and consequently in the implicit negation of history. The reificational incapacity to understand the present as a moment of history is mentioned by Lukács.[78]

In a study devoted to the problem of logic and language in propaganda,[79] S. Moscovici maintains that, in the world of propaganda, space and time 'assume an *absolute character*'. This does not have a very precise meaning. In social psychological studies it is as well to abandon common-sense concepts only when this step serves a real purpose. Everyone knows that modern physics has profoundly transformed the notions of time and space. This new view may shed light in social psychology, but not necessarily so, since the scale of size and speed in micro-physics differs too profoundly from the scale of social events. Therefore, the social psychologist should not shun current notions of time and space without proving their flagrant inadequacy for the desired end.

Now, in common-sense terms, the essential characteristic of space is to allow movement in all directions and also backwards. One does not choose 'one's place' in time; in theory one can choose it in space. One cannot go back in time but one can move freely in space. A man who leaves his apartment on 21 January 1959 at 3 o'clock, leaving the gas on, will never succeed in making 'the apartment that was left on 21 January 1959 at 3 o'clock with the gas on' become 'the apartment that was left on 21 January 1959 at 3 o'clock with the gas off'. But it can

---

[77] J. Domarchi (133), p. 824.

[78] Lukács (309), p. 173. 'The best illustration of the essentially ahistoric, or even anti-historic, nature of bourgeois thought is the situation of the problem of the present as a moment of world history.' Lukács reproaches bourgeois historians for being incapable of understanding the present as a historical moment, despite the rhetoric of their leaders ('I will lead you to historic times,' said Hitler in his first speech as Chancellor); fascist movements do not belie this observation.

[79] Moscovici (356), p. 444.

happen that—and in theory limitlessly—'the apartment situated in such and such a place with the gas on' becomes 'the apartment at such and such a place with the gas off' and vice versa.

Time is a dialectical dimension not only because, contrary to space, it is impossible to conceive of it in a state of rest, but also because its progression effects a dialectical synthesis constantly being reborn from its three dimensions: present, past, future. It is a totality which can be dissociated by reification of the past or the future—ideology, utopia, neurosis, madness are examples of it—but such a dissociation entails the de-realization of the whole world view as that suggested by the very examples that I have just quoted. The dissociation of spatial structures does not necessarily entail similar consequences. In a general way, temporal forms are 'stronger' than spatial forms and the question arises—it will be faced later on—whether the cohesion of spatial forms is not due to the permanence of temporal elements within spatiality. Finally, as an irreversible continuum, time is axiogeneous[80] while space is devaluing, and since it offers no framework to the 'function of suspension'[81] could protect only values of pure immediacy.[82]

Now, this anti-dialectical, anaxiological reversible continuum that common-sense space is offers a common denominator for the description of various phenomena of alienation. Concepts such as 'absolute space' or 'absolute time' by contrast possess only a limited explanatory value. Spatialization of experienced duration is the basis of morbid rationalism; our study presents it as reification of duration, since it is the real fundamental disturbance (*Grundstörung*) underlying other forms of schizophrenia and guarantees their unity. The alienation of human labour appears for its part in a spatializing context, as Lukács expressly

[80] This is the point of Ostwald's axiology. Cf. earlier, p. 72.

[81] In Janet's sense.

[82] This is the classic case of the schizophrenic who greets his mother with indifference and seizes upon the sweets that she has brought, and, in general, the phenomena of alimentary de-differentiation in schizophrenics, the extreme of which is the 'reflex placing of objects in the mouth' described by Arieti (15). One glimpses here the logical relationship of this syndrome with spatialization.

points out. Finally, 're-written history' also postulates possibilities of reevaluation of acquired knowledge incompatible with the influence of temporal irreversibility.

I shall briefly analyse a few cases of political false consciousness without any link between them other than that they appear in this de-dialecticized continuum ('abstract juxtaposition')[83] that is common-sense space. It is in this sense that it is permissible to maintain that these phenomena are various manifestations of *morbid rationalist* tendencies in ideological thinking. These facts are:

(a) reversal of the antecedent and the consequence in the reasoning of political justification;
(b) the 'cauldron';
(c) spatialization of the substratum of political responsibility;
(d) prevalence of the present in journalism;
(e) retroactivity of laws; and lastly
(f) the so-called 'policing' view of History.

As one can see, these phenomena are rather varied. Certain ones ('e' and 'f') belong to the totalitarian environment; others ('c' particularly) are, on the contrary, typically democratic phenomena. The examination of all questions about causal primacy is left aside, for it is difficult—if not impossible—to know whether these phenomena are cause or effect of the spatialization of collective duration. The same question is raised about the relationship between identification with the 'political father-figure' and the spatialization of collective duration in ideology; it may be that the spatialization favouring all forms of abstract identification also favours identification with the leader, but one might just as validly support the opposite hypothesis. One thing is certain: they belong to the same context of pre-dialectical regression: the renunciation of the dignity of the autonomous adult through an

---

[83] Hegel, *Encyclopédie*, trans. Gibelin, p. 147; but the translation is free since the German text (German edn., p. 160), says: 'Was von der Materie gewöhnlich gesagt wird, ist/dass sie zusammengesetzt ist—dies bezieht sich auf ihre Identität mit dem Raum.' (Currently it is said of matter that it is abstract juxtaposition; this refers to its identity with space.)

alienating identification with the leader, and the renunciation of the concretely dialectical perception of reality in the false spatializing identification of ideologies are certainly two aspects of the same process.

REVERSAL OF THE TEMPORAL ORDER OF THE ANTECEDENT AND THE CONSEQUENCE IN JUSTIFICATORY REASONING

Justificatory reasoning in politics confuses at will the antecedent and the consequence. One could quote numerous examples. The anti-German attitude of Jews has always been exploited as a justification for anti-semitic measures in Germany when it was the consequence of them; before Hitler, Judaism was on the whole rather favourable towards German culture. Egocentric thought structures time not as a function of objective processes, but as a function of the criteria of the privileged system; similarly in children's thinking the notions of 'before' and 'after' do not have the absolute character which makes the atoms of duration irreversible for the adult.[84]

The temporal structure of dissociated reasoning postulates the possibility of a return to the past, of completely new beginnings, which implies a spatializing element: time does not begin again. Meyerson and Dambuyant have described[85] a technique of egocentric reasoning: the 'cauldron'. It is of the following type: a man borrows a *cauldron* and he returns it cracked. In a court of law, his defence is summed up in three points: (1) I never borrowed the cauldron; (2) it was cracked when I borrowed it; (3) I returned it intact. Each stage of the reasoning ignores the one before: logical time is subject to a completely new beginning ('zero hour'), a step incompatible with the dialectical structure of concrete duration. The logical wholes then become additive wholes, that is to say they are antipodal to this logic of the totality which had been the model of the logic of disalienation

[84] Piaget (385), p. 27 and *passim*.
[85] Meyerson and Dambuyant (332).

(*Enthüllungslogik*).[86] Dissociated reasoning is based on 'de-objectivized', egocentricized concepts: the same total situation can be described at one and the same time as 'war' and 'peace', solely according to the criterion of reasons of state.[87] The universe of the 'cauldron' has no need of the dialectical criterion of coherence ('totality'); it is the universe of faulty abstraction.

This type of reasoning is common in the law courts (for the barrister, the 'system' of the accused is a privileged system), in politics and in journalism. I agree entirely with the conclusions of Meyerson and Dambuyant, save on the point that the authors seem to underestimate the importance of the phenomenon; rather than a demagogical artifice, the 'cauldron' type of reasoning is a structural element of egocentric logic and consequently of most forms of false consciousness.[88] It involves schizophrenic elements: dissociation and spatialization of duration (completely new beginnings). The analysis of Meyerson and Dambuyant also shows the logical link between the notions of dissociation and spatialization on the one hand, and those of concrete totality and duration on the other.

[86] P. Szende (440), p. 457.

[87] The whole of Arab politics with regard to Israel was, at a given moment, 'in cauldron': we have the right to attack because we are at war; they do not have the same right because they are at peace. The 'cauldron' of a totalitarian election is the following: there is a massive vote for us because we are the people, opposition parties cannot be authorized because the regime has too many enemies. For other examples, cf. the very valuable article by Meyerson and Dambuyant (332); the 'cauldrons' of the law courts are typical: my client is innocent, and anyway there are mitigating circumstances. (The term 'anyway' here corresponds to the spatializing element.)

[88] In short the gnoseo-sociological theory which underlies the explanation of this remarkable article is still the partial view of ideology. Schizophrenics also indulge in the cauldron type of reasoning (notably in Rorschach tests); with them, it is certainly the structural element of another logic.

SPATIALIZATION OF THE TIME OF POLITICAL RESPONSIBLITY

Recent events show that, in periods of tension or crisis, the time which underlies the collective judgement of political responsibility tends to be spatialized; it is an objective social fact confirmed by electoral results in the most developed countries.

It is advisable to distinguish—and here A. Hesnard's work is the best guide[89]—between *guilt* and *responsibility*. The feeling of guilt is characteristic of child psychology; the feeling of responsibility is an essentially adult phenomenon. The first is a phenomenon of reification; it is the subjective experience of a form of existence in a world without a dialectic and consequently devoid of higher values. The second corresponds on the other hand to the experience of the dialectical structure of existence itself (the 'mélodie vitale') which is responsible for the fact that our past is linked to our present in the frameworks of a creative totality of values. To feel guilty is to live without value, to feel responsible is to live for a value. Hesnard clearly emphasized that endogenous melancholy often sprang from what—freely interpreting his thought—he describes as *false moral consciousness*.[90] It occurs in a reificational–spatializing context, as A. Hesnard indirectly emphasizes.

A comparison between political responsibility and primitive forms of responsibility, such as has been described by P. Fauconnet in his classic work, is necessary, but I shall avoid as far as possible questions of ethnology which I am unqualified to discuss. The socio-psychiatric parallel is already sufficiently instructive. The responsibility of regimes and governments in the face of public opinion is completely in keeping with the *morbid universe of blame*. One can usefully compare it with forms of medical responsibility with regard to the least experienced clientele. Only the result counts: successful treatment of angina or of a cancer is basically the same; the doctor is supposed to intervene at 'zero

[89] Hesnard (228).
[90] Cf. further, op. cit., p. 148.

hour', the antecedents of the patient (including the medical attention received at the outset) are not taken into account; finally, medical power is deemed to be magical, that is to say that it does not consist of an ability for dialectical integration (analogous to 'praxis') in a natural process, but in an ability (and consequently a duty) to command nature without obeying it. This form of responsibility is exactly that of the political man in a period of collective exaltation.[91] It is not a particular form of 'normal' responsibility but something radically different. We have seen that the re-evaluation of the facts of history can be done according to two diametrically opposed techniques: dialectical integration in significant totalities expanding with time ('it is not until the 10th century that one perceives the importance of Charlemagne's coronation in 800') and anti-dialectical assimilation (identification) of the past into the present ('Trotsky was never the organizer of the Red Army'). The same applies to responsibility. Only the name is common between this act of dialectical valuation that is adult responsibility and its degraded form in the universe of false consciousness. This latter is the very negation of the dialectic both on the level of the totality and on that of becoming; it ignores both the concrete context of political action and its antecedents as well as the importance of relationships of force; since its view of political power is not scientific but magical, it believes it has the right to expect a miracle. It comes within a continuum analogous to that of the 'cauldron'; the notion of 'zero hour' and the implicit exercise of omnipotence indicates a *spatial* structure.

[91] I am thinking here of a definite historical fact. The American failure in China unleashed several treason trials, brought about an electoral landslide and was the origin of McCarthyism. Now, this event was in the logic of history; the diffused judgement of American opinion required from its leaders an exercise of extra-historical, magical omnipotence. For the relationship between magic and schizophrenia cf. Roheim (405), Schilder (418), Tourney and Plazak (450).

PRESENTIFICATION OF DURATION
AND JOURNALISM

The development of journalism is without doubt a powerful agent of diffusion of knowledge; furthermore, the pluralism of papers of opinion (journalistic comment) is a factor of decentration and consequently, de-ideologization. But informative journalism is at the same time imprisoned by current events, consequently there is a tendency (which naturally varies according to the newspaper) to neglect the historical and dialectical roots of events. So the temporality of political information tends towards a non-structured succession of present moments which results ultimately in a spatial type of continuum.[92] Taken in isolation, this phenomenon of journalistic sub-temporalization has no great importance. But it occurs in the wider context of the inadequacy of collective memory,[93] an inadequacy that is expressed in dictums of the type 'the French have a short memory'; it provides a sort of ratification for this collective amnesia. Its effects converge with those of other factors of de-dialecticization. In a general way, informative journalism actually tends to prefer spatial information (reportage) to temporal information (historical considerations); now, despite appearances, the latter constitutes a surer

[92] This non-structured succession of present moments is in clinical cases the temporality of maniacal states. But there is no more of a clear difference between this form of 'time' and space, than between maniacal symptomatology and that of disturbed schizophrenias. I shall return to this question. 'Present-type time' has this in common with pure space, that it is not structured and it is not valorized. This is a rather important analogy.

[93] I could be criticized for dealing with the question of class consciousness on the exclusive level of collective psychology when it belongs to a sort of social phenomenology. Cf. The notion of 'possible consciousness' (Goldmann (201), p. 113 and *passim*). But the data from the psychology of crowds constitutes one of the limits of 'possible consciousness'. The Marxian–Lukácsian theory of class consciousness postulates implicitly that the process of developing class consciousnesss can neutralize the factors of collective psychology; the teachings of the recent past show that this postulate is arguable.

source of information.[94] In any case, all attempts at scientific understanding of current events should be based on a dialectical synthesis of the two.

RETROACTIVITY OF LAWS AND THE PRINCIPLE OF PRESCRIPTION

The principles of non-retroactivity and prescription express the validity of the temporal factor in judicial matters. They thus constitute the personalizing–dialectical element in the administration of justice just as the theory of mitigating circumstances constitutes a concession both to the dialectical demands of the concrete totality and the time factor. The equilibrium of these factors is variable according to the juridical system. Totalitarian law tends to restrain their validity. Like the state itself, anti-statist activity is extra-temporal for totalitarian thought. Whatever the theoretical formulations may be, it is certain that in political matters, totalitarian justice is little troubled by questions of prescription or non-retroactivity. Moreover, tenth-century law, having undergone the totalitarian influence, is on the whole less demanding on this point than nineteenth-century law.[95] This is therefore one aspect of a more general phenomenon: emphasis of the reificational constituent of law at the expense of its personalizing–dialectical element. The disappearance of the institution of Assizes in certain countries, its decline in others, the loss of the

[94] Recalling the history of a regime or a politician offers a more valid source of information on their future than the analysis of statements in interview form; information journalism, in basing its analysis on the second element, in preference to the first, confirms public opinion in its tendency to 'presentify' and, consequently, to destructure and spatialize duration.

[95] Certain states having recently gained independence have sanctioned acts of 'collaboration' with the colonial power; if it were justified, the break with the principle of non-retroactivity is obvious and any comparison with the repression of collaboration in France is a *false identification*, for the French statist existence *had not begun in 1944*. But the Nuremberg judgements, although justified, constitute no less of a concession to the principle of retroactivity.

function of the advocate in a totalitarian context, in addition to an important diminution of the 'mitigating circumstances' factor, are all part of the same ensemble as the much troubled question of the revival of torture. Alienation appears once again as the decline of the dialectic, and the spatializing–identificatory constituent permits the integration of this phenomenon in the total context of the schizophrenic nature of false consciousness.

THE POLICING CONCEPT OF HISTORY

The policing concept of history[96] is the negation of the historical dialectic, in other words the negation of history. It is thus at the antipodes both of historical materialism, since in that case History's driving force is not the ensemble of objective forces but good or evil individual action, and dialectical philosophy, since the 'event' is no longer understood as the normal substratum of the course of History, but as miracle or catastrophe; it is no longer dependent on scientific explanation but on black or white magic. In the Manichean diptych of this view, the hero (leader) and the traitor represent two poles of the same principle of reificational negation of the autonomy of history. It is therefore a pseudo-history, a non-dialectical result either of success due to the genius of the leader or failure explicable through treason; an authentic 'syndrome of external action' permits the privileged system to evade eventual responsibility. The policing concept of history represents the extreme form of political alienation; it is both a sociocentrism which dichotomizes the world into a privileged system and a non-privileged remainder and a phenomenon of false consciousness of a schizophrenic nature. Since the privileged system is considered as perfect, extra-temporal and extra-dialectical, the event—particularly the unfavourable event—can only be explained by means of external action; it is experienced as an unexpected, 'undeserved' catastrophe, which is no longer integrated into the normal course of events whose succession constitutes the thread of concrete, dialectical temporality. One can compare this ensemble with two specific elements in the

[96] Cf. M. Sperber's (431) article and my contribution (180).

clinical picture of schizophrenia, *the syndrome of external action* and the *deranged experience of the end of the world* (*Weltuntergangslebniss*, abbreviated to WUE by German authors), the clinical translation of the appearance of the dialectic in a reified world which can accept the event only as a catastrophe.

The preceding analyses are naturally very brief and each of the points considered would require a more detailed study. For the moment, their convergence is of major interest to my subject. This convergence points towards the anti-dialectical and therefore schizophrenic common denominator of political alienation. The loss of the dialectic is seen either in the prevalence of the reversible spatial constituent of experience with anti-dialectical identification ('false identification') as the logical expression, or in a loss of temporalization with an incapacity to understand the 'event' in a way other than as a miracle or a catastrophe. Analogies with schizophrenia are clear—analysis of them can be followed even into the details of the clinical picture. They are dependent on this general fact that the instrument of dialectical thought, far from being an immediate datum, is the fruit of a perpetual reconquest; its acquisition demands a determined degree of maturity in the child, an ensemble of organic and pyschic conditions in the adult, and an ensemble of gnoseo-sociological conditions for collectivities (classes). It can be seen that a disturbance in any one of these factors can lead to similar results and that, notably, various organic and psychic causes can give rise to a complex of symptoms for which the common denominator of non-dialectical thought assumes a valuable nosological unity, despite etiological divergences.

In the light of recent work, schizophrenia appears as a loss of the sense of personal history, and psychotherapy therefore consists of a reconstruction of the totality of the person with a reintegration into history. From the viewpoint of the investigator the schizophrenic loss of the historico-dialectical perception of reality can be seen in the form of a preponderance of the spatial factor or as loss of experienced time: as over-spatialization or as sub-temporalization. This work[97] therefore constitutes a confirmation—and at the

[97] I am thinking of the research of G. Pankow and L. Binswanger.

same time a dialectical transcendence[98]—of the concept of morbid rationalism. On the other hand, my study of the different forms of false consciousness shows that spatialization is the real fundamental problem of political alienation; it is as a crystallization of a *morbid rationalist* perception of reality that ideology appears as a system of thought divorced from reality. The really pure clinical cases of morbid rationalism have always been rare and they will certainly become more so due to progress in theraupeutic treatment. It may be that one day the syndrome described by Minkowski will become something like an ideal type, that is to say a common denominator without autonomous clinical existence, towards which different forms of the illness would converge.[99] But doubtless it will retain its validity as a critical category of ideological thought for a long time.

National-socialist ideology constitutes a special example in this respect. Not only did the inhuman world of the concentration camps evoke—directly or through the intermediary of Kafka's work—the world of schizophrenics, but national-socialist ideology as a whole depends on morbid rationalism in its worst form. By placing the essential value of man in the biological domain, racism denies History; one extra-historical axiogeneous source is supposed to enlighten the 'outside' world without itself being exposed to the fates and fortunes of historicity. The result is that any unfavourable event for this racial pseudo value is itself extra-historicized and 'understood' in terms of treason or conspiracy: the ideology of national-socialism is logically inseparable from the theory of the 'stab in the back'.[100] An extreme case of ethnocentrism, it adopted the dichotomizing–reifying

[98] In the sense of *Aufhebung*.

[99] i.e. it would come close to being an abstract *fundamental disturbance* (Grundstörung).

[100] Nietzsche, whom the Nazis wished to adopt as their master thinker, suggests 'living dangerously'. From the axiological point of view, this 'dangerous life' corresponds to the dimension of precariousness (Dupréel). But if the individual and collective life of the Germans under Hitler was not exempt from danger, far from it, racial *value* which was not precarious was sheltered from all danger. From the point of view of its implicit axiology, Nazism was thus antipodal to the Nietzschean ideal.

(anti-dialectical) perception common to all forms of egocentrism by pushing it to its extreme point. An obsession with space existed in nationalist-socialist thinking, an obsession which, after what has just been said, corresponded to its essence as ideology; its incomprehension of History assumed in certain critical moments a literally mad nature. It is as a reifying and devaluing (anti-dialectical) perception of reality that national-socialism is a form of false consciousness; it is as an illusion of History and value that its theoretical expression deserves to be described as *ideology*. A doctrine which reifies value by locating it in the biological area, can only *dream* of History. But these are atrocious dreams.

V

Schizophrenic Structure of Racist Ideology

'. . . . it appears that in periods of extreme crisis, capitalism tends to intensify reification and even to bring it to a head.'

Histoire et Conscience de Classe.

'The Germans even more than people who claim to be rationalists, are capable of such complete suppression of the subject that only the intellect remains of interest and the demon of Abstraction celebrates untold victories.'

Albert Béguin (39), p. 180.

Ideology, which was bound to reach its logical conclusion in criminal medical experimentation on man, marks without doubt one of the outermost limits obtained by the process of reification in our culture. One might wonder to what extent the whole thing measures up to the concept of schizophrenization by means of which I have tried to define the phenomenon of false consciousness. Is Nazi doctrine an ideology of schizophrenic structure?

Hitlerian racism is without doubt a mad form of ethnocentrism, that is to say a system of collective egocentrism with an ethnic base. It would take a long time and be unnecessarily tedious to quote all the examples of egocentric arguments advanced by national-socialist propaganda. The most typical was certainly the one directed towards the role of Jews in resistance movements. The official theory stipulated that not only were German Jews bad Germans (which was false anyway before 1933) but also that

Judaism as a whole was linked with French and English 'imperialism'. Egocentric psychology did not realize that such an assertion was a seal of patriotism for English and French Jews who had no other patriotic duty than that towards their own country. The attempts at exploitation through propaganda of the activity of Jewish resisters (one is reminded of a certain famous poster showing the Jewish members of a cell, with the caption 'Liberators?'), could only produce a result diametrically opposed to the desired end.[1] For the promoters of this propaganda, the concept (unconscious for the most part) of *legitimate patriotism* was defined in terms of Germany, that is to say, for non-Germans, in a heteronomous way; sociocentric thought, a fine working instrument for internal propaganda, proved to be a source of monumental errors when used in a non-German political context.

In fact, the non-German world to a large extent seems to have been interpreted in terms of the postulate that the enemy world was homogeneous. This was less because of working hypotheses about propaganda than ideological convictions of a delirious structure; specific facts are available to prove this.[2] The concept of the completely depersonalized and mythologized Jew became the substratum of this hostility. It was the 'international Jew' who was behind the anti-German enterprises of English imperialism and bolshevism as well; the explanation for the real antagonism of the two groups in question is dependent on concrete political science; neo-primitive thought need make no reference to it and it has largely made use of this privilege.

In a general way the image of the Jew, a typical representative

[1] German propaganda in occupied France was a long succession of mistakes. This same propaganda was perfectly organized and astonishingly efficient in Germany; Sociocentrism having acquired a delirious nature (otherwise known as false consciousness) prevented effective transposition.

[2] The story of Joel Brand's mission is fairly typical. Towards the end of the war, Nazi leaders in Budapest promised leaders of the Jewish community in Budapest acts of clemency if they would obtain certain material from the Allies. It was absurd to a degree but the Nazi leaders were by all accounts convinced that the Allied Command had no reason to refuse the Jews. In fact what happened was quite different; first of all the emissary had difficulty with his visa in Turkey and was later arrested.

of the 'hostile world', was reified in Nazi thinking, that is to say, it was homogenized and dissociated; obviously a homogeneous reality can be dissociated much more easily than a concrete structure.[3] The picture of the Jew portrayed in propaganda is in 'a cauldron'; this is a general characteristic of all ethnocentrism,[4] but particularly clear in national-socialist writings.

Not only is the archetype of the Jew constructed in an autistic fashion, without regard for reality (neglecting completely the social and rational differences of Jews among themselves), but it is still more absurd because it involves contradictory characteristics. Jews are reproached for being behind pacifist movements and also behind all activities of war supporters, for being revolutionary socialists and retrograde capitalists, for isolating

[3] This is because, as we saw earlier, the organized whole is both consistent and precarious (the axiological nature of the totality), and therefore offers more resistance to the dissociation of its elements than non-organized wholes, but it suffers more in its 'formal qualities'.

[4] If all anti-Jewish criticism were categorized one would be faced by a list of contradictions, each description being contradicted by its opposite. Thus Jews are accused of sordid greed, ostentatious spending, excessive individualism and exaggerated devotion to social 'causes' . . . 'These contradictory criticisms sometimes come from different people, but almost as often from the same person, who presents them as a single characteristic.' (Loewenstein (306), p. 77.) Cf. also the results of Adorno's investigation (7), p. 75; 'The correlation of .74 between subscales "Seclusive" and "Intrusive" reveals a deep contradiction in anti-Semitic ideology. As a matter of simple logic, it is impossible for most Jews to be both extremely seclusive and aloof and at the same time too intrusive and prying.' Anti-semitism appears in these examples as a clearly prelogical phenomenon, an authentic survival from an emotional universe which predates attempts to understand 'reality as rational', according to Hegel's phrase.

This structural ambivalence of the archetypal 'Jew' in antisemitic ideology would be, according to Loewenstein, the materialization (authentic reification in my terms) of Oedipean ambivalence [(306), p. 65]; a legitimate ambivalence while it remains on the level of affect, but one which becomes absurd as soon as it relates to reality and not to states of mind. Oedipean explanations of antisemitism are predominant in Loewenstein's work; his theory confirms the more general one which emphasizes the reactionary role of the patriarchal family (Reich and the 'Sex-Pol' school, Flugel, etc.).

themselves from their neighbours and for wanting to be integrated. When one accuses 'The Jew' (significant singular!) of being at the same time a pacifist and a war supporter, this is not the dialectical unity of opposites but pure absurdity. A non-existent united will (there are pacifist Jews and militaristic Jews just as there are pacifist Germans and militaristic Germans) is postulated, and then characteristics which can never form a totality are brought together in the same image: the ethnocentric archetype is the negation of the *concrete* dialectical totality. In a general way, for national-socialism, the Jews constituted an inferior race possessing all the qualities which, for racism itself, define superior races: will for power, capacity for imposing its domination, *concern for racial purity.*[5] In all of these judgements one searches in vain for some coherence. In fact coherence is characteristic of reality and of scientific thought which tends to reflect it; projective thinking creates its own universe and does not have to be concerned with it: 'the unconscious is the non-structured' said a psychiatrist.[6] As Meyerson and Dambuyant[7] have shown, the 'cauldron' is the expression *par excellence* of autistic thinking.

THE AUTISTIC, REIFICATIONAL NATURE OF RACISM

S. Arieti, whose research on the logical structure of schizophrenic thinking will be considered later, writes: 'In our Western society, we find an infinite number of examples of autistic thinking when

[5] Loewenstein emphasizes that: 'The accusations made by Hitler against the Jews were but a projection of his own intentions' [(306), p. 40]. In a general way, one might say that this is the inverse mechanism of the one described by Anna Freud: an *aggression against one who is like oneself*: exorcism of possible remorse by projection of oneself on to a scapegoat, with aggression against the latter. An identical mechanism must have led some of the would-be organizers of medical experiments on men to join the anti-vivisectionist movement (on animals). (Goering.)

[6] E. Conrad (112) and (113). But the unconscious is also atemporal: the irruption of the unconscious into the collective consciousness de-dialecticizes thought.

[7] Meyerson and Dambuyant (332).

the emotions take the upper hand. A man may be criticized, disliked or even lynched if, as a consequence of one of his characteristics associating him with a racial or religious minority, he is autistically identified with evil.[8] It is interesting to note that a psychopathologist, who was generally not interested in questions of ideological criticism, spontaneously arrived at an observation which belongs to the theory of false consciousness.

The racist perception of human reality is schizophrenic in several ways. It postulates an identificatory, anti-dialectical step, dependent on Domarus-Vigotsky's law[9] ('The devil is black— the black man is the devil'). It implies a veritable 'deranged perception' of the racial minority in question; the ethnocentrist perceives the colour black as a sort of 'essential characteristic'. It is clear that this essence is not that of the perceived, but rather the perceiver: it is not the Black who is 'essentially' evil, but the racist who is essentially racist and who consequently perceives in this way.[10] It postulates a dichotomization whose equivalent is found in clinical schizophrenia, a dichotomization having as its corollary an actual 'reificational depersonalization' of the individual representative of the minority in question, which is reflected particularly in caricature, the strongest weapon of ethnocentrism.[11] It also admits fairly often the existence of *action at a*

[8] Arieti (11), p. 298.

[9] Cf. further the works of S. Arieti: identification based on the identity of predicates.

[10] These developments are difficult to follow without understanding P. Matussek's theory about deranged perception. Cf. further p. 282. Deranged ethnocentric perception is authentic mirror behaviour.

[11] It is significant that racist regimes, being generally insensitive to humour ('clowns do not laugh') are by contrast, keen on caricature, mainly in its most crude forms. In fact—and I don't think I go against Bergson's thinking in this—laughter is a reaction of de-reification against the mechanism whereas sociocentric caricature clearly arises from a wish for totalitarian homogenization in politics and reificational homogenization in philosophy: a person who is not constituted as we are is laughable and caricature magnifies bodily nonconformity by making it ugly and maladapted. In reality it is best to distinguish between two sorts of caricature: that which reveals a real weakness that is socially dangerous and objectively viewed, a reaction similar to laughter, and reifying sociocentric

distance of an undeniably magico-schizophrenic nature.[12] The nonconformity to the reificational scheme of perception sometimes sets off a reaction of defensive aggression: the Southerner does not like the Negro who is indiscreetly brilliant; the anti-semite does not much appreciate the Jew who is too disinterested in financial matters; he defends (aggressively if necessary) his prejudices, he assimilates the object of the perception instead of accommodating the perception to its reality: this is the very definition of paranoid deranged thought, an extreme form of non-dialectical thought.

DERANGED PERCEPTION AND REIFIED PERCEPTION OF THE ADVERSARY

P. Matussek's research[13] on the deranged perception of paranoids will be discussed in more detail later on. But Matussek formulated the hypothesis that deranged perception was characterized by the

caricature, dependent on a pseudo 'intuition about essence'. The caricaturist, without realizing it, is really drawing himself (cf. the 'mirror sign' in the psychopathology of schizophrenia, p. 258). The nobility of the characteristics of a Roosevelt, or an Einstein is obscured by the Nazi artist's pencil which emphasized an expression of hate in the former's expression (which never existed in photographs) and racial characteristics in the second. Clearly the caricaturist sees his own essence. In this category of ideas, one could say that socio- and ethnocentric caricature is the deranged perception of false consciousness.

[12] In truth, this 'magical action from a distance' is very much a fact of southern racism; it seems that it did not exist in Nazism. Fairly recently I read in the press a pitiful news item: a Negro was prosecuted for having *looked* at a white woman. The role of the look in paranoid madness is notorious (cf. (218), (270) and p. 241). The 'schizophrenic-magic' relationship is emphasized most strongly by G. Roheim [(405), p. 225]. Cf. also the interesting contribution by G. Tourney and P. J. Plazak: *Evil eye in myth and schizophrenia* (450) which contains rich documentation about medieval superstitions. The word 'fascination' has a well-known sexual connotation: for the Romans a phallus or 'fascinum' protected the garden (in a rather homeopathic way) against evil eyes (Roheim '405), p. 31).

[13] Matussek (322) and (323).

predominance of properties called 'essentials' in the act of perception.[14] I have tried to show elsewhere[15] that in reality this involves a reified anti-dialectical perception, and for this reason an integral part of a general theory of schizophrenia, a reificational psychosis of non-dialectical consciousness. The perceived 'essences' are elaborated in an egocentric way; the deranged person sees his own states of mind in the guise of 'essentialist' perceptions. Likewise, the ethnocentric perception of the member of a non-privileged group is egocentric, obscuring and depersonalizing; it relates to the homogeneity of the conviction itself and not to the concrete heterogeneity of reality; it reifies its object in a situation of uniform non-value without 'mitigating circumstances'. The racist wants to see the Negro as an ignorant brute, the Jew as an amoral being, cowardly and with base interests; behaviour that contradicts this can spark off a violent reaction. S. Kennedy gave a curious description of the code of conduct that governs the behaviour of the Southern Black;[16] if the latter is brilliant or possesses knowledge superior to that of a white man in a specific field, he will do his best not to show it; his duty and his interests are to respect the illusions of his adversary. Likewise, in certain towns, under the occupation, the Gestapo arrested at a given moment only Jewish men; women were taken only in the absence of their husbands. But when the husband presented himself later to obtain the freedom of his wife, the two of them were usually detained. A Jew cannot be heroic; so much the worse for him if he claimed to be so.[17]

BIOLOGICAL ORIGINS OF RACISM: RACISM AND SOCIAL DARWINISM

Historically and logically, racism derives from Darwinian theory. 'Social Darwinism' is based on the radical interpretation that one

[14] Wesenseigenschaften (Klages and Metzger).
[15] Cf. (172), pp. 275–8.
[16] S. Kennedy (257), chap. XIII (Les préceptes de l'étiquette raciste, particularly pp. 273 ff. and 282 ff.).
[17] For other examples, cf. my contribution (172), p. 278, note.

of his German disciples, Auguste Weismann, gave to Darwinian theory. Weismann strongly challenged the transmissibility of acquired characteristics thus making any kind of Lamarckian explanation of evolution quite impossible, while Darwin, less dogmatically, was content to show the role of selection without actually completely dismissing Lamarckian theory. Orthodox Darwinism introduced the notion of 'panmixie' due to Weismann: racial decadence as a consequence of the suppression of selection for a given factor; the dental degeneracy of civilized peoples as a consequence of the progress of dental art is cited as an example.[18] The sociological consequences of this theory have been recast in a more moderate form by Spencer and—in their extremist form—Ammon, Ratzenhoffer, Kidd, Gumplovicz[19] and their school; the writings of these latter people contain— as Lukács[20] emphasized—all the essential elements of racism, and this almost half a century before the political episode of German racism.

Social Darwinism (and consequently, the whole of racism) is, as Lukács[21] shows, doubly anti-dialectical. It sees man in quanti-

[18] One could make a similar deduction about spectacle wearers, but once again, the mechanism neglects the dialectical principle of the totality, 'Darwinian' Darwinism itself being unable to escape entirely from this criticism. Selection does not have any bearing on isolated characteristics, but on the organism as a whole when it concerns animals, and on the organism and its social possibilities when humans are concerned; the oculist who saves a short-sighted engineer from elimination thus permits the perpetuation of a minimal biological non-value, but a considerable social value.

[19] It is amusing to note that the author of the book *Der Rassenkampf*, L. Gumplowicz, was Jewish. This fact prevented the official doctrinairians of national-socialism from quoting him as their authority, but not from stealing his unenviable precursory titles.

[20] Lukács (310), pp. 525–601: *Sozialer Darwinismus, Rassentheorie und Faschismus.*

[21] Cf. the following passage from Lukács: 'Gumplowicz has as his point of departure the *absolute identity* and *qualitative indifferentiaton* of natural and social processes. According to Gumplowicz, sociology is but the *natural history of humanity*' (Lukács (310), p. 542; my italics). This remarkable chapter contains even more statements of this nature. It is essentially as an anti-dialectical doctrine that racism springs from reification.

tative continuation of the animal line, neglecting entirely the qualitative leap made by man;[22] this qualitative leap includes among other things the creation of 'non-selective' values in the struggle for life; in certain circumstances, a metaphysician can be more helpless than a fairground wrestler. On the other hand Weismannism, by rigidly opposing germinal and somatic stock, transforms germinal stock into a metaphysical entity; it becomes extra-dialectical, extra-historical and extra-temporal.[23] It was vainly hoped to use it artificially as the substratum of all values, but those 'values' in which the Dupréelian factor of precariousness is lacking are pseudo-values. Theoretical axioms aside, there is something deeply revolting in a doctrine which proclaims the integrity of a 'good germinal stock' at the end of a life of debauchery, while a whole life of honest effort is supposed to be unable to overcome the handicap of poor quality stock; doubtless it was a mistake that a saddler's son became the greatest of thinkers. Understood dialectically, value can be nothing other than a perpetual conquest and affirmation of the person in the act; on the contrary the extra-historical and extra-temporal 'value' of the so-called noble race acts with regard to the very ones who are supposed to be its bearers (or rather plain depositaries) as a factor of alienation and depersonalization. In this sad chapter of contemporary history, reification and depersonalization appear together, just as in clinical psychiatry.

From Weismann to the racists of yesterday (and today), the line is direct; it passes through works of very varied (though usually poor) quality, authors such as Ammon, Gumplowicz, Ratzenhoffer and others. Otto Ammon,[24] the author of *Sélection*

---

[22] What is annoying is that Pavlovism in psychiatry does almost the same thing.

[23] Cf. ibid., 'This so-called scientific method, social Darwinism, practically eliminates history' (Mit dieser angeblich naturwissenschaftlichen Methode hebt der soziale Darwinismus die Geschichte auf); in actual fact, an anti-historical method in sociology could hardly claim to have anything other than a so-called scientific character.

[24] Cf. Otto Ammon: *Die Gesellschaftsordnung und ihre natürlichen Grundlagen* (Iéna, 1896); *Die natürliche Auslese beim Menschen* (Iéna, 1893); Loria (307), pp. 82 ff. Italian Marxism around 1900, which was very Darwinian itself, was very much preoccupied

naturelle chez les hommes and *Bases naturelles de l'ordre social,* seemed condemned to well-deserved oblivion; racism dragged him out of it, at least in Germany. For Ammon, individual selection is the only factor in human progress; from this belief he derives a frightening programme of social 'reforms'; the justification for wars, which serve to eliminate non-values (such as Péguy or Apollinaire among others), is not the least of these insanities.[25] With Gumplowicz (and his disciple, Ratzenhoffer), social Darwinism takes on a more serious note. For Gumplowicz[26] the driving force of history is racial struggle (*Rassenkampf*) caused by feelings of racial love and hate (*Rassenhass* and *Rassenliebe*). Gumplowicz thus explains history by metaphysical or rather mythical entities; in comparison with explanations based on the production of material goods, or even sexuality, this theory indicates a certain decadence. In any case, his work constitutes one of the principal expressions of an intellectual movement which includes such diverse figures as Engels's renowned adversary, E. Dühring, author of a theory of violence in history,[27] F. Oppenheimer's theory of the State,[28] certain currents of nineteenth-century French historical thought[29] and, lastly, the morbid excrescence of a highly debatable, though on the whole serious, school, the racist concept of History. This whole school is more or less dependent on a Darwinian doctrine that has been carefully purged of all dialectical elements.

with criticizing social Darwinians, but, seeing the Marxian class struggle as the direct continuation of the struggle for life, it remained almost completely imprisoned by the adversary's point of view; cf. Ferri: *Socialisme et Science positive,* Paris, 1896, pp. 70 ff.

[25] Ammon also recommended favouring the natural selection of the most able by exempting them from taxes.

[26] Gumplowicz: *La lutte des races,* Paris, 1893; cf. Loria (307) and Lukács (310) *passim.*   [27] Engels (143).

[28] F. Oppenheimer: *Der Staat* (Frankfurt, 1907). Oppenheimer's theory of the State is a curious synthesis, its author having been influenced both by Marx and E. Dühring.

[29] Notably the *Conquête de l'Angleterre par les Normands,* in which Thierry explains certain post-Conquest historical facts (the antagonism between Henry II and Thomas Becket) as a persistence of racial dualism masquerading as class antagonism. Historically it is rather questionable.

RACISM AND REIFICATION

Based on social Darwinism, racism postulates the essential identity of the organic world and the social universe: its point of departure is therefore already eminently anti-dialectical. Furthermore, organic-social identification has a conservative significance; this was the meaning of Menenius Agrippa's famous fable—as Lukács emphasizes.[30] This biological conception of social existence is a reificational perception: the human laws of society are integrated into a natural domain, a dialectical one certainly, but one whose dialectical characteristic is situated in a superhuman temporal scale and, in any case, inaccessible to man's action: 'such a "naturalist" conception of sociology (eine solche «naturgesetzliche» Soziologie) leads man to resign himself to destiny[31] in the capitalist world . . .' For Gumplowicz the last word in sociology is 'the concept of History as a natural process'.[32] The result is that as a reified concept, racism misunderstands and ignores real human history. For ethnocentrism, History is a permanent prehistory which maintains the illusion of being history; this is one aspect of its false consciousness. Furthermore, for this ideology, racial historical value is given from before History. History does not therefore constitute, for racism, real progress, but rather an attempt at reconquering the position normally attributed to a given *a priori* value. Gobineau already considered evolution as degeneration, the mixing of races as an agent of racial decadence; 'the activism of subsequent racism is also based on Gobineau's pessimistic and anti-evolutionary view'.[33] This 'so-called scientific method practically suppresses History'.[34] 'The biological position of the problem implies . . . that what it

---

[30] Lukács (310), p. 525.

[31] '. . . fuhrt . . . zu einer Ergebenheit in das Kapitalistische Schicksal'. The 'mundanization' (*Verweltlichung*) of L. Binswanger (which I interpret as an expression of reification in psychiatry) is also defined as an 'exteriorization of fatalism' (*Veräusserlichung des Schicksals*), Binswanger (61), p. 55.

[32] Lukács (310), p. 541.   [33] Lukács (310), p. 530.

[34] Lukács (310), p. 542.

considers as essential is no longer submitted to any modification or evolution.'[35] Furthermore, Gumplowicz bases this view of the 'conservation of the sum of values in the world' on a doubtful analogy, that is, the physical principle of conservation of energy.[36] All the elements of a reificational interpretation of racism are to be found in Lukács's text: projection into the natural domain of certain interhuman data; denial of the dialectic and History, resignation to the 'natural' inevitable characteristics of the given social context. However, if the author of *Destruction de la Raison* also tenaciously avoids any allusion to the philosophical concept which made the reputation of the author of *Histoire et Conscience de Classe*, this is attributable to the whole context of the sociology of knowledge, which we have explained elsewhere.[37]

On the other hand it is correct that Weismannism (and not Weismann–Morganism, an imaginary school) was the precursor of racist doctrines. The 'germinal line' such as Weismann conceives it, is reified; it is a 'value' given once and for all, without any real interaction with the surrounding milieu, or even with the non-germinal tissues of the organism;[38] it therefore imposes on its bearer no duty other than a passive one: to avoid the degeneration of the noble line by refusing racial misalliance. Consequently, this extra-historical pseudo-value bears the significance of an authentic factor of alienation *vis-à-vis* its would-be bearers; the man whose value does not reside in his actions, but outside them, in his 'participation' in a mystical entity, is alienated (in the Marxist-Lukácsian meaning of the term) since he can not create himself dialectically; one cannot properly speak of a bearer of values, but a person borne along by an extra-temporal, heteronomic 'value'. He is also a dissociated person, his axiological centre of gravity being situated outside himself.

As reified and reifying consciousness, racism is, in theory, hostile to sexuality. It is the 'patrist' type of doctrine, to use

[35] Lukács (310), p. 543.
[36] Ibid.
[37] Cf. my whole contribution (170).
[38] Morganism actually admits the existence of sudden variations under environmental influence, for example, radiation; the difference is important.

Rattray Taylor's expression.[39] There certainly exists a 'reification of sexuality',[40] but this would constitute a whole chapter in sexual pathology; normal sexuality is altero-centric and anti-reificational. As a result racism mistrusts sexuality;[41] perhaps homosexuality, with its postulate of total homogeneity, constitutes the most adequate kind of sexuality.[42] Furthermore, for the anti-semitic racist, rejection of the Jew often symbolizes rejection of sexuality. The reificational nature of anti-semitism is very clearly emphasized by D. J. Lewinson.[43] This study based on the use of statistical methods of social psychology, is aimed mainly at American anti-semitism, but its conclusions are generalizable. Anti-semitism, one aspect of ethnocentric attitudes, postulates a rigid anti-dialectical dichotomization of the human universe into 'ingroup' and 'outgroup'. Outgroups are homogenous postulates; ethnocentrism ignores the differences between Jews of different nationalities or the conflicting interests between those of different classes;[44] in questionnaires, arguments postulating the essential homogeneity of Jews predominate, such as 'Jews help one another too much'; 'they are all alike'. The

---

[39] Rattray Taylor (395) and his summary, pp. 16 ff. (note).

[40] I. A. Caruso (91) *passim*.

[41] Cf. the famous play by Sartre 'La Putain respectueuse', which clearly brings out the relationship between infantile sexual regression and racial prejudice.

[42] Cf. the precocious flourishing of homosexuality in certain S.S. circles, but the attitude of Nazism *vis-à-vis* the sexual act was condemned to be ambivalent; a reactionary rejection of sexuality on the one hand, and a very clearly felt necessity on the other to assure the demographic movement required for a future of wars and conquests. Any scientific study of sexuality was held to be dishonourable. The work of Freud and Hirschfeld was forbidden. The obsession with venereal disease, an obsession expressed particularly strongly in *Mein Kampf*, constitutes a rationalization of the rejection of sexuality by Nazism. The feminine ideal of German racism was also a desexualized ideal. Cf. in this connection W. Reich (399) and his school (*Sex-Pol Bewegung*) whose point of view is always interesting if a trifle excessive.

[43] T. W. Adorno *et al.*, *The Authoritarian Personality*, New York, 1950.

[44] Cf. the phrase quoted by R. Loewenstein (306), p. 40; 'the mysterious alliance between capital and Revolution'.

F

ethnocentrist individual readily thinks in concepts: 'the Jew', 'the Negro' etc., the ability for making personal contact being psychologically lacking. He thinks in stereotypes, reifies, depersonalizes,[45] and dissociates his object. Finally, ethnocentrism is a global phenomenon; the anti-semite is readily anti-Negro, zenophobic and even anti-European; the source of its prevention is therefore not to be found in the concrete experience of the group or groups alluded to, but in the very psychological structure; it is not an empirical, *a posteriori* step, but subjective and *a priori*.

In the face of such an attitude, abstract reason or reason supported by concrete examples, is powerless, for it is not a question of reasoned conviction but of an emotional attitude,[46] therefore an act of false consciousness. Indeed, anti-semitic attitudes—and anti-minority attitudes in general—arise from a two-fold false consciousness; it reifies—and consequently depersonalizes its object, thought of as a symbol, not as an individual; furthermore, it takes little account of the real nature of the

[45] 'Another aspect of stereotypy which is implied by the scale items and brought out more directly in the interviews may be termed "stereotypy of interpersonal relationships and experiences". It involves an inability to experience Jews as individuals. Rather, each Jew is seen and reacted to as as a sort of sample specimen of the stereotyped *reified* image of the group.' Adorno (7), p. 94.
  'The ethnocentric need for an outgroup prevents that identification with humanity as a whole which is found in anti-ethnocentrism. This lack in identification is related to the ethnocentrist's inability to approach individuals *as* individuals and to their tendency to see and "prejudge" each individual only as a sample specimen of the reified group. Their experience of interpersonal relations involves, so to speak, the same stereotypy as their opinions regarding groups generally.' [(7), p. 148.]
  The American authors do not avoid, as Lukács does (310), the use of the term 'reification', which is quite indispensable in this context.
[46] '. . . numerous attempts to fight anti-semitism by giving the "true facts"—attempts which are distinguished for their lack of success. What this theory has overlooked is the *receptivity* of many individuals to any hostile imagery of Jews, and the emotional *resistance* of these individuals to a less hostile and less stereotyped way of thinking.' [(7), p. 93.] Deranged ethnocentrist perception is one element of this emotional resistance.

frustrations on which it is dependent.[47] The convergence of Adorno's work and Lukács's results show—in an undeniable way—the reified character of racist consciousness.

One other aspect of reification, the degradation of man to a position of utilitarian value, found its tragically famous expression in the concentration camp. Undeniably a reificational phenomenon, it required a whole terminology appropriate to the situation. Rousset readily evokes Kafka's work in this connection, a novelist of alienation and reification. It is also a schizophrenic act, for the world of schizophrenics is an inhuman world: 'what most particularly bears the mark of schizophrenia is the rigid, theoretical, inhuman nature of their conceptions', writes H. Baruk.[48] M. G. Gilbert emphasized the major role played by schizoid personalities in the concentration camp hierarchy.[49] Doubtless it was a matter both of selecting sub-human people destined for this atrocious task and also of normal or para-normal people experiencing a schizophrenic reaction when caught within the system. Besides, the irony is ferocious: here was an institution which claimed to depersonalize artificially the members of an élite who fell under its axe, but which achieved this goal with its own supporters only too well. In fact the pseudo-élite (the S.S.) living in the cult of this heteronomic, reified pseudo-value found themselves face to face with this pseudo-value in a situation of alienation. The concrete psychological study of the 'S.S.

---

[47] We cannot enter into the details of these theories: the role of the Oedipus complex which dominates Loewenstein's thinking [(306), pp. 24, 65. 135]; the role of circumcision which, by making possible more prolonged coitus, enables the Jew to seduce certain Aryan women and thus incurs the jealousy of competitors (Feller); the role of frustration (a certain renewed vigour of ethnocentric attitudes among children subjected to artificial frustration has been observed experimentally . . .). What is important in this connection is that these mechanisms play *vis-à-vis* anti-semitic theory the role of Pareto's residues *vis-à-vis* derivations (otherwise known as rationalizations). One finds again and again the close inter-relationship between the concepts of alienation (Jew–stranger), reification, false consciousness, and certain schizophrenic characteristics of thinking: dissociation and depersonalization.

[48] Baruk (32), p. 139.

[49] G. M. Gilbert (193).

personality'[50] shows clearly that in the circumstances this is not a vain phrase. 'The author of an injustice is always more unfortunate than he who receives it' was said two thousand years ago in the course of a famous conversation, by the spokesman for Calliclès.

In periods of acute crisis capitalism tends to accentuate reification and pushes it to its paroxysm.[51] During a crisis which appeared to threaten its existence, the German ruling class projected its desire to escape from dialectical law into a belief in the eternity of racial 'values'; racism thus appears as reification pushed to its ultimate end. Thus its history—which one would like to believe is finished—constitutes an essential episode in the schizophrenization of culture.

Lukács showed how this movement, referred to by its leaders as 'History', was basically foreign to History. The historical time of national-socialism was dominated either by the chimerical hope of an empty eternity ('we shall rule for 20,000 years' said Goebels).[52] or (at the approach of defeat) by a veritable 'repetition–compulsion' on the collective scale. A deranged temporality (very

---

[50] F. Bayle's (36) thesis and G. M. Gilbert's contribution (193) have an experimentally based contribution to make to this question.

[51] Lukács (309), p. 227. Cf. the epigraph of this chapter.

[52] The massive architecture of national socialism expresses this same nostalgia for extratemporality of which racism is the biological translation. W. Daim's work (120) contains interesting perceptions on national-socialist doctrine; without using Marxist terminology, it is an ideological criticism of Hitlerism, that is to say, its analysis as false consciousness. On the subject of temporality we quote the following hymn which was very popular in Germany during the Nazi period [Daim (120), p. 146]. Daim saw it as the sign of a displacement of feelings for the absolute; the word '*Götzenbildung*' consciously no doubt re-echoes Bacon, the first theoretician of false consciousness:

Deutschland heiliges (!) Wort	Germany, sacred word
Du voll Unendlichkeit	Full of infinity
Ueber die Zeiten fort	Beyond Time
Seist Du gebenedeit	Be blessed
Heilig sind deine Höh'n	Your mountains are sacred
Heilig dein Wald	Your forests are sacred

close to that described by Binswanger and Minkowski),[53] translated itself into deranged attitudes. In Merleau-Ponty's words: 'It is not his critical faculty which guarantees man against derangement, but the structure of his space,'[54] a saying which is equally valid for groups.

This factitious temporalization, both the foundation and the result of an illusory historicity (there is no real historicity which can offer its values on a platter), involves as an axiological corollary a universe of false values. It is rare for a philosophical doctrine to find its experimental verification. However, the axiological destiny of Nazism constitutes the verification of both Binswangers' and Dupréel's theses: the relationships between personalization and temporalization in the dialectic of 'consistency–precariousness' as the foundation of axiology. Nazism attempted to depersonalize and to devalue its enemies (the medical experimentation in the concentration camps certainly constitutes the most extreme kind of reification seen in recent History).

[53] Cf. below, pp. 253 ff.
[54] Merleau-Ponty (330), p. 337. I would prefer to say structure of his spatio-temporal universe; the temporal, dialectical, valuing element protects consciousness against the anti-dialectical, devaluing element that is space, the seat of hallucination and derangement which are reificational phenomena.

Foreign observers present in Germany in 1945 (foreign diplomats and distinguished prisoners) readily describe the atmosphere at the time as deranged. This is an interesting observation for the psychopathologist, since this derangement had, to use Binswanger's terminology, a foundation of pathological temporalization. Convinced of the absurdity of the hypothesis that Germany would be defeated, the leaders expected a re-enactment of the 'Brandenburg miracle' which, in 1762 (death of the tsarina Elisabeth), saved King Frederick from desperate straits. At the news of Roosevelt's death, the press received the order to deal gently with his successor and a prominent minister stated to a diplomat: 'Hearing this news I thought I heard the beating of the wings of the spirit of History.' This is simply an anecdotal fact which reveals its significance only in the context of a general theory of the schizophrenization of the contents of collective consciousness. Even in this supreme moment, ethnocentrism showed itself incapable of being sensitive towards real history. The absence of actual temporalization in an ideology based on the consistency (without precariousness) of extra-temporal racial 'value', leads to a literally deranged perception of reality.

It succeeded in depersonalizing and devaluing those whom it considered to be agents of absolute historical value; psychological studies and also the behaviour of certain leaders before the tribunals[55] show that it was not a question of spiritual views. This is again a Dupréelian theme: the impossibility of a unique value;[56] there is value in valuing and not in devaluing, just as there is freedom only in respecting the freedom of others. Therefore there is no place for a real valuation within the frameworks of implicit spatialism of racism, a spatialism which the theory of the perenniality (extratemporality) of the germinal line translates into biological language. A false historicity can give only false values. Racism thus offers us a coherent example of false consciousness, in which the insight of the psychiatrist provides the autistic element[57] and the investigation of the experimental sociologist reveals the reificational structure.

[55] 'Personal responsibility expresses a strong temporal structure (in the Gestalt meaning) of personality: my past belongs to me and to me alone; I accept it. The pseudo-élite of national-socialism, by contrast, underwent the action of a veritable 'alienating identification' (Hitler is Germany, Germany is Hitler') whence a tendency —evident during certain trials—to clear oneself of the responsibility for war crimes and to blame them on a small number of higher officials. (172), p. 273.

[56] Dupréel (136), p. 100. The supposed unique value becomes a thing (!!). Cf. also Ruyer (408), p. 94, for criticism of this view.

[57] We are thinking of Arieti's suggestion (11), p. 298.

Part Two
Reified Consciousness

I

Status of the Problem

'... Bergsonian ideas made us suppose the existence
of two major groups of mental disorder: one character-
ised by a deficiency in intuition and experienced time
and by a concomitant hypertrophy of factors of a
spatial order, the other by the opposite state of affairs'

Minkowski, *Le Temps Vécu*, p. 271.

The analysis of the process of ideologization has shown us that
the false consciousness of political groups is related both to child
thought, through the prevalence of egocentric mechanisms, and
to schizophrenia—and more particularly to morbid rationalism
and geometrism—through the reification of interhuman relationships and the spatialization of historical duration. They are,
furthermore, complementary data: individual or collective egocentrism is the agent of de-dialecticization and, consequently,
reification of consciousness. False consciousness—i.e. the ensemble
of these regressive and derealist structures in political psychology
—thus appeared to me to be essentially an undialectical, anaxiological, abstract consciousness of significant, concretely dialectical
realities. The analysis of the ensemble of these mechanisms
constituted the first stage of the present work; the study of
various aspects of totalitarian thought shows the generality of
the ideological phenomenon as well as the usefulness of the use
of clinical concepts in political psychology. Without the support
of psychopathology, the totalitarian phenomenon—one of the
dominant political phenomena of this time—risks remaining
partly unexplained.

The following stage consists of a reversal of this step: having enlisted the aid of psychopathology to facilitate the comprehension of social false consciousness, I shall now try to use the conceptual framework of Marxian theory of alienation as a suitable approach to the interpretation of certain data in psychopathology. This programme has meaning only from the viewpoint of an open Marxism; the contribution of orthodox Marxism, entirely centred on Pavlovism, is not of any help and this is so whatever may be the properly scientific importance of its results.[1] In fact, the psychiatric effort of orthodox Marxism is a prisoner of internal contradictions. On the one hand, as sociologism, Marxism opens up a psycho-genetic perspective in psychopathology; Soviet psychiatry is now uncompromisingly organic. On the other hand, the dialectical malaise of orthodox Marxism affects particularly its psychiatric applications for reasons relating to the sociology of knowledge, which I have developed elsewhere.[2]

Now a consistent sociologism could be nothing but dialectic. There arises in the psychopathological works of the Pavlovian school a *surface sociologism*, pointed out by L. Beirnaert[3] among others. In fact it is not sufficient, in behaving like a historical materialist in psychopathology, to establish that mental illness is an integral part of society (no one has ever claimed the opposite), nor again to emphasize the pathogenic role of unfavourable economic conditions. Even the observation that 'the secondary signal system is social in its essence'[4] is not much more than a generality. In Binswanger's work we meet a particularly concrete example of 'deranged thought determined by existence',[5] as, for example,

[1] This is not a *criticism* of Pavlovism (which could be criticized only in an experimental way), but a criticism of the conception which identifies *valid theory* with *dialectical theory*, thus reducing the description 'dialectical' to nothing but a generality. There are great discoveries which contribute nothing to Marxism and have nothing to do with the dialectic, as for example, the discovery of the syphilitic origin of general paralysis.

[2] Cf. (170), pp. 691–3.

[3] L. Beirnaert (40), p. 364.

[4] S. Follin, in *La Raison*, no. 8, p. 120.

[5] *Seinsgebundenes Wahndenken*, similar to Mannheim's *Seinsgebundenes Denken*. The expression is mine, but most of Binswanger's analyses are implicitly based on this principle.

the observation of a form of dissociated temporalization in one patient[6] who did not succeed in integrating a sudden change in his social milieu and who lived in 'two speeds'. Analyses of this order are totally foreign to the spirit of orthodox Marxism. Later on I shall have the opportunity to show that the dialectical school *Daseinsanalyse* is at the same time very close to sociologism and therefore to historical materialism, but this materialist-sociologizing essence is masked by a terminology of idealist origin. This is the case particularly with Binswanger's work and perhaps even more so with Médard Boss's.

On the other hand, it is significant that on this question the Durkheimian school also turns out to be less sterile than orthodox Marxism. The famous work of Blondel constitutes, as is well known, a consistent attempt to base a general psychopathology on the data of Durkheimian sociology. This is therefore a concrete psychopathological expression of the sociological postulate common to Durkheimianism and Marxism, whereas the homologous effort of Marxist orthodoxy based on a polemical conception of social reality, sometimes tends towards mythology.[7] It is in no way paradoxical to confirm that on this question the author of *La Conscience morbide* is closer to the Marxist position than the Pavlovians even though, as a prisoner of non-transcended capitalist reification, Blondel sees only a single aspect of the social factor. On this point, Marxism is without doubt in a position to push Durkheimian sociologism to its logical conclusions by dialecticizing it. This is, furthermore, one of the tasks of this study. The opposition between Marxism and Durkheimianism—an opposition much emphasized by orthodoxy[8]—appears, from the

[6] The 'Mary case' [(63) and p. 263]; cf. also the social origins of the loss of temporalization in Jürg Zünd and S. Urban (60 and 62).
[7] Let me quote as an example the criticism of internment which, such as it was practised around 1952, was based on certain precise data, but its comparison with the concentration camp has made it into a social mythology of the worst kind. This form of criticism did not survive the changes brought about in 1953; it would be wrong to regret it.
[8] Cf. L. Henry (220), pp. 75–81. Not everything is untrue in these criticisms; reproaches such as that of social conformism, of

perspective of open Marxism, to be completely relative. A suggestive inventory of their analogies is to be found in A. Cuvillier's article.[9] Durkheim himself certainly believed himself to be further from Marxism than he was in fact; with a moderate knowledge of Marxian texts he tended—like many others before him and after him—to confuse Marxism and popular Marxism. Cuvillier particularly draws attention to an implicit theory of false consciousness within the frameworks of Durkheimian thought. The principal analogy resides, to my mind, in a common 'objectifying' conception of the social fact; but for Lukács reification is transitory illusion, condemned historically by the rise of the proletariat, while the 'social fact' of the Durkheimians is a constant. Durkheimianism does not entertain—and for good reason—any conception homologous to the theory of the decline of the State in Engels. For liberated Marxism, Durkheimianism is therefore essentially the sociology of reification which is understood but not transcended; in this sense it marks—with works such as the *Philosophie de l'Argent* by Simmel—one of the limits of bourgeois sociology. This limited historical perspective actually condemns a psychopathology of Durkheimian inspiration to seeing only one single aspect of the problem; from this perspective of *non-transcended reification*, the social fact benefits directly from an unconditional positive value as opposed to the psychotic fact as a 'negative value'; for Blondel the pathological is the non-

a non-dialectical spirit, of obscuration of the class struggle, are well deserved. Durkheim was without the slightest doubt the sociologist of the successful bourgeoisie. Having said this, it should be recognized that he diagnosed the *existence* of reification if not its historical relativity; like Marx—more clearly than Marx—he saw in the religious phenomenon an act of false consciousness. In the *Formes élémentaires*, religion appears '. . . like an illusion, certainly normal, even beneficial in a sense, but an illusion all the same, since it consists in elevating what is purely human into absolute, supernatural realities'. (Cuvillier (118), p. 40.) We are certainly closer to the Marxist concept of alienation, while the *Marxian* phrase (more Marxian than Marxist) concerning the *opium of the people* smacks a little of the influence of ahistorical rationalism of the eighteenth century; it is a reiteration of the theory of the *Priestertrug*.

[9] Cuvillier (118).

social. Nowhere—except perhaps in the famous *Règles* devoted to the 'normal' and the 'pathological'—is the social conformism of this great doctrine ever demonstrated more clearly than in the Blondelian theory of morbid consciousness. The Durkheimians could not anticipate the period when the social itself would become deranged: their vision of society was not sensitive to this *Kafkaesque nuance* which is, however (as we now know), a real dimension. It is a reasonable doctrine, the expression of a reasonable period; but the psychopathological application of such a doctrine runs a serious risk of remaining partial. Blondel, however, did not in any way consider his theory as definitive, but rather as the possible point of departure for later research; a pluralist conception of morbid consciousness did not seem to him to be excluded *a priori*.

A passage from the preface of *La Conscience morbide* is significant: it indicates the dialectical path which, in psychopathology (and elsewhere), leads from Durkheimianism to open Marxism: 'Our observations at this point vainly tried to respond to a large group of morbid entities, since it is not obvious *a priori* that morbid consciousness, out of all of the psychoses, appears only in one form. My theory therefore opens up the way to new research. But we cannot predict whether it will confirm the theory and allow it to be extended.'[10] Blondel therefore indicates the possibility of a dialectical transcendence (*Aufhebung*) of his own doctrine. The introduction of the concept of reification into psychopathology is one stage of it, a Durkheimianism that becomes dialectical is not very different from open Marxism. As soon as Marxist criticism reveals the reificational—therefore historically and axiologically relative—nature of the capitalist reality, which served as the point of departure for Blondel, a general, pluralist psychopathology becomes possible

Starting with the postulate that a certain degree of reification is normal, one succeeds in conceiving theoretically two forms of pathological existence in the world: through lack or through excess of reification, 'surrealist' or 'sub-realist' attitudes. Aphasia or more precisely 'the aphasic mode of being-in-the-world' is the

[10] (66), p. 11.

most typical example of the surrealist attitude; schizophrenia, and more particularly, morbid rationalism, constitutes the form *par excellence* of the reificational syndrome (sub-realist attitude). In relation to Minkowski's theory, this proposed conception is essentially the result of the materialist integration of an idealist, dialectical conception. Due allowance being made, this is a sort of '*Umstülpung*',[11] similar to that used in the works of the German anthropological school which we shall deal with later. In fact we have seen in the chapter on political alienation that, placed in a materialist context, morbid rationalism does not lead 'towards a cosmology'; on the contrary it shows itself to be a valid instrument of ideological criticism.

[11] '*Umstülpung*' the materialist up-ending of idealist conceptions; in Marx the up-ending of Hegel's idealist dialectic. Currently *Umstülpung* is translated by '*remise sur pied*'. It is only a moderately good translation for it is somewhat embarrassing to '*remettre sur pied*' authors with a world reputation. I systematically use the term of integration meaning integration of an 'idealist' dialectic in the frameworks of an open Marxist conception. But I would want to emphasize here, once and for all, that this is a step prompted by the Marxian notion of *Umstülpung*.

II

Outline of a General Psychopathology based on the Concept of Reification

---

'The social world seems to me as natural as nature,
which endures as if by magic. It is in reality a magical
structure, a system which is based on writings, promises
that are fulfilled, ideas that are effective, habits and
conventions that are observed—all pure fictions.'

P. Valéry.

REIFICATION IN 'HISTOIRE ET CONSCIENCE DE CLASSE'

The starting point for the theory of reification is now a classic
Marxian observation; capital is both a *material object* (commodity, a machine) and at the same time the *centre for the crystallization of human relationships*. A given instrument can remain
materially the same in two different historical contexts; it will be
capital only in a capitalist context, i.e. when *human relationships*
characteristic of the capitalist form of society are established
through it. Commodity as an object corresponds to a human
need that is likely to remain the same through the ages. It is at
the same time dependent on a certain form of social production;
as a *social fact*, wine produced by a slave in the Ancient world
is not the same as that produced by the effort of the modern
agricultural worker. Because of its dual aspect—material and
social, substantial and relational—commodity assumes a mysterious character in Classical economy which is well explained by
Marxian terminology. N. Berdiaeff, a thinker alien to Marxism

if ever there was one, described the theory of the fetishist nature of commodity as brilliant.[1] Lukács, in 1928, saw it as the most essential element of the theoretical structure of Marxism, 'the chapter on the fetishist character of commodity contains all of historical materialism, all the self-knowledge of the proletariat as knowledge of capitalist society'[2] (identity of the historical subject and object).

The theory of reification in Lukács is closely linked to these considerations. Lukács shows that the interhuman, relational character and therefore the historically transitory, and relative (dialectical) nature of capitalist categories, is hidden by the materiality of capital, which gives them the mistaken appearance of a natural phenomenon. The result is that the man in the reified world lives in an *inhuman world*. Kafka's work is the most striking illustration of this inhuman world of reification. This emerges both in the analysis of the *Trial* (the man crushed by the impersonal power of the judicial *apparatus*) and the *Castle*. Similarly, the worker in the capitalist system is faced with the products of his own activity which, having acquired a 'phantom substantiality' (*gespenstige Gegenständlichkeit*), crush him just as a natural power would do. It is therefore a sociological phenomenon completely analogous to what Wyrsch and Binswanger find in the world of schizophrenics. I shall return to this point in more detail.

There are several important consequences.

PHENOMENA OF DISSOCIATION AND DEPERSONALIZATION

An important passage from *Histoire et Conscience de Classe* is devoted to the *rationalization of work*, a reificational pheno-

---

[1] Berdiaeff (47), p. 133.

[2] (309), p. 186: 'Man konnte ... sagen, dass das Kapital über den Fetischcharakter der Ware den ganzen historischen Materialismus, die ganze Selbsterkenntnis des Proletariats als Erkenntnis der kapitalistischen Gesellschaft (und die der früheren Gesellschaften als Stufen zu ihr) in sich verbirgt.'

menon. 'Rationalisation, in the sense of being able to predict with even greater precision all the results to be achieved, postulates a precise dissociation of every complex into its elements with evidence of the special laws governing their production. . . . It is thus, on the one hand, forced to declare war on the organic production of whole products based on the traditional empirical experience of the worker: rationalization is unthinkable without specialization. On the other hand, this dissociation necessarily involves a *dissociation from the person of the producer*. Because of the existence of rationalization, the human qualities and idiosyncrasies of the worker appear—when contrasted with these special laws functioning according to rational predictions—increasingly as *mere sources of error (blosse Fehlerquellen)*. The human being . . . thus ceases to be the master of the economic process: he is henceforth merely the cog in a mechanical system whose laws he must subject himself to, whether he likes it or not.'[3]

This dissociation from concrete totalities is not only evident in the economic area; it naturally possesses an epistemological extension. Lukács quotes, from amongst thousands of possible examples, Sismondi's theory of crises to demonstrate to what point a theory that is based on accurate observations, but which is imperfectly integrated into the concrete historical totality, can lead to erroneous conclusions. There exists, therefore, and this is certainly one of the essential meanings of reification—a pseudo-epistemology of reified consciousness, based on the dissociation of totalities and atomism: that is to say, the preponderance of analytical functions over synthetic functions.

QUANTIFICATION AND SPATIALIZATION

The 'inhuman condition' that reification creates is manifested in a certain preponderance of the *quantitative* aspect of existence; this eminently anti-dialectical world fatally ignores the dialectic

[3] (309), p. 99. I find that the French word '*dissociation*' (the only possible translation of '*Zerreissen*') is more 'psychiatric' than the German term; this has no importance but given the subject of this work, it would have been dishonest not to point it out.

of the transformation of quantity into quality, the dialectic in which the category of totality is mediatory. The reified world is, above all, a *world of quantity*. Customary values, and people's labours are *qualitative*, heterogeneous. The values of exchange and socialized work are *quantitative....* The exchange value is measured quantitatively; its specific measure is money. Quantitative work corresponds to a social average in which all the qualitative characteristics of individual work disappear, except one, which is common to all forms of work and which makes them commensurable: that is *every act of production requires a certain time.*[4] Man therefore becomes the slave of time. 'Time is everything, man is nothing, at the very most the incarnation (*Verkörperung*) of time.'[5] This time is no longer the concrete duration of creative activity, but a *spatialized time*. 'The contemplative attitude adopted towards a process that is subject to mechanical laws (*einem mechanisch gesetzmässigen Prozess gegenüber*) and is developed independently from consciousness and outside the sphere of influence of human activity (that is, a closed, definitive system) also transforms the main categories of man's immediate attitude towards the world: it reduces space and time to a common denominator and *degrades time to the level of space*.'[6] 'Consequently temporality loses its qualitative, changing, fluid character; it is transformed into a rigid, exactly delimited continuum, filled with quantitatively measurable "things" (which are the reified, mechanically objectified "productions" of the worker, wholly detached from his total personality); it is transformed into space.'[7] Elsewhere Lukács talks about *maleficent*

[4] Lefebvre (295), p. 72.

[5] '... the ticking of a clock has become as accurate a measure of the relative activity of 2 workers, as it is of the speed of 2 trains. So, rather than saying that an hour from one man is the equivalent of an hour from another man, one talks of one man-hour being the equivalent to another man-hour. Time is everything, man is nothing; he is at the most the incarnation of time. Quality no longer matters. Quantity alone decides everything; hour for hour, day for day....' (*Misère de la Philosophie*, Paris, 1947, p. 47). The fact that time thus conceived is a spatialized time hardly needs to be emphasized.

[6] Lukács (309), p. 101.

[7] Ibid. An important passage both as a key to the conception

space (*Schädlicher Raum*).[8] The need for the 'abstract calculability' of human activities which keeps reappearing in this chapter anticipates, from 1923 onwards, contemporary economic planning. This is certainly another reason why this book fell into disfavour.

PREVALENCE OF IDENTIFICATORY FUNCTIONS

The experience of reified reality is translated into a particular logic which is naturally situated at the opposite extreme to a dialectical logic. Let me emphasize once more that there is a risk of being completely misunderstood on the significance of this important aspect of dialectical philosophy if one loses sight of the close correlativity between terms such as 'non-dialectical thought', 'false consciousness', 'reification', and 'alienation'; in fact, they concern the same fundamental phenomenon seen from different angles at least in the Lukácsian thought of this period. As a collective lived experience of reification, false consciousness is —as we have seen—essentially non-dialectical thought on the level of social groups. The reified world sees the triumph of the logic of solid bodies: identity overflows into *reality*, to paraphrase

of false consciousness as schizophrenic thought and as a mark of the indirect Bergsonian influence experienced by Lukács: 'Die Zeit verliert damit ihren qualitativen veränderlichen, flussartigen Charakter; sie erstarrt zu einem genau umgrenzten, quantitativ messbaren, von quantitativ messbaren "Dingen" (der verdinglichten, mechanisch objektivierten, von der menschlichen Gesamtpersönlichkeit genau abgetrennten "Leistungen" des Arbeiters) erfüllten Kontinuum: zu einem Raum.' Elsewhere [(309), p. 182], Lukács quotes Marx: 'Die Zeit ist der Raum der menschlichen Entwicklung' (Marx, *Lohn, Preis und Profit*, p. 40).

[8] Here is this passage [(309), p. 223]: 'Solange der Mensch sein Interesse reinanschauend kontemplativ—auf Vergangenheit *oder* Zukunft richtet, erstarren beide zu einem fremden Sein, und zwischen Subjekt und Objekt ist der unüberschreitbare "schädliche Raum" der Gegenwart gelagert.' (As long as man concentrates his interest contemplatively towards the past *or* the future, both are ossified into an alien existence and between the subject and the object lies the unbridgeable 'malificent space' of the present.)

the title of a famous work.[9] The reified world 'meyersonizes' to excess; it is obsessed with the identical. 'The formal act of exchange (which for the *Grenznutztheorie* (theory of marginal utility) remains the fundamental economic fact) likewise suppresses use-value as use-value and creates this relationship of *abstract equality* (my italics) between concretely unequal, and indeed non-comparable data.'[10] Lukács confines himself to denouncing abstract identification in the reified economic superstructure. The criticism of ideological thought goes further in this direction as we have seen elsewhere. Once more, identification appears as a devaluing depersonalizing process; the concept of *alienating identification* is well known in psychopathology.

AXIOLOGY OF THE REIFIED WORLD

The reified universe of dissociation of totalities, of spatialization and quantification is necessarily the locus for the deterioration of the axiological contents of existence. Elsewhere we have seen the relationships between totality and axiology; the concept of totality, a *dialectical* category (a revolutionary principle of science according to Lukács) is as central in axiology as in dialectics. In fact, the world of reification has a spatial structure; now, space is a milieu that allows for a *complete return* whilst axiology postulates the principle of the impossibility of such a return— ('consistency of values', according to Dupréel). On the other hand—and this is nothing more than my earlier observation seen

[9] This preponderance of identity over reality is characteristic of *schizophrenic* states especially in the lived experience of the symbol. Cf. Arieti (14 and 12) and my contribution (183). Caruso writes (89), p. 300, 'What we see here is a reification and a logico-formal, anti-dialectical objectivation of the symbol (in der Psychose kommt es eben zu einer formalistisch—logistischen und undialektischen Verdinglichung und Verselbständlichung des Symbols); like the dreamer, the psychotic believes in the omnipotence of his mental projections, for he objectivizes and reifies the symbols by constantly applying the principle of identity: symbol A normally meant to represent the symbolized B becomes a tautology by virtue of the equation $A=A$ and loses its real significance.'

[10] Lukács (309), p. 116.

from a different angle—the world of reification is dominated by the principle of identity; now, value is what, by definition, is not identifiable. The result is a deterioration of the axiological contents of existence and a promotion of immediate, utilitarian ('identifiable') values. Reified morality is typically what I shall call later 'objective morality'; the category of efficiency is a substitute for that of moral intention. 'In the world of extreme rationalisation, the worker's intention, his moral life as a person matters little; for society, he counts only as a cog destined to carry out a particular motion. *In a reified world, he himself becomes a thing.*'[11]

AHISTORICITY OF REIFIED THOUGHT

As a prisoner of a universe where space takes the place of duration, man in the reified world cannot understand history as the expression of creativity and spontaneity. Consequently the undeniable fact of change forces itself on this 'consciousness of immediacy' as a *catastrophe*, as a sudden change coming from outside that excludes mediation. In fact, the notion of 'event' implies a dialectical transformation of quality into quantity; it is both a continuation of the past and a break with the past. Reified existence, where everything is measured in quantity, does not understand the event and substitutes the notion of catastrophe, which is the result of heteronomic action (external action). Seen in this perspective, history appears as a function of a *demiurgic action*. An external force (God, the hero, a party) transcends the efficiency of its autonomous dialectic. Reified consciousness is essentially ahistorical: 'mens momentanea seu carens recordatione', said Leibnitz on this subject.

This rather long summary of Lukácsian theses was necessary since I wish to carry out a psychopathological application of his ideas that are rather inaccessible. It would be bold to summarize

[11] Lukács (309), p. 182. 'Der Arbeiter ist deshalb gezwungen sein Zurwarewerden, sein Auf-reine—Quantität Reduziertsein als Objekt des Prozesses zu erleiden.' This is one of those impenetrable Lukácsian phrases which is not easy to translate.

philosophical thought of this importance in a few points. However, one might say that the most essential elements of this theory are the following:

(a) The relationships between the concepts of *alienation, reification, false consciousness and non-dialectical thought.*

For Lukács—at least in *Histoire et Conscience de Classe*—alienation is a corollary of reification. On the other hand, the logical expression of reified consciousness is always a non-dialectical logic.

There is too much to choose from if one wants to quote passages from *Histoire et Conscience de Classe* where Lukács does not make a distinction between reification as a way of being-in-the-world and the notion of non-dialectical logic as a form of thought. It is therefore a theory of alienation, and should be judged as such, but it has the advantage of a clarity and an undeniable coherence which makes psychopathological applications possible. One works with delimited concepts and if we are able to show that these concepts correspond to something precise in psychopathology (which is what I shall try to do later), this will be both the indirect proof of the value of *Histoire et Conscience de Classe* and a specific scientific contribution. Marxian orthodoxy has, by contrast, challenged *Histoire et Conscience de Classe* without ever responding with a coherent theory of alienation. The constant use of a concept not having any concrete content has produced—specifically in psychopathology—paradoxical results. In fact, the concept of alienation in psychiatry simply denotes a man estranged from the milieu of his fellow men. In this sense, it is perfectly logical to say that all mental illnesses —even criminals and asocial forms—are *aliens*, but alienation thus understood has nothing in common with the Marxist concept. For Lukács, alienation means an anti-dialectical view of the world, which isolates the individual from a dialectical social reality. An analogy might be found in the Bergsonian theory of the comic. In psychopathology, alienation is not therefore mental illness in general, but *morbid rationalism* in particular.

(b) The role of the category of totality.

If the concept of alienation is a corollary of reification (and through the intermediary of reification, of dissociation and depersonalization of the producer in the reified economic process), then the dialectical category of the totality appears, on the contrary, as the essential instrument for all dialectical consciousness and also as the central category for all dialectical epistemology. Now, this raises an important problem for this subject: that of the dialectical value of psychological doctrines of *totality*, of which Gestaltism is the best known. These doctrines have been accused of idealism, and their dialectical nature has been minimized. In fact, once again the sociocentric criterion has come into play: these theories have been judged in relation to Pavlovism, which has always had its dialectical quality taken as axiomatic.

(c) The role of the historical subject and object.

In the reified world, the individual is crushed by the economic universe, the result of his own activity. This is, *mutatis mutandis*, as true for the capitalist as it is for the worker. This state of man being crushed by an almost hallucinatory pseudo-reality is reflected in Kafka's work. The historical consciousness of the working class (the formation of class consciousness) is essentially a de-reification analogous to the de-objectivation which characterizes the consciousness of the sick person undergoing psychoanalysis. The working class, having rediscovered, beyond reificational atomism, its own totality as the acting subject of history, discovers at the same time the subject–object identity (revolutionary class-society). Conscious and free historical action follows the state of being crushed by obscure forces.

These are the outlines of Lukács's thought. One can see how simplistic it would be to see it only as the expression of a 'thing-like' experience of the human world. In fact, it is a whole 'way of Being-in-the-world' involving two schizophrenic elements: *the state of being crushed by the 'World'* and *spatialization of duration.*

The examination of different theories of schizophrenia seen in the light of this hypothesis will be the subject of a later chapter. From now on it is possible to emphasize certain analogies between the world of reification and the world of *schizophrenia* and related nosological entities, with the exception, however, of certain categories of mental illness. Thus, the *spatialization of duration* is—as we know—central in Minkowski's doctrine. The state of *being crushed by the world* is dominant in the analyses of Binswanger and his disciples. We find again two essential elements of the Lukácsian description of the reified world. Now, in Lukács's work, the coexistence of these elements is not at all fortuitous. The link which unites them leads us to see reification as the common denominator in the works of Minkowski and Binswanger, because of the methodological principle defined earlier, the social dimension clarifying the individual dimension ('the anatomy of man is the key to the anatomy of the monkey', said Marx). The outline of a 'logic of pure identity', appears in the description of the reified universe. It is dominant in false political consciousness; we saw earlier, in fact, that sociocentric logic was essentially an identificatory logic. The same *obsession for identity* is found in schizophrenics. The notions of formal destructuration and devaluation, central notions in A. Hesnard's work, are thus also of a reificational nature. The ahistoricity of reified consciousness and the emergence of the historical nature of reality in the form of a *catastrophe* exist in the clinical annals of schizophrenia: a dialectical interpretation of the 'deranged experience of the end of the world' will be outlined later. However—anticipating later developments—I would like to draw one conclusion straight away. One current criticism directed at studies that are philosophically inspired in psychopathology is that of practical sterility. They are contrasted with the healthy practical orientation of biological studies. It is curious to observe, however, that biological pathogenics often reveal themselves to be sterile on the therapeutic level and biological treatment tends to proceed from empiricism—except for one famous case where the biological treatment had a speculative, even erroneous, departure point.[12] Now, the introduction into psychopathology of the concept of reification immediately offers practical information (which may even have, in certain circumstances, a therapeutic effect): the different elements characterizing the universe of reification *are* to be found in the clinical descriptions of schizophrenia; they are *not* found in cases of real paranoia: schizophrenia is a reificational phenomenon, but a categorized chronic derangement is clearly

[12] Von Meduna's discovery.

not one. In the ever open debate about the essential identity or dualism of the two entities, this fact thus provides an argument in favour of the second conception. On the other hand, the reificational hypothesis allows for the re-evaluation of the syndrome of morbid rationalism which appears despite its rarity —or perhaps because of its rarity—as *a type of schizophrenia,* from which one can deduce a certain number of elements in other clinical forms of this disorder. Once reinstated, morbid rationalism can, in fact, integrate a fairly large number of clinical data and theoretical interpretations. Thus, the nosological unity of schizophrenia is to be found at a dialectically superior level.

SURREALIST AND SUB-REALIST CONSCIOUSNESS

We started with the working hypothesis that a certain degree of reification of consciousness was inseparable from the normal social functioning of intelligence. An insufficiency or excess of reification would thus result in phenomena of inadaptation. It results in a bipartite nosological division or, more exactly, a dualist theory of morbid consciousness which furthermore would not claim to be exhaustive. It includes on the one hand cases characterized by an excess of reification manifesting itself through anti-dialectical thought, abstract attitudes, spatialism, identification, artificialism, dissociation, devaluation, incomprehension of the historicity of existence, as well as through depersonalization, and destructuration of concrete valuing totalities ('axiogeneous forms'). All of these are sub-realist tendencies. On the other hand, it includes structures characterized by insufficient reification of the real world, involving over-concrete attitudes, temporalization, over-valuation, and an abnormal reinforcement of significant dialectical structures. These are surrealist tendencies. It seems appropriate to point out here that the dialectical mechanism postulated by the Jacksonian and neo-Jacksonian school seems to be quite valid in the sub-realist group, whilst its application to the other group seems to be rather forced.

THE WORLD OF THE APHASIC
AND THE MORBID RATIONALIST

A basic statement of this opposition is represented by the accompanying table taken—with a few modifications—from an earlier work.[13] Where it concerns aphasics, it is based on Cassirer's[14] much quoted article and where it concerns morbid rationalists it draws on E. Minkowski's book. Here I am comparing the different ways of structuring the world in the two disorders: the question of the anatomical basis of aphasia is beyond my scope. The same applies to the controversial problem of the uniqueness of aphasic manifestations. Nevertheless, the possibility of reducing these diverse manifestations to a single and 'fundamental disturbance'[15]—a lack of reification in my terms—and one which is the symmetrical opposite of the structure of the schizophrenic world, constitutes an argument in favour of the unitary conception.

CASSIRER'S POINT OF VIEW

Cassirer did not carry out original clinical work. The results of his work, based essentially on the observations of Gelb, Goldstein and Head, illustrate both the possibility and the legitimacy of reflection based on the clinical material of others. Two types of observation contained in this study are important for this subject: (1) Amnesia of the names of colours. A patient of Goldstein's and Gelb's was incapable of using the names of colours spontaneously or of making a choice from samples on verbal instruction. He was not colour blind: his choice was perfect when it came to selecting colours corresponding to pre-existing samples. Goldstein and Gelb saw it as the manifestation of a decline in conceptualizing capacity. These patients saw only

[13] I am stating, practically without modification, a hypothesis formulated in two earlier publications (171), 1946 and (181), 1948.
[14] Cassirer (98).
[15] *Grundstörung.*

Surrealist tendency	Normal state	Sub-realist tendency
Lack of identification	Normal identification	Compulsion for identification (Identitätszwang)
Asymbolism		Symbolism of identity
Morbid realism		Morbid rationalism
Absence of the notion of the possible		Preponderance of the notion of the possible
Over-structured perception of reality		Insufficiently structured perception of reality
Preponderance of the *temporal* aspect in the perception of the world*		Preponderance of the *spatial* aspect in the perception of the world
Preponderance of the experience of the 'Here and Now' (Cassirer)		Loss of the function of the 'Me– Here–Now' (Minkowski)
Preponderance of the category of *being* over *having*†		Preponderance of the category of *having* rather than *being*
Incapacity for objectivation		Morbid objectivation‡
Impossibility of separating 'Me' from the 'internal attitude'‡		Radical separation of 'Me' from the 'internal attitude'§
Morbid authenticity (patients incapable of lying)		Individual false consciousness
Insufficient reification		Excess of reification

Taken with numerous modifications, from my article (171), Madrid, 1946, p. 116. The term 'identification' is used strictly in E. Meyerson's sense. Cf. the empirical confirmation of these views, Faure *et al.* (151).

* Cf. Binswanger [(54), p. 606]. The notions of 'in front of' and 'behind' have an absolute significance for the aphasic just like 'before' and 'after' in time.

† Van Der Horst's interpretation (456).

‡ Cf. Wyrsch (476), Ey (146) and my critical summary of these views in the following chapter.

§ Zutt's notion of 'innere Haltung' (483); the application of this notion to the aphasic's 'mode of being-in-the-world' is my own.

differences; the identificatory act[16] which permits one to detect the similarity between navy-blue and sky-blue escaped them. Aphasia thus provides the example of an existence which dwells in an over-concrete universe. The reificational act[17] of language which impoverishes experience in order to make it communicable does not apply here. It is therefore rightly that Goldstein and Gelb emphasize that these patients are in a sense *closer to reality* than normal people (a surrealist attitude, or in my terminology, morbid realism), but they pay for this concrete mode of being-in-the-world by the loss of the use of the linguistic tool.

(2) This morbid realism reappears in another form in the cases that Head refers to by the term *asymbolism*, to use Finkelberg's expression. He cites patients who are capable of carrying out a gesture that is integrated into the concrete totality of the situation but incapable of repeating it in a vacuum, such as the patient who succeeds in knocking on a real door but fails when faced with an imaginary door. Again one might postulate that in some way it is a question of an *overdialectical* experience of the world: the formal whole[18] of experience as a dialectical totality does not allow for dissociation, and resists identification, which is an anti-dialectical condition of interhuman communication. The extinction of the identificatory function is translated into a sort of morbid realism. These cases illustrate the opposition between the 'Gestaltist' and 'identificatory' types of experience (dialectical and anti-dialectical) analogous to those of authentic political consciousness and false consciousness in social psychology. To use Meyerson's terminology, these patients have *only* intuition about various things. The faculty of identification is largely lacking.

MORBID AUTHENTICITY: SICK PEOPLE WHO ARE 'INCAPABLE OF LYING'

A patient seized with paralysis of the left hand is urged to write: 'I can write with my *left hand.*' Being literally incapable of

[16] The use of the term is my own.
[17] Again, my own term.
[18] 'formal' in the Gestaltist sense obviously.

lying, he wrote on the paper a phrase consistent with the truth: 'I can write with my *right hand*.' Another patient was asked to write on a sunny day, 'It's bad weather, it is raining.' The failure was the same. It is not, certainly, a matter of moral scruples, but an incapacity to deduce a possible situation from the real situation.[19] Here again, the patient is the prisoner of a reality which does not allow for dissociation. Faced with the structural vigour of reality, he loses the notion of the possible.

SUMMARY

There exists a group of disturbances of the aphasic kind described in various ways either as asymbolism, or a non-conceptual or non-categorical attitude in the face of reality. The expression 'lack of function of identification' suggested by me, is not fundamentally different. However, it does have the methodological advantage of relating the analysis of these disturbances to E. Meyerson's epistemology and of emphasizing the contrast with schizophrenia; the role of identity as an element of morbid pseudo-logic in schizophrenic thought was noted for the first time, to my knowledge, by E. von Domarus, and subsequently by Arieti, Kasanin, and the other writers in the Kasanin anthology.[20] It should not be forgotten that identification (in the epistemological meaning of the term), the central category of anti-dialectical, reified logic is a spatializing, devaluing function. In fact, the lack of the function of identification among the patients studied by Cassirer was accompanied by a disturbance that is diametrically opposed to the spatialism of schizophrenics: a certain degree of *spatial incapacity*. Head discovered among the asymbolists, elementary mathematical deficiencies to do with problems whose solution required a precise transference of spatial coordinates. The space

[19] Cf. Cassirer [(98 and 171), p. 112]; briefly this is the opposite of what Tosquelles (448) means by the term *thetic existence* (used by Kierkegaard).

[20] J. S. Kasanin (editor): *Language and Thought in Schizophrenia* (251). For the role of epistemological identification in the psychology of schizophrenics, cf. especially Kasanin's article (25), pp. 41–9 and Benjamin's article (ibid., pp. 65–88).

of these mentally sick people is a milieu which is concrete, organized, structured, centred on the 'here and now', of the acting subject; it is precisely a lack of the 'Me–Here–Now' function which characterizes the world of schizophrenics (Minkowski).

In a work which appeared in 1841–2, the Montpellier professor, Lordat, referred to a *disturbance of corporification* or of embodiment of ideas.[21] My Marxist analysis therefore links up with a century-old hypothesis in its indictment of an *insufficient reification of the real world* in the aphasic with, as a corollary, a deficiency in abstract spatial sense and a weakening of identificatory ability. It is thus the opposite of the schizophrenic state, which is a reificational syndrome. I have tried to represent in the table earlier (p. 157) this phenomenological opposition,[22] which can be followed up by studying the details of clinical cases.

[21] Lordat himself suffered from aphasia. His theory is the result of a moving process of self-analysis. He distinguishes five stages in the process of moving from thinking to speaking: (1) the extrication of the general intention through the 'compression or voluntary forgetting of the interconnecting feelings that are capable of complicating the subject'; (2) the main thought is developed into elementary thoughts; (3) corporification or embodiment of ideas; (4) act of syntactical ordering of sounds; and (5) use of synergic movements to articulate the sounds (summary from Ombredane (369), pp. 47–8). Language disturbance can be located at any one of these levels; Lordat considered that his disturbance was at the third and fourth levels. A. Ombredane saw it as 'a remarkable attempt at analysis' in the 'old fashioned style' by the Montpellier professor, and this is true. Point (1) ('compression or voluntary forgetting, etc.') corresponds to the obscuring element inherent in the identificatory act; point (3) emphasizes what, in Marxist terms, I have called 'insufficient reification of the real world'. Aphasic consciousness is *too authentic* (cf. Cassirer's cases who were 'incapable of lying'). The question arises as to whether Lordat is not in fact the true founder of phenomenological psychiatry.

[22] Phenomenological opposition in the sense that Minkowski speaks of 'phenomenological compensation' [(343), p. 227].

POINTS OF VIEW OF DIFFERENT AUTHORS

The question of aphasia has been the subject of countless works. A. Ombredane's thesis certainly contains the most complete list of them. Leaving aside the research of an anatomo-clinical nature I shall consider certain research that deals with 'the aphasic's mode of being-in-the-world' in relation to my hypothesis. In the same context it would be as well to examine K. Goldstein's hypothesis postulating the *over-concrete* nature of the thought of schizophrenics, which is incompatible with my hypothesis, and also with the theory of Minkowski, Wyrsch, and Binswanger, who all implicitly postulate the abstract nature of schizophrenic thought.

K. GOLDSTEIN'S CONCEPTION OF SCHIZOPHRENIA

Goldstein[23] maintained that the thought of schizophrenics is characterized by a very high degree of concreteness. As a corollary of the theory which tends to find analogies between the language of schizophrenics and aphasic disturbance this conception is certainly strictly incompatible with that expressed in the table earlier. But it is also incompatible with numerous notable theories about this disturbance (Minkowski, Wyrsch, Binswanger, Matussek . . .), theories based on the Marxist concept of alienation–reification as the common denominator. A morbid thought can be either too concrete or too abstract; but it can not be both at the same time.

Furthermore, Goldstein's argument is not entirely convincing; it rests—at least in the article quoted—on fragmentary observations. Also, it involves what are doubtless accurate facts, but their interpretations are forced. 'One of Hanfmann's schizophrenics said: "Half past eight, time to get up", or "Time for the sun to rise". *These responses are exactly the same type as those of the*

[23] Goldstein (251), p. 23.

organically sick.'[24] Another patient observed that it must be later than 4 o'clock because 4 o'clock was tea-time. A third patient noted that it was 12 o'clock because that was the usual time for the departure of his friend who was actually preparing to leave. It requires a certain amount of imagination to see 'pathologically concrete' attitudes here. They are, doubtless, the residues of an otherwise normal attitude that the schizophrenic process, though dissociated by definition, has partially respected. Other, less naive, arguments involve no less of a diametrically opposed interpretation. One of Tuczek's patients calls a bird 'the song', the summer 'the warm', the physician 'the dance' (because during hospital rounds the physicians seem to dance round the professor),[25] another (of Goldstein's) said 'kiss' instead of 'mouth'.[26] It is surprising to see writers of repute talking of *concrete attitude* in this context; nothing could be more abstract. The word 'kiss' certainly designates a concrete gesture if ever there was one; but the intellectual act which *indentifies* 'kiss' with 'mouth' is an act of dissociation and abstraction since it obscures other no less important functions of this organ. We must presume—and this is where we begin to regret the fragmentary nature of these observations—that we are dealing with an obsessive or sexually frustrated person (who is not specifically schizophrenic); on the other hand what is clear is that he is conceptualizing egocentrically as a function of the sexual element that has become a privileged system.[27] It would be both facile and tedious to repeat this demonstration in connection with other quoted examples. They obviously spring from what Paulhan calls *the illusion of totality,* a pseudo-dialectic, a *false concretization* of thought. There is clearly a philosophically insufficient definition of the actual notion of the concrete under-

[24] Goldstein (251), p. 25.

[25] Tuczek, quoted by Goldstein (251), p. 26.

[26] Goldstein, in Kasanin (251), p. 26. Concrete attitude? On the contrary, it is clear that a point of view of 'pure immediacy' dissociates the totality in question; of the numerous relationships which constitute the *concrete* personality of a doctor, only one (the immediate) is retained.

[27] Cf. later, pp. 282 ff.; the criticism of Matussek's theory of deranged perception.

lying Goldstein's research and particularly a failure to recognize its relationship to the dialectical category of totality. 'The concrete is concrete because it is the synthesis of many factors and therefore, a unity of diversity' said Karl Marx in a totally different context;[28] the concrete is the *dialectic*.

We cannot go through all of K. Goldstein's arguments; the examples quoted are sufficient to show their weakness. The main basis for this view is experimental: the failure of schizophrenics in tests of conceptual thought. Since this failure is common to the organically sick and to schizophrenics, one might draw hasty conclusions as to the nosological relationship of these states. Once again, one can but deplore the eminently *anti-dialectical* nature of the reasoning which underlies this chapter in Goldstein's research, which contrasts curiously with the otherwise dialectical inspiration of his school. A muscular spasm or the cutting of a nerve might lead to the same failure in doing a concrete task; the nature of the failure covers a fundamental physiological difference. The same applies to tests of conceptual thought. Their success is the function of a whole complex of elements in which the social factor particularly intervenes. In tests of conceptual thought, based on a criterion of abstraction agreed upon in a given society, the 'organic' incapacity to classify, or the persistence of a different (egocentric) criterion of classification might lead to a similar failure without there being any reason in the world for inferring (as Goldstein does) the existence of a nosological, or even anatomical relationship. This is one of the limitations of quantitative testing.

THE CONTRIBUTION OF REIFICATION

The concept of reification and its corollaries (epistemological identification and the fragmentation of totalities), perhaps due to the dialectical element which is inherent in them, provide a certain clarity in a question which seems at first sight rather confused. The notion of a *concrete* and *abstract* attitude, which is fundamental for Goldstein, is equivocal; the 'concretely concrete'

[28] Marx, *Contribution à la critique de l'économie politique.*

G

attitude (if one dares to say it) necessarily involves abstract
elements. A doctor must constantly go from a 'categorial' attitude
when he is making a diagnosis, to a less categorial attitude when
prescribing a treatment; it is his capacity to go easily from one
attitude to the other, according to the differing needs, which
measures the degree of his *concrete* integration in his professional
world. The same applies to numerous other intellectual and
professional activities. Goldstein defined the abstract attitude as
the most active, and the concrete attitude as the most passive;
this would explain how a schizophrenic can have a pathologically
concrete attitude, but the explanation then rests on an arbitrary
definition: real activity is a dialectical synthesis of abstract and
concrete attitudes. The hypertrophy of the function of identification in the sub-realist psychoses (morbid rationalism) and its extinction in the surrealist type of mental illness satisfactorily explain the
facts used by K. Goldstein, without having recourse to the hypothesis of over-concrete schizophrenic thought, a coherent hypothesis in itself, but contradictory with many others. The patient
who classifies 'fish' with 'pumpkin' is not captivated by the concrete image of a laid table; he is making a regressive classification
based on the undifferentiated predominance of the alimentary
function.[29] A patient completes the pictures that are presented to
him according to the principle of similarity or equality. 'I see three
boys, then I add one more, and there will still only be boys.'
One wonders really, by virtue of what intellectual aberration, the
famous theorist manages to see this as the expression of a *concrete
attitude* (as if *concretely* boys and girls were never together).
This is one typical case of reification of the real world: the
principle of homogeneity and obsession with the identical. I
apologize for being difficult, but the fact that the same patient
drew a horse in a *bedroom* ('there is a boy who needs a horse,
because he wants to travel') does not seem to me to be any more
indicative of a concrete attitude, whatever K. Goldstein may say.[30]

[29] Cf. Arieti (15) on this form of regression of the alimentary
function.

[30] It is difficult to argue about incomplete observations, but it
seems obvious that there is either an extinction of spatialization,
according to Binswanger's theory (two spaces are superimposed)

Therefore, this view is not easy to defend. It is naive to see the expression of over-concrete thinking in the act of the patient who identifies kiss with mouth. Other features of this organ are just as much a part of its essence; to make an abstraction of it is to reveal not a realist, but a sub-realist attitude. These patients are close to their own autistic reality; according to this, one could just as well consider the hallucinatory state as the result of too concrete a perception. One wonders, in fact, by virtue of what miracle, schizophrenic thought, which is *too realistic* on the logical level, becomes de-realistic in hallucinatory activity. It is difficult not to see a certain connection between the logic which underlies the equation 'mouth = kiss' and certain mechanisms of deranged thought. This is the possible starting point for a reificational theory of hallucinations, whereas Goldstein's views provide no possibility for interpretation. The hallucinatory attitude is perhaps *concretizing*, but it is certainly not *concrete*. Without subscribing to the somewhat crude opinion of J. J. Lopez-Ibor who describes them simply as puerile,[31] it is fair to note that these studies do not constitute the most valid—nor the most dialectical part—of Goldstein's work. However, it was necessary to examine this at length, given Goldstein's reputation, and its total incompatibility with the point of view defended here. The question is whether schizophrenic thought is abstract or concrete. It follows from a critical examination of Goldstein's own examples that it is in

or, on the contrary, an extinction of temporalization according to Minkowski and Pankow; it is the continuous eruption of time (*Zeitigung*) which by saturating it with value, prevents space from being fragmented. Whatever it is, a *horse in a bedroom* is in no way a concrete vision. It is rather the result of a pre-hallucinatory structuring of reality.

[31] Lopez-Ibor, quoted by Cabaleiro [(82), p. 149]. Miss Balken is no less critical ('interpretations such as these are largely a function of methodology') (27), p. 283; that is to say, in a polite way, that they are without objective value. For Balken (p. 270), the fundamental disturbance of schizophrenia is to be found in 'subject-object' relationships and not in the incapacity for categorizing or in regression to a pre-logical stage; my conception of the *reificational syndrome* allows for a synthesis of the two: loss of the subject-object dialectic and subsequent predominance of the identificatory functions.

fact *abstract* thought and, furthermore dependent on the particular form of abstraction that results from the anti-dialectical preponderance of the identificatory principle.[32]

KLAUS CONRAD'S VIEW

These studies[33] were influenced by Gestaltism, which led Conrad to a clearly dialectical approach to the problem. Their starting point is a phenomenon, the importance of which has been emphasized by Wenzl and Lothmar, namely, *the intermediary experience* (*Zwischen-erlebniss*). Conrad criticizes other authors for having neglected this phenomenon and for having concentrated their effort on the deficiency without studying the techniques used by the patients to remedy it. The existence of these *Zwischen-erlebnisse* is common in aphasia and in phenomena of forgetting as described by Freud. It is common knowledge that the forgetting of proper names usually involves the appearance of immediately rejected substitution names which point the way to the forgotten word. Conrad's research is centred on this neglected phenomenon. A rather long passage devoted to the anatomical substratum of the disturbance betrays his scepticism over the usefulness of an over-exclusive anatomo-clinical view of the problem.

---

[32] Cf. Binswanger in the Jürg Zünd case (60), p. 28. 'The inconsistent character of the self (*Selbstflüchtigkeit*), and the frailty of existence are shown here in attempts to master the situation with the help of a homogenizing, devaluing abstraction (*nivellierende und devalorisierende Abstraktion*). It is when he finds himself faced with the impossibility of fleeing from the concrete intellectual situation towards abstraction (with its definitive general "solutions") that Jürg Zünd experiences his failure most painfully.' This is clear and the opposition to Goldstein's point of view is definitive. Without wishing to settle this debate let me say by virtue of a simple socio-psychiatric contribution, that *false consciousness* is an '*abstractive* tendency'. Cf. Szende (439 and 440), *passim*.

Gabriel Marcel (319), pp. 114–21 ('spirit of abstraction, factor of conflict'); A. Béguin (39), p. 180, etc.

[33] Cf. Conrad (112 and 114).

A patient is shown a funnel.[34] He searches unsuccessfully for the word 'Trichter'. The first word which comes to mind is 'Bettflasche' (bed urinal). Another says the word 'Becher' (kettle-drum); a third says 'Kindertrompete' (toy-trumpet).[35] The common characteristic in these responses this time is the obviously concrete nature of the first impression, which is in accord with Cassirer's ideas.[36] It is therefore, obviously one of the constants in the aphasic's mode of being-in-the-world (cf. Van de Horst's point of view below). These patients are fascinated by the 'active' aspect of things (*Tunsqualität*, to use Russel's expression). The following example demonstrates still better the concrete and dynamically realistic nature of the aphasic experience. Asked to name a fowl, a patient provides this somewhat unexpected response: 'fox . . . no, duck'.[37] We learn later that the subject had in mind a very concrete picture; a picture in a child's book showing a fox carrying off a goose. From this concrete context, one step of abstraction must select the goose; the seemingly absurd appearance of the word 'fox' causes it to be rejected. It is, therefore, the most active figure—the fox—which attracts the attention of the subject; a good example of this 'deviation from accurate observation' (*Entgleisung der Beobachtungsrichtung*) to which Binswanger refers.

The common denominator in these disturbances is a deterioration in formal experience in the direction of a larger formal coherence of the real world. A patient asked to give the concept which included 'bread', 'butter', 'bacon' etc., responded curiously: 'vegetables'! He explained later that he had not been able to make an abstraction from a primary concrete image: 'bacon with peas' (*Speck mit Erbsen*).[38] We are, therefore, faced with a 'process of structuration that the patient is no longer able to control'.[39] He is a prisoner of the over-pronounced dialectical structure (formal coherence) of his own universe.

---

[34] Conrad (112), p. 158.   [35] Conrad (112), p. 164.

[36] Cf. also Hecaen *et al.* (215), p. 172; typically the patient says 'for drinking' for bottle, 'for writing' instead of 'pencil' etc. The tests show a characteristic lack of abstraction in this patient (p. 175), which is hardly surprising.

[37] Conrad (112), pp. 169–70.   [38] Conrad (112), p. 169.

[39] Conrad (112), p. 169. The expression is very typical: 'Auch

This is, therefore, a clearly dialectical conception of aphasia the essential elements of which are: (1) The concrete, dynamic nature of the aphasic experience (role of the *Tunsqualität* and the *Gebrauchsqualität*); (2) the importance of the category of the totality[40] and, finally (3) an obvious scepticism for a too exclusively clinical view of the problem, a scepticism confirmed by the experience of this former director of a head injuries clinic.

His other contributions from the speculative point of view seem less solid. A Gestaltist interpretation of the unconscious is contrasted with the so-called spatialism of Freudian notions;[41] the unconscious is non-structured. The recall of a forgotten word would, therefore, be essentially a process of structuration (*Gestaltung*) and the intermediary phenomena would be pre-structures (*Vorgestalt*). Now, a word is certainly a 'strong form', like the object that it designates; the object-word unity is by contrast a relatively weak structure, liable to dissociation, without which the learning of foreign languages would become impossible. Two concomitant processes dialectically indicate the passage from experience to word: *structuration* of the word and *destructuration* of lived experience, this latter process being of a reificational

hier werden Gestaltungsprozesse in Gang gesetzt, die nicht gezügelt werden können, so dass der Pat. ihnen gewissermassen unterliegt. Er bleibt nicht voll Herr über sie wie der Gesunde.' But this point of view, so consistently Gestaltist, somewhat contradicts Conrad's conclusions, as we shall see later.

[40] Conrad, faithful to a pure Gestaltist terminology, does not use the word 'totality'. Hecaen *et al.* are more explicit. 'What is lost is the ability to break down the significant material into its elements' (215, p. 180). 'Aphasia . . . is thus conceived as a loss of the possibility of structuration of thought in linguistic forms, as *loss of the ability to divide totality into articulated parts.*' Ibid., my italics.

[41] Conrad (112), pp. 147–9 and *passim*; unconscious elements do not become conscious like objects which come up to the surface of the water (movement of a spatial kind) but rather like a crystal which is formed out of a solution. Using the famous comparison with the iceberg, Conrad modifies it in this way: the unconscious is not the invisible part of the iceberg but the ocean (112), p. 148. This criticism of the spatialism of the Freudian notion of the unconscious corresponds to a certain degree of reification of Freud's primary doctrine, as discussed by certain psychoanalysts (cf. D. Lagache's lectures 1959–60).

nature. Of the two—and this comes from the actual analysis of the examples given—it seems that the German author has grasped the subordinate point and not the essential one. To arrive at the concept of 'fowl' the patient has to dissociate the totality of the memory 'fox carrying off goose'; the illegitimate entry of the word 'fox' into the foreground of consciousness points up the failure of this operation. As a dynamic figure, the fox represents, in this case, the non-dissociated unity of the image: the image of a fighter and his vanquished enemy at his feet is the *primary* image. When faced with processes of structuration that are impossible to master, with an 'agglutination of formal qualities',[42] the operations of abstraction and identification (reification) which underlie the constitution of higher language are restricted. The real difficulty that these patients experience does not, therefore, lie in the *structuration* of elements but in the destructuration of totalities which is its preliminary condition. This aside, Conrad's results confirm those of Cassirer's study and consequently, the view that I have outlined.

THE APRAXIC'S MODE OF BEING-IN-THE-WORLD ACCORDING TO VAN DER HORST[43]

Van der Horst comes across this classical symptom among apraxics: they can drink a real cup of coffee, but it is impossible for them to 'pretend' to drink from an imaginary cup (incapacity for abstract acts). The difficulty that they experience is essentially that of 'distancing themselves from the concept of mobility'[44] given in the dynamism of the corporal scheme.

The normal man is capable of objectifying his corporal existence, of analysing the psychodynamics of his body and of

---

[42] Conrad, article quoted (112), p. 163, uses this characteristic term '*Agglutination von Gestaltqualitäten*'.

[43] Van der Horst (456). (This article is the Spanish translation of a conference paper given in Professor J. J. Lopez-Ibor's department in Madrid.)

[44] 'Distanciarse del concepto de mobilidad, tal como esta dado en la dinamica de su esquema corporal.' Van der Horst (456), p. 18.

applying the results of this analysis to hypothetical (abstract) situations. The apraxic is incapable of this; as for the schizophrenic, this *faculty* of objectifying the subjective that the normal person possesses becomes for him a *necessity*; he is a prisoner of it (Wyrsch).[45] This very particular deficiency in the apraxic gives an inkling of one aspect of the 'mysterious relationship which unites man and his body' . . . 'the apraxic *is* body, but he does not *possess* his body'.[46] The category of being borders on the reificational one of *having*. A normal individual can say about his body: 'I am' but he is nevertheless in a position to situate his body among the 'things' surrounding him. He disposes of it and can put it in abstract situations at will. It is the absence of this reificational flexibility which makes the apraxic maladapted in a particular social context.

THE TEMPORALITY OF AGNOSICS—
C. A. PALLIS'S CASE

Pallis[47] published the case of an engineer with a cardiac condition, suffering from cerebral embolism. Subsequently a complex syndrome developed: achromatopsy, prosopgnosia and a peculiar and hitherto unrecorded disorder of spatial thought; an actual 'despatialization' of thought, or so it seems. The term 'lack of identification' is indispensible[48] and although the English neurologist certainly did not know Meyerson, it seems that the use of this term corresponds clearly here to the use that the author of

[45] I have based this chapter on the hypothesis that I formulated in 1946 (171), of a symmetrical opposition between the fundamental disturbance of morbid rationalism and the aphaso-agnoso-apraxic range. Van der Horst's study confirms this point of view: incapacity for objectivation on the one hand, compulsion for objectivation on the other (Wyrsch's conception of schizophrenia). In this range of ideas, one can, by contrasting it with Binswanger's 'Verweltlichung', define the aphasic's mode of being-in-the-world as a real 'Verichlichung'.

[46] The Spanish text is more expressive: 'existe . . . como cuerpo pero no tiene su cuerpo' (456), p. 18.   [47] F. Pallis (375).

[48] 'Identification failed in the presence of perceptual data adequate for gnosis in the ordinary sense' (375), p. 223.

'*Cheminement de la Pensée*' makes of it. The identification of faces is difficult. If it succeeds it is generally as a function of some 'critical detail'. Faces and places always appear as if new which prevents the patient from identifying the photographs of personalities famous for various reasons: Churchill, Bevan, Hitler, Stalin, Marilyn Monroe, Groucho Marx (excellent choice!). The white coat of the doctors enables them to be identified; the patient's wife, on the other hand, appears 'like new' on each of her visits. To locate the philosophical interpretation of this case, it should be remembered that the *Gestalt* is a *temporal* theory *par excellence*. Time is naturally structured through events and through irreversibility; these are our measuring instruments which artificially introduce a reificational-spatializing element.

The identificatory function is, by contrast, a corollary of spatialization; a purely spatial existence would in theory allow for absolute identification and repetition; it is the inevitable imbrication of the temporal element which renders them illusory. The nostalgia for repetition among certain schizophrenics[49] is therefore one aspect of the spatialization of their own world. The agnosic is condemned to living in a world of diametrically opposed structures: a temporality deprived of spatial elements prevents him from extricating from the succession of various aspects of a face the common element (abstract, if you like, but my example shows the futility of this terminology) which constitutes its unity. If he identifies the doctors, it is because of their coat, which as a material object, introduces into his field of consciousness a reified element that his over-concrete thought is incapable of creating. Pallis rejects the Gestaltist explanation: the tests of formal thought in these cases do not reveal any deficiency and for good reason. It is not, however, clear that all Gestaltist explanation should be abandoned. It remains valid in the dialectical perspective that has just been outlined: the contrast between structuration and reification or—if you will—between totality and identification and an insufficiency of reificational elements in the world of the agnostic. It is understandable that in

---

[49] Cf.—still in the framework of the 'schizophrenia–aphasia' contrast—the case of Kulenkampff's paranoid (271) patient who compulsively 'recognized' even total strangers.

the presence of an excess of structural coherence in the real world and in thought, tests of formal thought might not reveal any deficit.

PARAPHRENIC DERANGEMENT COMPLICATED BY APHASIA

The case of H. Faure *et al.*[50] brings us right back to full clinical reality; this is in some way the experimental verification of earlier considerations. An interned deranged woman suffered a blow and developed an aphaso-agnoso-apraxic syndrome. Her derangement seemed in some way to be cured (!); it 'foundered with the patient', the deranged themes suddenly faded away and 'it appeared as if the patient who had suddenly become aphaso-agnoso-apraxic had by the same token also become *incapable of being* deranged'. She had 'passed from the level of imaginary and abstract occupations to the level of immediately concrete pre-occupations'.[51] The doctrinal importance of such a study should not be misjudged; explicitly or implicitly it shows: (a) the essential unity of the various manifestations of the asymbolic disturbance;[52] (b) the relationship of the paraphrenic syndrome with schizophrenia in the sense of H. Ey's conception; (c) the abstract (and not, as K. Goldstein believes, the *concrete*) nature of sub-realist deranged thought (schizophrenia and paraphrenia) and finally, (d) the clinical validity of the sub-realist-surrealist contrast, such as I have indicated. Furthermore, this observation opens up curious perspectives for the interpretation of certain therapeutic facts,[53] perspectives that the authors of the article have not been tempted to exploit.

'In the present state of affairs it may be that the doctrine of

[50] Cf. Faure *et al.* (151).   [51] Cf. Faure *et al.* (151), p. 102.
[52] At least this is the conclusion of Faure *et al.*
[53] The conclusion from this case—if others were to support it— would be an experimental confirmation of lobotomy by the concepts of 'phenomenological compensation' (Minkowski) and 'regressive syntonisation' (Barahona Fernandes). Cf. the existence of Gerstmann's syndrome noticed as a result of the application of electric-shock treatment.

aphasia has almost more to gain from the doctrine of schizo-phrenia than inversely,' wrote the Viennese psychiatrist Joseph Berze in 1829.[54] Aphasia is still a mystery just as schizophrenia is still a mystery; it may be that they are two complementary mysteries. The summary of data grouped in the table on p. 157 involves a certain number of consequences. It offers an argument in favour of a globalist conception of the aphasic disturbance and related disorders, a conception aimed at defining an actual *basic disturbance* beyond the atomism of a polymorphous terminology. The role that a change in the formal quality of experience might play follows implicitly or explicitly from most theories: the role of reification was hinted at a century ago by Lordat. The proposed interpretation is that of an insufficient reification of experience with a predominance of structuring functions (*Agglutionation von Gestaltqualitäten*, Conrad), and a deficiency in the function of identification, and is therefore hardly anything other than a Marxist reinterpretation of theoretical data from various sources. Nevertheless, it constitutes an experimental-clinical verifica-tion of certain philosophical themes; it is as over-authentic consciousness that aphasic consciousness rejects the inauthenticity of the spoken word. The existence of a symmetrical contrast between morbid rationalism and a non-delirious disorder that is undeniably anatomically based (though still indefinitely located) constitutes to my mind a serious presumption—but in no way a proof—in favour of the *organogenesis* of schizophrenia. Finally, this contrast provides the *pattern* of a general dualist division of the psychoses that I shall try to extrapolate later on by using it in a critique of certain traditional concepts.

CRITIQUE OF CERTAIN TRADITIONAL CONCEPTS

Minkowski emphasized in *Le Temps Vécu* how it was scien-tifically open to criticism to combine in a single concept the

---

[54] 'Wie die Dinge heute liegen, könnte fast die Aphasielehre aus dem Hinblick auf die Sizophrenielehre mehr Nützen ziehen als umgekehrt' (Berze (51), p. 55).

hypochondriacal preoccupations of an anxious person and a schizophrenic or the delusions of grandeur of a general paralytic and a paranoid. A certain element of sociocentrism is involved in such a step: classification is a function of the criterion of normality accepted in a given society and not of the psychodynamics of the illness. A man who is afraid of being poisoned, when, in the opinion of the group, this danger is non-existent, is labelled as a person suffering from a poison mania. Now, a schizophrenic variant of the poison mania exists, a variant where the role of the reificational element is fairly obvious; all those who believe, wrongly, that they are in danger of being poisoned, are not necessarily schizophrenics. It would be easy to make a similar point with regard to the role of electricity in mental illness. The very concept of mental illness thus appears as a sociocentric, identificatory concept, summing up according to the normal person's usage 'those who do not think like them'. It becomes the geometric location for disparate data. The same applies to the classical concept of alienation which designates—as we have seen earlier—arbitrarily, all those who are 'strangers in society', without questioning the nature of the process which has made them 'strangers'. An aphasic is certainly 'strange' to the society whose language partially escapes him: from the Marxist point of view, it would be rather more appropriate to speak of *insufficient alienation* (reification).

It is impossible not to see the links which unite this terminological globalism to a previous era of conduct in mental institutions, before effective therapy and present-day diagnosis. Here again, as in many other areas, language preserves the memory of the criteria of an earlier epoque.

SUB-REALIST DISTURBANCES

I shall consider three of these: the reification of sexuality, the mode of being-in-the-world of hysterics and manic-depressives.

REIFICATION OF SEXUALITY

There exists a reification of sexuality. This term we owe to the Viennese theorist, well-known in France, Igor A. Caruso, who suggested it in 1952,[55] with reference to one of my publications that appeared sometime before. Caruso is a disciple of Gebsattel's whose early works on perversions—and particularly an article often quoted in Germany on fetishism—are based on the dialectical value-giving category of totality (an axiogenic form in my terminology) in a sense very close to the work of A. Hesnard and theories of the dialectic. Therefore, the two corollary concepts of Lukácsian thought reappear: *totality* and *reification*, the principle of value-giving, authentic dialectical thought for the former, and of alienation and false consciousness for the latter. Seen in this perspective, certain perversions appear as *sexual alienation* in the full Marxist meaning of the term. The fact that one of the principal nosological entities of sexual pathology (fetishism) and one of the main phenomena of capitalist reification (the fetishist character of commodities) bear—spontaneously in some way— almost the same name, is not merely a coincidence.

FETISHISM ACCORDING TO GEBSATTEL[56]

What is the 'essence' of fetishism? To give primacy to research on signification would be misleading. Nothing proves—states Gebsattel—'that a shoe necessarily signifies the same thing for a fetishist as for a non-fetishist, the only difference being the existence of a particular psychic structure allowing the fetishist to enter into sexual excitation through the mediation of an ordinary shoe'. In other words, Gebsattel refuses very dialectically to separate the instinctual point of view from the noetic point of view in the study of the fetish. What is important in the first place for existential analysis is not the more or less conscious significance of the fetish for the patient, but the fact that it *is* a

[55] Caruso (91).   [56] Gebsattel (191).

fetish, i.e. an artificial reality promoted to the level of authentic reality, a *pars pro toto*, and therefore an illusion of totality.

Fetishism is therefore essentially a 'deviation from the total structure of the You' (Eine Abirrung von ganzheitlicher Du-Gestalt').[57] To be attached to a piece of clothing is not to posit a false sexual value (for the woman herself, the clothing is an integral part of her sexual mode-of-being), but to place the value in an egocentric perspective. Fetishism makes an abstraction of what the woman signifies for herself, she thus becomes a *sexual object* and the instruments of her attraction acquire a pseudo-value[58] independent of the whole. The analogy with the psychology of the child is strong in the sexual noetic of the fetishist, the fetish plays a role similar to that of the doll (or, rather, any object playing the role of the doll) in infantile noetic.[59]

Fetishism thus appears as an auto-erotic attitude which does not like to recognize itself as such; an illusory self-transcendence. As a pretext for this false transcendence, the fetish plays the role of a pseudo-other.[60] It can be seen that the essentially dialectical inspiration of these developments relate to specific concepts of Marxist philosophy. The fetishist consciousness appears very typically as a sexual *false consciousness*: an illusion of totality (therefore illusion of love), a reificational and dissociative element. It is also a *slice of primitive life*.[61] Adult love involves the intention of a union (Wirheit) which presupposes the preliminary differentiation of the Self from the Other; now the amorous reality of the child—and the fetishist—is antecedent to this differentiation.[62] Infant auto-eroticism expresses this non-differentiation, which tends to reappear in fetishist sexuality, but, said Marx, 'man never becomes a child again; at the very most he may lapse into infancy'.[63] The fetishist world is thus characterized by a funda-

---

[57] Gebsattel (191), p. 9.

[58] In this context of extreme 'false consciousness', the fetish appears as pseudo-value, for it is without precariousness; the fetish is not—and could not be—a permanent dialectical conquest like sexual union. (Wirheit.)

[59] Gebsattel (191), p. 11.   [60] 'Ein Schein Du', ibid., p. 16.

[61] 'Ein Stück primitiver Lebensgestaltung' (191), p. 11.

[62] Ibid.

[63] Marx, *Contribution à la critique de l'économie politique.*

mental asynchronism: the co-existence of a degree of *intellectual* maturity which requires the differentiation between the Self and the Other, and of an emotional 'maturity' which does not include this differentiation. Fetishism is based on a pseudo-separation of the Self and the Other,[64] it is a pretext for auto-eroticism. Thus understood it is the end of a long series of egocentric and therefore reifying attitudes: the primacy of the body over the total Other (*Totale Du-Gestalt*), of possession over encounter. 'I despise a woman's mind, but I like a pair of lovely legs; as for her personality it makes me literally impotent' said one patient.[65] This banal attitude, if we are to believe Gebsattel, contains the germ of the whole complexity of the fetishist attitude. Futhermore, the axiological promotion of the body denotes a reificational structure. In short, the fetish is the *objectivation of the stage of indifference*, a form of transposed auto-eroticism[66] in a person who has been unable to free himself from the influence of maternal love.

This is Gebsattel's conception: a non-Marxist dialectical conception of the fetishist phenomenon. To go from there to a Marxist conception is essentially a question of 'setting it back on its feet'. (*Umstülpung.*) The introduction of the concept of reification into sexology is one stage in this.

In the first place there exists a pre-clinical social aspect of sexual reification; prostitution where the 'partner' is reified as a commodity; the same applies to certain aspects of worldly Don Juanism where the woman, without undergoing this extreme degradation, nevertheless becomes an object of an acquisitive tendency that is foreign to love. We might say that this is a purely social aspect since prostitutes and their clients are not necessarily neuropaths, but one which can become a perversion through the internalization of these reificational elements, especially if they survive in a different social and emotional context. The case of Erika P. (of Medard Boss), will later provide a striking example of this. In all these cases—the study of which is barely separable from a critique of the capitalist organization of

---

[64] Von Gebsattel (191), p. 12. 'Pseudosonderung von Ich und Du'.
[65] Ibid., p. 18.
[66] 'Transponierte Selbstliebe', ibid. (191), p. 19.

society—the 'loving union', based on alterocentrism and recipro-city, is egocentrized and undergoes a degradation which is of a reificational kind. One 'possesses' and one is 'possessed'; slipping from the category of being (in its dialectically and axiologically superior form: being together) towards that of having[67] is a typical process of reification. It is the axiological aspect which dominates in other cases; 'all perversion is devaluation', said E. Strauss. Finally I have observed a curious case of a sexual schizoid personality, homologous to the 'morbid rationalism' of Minkow-ski: an incapacity for 'cohabitation' as a consequence of a geometrization of sexual space.[68]

TWO OBSERVATIONS OF MEDARD BOSS:
1. COMPENSATORY KLEPTOMANIA[69]

A patient of M. Boss's (Erika P.) had a disturbed youth. Her father, a drunkard, ruined his family; her mother got mixed up in organizing a 'family guest house' which rapidly degenerated into a brothel (*maison close*). Up to the age of nine, Erika lived among the promiscuity of the clients, amusing them with tricks, though physically intact. At the age of nine, the authorities placed her in the hands of some nuns; Erika became pious and sociable. At the age of eleven she was adopted by a rich and somewhat formal uncle who kept her apart from all masculine company before marrying her at the age of nineteen to a dis-tinguished, older man. Erika proved to be frigid in marriage. She obtained pleasure in life in peculiar ways. One day she stole an insignificant amount of money from her husband (an illogical theft since she did not lack money). A hitherto unknown pleasure took over her body, followed, however, by a terrible remorse (the

[67] Cf. Gabriel Marcel 'Etre et Avoir', *passim* and also current forms of feminine frigidity which are a protest against the reifying tendency of man; frigidity related to the position of submission in the sexual act (cf. Hitschmann–Bergler (231), p. 299; Laforgue (277), p. 220, women who achieve orgasm only with lower-class men, etc.). Cf. also the Hebraic legend of Lilith and its literary use in Marc Chadourne's novel: a novel about the frigid woman.

[68] Cf. (174 *bis*).   [69] Boss (74), p. 62.

untranslatable *Katzenjammer* in German). She relapsed into crime and two months later stole from her servant. Her technique improved: during her own fashionable gatherings she slipped into the kitchen and made a clean sweep of the servant's tips. An extreme anguish preceded this action, an anguish which literally filled her body with sensuality.[70] It was an anguish mixed with pleasure; the feeling of strangling in her throat and pressure in her body was more intense, the more she realized the voluptuousness of this immoral act. In this ecstasy the world seemed golden; she *pressed the money against her hand* until she hurt herself; she trembled all over her body and she experienced an intense vertigo. After a few moments, the ecstasy was over, she left the kitchen with feline skill, without ever allowing herself to be caught.

In Erika P's case, reification seems to be more advanced than in the coprophile, Rico, whose case we shall look at later, and even in 'normal' (if one can use the term) clothing fetishism. The sensuality of this patient is related to the most reified constituent of venal love, i.e. money, instead of either to clothes, which mould the body, follow its contours and maintain contact, or to the excremental bolus, a 'post-biological' reality that is warm with life. 'Only the mediation of money, a dead reality, foreign to the body and of purely conventional value[71] could allow Erika P. to exist in the world as a loving person.' The other fetishists 'retain at least the faint memory of the happiness of a partially spiritual union; the way of being loving for this kleptomaniac is reduced to the purely corporal-impulsive-orgiastic sector'.[72] Furthermore, Erika's fetish—money—involves another significant characteristic: it is the property of the other person, protected by one of the two most powerful prohibitions (with sexual prohibition) of capitalist society. Legitimate money—of which she was hardly deprived—was of little interest to this patient; legitimate money could not undergo the axiological promotion that raised it literally to the level of a sexual partner. In fact, the act of

[70] Boss (74), p. 62.
[71] 'Bloss sozial gesetzte Werbedeutung.' Boss (74), p. 62.
[72] 'Auf den rein leiblich-triebhaften-orgastischen Ausschnitt reduziert.' Boss (74), p. 62.

theft constitutes a breakdown of these social and moral defences; now, it is precisely these social and moral prohibitions which—after a childhood free from all prohibitions—are thrust upon Erika, surrounding her with a 'truly hostile, inorganic, artificial armour'.[73] It is well known that 'kleptomaniac fetishism' is much more common among women (whilst other forms show an inverse proportion); in fact, the manifestation of feminine sexuality today still involves, in a conservative milieu, a certain amount of nonconformism and revolt, from which masculine sexuality is free. The sexuality of women is therefore more easily symbolizable by a punishable act.

The theory of the penis symbolism of the fetish does not entirely satisfy existential analysis which would prefer to see it as one of the concretizing (reifying in my terminology) elements of Freudianism. (This dialectical-existential critique of analytical doctrines certainly dates from Gebsattel.) Whatever may be the justice of a symbolic interpretation it does not exhaust the richness of the existential view of one form of amorous reality.

Now, 'the perverse ecstasy of this kleptomaniac is, despite everything, part of the domain of love. Just like real love, it breaks barriers even though it is only a pale reflection of true union.'[74] In Erika, kleptomania appeared in fact as the 'perverse existential cover'[75] for a powerful erotic feeling for another uncle, a friend from the debauchery of her childhood. In her dreams this masculine figure appeared often. It was not then a question of kleptomania; the uncle appeared as a generous lover who overwhelmed her with presents (money and lavish clothes in plenty); a perfectly normal erotic scene usually ended the dream. The kleptomania thus appeared at 'the point at which real love was about to break through its state of imprisonment into a whole range of corporal instinctual realizations'.[76]

---

[73] 'Denn es waren gerade diese Schranken . . . die ihr . . . so spät und dann derart abrupt und gewaltsam aufgeprägt wurden, dass sie zu einem besonders liebesfeindlichen unorganischen, verkünstelten Persönlichkeitspanzer werden mussten.' Boss (74), p. 63.

[74] Boss (74), p. 66.

[75] Boss (74), p. 66. It is to be noted that Boss uses a terminology based on that of ideological criticism, particularly in P. Szende.

[76] Boss (74), p. 67.

Few things in such an interpretation have to be changed for it to become Marxist; in fact, beyond the introduction of the concept of reification, these modifications are almost exclusively of a terminological kind. The very facility of this *Umstülpung* proves the profoundly dialectical inspiration of the research of the whole school. In fact, so-called existential analysis in psychiatry—this comes out of Boss's work as much as Binswanger's analysis—is often nothing other than a consistent analysis of the sociological conditions of the genesis of a mental disorder. Thus Boss's analysis of Erika P.'s case shows concretely how 'being' determines consciousness in sexology, whilst Marxist analyses of an orthodox hue, while admitting the theory of the social determination of psychiatric facts, rarely go beyond the stage of generalities in the concrete application of this theory.

Let us add that a case like that of Erika P.'s is barely imaginable outside a capitalist context. It is a striking example of the interiorization of capitalist reification. This patient had the misfortune to undergo two contradictory experiences without a period of transition: prostitution which, in exchange for an impulsive pseudo-freedom, reduces woman to the level of a commodity by alienating her sexuality for money; and the convent, the supreme expression of the anti-sexual nature of reified morality. During this dual experience, her faculty for loving was suppressed; the absence of any transition itself must have constituted an existential element of pathogenic value. It would be in bad taste to compare these two experiences. Nevertheless, they do have *one thing* in common: the denial, certainly for radically different reasons, of the possibility for maturing love in the normal young girl, who, through flirtatious, even legitimate, relationships, gradually arrives at mature love. For Erika, the sudden restraint on entry into the convent fixed her sexuality at the reificational level; in her later existence, organized at a superior social (but not instinctual) level, the 'fetish' character of the woman as commodity reappeared in the form of an individual fetishism. On the other hand, her revolt against the category of 'having' does not go beyond the axiological level of this latter; she is as if imprisoned by it. To the 'you are possessed' (like a thing) of her childhood memories, she does not respond with an

'I am' but with a 'Now it's my turn to possess.'[77] By way of conclusion, let us say that the heroine of this exceptional clinical observation is a fetishist in both the Marxist and classical sexological meaning of the term.

2. A COPROPHILE

Another of Boss's patients, Rico D.[78] was the son of a couple who were brilliant diplomats. His parents entrusted his education to the domestic staff though not without forbidding him to play with neighbouring children no doubt because they were too undistinguished. Rico sought consolation in the stables, in the form of long conversations with the cows and the pigs. His first sexual emotion at the age of eleven was due to them. His masturbatory fantasies also were exclusively related to cows in a state of defecation. His first sexual experience succeeded only when his partner agreed to anal coitus. Married at the age of thirty-six, he settled down to a colourless sub-existence, without energy, and devoted himself to agricultural research, mainly on parasites. His *Privatgelehrte* room was full of books and bad smells.[79] A large eater, he compulsively had to eat during the writing up of his work, as if to compensate for the outlay of 'spiritual energy'[80] by a material input. His sexual life remained restricted to anal coitus. His wife consented to it, but a chronic inflamed condition soon marred the limits of her devotion. Deprived of his pleasure, Rico became irritable. He took on mysterious trips from which he returned soothed. One day his

[77] Erika's revolt is an historical revolt of the same order as that of the slaves of earlier times (or certain colonial peoples of today) which did not aim at a historical liberation within the framework of a general idea, but a simple change of roles. 'Alienated' Erika wanted to 'alienate'; the idea of a world without alienation was foreign to her.

[78] Boss (74), pp. 55–9.

[79] This is the description of the Balnibarbian scholar's room in *Gulliver*; for Swift's coprophilia, cf. Ben Karpman (24), and for his schizophrenia, my contribution (182).

[80] The inverted commas are not accidental. There is some 'experimental Bergsonism' in this case.

wife learned that his trips were designed to enable him to carry out his coprophilian practices far away from his own town. Thereupon the couple decided to seek advice.

A curious thing was that this consultation was aimed less at psychotherapy than local treatment for the wife which would make possible the practices to which she seemed resigned. As for him he was perfectly satisfied with it. During the act, Rico experienced the impression of 'penetrating a scorching furnace like the centre of the earth'.[81] He was indifferent to his wife's body —except for the gluteal region—it was raw material (!!!).'[82] The skin, even the sexual organs of his wife, no longer interested him at all. Life began inside her, but much more deeply at the level of substances. For Rico excrement was not dead matter but the beginning of everything.[83] He was happy only on contact with excrement or in the fields in the company of his worms.

These two observations of Boss's seem to justify Caruso's opinion as to the generality of the phenomena of reification in the domain of sexual perversion. The reificational element could not be clearer than in Erika P.'s case. The sexuality of this patient remained fixed at the level of 'normal' reification of the social milieu of her childhood; in the milieu of her life as an adult woman, it survived therefore in the form of a money fetishism. In Rico's case, reification consisted mainly in the negation of duration and value. E. Strauss sees an axiological element in all sexual perversion. This is Caruso's conception though expressed in a different way: reification is equivalent to devaluation. Reification is anaxiological in three ways: as destructuration of totalities when value is essentially structured; as a spatializing perspective when irreversible duration alone is axiogenic; and finally as an inauthentic and anti-dialectical conception. By erotically aspiring to the most unaesthetic element that a woman's body possesses, Rico *denies value* and its negation extends without any possible misunderstanding to the irreversible duration which

---

[81] Boss (74), p. 57.   [82] Boss (74), p. 57.
[83] 'Kot ist nicht tot. Er ist der Anfang von Allem' (1). This coprophile had a deranged temporality. Cf. the Balnibarbian scholar in *Gulliver*, who wanted to make nutritious materials from excrement.

it tends to invert: 'excrement is the beginning of everything'. It would be ungracious of a Bergsonian to require a more eloquent 'experimental' confirmation of his doctrines than this. To 'vitalize' the fecal bolus (normally the least vital element that an organism contains) is equivalent to inverting (therefore, spatializing) duration; the interpretation that the patient himself gives to it moreover hardly justifies any other explanation. 'The whole feminine body, except the gluteal region, is to me raw, lifeless, material, like a statue. By the same token I am indifferent to skin and genital organs. On the other hand excrements are living: it is the starting point for everything.' A reificational structure underlies the coprophilia of this 'schizoid with anal erotic tendencies'; his irresistible drive to eat during his intellectual creation (to compensate materially for the expended spiritual energy) is for its part a magico-reificational technique of a schizophrenic kind. One thinks of E. Minkowski's curious observation:[84] a patient suffering from schizophrenic melancholy imagined that all the refuse in the world was put into his stomach. The two themes are almost identical. It is the way in which they enter into the personality that differs mainly: a deranged idea in Minkowski's schizophrenic, an obsession in Boss's coprophile. The concept 'reifying attitude', the denial of duration as a bearer of value, is the common denominator. At its extreme, it becomes a crime against duration; the creative sexuality of life and future becomes a pretext for destruction and death.

ELEMENTS OF REIFICATION IN MANIA AND MELANCHOLY

It follows from a number of works that the maniacal crisis is essentially an axiological crisis (due, perhaps to a devaluation of things in the world). Maniacal consciousness thus appears as one of the aspects of subrealist consciousness even though the reificational element is not *directly* obvious.[85] At a certain time it was

[84] Cf. E. Minkowski (343), pp. 169–81.
[85] The 'mourning' factor (D. Lagache) certainly represents the reificational element in mania; mourning is—socially—of reified structure (cf. p. 137).

classic to contrast mania and schizophrenia. The well known 'good contact' of the maniac, his 'optimism', his 'activity' (many inverted commas are used when talking about mania), his vital exuberance are so many arguments in favour of this notion, established by Kretschmer's doctrine. Recent books, however, emphasize certain difficulties of differential diagnosis and cases in mental hospitals where the diagnosis 'changed' two weeks after admission are not exceptional, or not more so than in mixed cases. The theory of the relationship between these two disturbances has been upheld by authors belonging to different schools.[86]

TEMPORAL STRUCTURE OF THE MANIACAL UNIVERSE

The study of the temporal structure of maniacal consciousness supports this thesis. We know (especially since Binswanger's works) that the maniac lives in an eternal present. His personal time is a succession of present time without memory of the past and without plans for the future. At first sight this bears little resemblance to the time of schizophrenics, though the difference is more apparent than real. We read in an article on mescalinic intoxication, 'A time which no longer advances, which is fixed in the present moment, in momentaneity, could not be described as "time" in the proper meaning of the word.'

It is, if you like, eternity, atemporality (*Zeitlosigkeit*) a 'pure void';[87] and the same author adds (very dialectically): 'Aspatiality or—what amounts to the same thing—total space.'[88] Therefore the eternal—and eternally renewed—present of the maniac corresponds to a sort of spatialization of duration.[89]

[86] E.g. Wyrsch [(475), p. 101], Fenichel (152), p. 533, etc.
[87] Wolf (473), p. 170.
[88] 'Raumlosigkeit oder was dasselbe bedeutet: Allraum', Wolf (473), p. 170.
[89] Binswanger (54), p. 626 describes 'the homogeneity and monochrome nature' (*Nivelliertheit und Reliefarmut*) of the maniac's world. He compares it with the 'present type movement' of the *dance* which takes place in time without being really in duration; the same applies to the maniac's approach. It is characteristic that

Between schizophrenic spatialization and maniacal presentification one always discovers at least one essential element in common: axiogenic incapacity. Whether the axiological void of the reified (schizophrenic) universe is a consequence of the preponderance of the 'consistency' factor, whilst maniacal loss of value appears to be more dependent on the preponderance of the 'precariousness' factor, it amounts to the same thing as far as the result is concerned. It is in fact the dialectical synthesis of 'consistency' and 'precariousness' (a synthesis achieved in concrete dialectical totality) which conditions the existence of values; now, maniacal consciousness, like schizophrenic consciousness, is incapable of synthesis. Seen in this perspective, the phenomenon of 'maniacal mourning'[90] is not paradoxical, but the expression of a dialectical necessity.

This fact is significant, for if maniacal consciousness is exempt from obvious reificational elements, mourning, on the other hand, which is a social phenomenon, clearly is dependent on reification. There is the real sadness that the loss of a beloved normally causes, and the external socialized manifestations of this sadness. The state of mourning is a balance of these two elements, normally developing towards a predominance of the second. Mourning thus appears as a social technique aimed at masking the inevitably transitory (dialectical) nature of the axiological disequilibrium caused by the disappearance of those close to us, but also aimed, in effect, at slowing down this process. It involves an inauthentic (artificial) element, revealed in certain folklore techniques. It tends to give the illusion of the extra temporal and non-integratable nature ('eternal regrets') of certain states of mind that are, in reality, temporal and integratable. By

the *back step*, which is fairly rare in life, is legitimate in dance (Strauss). The 'temporal turmoil' (*Zeitwirbel*) that Heidegger contrasts with Bergsonian categories as a temporal expression of the inauthentic Me [Binswanger (54), p. 599], is devoid of axiological meaning (the double meaning of 'Sinn' in German); its structure therefore differs little from that of space. The difficulty that the doctor sometimes experiences delimiting these two disorders therefore corresponds to an unmarked differentiation in the area of the fundamental disturbance.

[90] D. Lagache (278).

welcoming it, society is an accomplice to this pious deception; it even requires it. Mourning thus denotes a negation of the dialectical law in moral life; it is a materialization and an exteriorization—therefore, a reification—of the contents of transitory and dialectical consciousness.[91] It is to a certain extent dependent on a process of spatialization. Being the result of a sort of 'lucid conversion', mourning also involves a 'theatrical' element; the need for a public characterizes the least sincere of its manifestations. The phenomenological studies of melancholic consciousness (I am thinking here of the older studies of Minkowski and Gebsattel, as well as the more recent ones of H. Tellenbach), corroborate the theory of its relationship with mourning (Freud, Lagache). This is one of the numerous examples of the convergence of research of an analytical and phenomenological inspiration. Tellenbach emphasizes *expressis verbis* one reificational aspect of melancholic consciousness. It is interesting to note in this connection that at least one of the observations contained in his recent work—like Minkowski's[92]—can be placed midway between melancholy and schizophrenia.

THE WORK OF GEBSATTEL AND TELLENBACH

Gebsattel devoted several articles to the question of endogenous melancholy, one of which is summarized in *Le Temps Vécu*. A young *engaged* girl is overcome by a melancholic depression. She *constantly records the passing of time* in its material manifestations and this state involves terrible anguish for her. All activity seems to her deprived of reason; action demands time and this *brings nearer the time of death*. Making plans seems to her no less absurd. Now, normally the passing of time is not so much a shrinking as a flowering; the idea of death which accompanies it is far from being itself a generator of permanent terror.

---

[91] V. Jankélévitch (241), p. 22, speaks of the 'true lie, one that offers . . . the momentary message for an eternal sentiment, as a truth in itself'.

[92] In *Le Temps Vécu* (343), p. 165.

Gebsattel here takes up the distinction between *imminent* death and *transitive* death. Capital punishment is certainly the second type. In fact, the temporality of Gebsattel's patient is that of someone condemned to death. These are the outlines of this case: it is curious to note that the fact that it is about a *fiancée* (someone 'who is waiting') did not draw the attention of the two great theorists who studied this case.

A priori, such a case lends itself to divergent interpretations. It is convenient—and intellectually satisfying—to envisage the hypothesis of an existence (consciousness) diametrically different from that of the morbid rationalists: the tyranny of time mitigated by a failing spatial function. Space is immobility, which is a bit like death. It is also rest; its presence allows us in certain circumstances to give expression to Lamartine's (and Faust's) wish. Even in ordinary circumstances, the spectacle of spatial immensity is restful, its absence is, on the contrary, a generator of anguish.

Imagine a man lying on a beach. Before him is the immensity of the sea, and he is happy; tomorrow there is the routine of daily life, but tomorrow is far away! He lives in the artificial eternity of the happy moment; his universe is all space. It is this fixatory (reificational if you like), spatializing element, which is lacking in this patient. Her time is a totalitarian tyrant which watches over every one of her moments. One is therefore tempted to see in melancholic existence a form of over-authentic consciousness, dependent on a constant, and consequently exhausting, axiogenic process. The melancholia is due, in a word, to a pathological exacerbation of *moral consciousness*.[93] It is tempting —and *a priori* perfectly logical—to relate the tyranny of time that Gebsattel's patient suffers with the exacerbation of moral consciousness that H. Baruk talks about, and the tyranny of the super-ego in analytic conceptions. Briefly, melancholia is a disorder based on lack of reification: a surrealist disturbance in my terminology.

Hesnard, however, disputes the validity of Baruk's hypothesis: the pre-morbid moral quality of potential melancholics seems

[93] H. Baruk (32), p. 51.

to him to be debatable.[94] One may say—without recapitulating all of Hesnard's argument—that it is not a question of exaggerated moral consciousness, but a real *moral false consciousness*,[95] just as fetishism, an illusion of totality, is a form of sexual false consciousness. It occurs, moreover, not in concrete duration, but in its negation.[96]

In fact, to return to Gebsattel's patient, it is perhaps not so much the progression of creative and axiogenic duration which embarrasses this young woman as its *objective recording* which shows the 'retardation' of a reified but not yet deranged consciousness. When she becomes deranged, she will overcome this anguish by denying duration (she will resolve the drama by finding refuge in derangement): the fear of death will then become, dialectically and not paradoxically, an illusion of immortality. It is quite permissible to accept as a hypothesis that this —engaged—patient of Gebsattel's has 'de-realized' a situation involving an untempting future, by avoiding duration. This attitude puts her out of synchrony with real time—this phenomenon has also been observed in schizophrenics—and constrains her to realize this asynchronism in the form of an anxious compulsion to register the progression of objective time. A hint of a dissociative syndrome completes the picture. All this may seem an arbitrary interpretation. But the clinical history of a *depersonalized melancholic*, studied by Gebsattel,[97] emphasizes its probability.

---

[94] Hesnard (228), p. 203.

[95] The use of the term 'false consciousness' is obviously personal, but Hesnard's whole development follows the same direction. Cf. also Abadi (2), p. 182, who compares melancholic self-accusations to a smoke-screen designed to mask (*Verhüllung*) the real guilt, which is Oedipal.

[96] 'Thus the melancholic having just lost a beloved, consistent with certain infantile reactions born of guilt, reacting to the loss as to a transgression, plunges into a fixed, monotonous world, thus escaping from duration, the significance of which for him is a world of accusation where expiatory aggression is dominant.' Hesnard (228), p. 210.

[97] Gebsattel (190).

GEBSATTEL'S CASE

This case concerns a cultured woman of forty-three, hospitalized for two years for 'endogenous depression' which responded to classical treatment. Her cultured upbringing enabled her to give an exceptionally lucid description of her morbid universe. This universe is characterized schematically by the experience of the *existential void* (*existentielle Leere*) culminating in the very characteristic impression of a bottomless chasm and a fall,[98] and by a disturbance of spatio-temporal experience and by a certain dissociation. The patient has the impression that her morbid self *is running after* her normal self without being able to catch it up. A curious 'loss of the faculty of becoming'[99] completes the picture; it is permissible to see here a homologue of the dialectical incapacity that certain schizophrenics manifest—on the level of morbid epistemology. Once again it is a question of *reification*. It is therefore a symptomatic whole where one discovers many schizophrenic elements fixed at a pre-deranged level. It is curious to note that this melancholic when experiencing a real 'existential crisis'—like a famous schizophrenic—uses a precise philosophical terminology; on the way to recovery, L. Br. (just like Renée) was reminded of Roquentin. Furthermore, during her illness she edited a curious 'Journal':

'It is not as if I was experiencing the void; I *am* the void. I could not say that I am suffering the torments of hell; I *am* hell . . . I am the void; consequently I do not exist (*ich bin die Leere und darum bin ich nicht*). Death would be easier, but death does not exist as death. It is because I am dead that I have no need of the concept of death. *I am death.*[100]

One is entirely deprived of being. (*Das Sein ist einem vollständig entzogen.*) This is what drives me mad. And yet *one* is a human being.

How is it possible to fall so low? I am, nevertheless, mind, spirit,

[98] *Abgrund* and *Sturz*: the analogy with the schizophrenic Lola Voss (61) is clear.
[99] 'Ausschaltung des Werdenkönnens', Gebsattel (190), p. 177.
[100] To be 'death' is one way of being immortal.

freedom. How can one take from someone all that, and, in addition, the world, human beings, everything? My universe is the void. I am there and yet I am not there. I have lost everything, except the consciousness of what I have lost. . . . You say that I have led a monotonous existence. I have never led any existence; I was simply not there. How can one fall so low?

Plenitude can be lived only through plenitude, the void only through the void. We travel in the void and we are the void, but in reality the void starts with us, penetrates into the world and makes us lose it. The void is not experienced; it is the most immediate thing that is. Normally we experience the void through plenitude. As sick people, we have only the void. External void, internal void, devoid of space, devoid of time. One is the void oneself, one is possessed by it.'

Her description of dissociation (*Gespaltetsein*) is no less striking. 'There is'—writes L. Br.—'a break between the Self (Me) and the body. My body is rotting in bed, my former Self is running far away and it is impossible for me to catch up with it. The feeling that I am not Me but someone else does not go away. This is the feeling of dissociation.'

The interpretation of such a case poses an ontological problem and it seems that the solution of this problem is dialectical. Any intellectualist interpretation is rejected by Gebsattel: the derealization of the perception of the world is not the consequence of some loss of the cognitive functions, but a change in the 'fundamental sympathetic relationship with the World' (E. Strauss) prior to the cognitive and volitional functions. Certain of the elementary structural relationships of existence are, despite —or perhaps because of—their elementary nature, singularly difficult to show. Consequently the study of the clinical cases of derealization and depersonalization offer a truly experimental contribution to the thinker contemplating the problems of human existence.

One total fundamental structural relationship (*allgemeine Totalitätsbeziehung*) of the Self and the World, precedes the different forms of individualized encounter of man with his universe, such as the perceptive encounter. The encounter of the existing relationships between this non-representable (*nicht*

anschaulich) fundamental relationship and its representable manifestations, constitutes an important ontological problem. According to Heidegger and Strauss this 'total fundamental relationship
between Man and World' which underlies our perceptive and
volitional acts relates to phenomena of possibility and potentiality,
these latter having meaning only in the frameworks of a general
doctrine of becoming. 'Existing' thus becomes the equivalent of
'being able to exist'; the expression 'I am' has meaning only to
the extent that, implying a capacity for self modification, it is
situated in the dynamics of becoming. This is to say, in my rather
complicated terms, that one exists only dialectically. The characteristic of the melancholic's mode of existence is precisely,
therefore, a loss of the *power of becoming* (*Ausschaltung des
Werdenkönnens*); the result is (by virtue of earlier considerations) a diminution of the sense of existing. In its turn, this
impression of sub-existence discolours the real world which
appears consequently in an artificial, factitious light. Depersonalization (impression of sub-existence through loss of the capacity
to become) and de-realization (impression of emptiness) are
consequently correlative phenomena; two aspects of the same
loss of encounter with the world. Sensory de-realization is a consequence and not a cause of this pre-sensory fundamental change
in the relationships between man and the world.

In its broad outlines, this is Gebsattel's interpretation, in which
any consideration of pathogeny remains visibly alien and in
which an undogmatic Marxist would have difficulty in finding
the dialectical core. 'Put the right way round' von Gebsattel's
interpretation would be formulated approximately in these terms:
there exists between man and his universe a system of dialectical
interactions based on human creative activity (the 'praxis'). This
whole situation involves a *dialectical* aspect (the dialectical interaction between man and the world), a *spatio-temporal* aspect
(balance of spatial-reificational elements and elements of concrete
duration), and finally an axiological aspect: human creation
creates at the same time an axiological milieu which is both a
condition and a consequence of organized action and which
structures concretely experienced space by saturating it with
value. One cannot emphasize too much that this concerns only

three facets of the fundamental phenomenon of the dialectical position of man in his universe. The identificatory factor thus appears as an element of spatialiaztion, as an atom of an anti-dialectical logic and as a possible psychodynamic factor. For its part, the notion of value is little different from the dialectical quality of reality which is like lived experience: the category of concrete totality is central in axiology (Köhler) as in dialectics (Lukács). I have already developed these views; let me say again —at the risk of repeating myself—that the loss of this dialectical position in reality, in the world of reification, necessarily involves a certain degree of spatialization of duration and ends in a mode of existence in the world, analogous to that achieved by morbid rationalism in psychopathology.

This axio-dialectical position in the world (a position, the concrete duration of which is mediatory) can be disturbed in several ways. This is one of the advantages of *Umstülpung* which leads us from Heidegger to Lukács: that it does not close the door to any psychodynamic hypothesis. It is permissible to admit, for example, that in the first case of Gebsattel, the destructuration of duration experienced through obscuration of an uninviting future, could constitute the psychodynamic position in reality, involving secondly a devaluation and a 'de-realization' of the real world: the universe is 'real' only when saturated with value. The experience of the void of which L. Br. talks is certainly an experience of the *axiological* void. In certain cases it is the axiological aspect of the phenomenon which deteriorates under the effect of a crisis of personal values, too violent a crisis for it to be able to be assimilated. Hesnard quoted the role of *national indignity* as a pathogenic factor[101] of *maniacal* states. For his part, the melancholic wants to stop time, the progression of which is intolerable to him, but in doing this, he inexorably ends in profound upheaval

---

[101] Hesnard (228), p. 213.
Cf. The case published by H. Mignot and myself (333), p. 54: a woman had intimate relations with Germans during the occupation; her family disowned her, which resulted in chronic mania. It is curious to note that the first diagnosis was that of *paranoid madness* and the instinctual test confirmed this diagnosis at the peak of a maniacal period. This constitutes an argument in favour of the relationship of the two entities.

of the structure of the real world in a reificational sense: spatialization and devaluation.

It is, moreover, certainly this atmosphere of reificational devaluation (the 'void' about which the patient L. Br. talks) which creates secondarily the feeling of guilt which Baruk's school sees —probably wrongly—as the real generative disturbance of the melancholic syndrome. It ends, finally, in a significant transformation of the *spatial* structure of the universe. There are some recent works which enable one to see more clearly in this relatively unexplored area.

THE SPACE OF MELANCHOLICS

Space experienced by melancholics is characterized, according to recent works, by the de-realization of the dimension of depth, of concrete valuing activity (of the 'praxis').[102] This de-realization can be translated into either the tendency to stretch spatial distances[103] to infinity (a phenomenon which may still permit a completely objective evaluation of real physical distances), or 'on the contrary', a loss of the feeling of depth (Tellenbach).[104] We say 'on the contrary' between inverted commas, since the opposition of the two is artificial. For concrete 'praxis', an infinite spatial depth involves exactly the same significance as the absence of any depth. They both assume the impossibility, or rather the absence of significance, of all concrete action in a continuum without perspective. The word 'perspective' curiously has a double meaning: it signifies both an opening on to future time and the third dimension of space; the language here confirms the partially temporal nature of the spatial perspective. The space in Kafka's novels is an example: the bidimensionality of the action presents to the reader beings without depth, and

---

[102] Rosenfeld (406) pointed out as early as 1905, a deficiency in the sense of stereognosia but it occurred in *catatonia*.

[103] 'I have not even managed to reach the nearest wall' said Von Gebsattel's patient (190), p. 177.

[104] This whole section is dependent on two fine contributions by H. Tellenbach (442 and 443).

infinite, supernatural distance to protect the entry to the 'Castle'.[105] The melancholic perceives his environment as a flat surface[106] which, for certain of them, evokes the universe of infantile drawings.[107] 'Everything is situated on the same line; objects are like an immobile surface.' 'A house is nothing more than a façade without depth,' said one patient who saw herself as a person of pure surface. Another patient *touched objects* to assure herself through the tactile sense of their tridimensionality. This time, the articulation of space as *near space* and *distant space* is blurred. Objects leave the foreground: a flat surface (recalling the cinema screen) takes the place of the circular horizon. In this destructured space, the experienced and well-tried dimensions lose their contours, and the world becomes vertical.[108] Sometimes, there is an exaggeration of weight: a mother despairs of lifting her child.[109] The German word *Schwermut* perfectly expresses this 'verticalizing' tendency in depression.

Elsewhere—the contradiction is only apparent—phenomena of levitation dominate the scene; a melancholic complains that the disappearance of her weight makes standing up difficult; she has the feeling of floating, even of being drawn upwards. The air is displaced towards the top of her body and fecal matter rises to the mouth.[110] At the extreme there is a total disappearance of spatial directions: such a patient feels herself fluttering in the air, another compares herself poetically to an autumn leaf dancing in a dead universe. Sensory experience is also affected: voices seem to come from an infinite distance; surrounding people

---

[105] Cf. Nemeth (366), pp. 86–7.
[106] Tellenbach (442), p. 15.
[107] Tellenbach (442), p. 13.
[108] Tellenbach (442), II, p. 294.   [109] Ibid.
[110] It would be interesting to interpret this phenomenon psychoanalytically; whatever this interpretation might be, it does not necessarily reinforce Tellenbach's but it could contribute to a psychoanalytic theory of the origins of space and time; a psychoanalytic theory of the reificational phenomenon in short. For relationships between anality and time: cf. Oberndorf (368), p. 147, between oral frustration and aggression and regression of temporalization, see Schilder (419), etc.

H

are reduced to Lilliputian dimensions. This non-structured bi-dimensional continuum seems incapable of assuring the formal-dialectical coherence of things; objects in the melancholic's field of consciousness are isolated without reciprocal relationships.[111] In this fragmented world, with infinite distances, movement loses its significance, even its *raison d'être*; 'One does not try to catch the moon' said Tellenbach expressively.[112]

In short, space experienced by melancholics is characterized by the loss of the dimension of experienced depth, and this —in a seemingly paradoxical manner—as a consequence of the exaggeration of experienced distances which, from being human ones become super-human. One conceives, in effect, that an 'extra-vital' distance can hardly give to the experienced continuum the concrete and articulated depth which our store of experienced and practised values give it. Whether this bi-dimensional universe is interpreted by certain patients as a *background* and by others as a *universe of pure façade*, amounts to the same thing as far as the essentials are concerned: a loss of the differentiation of space as normally experienced and used (Cassirer's '*Leistungsraum*') between *near space*, i.e. accessible to action, and *distant space*. This form of de-differentiation of experienced space certainly corresponds to a certain degree of infantile regression.[113]

These results confirm *grosso modo* those of Gebsattel who emphasizes the dialectical incapacity of melancholics (*Ausschaltung des Werdenkönnens*). The contributions of Gebsattel and Tellenbach have brought out, in connection with melancholy, two different but complementary aspects of anti-dialectical (reified)

---

[111] This passage is typical: 'Die einzelnen Gegenstände ... die hatten innerlich nichts miteinander zu tun. Die standen ganz verein-zelt da, ohne gegenseitige Beziehung.' One sees that the melancholic universe is a sub-dialectical universe, and this specifically in the sense of a dialectic of the totality.

[112] Tellenbach (442), II, p. 293.

[113] Cf. this passage: 'Erst mit der Tiefe ist das Ausgedehnte in seinem Wesen erschliessbar. Der Mensch gewinnt sie im Werden— das Kind das nach dem Monde greift, hat sie noch nicht' (Tellenbach (442), II, p. 296).

That is to say, in other terms, that spatial depth is the acquisition of a process of dialectical maturation.

existence: the 'incapacity for becoming' and as a corollary, a breakdown of the subject-object dialectical unity, according to Gebsattel; over-spatialization through loss of the dimension of depth, with destructuration of the concrete totality (formal quality) of experience, and atomization of experience, in Tellenbach's analyses. Once again the concept of reification serves as a common denominator: Tellenbach utilizes it furthermore *expressis verbis*, perhaps without knowing its importance in Marxist philosophy. Without going into discussions about pathogeny here, it is permissible, on the basis of earlier observations, to consider certain forms[114] of endogenous melancholia as *forms of reification* where all the essential elements of the schizophrenic picture are present without, however, being neo-structured to a deranged level.

HYSTERIA AS A SUB-REALIST DISTURBANCE

Without considering the psycho-dynamic problems which arise from analytical theories, I shall merely try to place this 'mode of pathological reaction' (Guiraud)[115] in the framework of the sub-realist attitude. In my view one of the major difficulties of the

[114] Cf. Tellenbach (442), II, p. 294: 'Die Melancholischen befinden sich stets *in einer Bewegung zur Verdinglichung* (my italics) vergleichbar der immer wieder beginnenden und nie endenden Bewegung eines Drehschwindels.' The corresponding deterioration of 'vital' feelings fits in with the feeling of the 'existential void' of Gebsattel's patient. Tellenbach adds (ibid., note) that these considerations open up new perspectives in the comprehension of melancholic compulsions. Elsewhere (ibid., p. 291), a patient compares herself to a *stone*: 'I now know what it is to be a stone' (Kafka uses almost the same image). Obviously the concept of reification in Lukács is differentiated in another way; the coincidence is no less significant.

Certainly, the differentiation between endogenous melancholia and reactional depressive states (cf. Ey (149), pp. 532–4 and *passim*) is the stumbling block in this whole problem. The spatio-temporal structure of the *Cotard syndrome* has been studied by S. Resnik (401); over all, it is quite close to those that we have just examined.

[115] Cf. H. Claude (105), p. 263. This prudent expression has the advantage of eliminating the sterile discussion about whether it concerns a *psychosis*, a *psychoneurosis* or a *neurosis*.

traditional division of the psychosis into *realist* and *de-realist* is that this classification, centred on the critique of the perspective functions alone, is forced to put hysteria and schizophrenia into different compartments.

Now, their relatedness—postulated by Pavlovian conceptions among others—is accepted by numerous authors.[116] An authentic phenomenon of reification is the basis of conversion hysteria; Ferenczi talks about 'hysterical materialization'.[117]

HYSTERICAL INAUTHENTICITY

A servant looked after her phthisic master. She soon exhibited, without the slightest anatomical basis, the clinical symptoms of pulmonary tuberculosis. Another, who worked as an aide in a psychiatric clinic, suffered a catatonia which baffled the doctors, required biological treatment and was diagnosed as hysteria only *in extremis* and then with reservations.[118] (A good argument, we might mention in passing, in favour of the possible psychogenesis of catatonia.) They are—Klages tells us—hysterical characters, similar to the pseudologist who parades his illusions throughout the world and communicates them to his dupes, the hospital mystic dominated by the devil, the 'witches' of Salem, or the nuns who led the unfortunate Urbain Grandier to the stake.

The *hysterical character* is as common in life as in mental hospitals; he has his place in history.[119] For Klages, it is essentially

[116] Cf. Kaiser (248), the thesis of Reynaud (401 *bis*), Perelmann (383), etc. It seems that H. Claude (105) has gone furthest in the identification of these two modes of pathological reaction. Cf. the notion of 'schizoses', art. cit. (105), p. 14 (hysteria would belong to the group of schizoses).

[117] Isolated from its context, it is an arbitrary assimilation. If we think it possible to consider conversional materialization as an act of reification, it is because it is placed in a reificational context: destruction of totalities (Klages), sub-temporalization (Racamier) (392), false conscious alienating identification (pseudology).

[118] A case of Müller, Burner and Villa; the authors emphasize the difficulties of differential diagnosis particularly between certain hysterical states and the catatonic stupor (361), p. 262.

[119] Erostratus's exploits were authentically hysterical [Klages (258), p. 163] as were Damien's, though perhaps more clearly so.

dependent on a diminution of the *structuring force* (*Gestaltungs-kraft*) of the personality with an increased need for compensatory representation. One wonders if it is a good idea to talk of *hysterical irrealism.* In effect this term translates an inadequate perceptual-reflexive attitude: the expression 'sub-realism' expresses a particular form of the mode of being-in-the-world, prior to any deterioration in the purely perceptual experience. It is, in fact a sort of 'subvitalism' (not without analogy to the athymhormia of schizophrenics) which, according to Klages, by preventing the patient from raising himself up to the vital level of the everyday, obliges him to compensate for this insufficiency by techniques which are symptoms. The hysterical pathomime carries within her the image of the symptoms; the loss of her faculty for structuration prevents her from assimilating this image. Seized by an 'elementary impoverishment of vitality', she does not dominate her images by assimilating them, but conducts herself passively in relation to them; she is like a puppet. This fact should not be passed over without recalling the phenomenon of the crushing of the *Dasein* by the world, a phenomenon condemned by certain German theorists of schizophrenia, since Binswanger. Some of them have contrasted the activity of the hysteric with the passivity of the schizophrenic;[120] Klages's conception shows the limits of this argument. The 'activity' of the pseudologist who transforms his universe through articulated thought and not through action is closer to hallucinatory *activity* than to concrete action: it is in fact lucid onirism.[121]

The need for imitation that Klages discovered (with many others) at the basis of hysterical pathomimia therefore has nothing very much in common with conscious simulation. It is rather a necessary structural corollary of the inauthentic 'mode of being-in-the-world' among patients who cannot achieve self-realization in any other way than by alienating themselves ('alienating identification'). The abnormal need for representation here makes up for a torturing feeling of being on the edge of existence; the vital loss of these patients is essentially a loss of the structuring, and, consequently, the *dialectical* function of consciousness: with

[120] Cf. Claude (105), discussion.
[121] Cf. the case of lucid schizophrenia described by Vinchon (458).

the dialectical importance of the totality we come back to the Lukácsian ethos. Like the schizophrenic, the hysteric is in-authentic because he is non-dialectical; hysterical imitation, like the *Identitätszwang* of schizophrenics, is a structural element of this inauthenticity which occurs on this side of the voluntary-involuntary alternative. The characteristic elements of political false consciousness are thus to be found in hysterical conscious-ness: reification with, as a corollary, a certain degree of destruc-turation (and consequently, spatialization) of duration, with concomitant destructuration of the totality of experience; Klages's loss of the structuring function (*Herabgesetzte Gestaltungkraft*). The logical result is phenomena of devaluation ('hysterical amoral-ism') with a characteristic loss of the limits of the true and the false in *fantasy pseudology*.

REIFICATION AS DEVALUATION OF THE TRUTH: FANTASY PSEUDOLOGY

We know a variant of hysteria[122] in which the boundaries between the true and the false are erased, just like those of the Self and the World in certain forms of paranoid disturbance: the consciousness of the pseudologist—'theatrical consciousness' in general—is still an individual form of *false consciousness*. It is no coincidence if the 'political' term seems to demand to be recognized as an analogy;[123] hysterical consciousness possesses, in fact, all the inauthenticity of politicized consciousness. The hysterical lie could be described as organic, or even instinctual; it is the result of a regression (this term is used here with reservations) to a stage

[122] The hysterical nature of pseudology is accepted by most authors (cf. Dide (128)); Sophie Muller (362) points out, however, a syndrome similar to the progression of the prodromic period of *schizophrenia*.

[123] Cf. Racamier (392), p. 31, talks of the '*politics* of ridiculiza-tion of reality' (my italics); the same word reappears in Codet (Claude (105), p. 258 in the same discussion) who discerns in the behaviour of the hysteric a controlling continuity, *real politics* (my italics) which allow one to understand that 'each symptom is not a fortuitous disturbance, but possesses real significance'.

where the differentiation of experience into true and false does not yet possess the axiological substructure which makes it definitive. The essential characteristic of the so-called impulsive lie is less its nonconformity with reality than the incomprehension of the axiological privilege of truth. The anonymography which destroys the subject-object dialectic by causing the subject to disappear (whilst the lie destroys it by reifying the object) ends in the same psychological and moral result as the lie, despite the possible congruence of its assertions with reality; even when consistent with truth, anonymography is behaviour of the *lying type*, for by not assuming its truth, the anonymographer devalues it as much as the liar.[124] But, on the other hand, since the axiological quality of reality is inseparable from its dialectical structure, hysterical consciousness, which is incapable of structuration, is also not valued; the loss of the sense of the axiological privilege of truth is its consequence. Comparison with the theatre is relevant; the theatrical event is also *true* in its material factitiousness (one could say: reificational), but it is an anaxiological truth which is cut off from the necessary dimension of *consistency*: death, in the theatre, is not irreversible, and the 'dead' person appears at the end of the show to acknowledge the applause. The fictitious historicity of the theatrical event is incompatible with irreversible time: theatrical temporality (that of fiction in general) allows for new beginnings and flashbacks, which give it a structure of a spatial type. The same applies to hysterical time. A certain patient . . . 'relives a certain shelling that he experienced twelve years earlier at the time of the evacuation: every few seconds he relives and mimes coitus and labour, and maintains that he is fourteen months pregnant or pregnant at the age of seventy-eight'.[125] All of this is quite close to schizophrenic temporality (see particularly, the extraordinary 'Gardair case' that G. Dumas

---

[124] Anonymography is an archaic schizoid technique according to J. Wyrsch (476); an objectivation ('bad objectivation' in the worst sense of the term) of a product of thought; furthermore, it is a technique of self-depersonalization. It is not surprising that anonymography flourishes in a totalitarian milieu. Cf. Binder's masterly study (53).

[125] Racamier (392), p. 20.

describes).[126] The loss of spatial depth that P. L. Racamier indicates (the hysteric is a person without perspective) recalls the structure of the spatio-temporal existence of melancholics (Tellenbach). The anachronism of the hysterical syndrome is, after all, a classical datum. The question then arises whether one must really consider the lie as instinctual, that is to say, due to the presence of a positive factor forcing the patient to lie, or *existential*, that is to say, due to the absence of any element likely to confer a primacy on truth in an anti-dialectical and therefore anaxiological, undifferentiated world. The two views have been defended;[127] the theorists influenced by Klages lean towards the second hypothesis: '. . . it is not at all, as is usually held, because the hysteric "lies" that he poisons and destroys the truth of his feelings, but, on the contrary, because he cannot experience this reality that he is led to lie'.[128] This observation of Racamier's confirms what we said earlier about the reificational structure of the hysterical disturbance. The analogy between the loss of the boundaries between the true and the false in hysterical states (for which pseudology is the 'pattern') is therefore not merely verbal; they are two different aspects of the spatialism of reified existence. In fact (I should mention the paranoid phenomenon in this context), pure space does not clearly delimit the contours of the person who is cut off from his valuing historicity: phenomena of *Verweltlichung* are produced; we shall examine later the interpretation of C. Kulenkampff's *poisoning derangement*. Space affords little shelter; a purely spatial existence poses existential problems of habitation, even of co-habitation touched on rather a long time ago by Minkowski and Zutt. Axiologically speaking (it is always possible to translate a problem of reification in terms of axiology), space being a milieu devoid of values, lends itself badly to the differentiation of the Self as value; space depersonalizes by devaluing. Something similar happens in the hysterical consciousness: in the destructured world peculiar to these patients, reality perceived at the level of crude factitiousness, and deprived

---

[126] Dumas (135), p. 220. One of the most typical examples of the ahistoricism of schizophrenics.

[127] Cf. in connection with this debate, Havermans (214).

[128] Racamier (392), p. 30.

of its axio-dialectical halo, is nothing more than a sub-truth incapable of imposing its primacy.

If the axiological indifferentiation of the reified universe explains the possibility of the substitution of an inanimate (or at least partial) object for the loved one as a totality, it explains similarly the indifferentiation of values of truth in hysterical consciousness, and that of pesudologists in particular.

Furthermore there exist cases where the sexual determinism of the lie is highlighted. A patient of Havermans,[129] a married man of common origins, was almost instinctually compelled to invoke his so-called noble ancestry in company. This lie was transparent and the confusion of his wife—whom he loved—usually gave him an otherwise rare feeling of pleasure. This case is interesting. In his own inauthentic (anti-dialectical) temporality, this man is, in a way, his own ancestry (his own descent too, no doubt); the artificial egodiastol compensates for the tortured feeling of being condemned to a definitive egosystole. The satisfaction thus derived is dependent on an artificial sexuality because it is not directed towards the future; the hysteric 'is masturbation'.[130] The two servants fixed in their sub-existence, want to demonstrate (the word emphasizes the classical 'dependence on the spectator') that they *at least* know how to be tuberculous or catatonic. Moreover, Havermans refers significantly to Boss's attempt at an existential analysis of perversions. Boss's notion (the loss of sexual encounter among perverts) is in fact related to those of von Gebsattel and I. A. Caruso. On the other hand, the dialectical location of the problem of perversions by this school links up with certain theoretical interpretations of schizophrenia: the loss of the function of encounter (von Baeyer), reified logic (morbid rationalism), and destructuration of totalities. This is an interesting convergence of theories and facts. We shall evaluate the significance of this later on.

The problem of explaining why a certain patient manifests his sub-realism through an hysterical disturbance, another through melancholia, and yet another through paranoid psychosis, lies in the realm of analytical research. My aim was to discover in

[129] Havermans (214), p. 215.
[130] Racamier (392), p. 41.

hysterical consciousness the elements characteristic of false consciousness: destructuration of totalities, spatialization of duration,
devaluation, inauthenticity (the 'organic lie' and pseudology),
identificatory and reificational elements.

DIVISION OF THE PSYCHOSES
IN *LE TEMPS VÉCU*

The idea of a bipartite division of the psychoses is based on a
remark of E. Minkowski's. In a passage of *Le Temps Vécu*,[131]
the possibility of a dualist classification inspired by Bergson is
suggested: the psychoses characterized by a lack of intuition and
hypertrophy of the spatial functions on the one hand, and the
opposite state of affairs on the other. In effect, the former would
coincide with schizophrenia; concerning the latter ('surrealist'
in my terminology), Minkowski's thought remains guarded. He
rejects the classical opposition between schizophrenia and manic-
depressive psychoses; on this point, recent research—phenomenological and other kinds—suggests that this is correct. The opposition between the spatialized time of schizophrenics and the
destructured time of maniacs ('a succession of presents') is, as we
have seen, more apparent than real. Berze speaks of 'flüchtige
Momentpersönlichkeiten' among *schizophrenics*.[132] In fact, Minkowski considers—though not without reservations—general paralysis as a type of existence in pure duration.[133] But the spatio-
temporal structure of the existence of general paralytics is little
explored and will no doubt remain so. A disorder which is as well
delimited anatomically (and also accessible to therapy) provides
rather an unfavourable territory for phenomenological research.

The introduction of the concept of reification seems to be
fruitful on this point. It allows for the enlargement of the

[131] Op. cit., p. 271.

[132] Quoted by Zutt (483), p. 371.

[133] Cf. particularly this well-known contrast (Minkowski (340), p.
93): the schizophrenic knows where he is but does not have the
feeling of being there (loss of the function of the Me–Here–
Now); the general paralytic experiences the opposite.

'sub-realist' group by encompassing other disorders involving a reificational element: certain perversions, the manic-depressive psychosis (where the reificational element is represented by the role of mourning, which has been demonstrated by the psycho-analysts) and hysteria. It may be asked whether the assimilation of the hysterical syndrome into the concept of reification is not merely a verbal exercise. Without going into an examination of the different theories of the hysterical disturbance, let us say simply that this assimilation is not based on a terminological analogy, but on the observation of a whole anti-dialectical, anaxiological context, a context in which the often studied analogies between the clinical pictures of hysteria and schizo-phrenia are the concrete expression. On the other hand, seen in the light of this hypothesis, the type of existence in duration is not so much general paralysis as an aphasic disturbance. I refer back to the preceding pages and to H. Faure's observation[134] which is to a certain extent the experimental verification of my hypothesis. Finally, such a classification certainly could not claim to be exhaustive. In addition to the disorders studied, it is quite possible to describe psychastenia, Cotard's syndrome,[135] as well as the alcoholic's hallucinosis,[136] as sub-realist, not to mention minor reifying-sub-realist behaviour, such as lying or anony-mography.

This classification is not superimposable on the classical one of the psychoses into *realist and de-realist*, based on the critique of the perceptual functions isolated from their context. The fact that one can be led into classifying hysteria and schizophrenia separately (despite their numerous similarities) emphasizes its artificial character.

The very notion of 'realist psychosis' should be viewed with

[134] H. Faure *et al.* (151).

[135] Cf. the study of Cotard's spatio-temporal structure (in an analytical perspective). Resnik (401).

[136] For the relationship between hallucinosis and schizophrenia, cf. Benedetti (44); Fusswerk (169) (categorical deterioration both in the paranoid disturbance and in hallucinosis) and particularly Bilz (52) (on existential analysis of hallucinosis with a study of spatio-temporal structures: the world of the 'beleaguered man', *Belager-ungserlebniss*).

caution; in the strict sense of the term, the only normality is supposed to be completely 'realist'. The idea of 'realist psychosis' presupposes an essentially biological theory of perception. Now, perception is both a biological and a social act; an act of encounter. The maturation of the perceptual functions is a social maturation; this emerges particularly strongly from J. Piaget's criticisms of the Gestaltists on the subject of perceptual constants. The 'reality' with which we are dealing is not only nature, but also the lived, valued, acted upon social reality (the reality of Marxian 'praxis'). Having accepted this, it may seem hazardous to describe as *realist* the hysterical experience, which is characterized by the accurate perception of crude artificialities (the hysteric does not hallucinate), but is devoid of this structural-dialectical coherence[137] capable of giving it the axiological dimension necessary for imposing the primacy of truth. The same applies to the experience of the melancholic who is also furnished with adequate perceptions, but who reveals a breakdown of the dialectical relationship between the self and the world ('Subject and Object'; the melancholic—I would say—has no *praxis*) with a loss of spatial depth, which is the dimension of action. Between these 'realist' structures and hallucinatory 'de-realism', there exists a transitional phase which emphasizes the danger of the utilization of the isolated perceptual functions as a criterion of classification. I have tried to base this classification on a clearly delimited whole, that emerges as a criterion from Marxist sociology: the sub-realist attitude in psychiatry provides a structural analogy with false consciousness, i.e. an anti-dialectical mode of being-in-the-world. Hallucination is certainly one manifestation of it (I refer here to recent developments concerning the relationships between hallucination and space as well as to those between the identificatory structure of thought and deranged perception); but it is not the only manifestation. It is, for example, a curious

---

[137] Cf. in this connection: (1) the importance of the category of the totality for dialectical thought [Lukács (309); Goldmann (196)]; the axiogenic role of structures (Köhler (261) and *excursus* pp. 51–9). The hysteric perceives accurate artificialities, but they are deprived of the axiological 'halo' which makes *truths* out of them.

observation—and quite consistent with the data in dialectical philosophy—that sexual reification is at the same time a form of sexual false consciousness in the Marxist sense of the term, with all the structural characteristics of this latter. In fact, fetishism is not only a dissociation of the totality of the person from the partner, but also an illusion of totality, not only ignorance of the real loving other, but also an illusion of otherness (the fetish is a 'Schein-Du', according to Gebsattel's expression); therefore it is not only an egocentric attitude but also an attitude which would prefer not to know and to which the patient clings.[138] Perhaps what is most striking to the Marxist reader of the writings of Gebsattel and Boss, is a consistent and curious coincidence between the terminology of the phenomenological sexologists and the Marxist theorists of false consciousness.

The passage in Boss's book where he describes the *fetischistische Verdeckung*[139] is not the only example of this. From the point of view of 'sexual epistemology', the fetishist's position thus appears typically as *false identification* according to the meaning given to it in ideological criticism: an anti-dialectical position appears in a regressive context of egocentrism and reification, as I have tried to define above.

A dualist theory of morbid consciousness is proposed, a theory which to my mind constitutes a dialectical transcendence ('Aufhebung') of Blondel's unitary conception.[140] It aims to show that

---

[138] Cf. D. Lagache (*Evolution Psychiatrique*, July–Sept. 1955, p. 580): a fetishist is depressed when he frees himself from his infantile sexuality and seeks a way out in *identification with an older woman*; later the hypothesis of an intimate relationship between certain identifications and the experience of time is suggested. Obviously anti-dialectical existence (and also thought) is convenient; one does not easily abandon such a comfort. It is easier to 'love' a shoe than to conquer a woman, just as it is easier to think in schemas than to dialectically capture truth (the role of 'the abstraction-refuge' in the derangement of J. Zünd. Binswanger (60), p. 28).

[139] Boss (74), p. 62: the corresponding Marxist term is *Verhüllung*; cf. Szende (439), *passim*.

[140] We must emphasize the difficulties of translating the term 'Aufhebung'. J. Gibelin's translation (cf. *Encycl. Sciences Phil.*, p. 94

the notion of 'reified consciousness' has a concrete clinical expression. The analysis of clinical facts is used here as an experimental check on the results of speculation, in keeping with J. Berze's suggestion.[141]

The classification thus obtained does not claim to be exhaustive and does not imply any 'principle of the excluded middle'. An artificial classification is by definition exhaustive; a natural classification is rarely, if ever, so. All mental disorder is by definition realist or derealist, but the concept of reality underlying this classification is an abstraction, for it is an extra-social reality.[142] On the other hand, when one chooses as a criterion of classification, the dialectical quality of involvement in the social universe and perception of reality, one is obliged to take account of the existence of disorders which are outside the classification thus obtained; thus mental confusion is certainly a 'de-realistic' mental illness, but it does not come into any classification based on dialectics or reification. Such a classification can not therefore be exhaustive.

Bipartite classifications are numerous in psychopathology; that of the late F. Minkowska is among the most well-known.[143] It is

and elsewhere) is debatable. What I propose is far from being perfect, for 'dépassement dialectique' (dialectical transcendence) implies a pejorative connotation which is alien to 'Aufhebung'. Since I must make my position clear in relation to this classical work, this comment is necessary.

[141] Berze, who describes schizophrenia as 'Nature's great experiment' (51).

[142] This is 'abstraction' in Marx's sense when he says that the population of a country is an abstraction without the classes which compose it. The 'bare' natural reality is not an abstraction for the physician. It is so for the psychopathologist to the extent that it is legitimate to consider mental illness as a social fact.

[143] F. Minkowska distinguished between a rational type and a sensory type of perception (the Rorschach of epileptic children). The contrast between the 'rational world' and the 'sensory world' naturally does not exhaust either 'all constitutions or all ways of seeing . . .; they simply have the advantage of touching upon two essential factors of life, that of perception-sensation and that of perception-definition-rationalism' [(334), p. 63]. I shall show later that the *deranged perception* of paranoid states is essentially a pathological exacerbation of the second type of perception.

not my concern to compete with them or to make a laborious attempt at synthesis. My aim has been simply to show that a classification based on a criterion of sociological origin may provide a useful working hypothesis in psychopathology.

Mine in fact provides an argument in favour of the dualist location of the paranoia-schizophrenia problem. I emphasized earlier that the classical clinical picture of paranoia does not involve appropriate reificational elements. The psychoanalysts generally tend to consider paranoia and paranoid disturbances a unique nosogical entity; the alienists tend to see it as two different disorders.

My point of view offers an argument in favour of the dualist idea by making possible a distinction between *false consciousness* as the destructuration of totalities, accompanied by spatialization and the prevalence of identificatory functions, and *false judgement* which has nothing to do with a de-dialecticization of the cognitive functions or a loss of *praxis*. We could go more deeply into this problem where each of the opposing theses has defenders of repute; nevertheless, in an open debate a straightforward decision in favour of one of these points of view already constitutes some progress.[144]

The notion of reification of sexuality highlights the significance of one well-known fact: the coexistence of sexual and social repression.[145] If—as I. A. Caruso believes—sexual pathology is reificational in its essence, it follows that sexuality is essentially dereification: the sexual act is not only a dialectical act but something more: the very expression of the dialectical character of our involvement in the world.[146] This observation brings up for consideration an extra dimension to the relationship between

---

[144] The dualist ideas of Claude and Montassut in France (106), (107) and (354) and those of Kurth in Germany (273) are those which fit in best with the starting hypothesis of the present work.

[145] Cf. the extreme point of view of W. Reich (399) and his disciples Parrell (379) etc., and the whole 'Sex-Pol' school in Austria and Germany between the two wars.

[146] Cf. Merleau-Ponty (330), p. 184: 'Psychoanalysis reveals a dialectical process in the functions that were believed to be "purely corporal"'; Chapter V of the book (Le corps comme être sexué) is centred on this theme.

sexuality and social repression, and one which has not been expressed in this form: by repressing sexuality, class society indirectly defends its false consciousness.

Finally, the structure of truth in hysterical consciousness (particularly in pseudology) permits us to understand better the mechanism of ideologization; it illuminates particularly the problem of the partial or total character of ideology. This question needs to be treated separately.

THE PROBLEM OF THE TOTAL CONCEPT OF IDEOLOGY AND THE PSYCHOPATHOLOGICAL APPROACH (IDEOLOGY AND LIES)

On the basis of lessons learned from the phenomenology of sub-realist consciousness, this is the place to take up again the study of a problem raised by Mannheim: that of the partial or total character of ideology.

The accusation of spontaneous lying brought against the adversary, the denunciation of conscious mystification in religious alienation, the supposedly predominant role of a psychology of interests in the process of ideologization, all belong to a phenomenon for which Mannheim reserved the name of *partial concept of ideology*. The clear, utilitarian lie (mystification) would therefore play a primordial role in this conception, whilst the total concept of ideology is based, on the other hand, on an analysis of structural transformations of thought, a transformation whose schizophrenic nature I have demonstrated. It is not a matter of evaluating the importance of the 'State lie' in political life—it has been notorious since Plato—but of establishing whether the political lie assumes a primary or secondary role in the process of ideologization, or in other words, whether mystification creates false consciousness or whether it is a by-product of it.

The global problem of the lie is an immense area; it goes far beyond the frameworks of our study in which the moral questions, among others, remain completely foreign. But, beyond its sociological extension, the lie also possesses a psychiatric extension, certain aspects of which we have just indicated. It is consistent with the general methodology of the present study to raise the question as to whether these two aspects might shed light on each other.

I shall briefly consider the two cases in Cassirer's quoted work: the question of aphasics who are 'incapable of lying'.[147]

According to my interpretation, these patients live in an over-dialectical universe that is insufficiently reified and too exclusively temporalizing.[148] It is on this account that it is possible to contrast the structure of their universe with that of the world peculiar to schizophrenics. It would appear that lying is a reifying, spatializing function, and that the too exclusively temporal and insufficiently reified universe of aphasics is not well suited to it.

Obviously the cases quoted by Cassirer are isolated observations. But the information to be gained from studying them is confirmed *a contrario* by that of sub-realist consciousness; we have seen the psychodynamic mechanism that certain authors postulate as the basis of the hysterical lie. It is characteristic that the disorder which constitutes the pure clinical expression of the hysterical lie also provides a link between hysteria and schizophrenia, since the elements of its clinical picture are part of the prodromic period of schizophrenia.[149]

What follows is a general conception of the phenomenology of the lie that is different from the one defended by V. Jankélévitch in his short, but stimulating book. Jankélévitch seems (if I have properly understood his thought) to find a *temporalizing* element at the basis of the lie.[150]

---

[147] Cf. Cassirer (98) and above.

[148] Cf. in this connection (the over-temporalizing character of the aphasic world) Binswanger's observation (54), p. 606: among aphasics, space is always orientated according to their bodies, in other words, the notions of 'before' and 'after' have an absolute significance *as in time* and not a relative significance as in space.

[149] Pseudology. Cf. Sophie Meyer's thesis (362).

[150] Jankélévitch (241), p. 21 '. . . to call things by their name, I would say first that it is time which keeps story-tellers supplied with material, due to the infinitely varied riches that it accumulates.

Now, on this point, psychopathology and social psychology say the opposite. It is in fact the subrealist—and consequently *spatializing*—disorders which seem to favour the lie, just as it is the historical periods that are predominantly spatial ('A' periods according to V. Zoltowski's terminology) which favour both manifestations of collective aggression and social forms of the lie.

Independently of any consideration of clinical psychiatry or social psychology, the spatializing, reifying character of the world of the lie can be established in a uniquely reflexive way. If the lie reifies the interlocutor by removing him from the sphere of 'being' to that of 'having' ('He's been had' says the liar), this does not need to be proved at length, or no more so than the egocentric,[151] devaluing character of the lie.[152] The lie is part of a false dialogue; it crystallizes a false encounter; even more than hallucination, it is dependent on a 'disorder in sympathetic communication' discussed by E. Strauss.[153] This reification of the interlocutor goes hand in hand with a self-reification of the liar. This seems less evident: *a priori* it seems that it is necessary to be very flexible, very 'dialectical' to be able to lie well. And yet, this marvellous freedom and power of the liar that Plato ironically admired is a false freedom and an illusion of power, similar to that supposedly conferred by a magical power or the

Time, first of all, makes for lying in that it is the agent of contradiction: a person, through chronology, becomes another, and then yet another; for that is becoming: to be other than oneself, to be what one is not, sometimes less and sometimes more; through a sort of continuation and otherness, the future makes people unequal to themselves, unlike themselves, just as it makes any prediction synthetic.'

[151] It is the egocentricism of the lie that the famous Kantian statement is implicitly denouncing.

[152] In support of these points cf. Jankélévitch's book (241), p. 37 and *passim*, but it seems to me that these views somewhat contradict what the author said on the relationships between the lie and temporality.

[153] 'Sympathische Kommunikationsstörung', Strauss talks only about the act of hallucination. Cf. Jankélévitch (241), p. 32, who accuses the lie of being 'a devious and loveless sympathy' and later (ibid., p. 40) 'that there is no possible community in the lie'. It is therefore almost the same idea which appears in the two contexts that are, in theory, different.

feeling of omnipotence in certain schizophrenic states. This is the moment to reiterate the terminological distinction that I introduced in connection with the term '*Verdinglichung*'; there is objectification and *reification*. Objectification is the experience of the other (or of oneself in paranoid states) as a thing; reification is an existential state which involves in addition to the phenomenon of objectification, a neostructuration of the whole mode of being-in-the-world, with a loss of temporalization and consequent spatialization.

Having said this, we consider that the liar objectifies the interlocutor while reifying himself, for his lie forces him to leave duration in order to find refuge in a continuum of spatial structure. It is for this reason that we have been able to describe the lie, along with anonymography as *minor sub-realist behaviour*. The opinion of G. Durandin who sees it as an 'archaic technique originating in conflict'[154] corroborates this point of view.

In his work on schizophrenia, Berze talks about the formation of subordinate lines alongside the main line of thought in the hallucinatory phenomenon.[155] Something similar happens in the world of the liar. A man who, consistent with truth, acknowledges that he is forty-five, by the same token expresses the fact, *ne varietur*, that he was forty-four one year earlier and that he expects to be—except for unforeseen circumstances—forty-six one year later. He thus places himself in an irreversible duration whilst the liar, by leaving the domain of truth, opens up the way to an infinity of possible temporal perspectives, which amounts to an assault on the axiological privilege of truth; these perspectives are juxtaposed according to a *spatial* pattern. To state truthfully that one has 40,000 francs in his bank account implies the statement *ne varietur* that a salary of 70,000 francs has been deposited and that three withdrawals of 10,000 each have been honoured.[156] To claim, on the other hand, that one possesses

---

[154] Cf. G. Durandin (138) who, in addition, emphasizes the relative rarity of the utilitarian lie.

[155] Berze (51), p. 22: 'Bildung von Nebenreihen neben der Hauptreihe im Denken.' The spatializing function expressed in the word 'neben' (non-organized juxtaposition) is, as one can see, common both to morbid rationalism and the lie.

[156] Obviously I can say truthfully that I have 40,000 francs in my

two million (in defiance of truth) presupposes a series of factitious antecedents which, since the moments of *true* temporality are 'filled' by acts, must be spatially juxtaposed. Furthermore, the absence of the *ne varietur* confers on this series of false antecedents a structure of a spatial type. In fact, the lie does not aim at revaluing the past by placing it in a wider historical totality. It retroactively modifies the very factitiousness of the elements of the past by going back over the course of time with an ease that space alone can offer. The spatio-temporal structure of the world of the lie is therefore analogous to that described in psychopathology by Honorio Delgado and to which I referred earlier.[157] The lie spatializes; spatial existence, for its part, with its possibilities of unlimited displacement in all directions, facilitates the lie. Furthermore, space favours aggression;[158] inversely, aggression spatializes and reifies.[159] Now, there exist obvious interrelations between the lie and aggression: in the psychology of social groups in particular, aggressive behaviour goes almost systematically hand in hand with a semi-conscious distortion of the truth about the object of aggression.

We therefore arrive at the following conclusion: lying behaviour is reifying, spatializing, devaluing and de-dialecticizing; in the lie 'one does not feel . . . the dialectical élan'.[160] But from the moment one considers the world of political alienation to be of a spatializing (schizophrenic) and sub-dialectical structure, the question of the place of the political lie in the causal chain of the process of ideologization conspicuously loses its importance. What I am saying in effect is that if the political lie involves a account and suggest the imaginary payment of a salary of 300,000 francs and a subsequent withdrawal, also imaginary, of 260,000 francs. I remain truthful because of two compensatory lies. But the difficulty is not resolved as such, for I must imagine 'alongside' my real employer, a fictitious employer and also the fictitious moment of the imaginary expenditure. Sooner or later, the liar must come out of concrete duration and juxtapose himself in it spatially (the '*nebeneinander*' of German theorists of schizophrenia).

[157] Cf. p. 84.
[158] Cf. Minkowski (337).
[159] Cf. Schilder (418), pp. 278–82.
[160] Jankélévitch (241), p. 39.

spatializing and reifying action,[161] reification of social consciousness creates for its part the necessary conditions for the effective
action of voluntary mystification. Thus abandonment to great
collective emotions of a non-dialectical structure in crowd
psychology naturally provides opportunities for voluntary mystification which operates in the same way. Nothing, however, proves
the *primacy* of conscious mystification in this causal chain.

The psychopathological approach to the problem of ideology
thus provides an argument in favour of the total concept. An
analogous observation could have been made earlier in connection with another problem: that of the place of the 'cauldron' in
the world of false consciousness. In their article[162] Meyerson and
Dambuyant are supported by examples drawn from the life of
the Palace, the domain *par excellence* for lucid utilitarian decisions. Their examples, taken from political life, seem also to
postulate a quite conscious wish to persuade. Here again, the
analogy with schizophrenic thought can serve as a guide.[163]
Among the mentally sick, elements of the 'cauldron' exist,
though they certainly are not found at the level of decisions, but
at the structural level. One can see therefore that any comparison
between ideology and psychosis has meaning only from the
viewpoint of the total conception of ideology. To the extent that
such a parallelism is valid, this idea is itself validated.

On the other hand, earlier considerations that there is a
correlation between notions of truth, dialectical structure (concrete totality) and valuing structure reappear. Truth is in some
way naturally dialectical, which does not prevent its *social*
expression, scientific truth, from often being dependent on legitimate, anti-dialectical abstraction in a given social context. However, one cannot say that truth *possesses* a certain value; it *is*
value; the axiological and dialectical dimensions are inseparable
from its essence. The aphasic, who is a prisoner of an over-

---

[161] We go along with the thesis developed by J. M. Domenach in
his article on the political lie (132) which, by the way, quotes in
this context my contribution *La Réification*, which appeared
sometime earlier in the same journal.

[162] Meyerson and Dambuyant (332), cf. earlier, pp. 108ff.

[163] Cf. earlier: the spatializing and dissociated character of the
world of the 'cauldron'.

coherent universe, and consequently incapable of lying, provides indirect proof of it, in exactly the same way as the analysis of the hysterical lie, which is dependent on the indifferentiation between the true and the false in a destructured world that has no real temporalization, and therefore axiologically empty.[164] Truth then becomes pure artificiality without the axiological dimension necessary to impose its primacy; the hysteric does not lie because he is instinctually forced into it but because he has no reason to tell the truth rather than a lie.

These lessons from the phenomenology of hysterical consciousness open up a way for the understanding of the individual psychodynamics of the mechanism of ideologization. I have recently witnessed the remarkable phenomenon of absurd theses being given a favourable reception by the public in advanced societies.[165] We can presume that the structure of the world peculiar to the man in a state of receptivity with regard to propaganda is similar to that of the hysterical universe: a destructured world in which the *axiological* resistance of truth having collapsed, nothing can withstand the action of propaganda.

Now, the process of ideologization goes hand in hand with a profound axiological transformation. In a world dominated by a 'privileged system' of powerful radiance, the 'consistency-precariousness' dialectic undergoes a process of dissociation ending, on the one hand, in consistent, but non-precarious 'value' ('social sacredness') and, on the other, in 'values' of pure precariousness (the idea of subordinate value, *Dienstwert*).[166] The artificialities that are not given value by the axiological proximity of the privileged system, do not accede to the level of experienced

---

[164] These developments are based on the ideas of L. Klages and P. C. Racamier interpreted in my own way. There are other interpretations, mainly concerning the instinctual nature of the hysterical lie. The choice here is a function of a criterion of coherence. On the other hand, this chapter postulates as a whole the theory of the hysteria-schizophrenia relationship as it has been upheld by Claude (105), Pavlov and others.

[165] By quoting as examples the Rosenberg trial and that of the 'White Shirts' I hope—perhaps vainly—to escape the criticism of partiality.

[166] The axiological polarization described in schizophrenia by Storch (435), p. 68. Cf. my contribution (172), p. 277.

truths as such; pseudo-acts, on the other hand, do accede to it due to a heteronomic valuation. Analogy with the clinical picture —particularly hysterical states—is necessary; this analogy does not explain the element of decision in political mystification (it hardly needs to be explained); but it does highlight the otherwise important problem of the mechanism of its acceptance. Once again it seems that mystification is effective only in conditions prepared by a polarization of the values of a given society (the 'displacement of the sacred' discussed by J. Monnerot). It is an epiphenomenon of the process of ideologization rather than its causal agent.

The 'crisis of truth' that it translates is inseparable from a crisis of values which is, in the last analysis, a crisis of the dialectic.[167] Ideologization is therefore a function of the profound structural modifications of social awareness, and not the superficial action of techniques of persuasion. Our socio-psychiatric location of the problem of ideology thus joins with that of social psychologists,[168] who by denying the omnipotence of 'crowd mentality' confirm, for their part, the total conception of ideology.

[167] The efficiency of Hitlerian mystification is inexplicable without the extraordinary crisis in values that Germany experienced after the First World War. This crisis of values is reflected in numerous works—and not minor ones—of literature at that time; let us quote at random *Berlin, Alexanderplatz* by Doblin; *Fabian* by Erich Kastner and even *l'Affaire Maurizius* by Wassermann. It is likely that the extreme precariousness of values (of *all* values) under inflation subsequently revived, as a reaction, a tendency to find refuge in the cult of a uniquely consistent 'value', whence the permeability of a people at a high cultural level to the worst of propaganda.

[168] Cf. Klineberg (259), p. 367. Propaganda could succeed 'only in certain conditions and in a state of pre-existing receptivity'. This pre-existing receptivity consists, according to what has just been said, of a state analogous to pseudology; devaluation through reification of consciousness.

III

The Dialectical Drama of Alienation (Schizophrenia)

'It may be that at the present time we accept the existence of too many primary symptoms; perhaps one day we shall succeed in reducing two or more of them (even all of them) to a single primary symptom that is currently unknown.'

Berze (51), p. 20.

For some time schizophrenia has been the object of growing interest, and occupies a special place among mental illnesses. For Bleuler, it is 'one of the major and most distressing enigmas of humanity';[1] for Berze, 'Nature's great experiment'; H. Ey considers it as 'the most authentic experience of man that separates him from other men'; according to C. Schneider, this illness is the expression of a constant in human nature that is revealed when it is isolated from its context. The idea of schizophrenization emphasizes its importance in cultural philosophy.

It is one of the rare entities of nosology where the debate about organogenesis and psychogenesis remains open, and this fact perhaps constitutes one dimension of its philosophical significance. It seems, in fact, that the schizophrenic disturbance occurs at the precise level of psychic involvement in the organism —at the junction of body and mind, as the Ancients would say. In this order of ideas the existence of schizophrenia perhaps offers as many solutions to the philosopher as it poses problems to the clinician.

[1] Bleuler (65 *bis*), p. 281.

On the other hand nothing is more striking than the observation that the very existence of an entity of this importance—or at any rate its unity—could be questioned. Thus Garcia Badarocco observes that 'in the extensive group of what is clinically called schizophrenia, one does not find constant pathogenic elements on which the notion of a nosological entity might rest'.[2] It is in the same spirit that many theorists (Kretschmer among others) likes to talk of 'schizophrenias'. By describing schizophrenia (along with psychasthenia) as a 'pathological and metapsychopathological myth', Leconte[3] certainly represents the extreme position on this issue. Yet, said Müller-Suur, 'despite *schizophrenias* one continues to talk of *schizophrenia*'. He would prefer to see it as a metaphysical problem. I shall strive to prove that the so-called metaphysical problem of the unity of schizophrenia is in reality a sociological problem close to that of the sociology of knowledge. The same applies to many other 'metaphysical' problems.

My position with regard to the general problem of alienation has led me to consider schizophrenic disturbance as an individual form of false consciousness, as deranged neostructuration being, for its part, an individual form of ideology. It is, therefore, an anti-dialectical form of existence both as consciousness, as structure of involvement in the world, and as logic. It is manifested on the existential level in the loss of the Subject-Object (Self-World) dialectic. The Self which no longer acts dialectically on its world is seemingly crushed by it; the 'World' (in reality Society) then appears as a supernatural power which assumes in certain cases a religious or, more precisely, a numinous appearance.[4]

On the logical level, reification appears as a characteristic anti-dialectical logic, which I have described elsewhere,[5] and, in the prevalence of the identificatory principle, which is an

---

[2] Garcia Badaracco in the *Encyclopédie*, p. 13.

[3] M. Leconte (293).

[4] As, for example, in Binswanger's case of S. Urban (62). Winkler is one of the authors who emphasizes most the importance of the 'Subject-Object' dialectic in schizophrenia (Winkler (472), p. 202; cf. also Balken (27), *passim*) who talks of the characteristic mode of *withdrawness of the self* (Ich-anachorese).

[5] Cf. my two publications (171), 1946 and (191), 1948.

anti-dialectical principle, the corollary of spatialization and de-valuation.

From this initial working hypothesis—the sociological origin of which I should emphasize once again—I shall try to 'deduce' the principal symptoms and principal explanatory theories of schizophrenia. H. Müller-Suur disputed the validity of any attempt of this kind: 'these different aspects of schizophrenic experience which are empirically verifiable data (*Sachverhalte*) make the reduction to a common denominator difficult; as for deducing them from each other or even reducing them to a single experience, it should not even be contemplated'.[6] This is a valuable reference since it provides an exact—though negative—definition of the very aim of my study: to show that a certain number of classical symptoms of schizophrenia are actually deducible from the hypothesis of an anti-dialectical structure of consciousness and existence, in the same way that a certain number of explanatory theories reflect the existence of such a structure. This is therefore a phenomenological method according to Minkowski's personal use of this term.[7] But the Marxist use of the concept of alienation requires the phenomenological method to be placed in a sociological perspective.

There are methodological advantages. By schematizing, we can discover three types of elements in the symptomatology of an illness: (a) elements due to nosological specificity; (b) elements dependent on personal specificity—Schneider's tertiary symptoms —and (c) elements depending on therapeutic action. Analytic treatment—like all consciously practised therapy—deals with individual elements (there is no science other than a general one, but there is no real treatment other than individual), which explains the fact that despite therapeutic successes, psycho-analysis has not yet provided a coherent theory of schizophrenia; the position of *Daseinsanalyse* is almost the opposite. In Seche-

[6] Müller-Suir (363), p. 11.
[7] Cf. Minkowski (347); Lacan (274), p. 133 (note), emphasizes the differences between the phenomenological method according to Husserl and Minkowski. I use the term throughout this study in Minkowski's sense without attempting to go further into the question of its relationship with Husserl's thought.

haye's cases—and even more clearly in Pankow's—one can easily distinguish the individual elements, the points of impact of therapeutic action, and the general elements: a space-time dialectic in Gisèle Pankow; a reification–dereification dialectic in Sechehaye. This dualism of formal elements and content constitutes a danger, and antinosologism is doubtless the expression of it. Exploiting the socio-psychiatric parallelism in the particular sense of a parallel sociological and psychiatric study of conditions of dialectical thought, may provide a valid means of evading this difficulty. In fact, collective existence erases individual differences. Consequently, the sociological study of the contents of subrealist consciousness (phenomenology of false consciousness) in relation to individual psychopathology is one aspect of the '$\grave{\epsilon}\pi\theta\chi\eta$' and may provide useful indications for determining the fundamental disorder. I indicated earlier that in one sense false consciousness represents a *purer* form of schizophrenia than clinical schizophrenia, precisely because of the elimination of the non-conceptualizable individual factor; certain straightforward empirical relationships on the clinical level, such as relationships between the structure of the Self-World dialectic and temporalization, assume a more obvious coherence on the sociological level.

The metaphysical problem that Müller-Suur[8] sees behind the existence of schizophrenia then comes down from the clouds and becomes a problem of sociology of knowledge (this is not the first time that this has happened in the history of ideas); i.e. a problem concerning the conditions of dialectical thought, which is common both to the study of ideologies, and research on the structure of schizophrenic consciousness. Finally let me point out that Müller-Suur talks about schizophrenic consciousness *or*

---

[8] Müller-Suur (363), p. 19, uses the term 'der Wahnsinn als metaphysischer Faktor des Schizophrenieproblems?' (though with a question mark). There must be, says Müller-Suur a kernel (*ein Kern*) which 'despite the existence of schizophrenias makes us continue to speak of schizophrenia'. My aim is to show that this kernel exists; it is the reificational act. Consequently, the metaphysical problem raised becomes a problem of sociology, a little like that of space and time in the perspective of Durkheimian sociologism.

existence.[9] Now, for a Marxist, the dialectical unity of the two is a condition of their analogies of structure, and if schizophrenic existence is characterized by a de-dialecticization of the relationships of the Self and the World, while schizophrenic consciousness operates by virtue of a pathological anti-dialectical logic, this is not the result of chance or pre-established harmony, but the expression of a law: 'it is the social existence of man which determines his consciousness' said Marx.

FUNDAMENTAL DISTURBANCE AND PRIMARY SYMPTOM

The whole issue rests on the problem of the 'fundamental disturbance'. The word *Grundstörung* involves, like most German psychiatric terms, several possible translations: the expression 'fundamental disturbance' is perhaps preferable to 'generative disturbance' for it does not suggest any ambition towards pathogeny. Certain people use it wrongly, as a synonym for primary symptom.[10] Berze[11] has very clearly posed the problem of the differences between them. The primary psychotic symptoms are verifiable in a direct way and differ from secondary symptoms only in the fact that it is not possible to trace them to other data. The 'fundamental disturbance' by contrast, is not demonstrable phenomenologically,[12] but one can draw conclusions about it from the total picture of the primary symptoms, and Berze emphasizes this particularly, by means of *analogical reasoning*. A psychosis may involve numerous primary symptoms having as a common basis a single and unique *Grundstörung*. This latter therefore has nothing in common with any kind of cardinal symptom. In fact, says Berze, 'the manner in which the

---

[9] Müller-Suur (363), p. 11.

[10] Cf. for example the Spanish work, which is otherwise excellent, by Cabaleiro-Goas (82), p. 150.

[11] Berze (51), pp. 4–5.

[12] 'Phenomenological' here, in the traditional psychiatric sense, without any connection with Husserl. In what follows, I am summarizing Berze's point of view, but as my translation is rather free, without quotation marks.

symptomatology of a psychosis is constituted never depends exclusively on the nature of the fundamental disturbance: the general psychological structure of the patient plays a constant role, particularly when the fundamental disturbance is not very pronounced. The intensity of a primary symptom also depends to a very large extent on the psychic constitution of the patient; because of the influence of this factor a particular primary symptom may dominate the clinical picture in certain cases whilst a different symptom may be dominant in others. Furthermore, the data of the "normal" psychic structure may qualitatively modify that of the primary symptoms to the point of making them unrecognizable.'[13] I shall show later that the concept of reification in psychopathology fits the definition that Berze gives of the fundamental disturbance. The hypothesis which considers primary disturbances as somatic manifestations and secondary disturbances as psychic manifestations, has not yet received any experimental confirmation.

The term reification was used in psychiatry for the first time to my knowledge by S. Schneider, who spoke of a 'reification of the states of our Self in external objects' (*Verdinglichung der Zustände unseres Ichs in Aussen-Objekten*)[14] and in a way this is very close to Wyrsch's conceptions. Schneider might have read *Histoire et Conscience de Classe*; but it is unlikely. Whatever it may be, the world of reification in Lukács constitutes a coherent whole which corresponds to one specific aspect of the general theory of alienation, which is not the case in Schneider. It is curious to note, however, that, returning to V. Domarus's idea, Berze and Schneider emphasize the preponderance of the identificatory function among schizophrenics: this conception which is, in short, that of a non-dialectical morbid logic, is central to the more recent research of Silvano Arieti.

---

[13] J. Berze (5), pp. 4–5.
[14] Schneider, quoted by Berze (51), p. 50.

ARIETI'S WORK

Still relatively unknown in France, S. Arieti is considered in the United States as a first-rate theorist on the problem of schizophrenia. He is close to the authors in the Kasanin anthology,[15] Goldstein particularly, whose hypothesis on the *over-concrete* nature of the thought of schizophrenics he adopts. Arieti is influenced by psychoanalysis, but without conforming to orthodoxy; he often quotes Piaget (whom he does not seem to know very deeply); finally, the logic that he notes among schizophrenics is essentially a reified, anti-dialectical logic. It is therefore the logic of false consciousness such as we described it earlier.

THE LAW OF VON DOMARUS-VIGOTSKY

Arieti refers to von Domarus who, in a short publication that appeared in 1925,[16] clearly seems to have been the first to use the principle of epistemological identification in the structural analysis of schizophrenic thought, and in a sense this is very close to Meyerson's ideas. Von Domarus distinguishes four functions: schematization, analogization, causalization and identification; these functions can exist among schizophrenics as among normal people without one being able to determine a precise line of separation. It follows, however, from the clinical example that this concerns a preponderance of the identificatory function over the structuring function.

[15] This work bears the title *Language and thought in schizophrenia*, with an introduction by J. S. Kasanin, and contains contributions by Sullivan, Goldstein, Cameron, J. D. Benjamin, S. J. Beck, Von Domarus and Angyal. I call it the 'Kasanin anthology' for reasons of convenience; the studies used for the editing of this thesis appear in the bibliography.
[16] Von Domarus (129 and 130). Arieti talks about von Domarus's law. The expression 'law of von Domarus-Vigotsky' seems to me to be fairer.

In a more recent work[17] von Domarus developed this idea. One of his patients believed that: 'Jesus = cigarette box = sex, for each one is "encircled": Jesus by a halo, the cigarette box by a band, and sex by the feminine body.' The nature of the encircled object and that of the encircling substance does not come in for consideration. According to Vigotsky 'the logician accepts the identity when it is based on the identity of the subjects; the paralogician when it is based on the identity of the predicates'. Roheim for his part notices 'a strong tendency to identify with other people or surrounding objects',[18] but the term 'identification' is used here in its psychoanalytic meaning. The question of the relationship existing between epistemological identification and psychoanalytic identification does not seem to have been raised clearly up to this point; its solution might offer a good approach to the enigma of schizophrenia. Yet the fact that these two forms of identification co-exist among schizophrenics constitutes in itself a valid experimental datum.[19] Here again schizophrenia appears as 'Nature's great experiment'. Furthermore, this dual aspect of identification[20] doubtless constitutes a point of convergence between Marxism and psychoanalysis.

The following example is given by Arieti: a normal man reasons according to the following syllogism: Every person born on the territory of the U.S.A. is an American citizen; John Doe was born in the United States: therefore J.D. is an American citizen. This is the classical syllogism of Aristotelian logic. A schizophrenic reasons according to the following model: 'The President of the United States must be American by birth (correct); John Doe is American by birth, therefore John Doe is

---

[17] Von Domarus (129), Kasanin anthology, p. 113.

[18] Roheim (405), p. 101, 'patient frequently identifies himself with his own persecutors'.

[19] The study of false consciousness involves an analogous lesson: coexistence of two phenomena, one an affective kind, the other a logical kind, i.e. identification with the leader (Freud (116), *passim*) and the anti-dialectical logic of false identities.

[20] That is to say, identification as kernel of an anti-dialectical logic in Marxism and identification as a formative factor in personality among psychoanalysts. But this observation raises a problem without claiming to resolve it.

President of the United States.'[21] This is the model for what Arieti calls the *paleological syllogism*, according to the law of von Domarus-Vigotsky. Through analogous reasoning a patient 'identifies' his father and the doctor (two people that are agents of authority);[22] another patient considers all the other patients as being really her sisters.[23] These 'identifications' naturally possess a psychoanalytic dimension, but the two perspectives can be complementary. Sometimes the principles of von Domarus-Vigotsky find a partial application: in these cases the identity of the predicates is translated through a partial identity of subjects; a man with the qualities of a horse is visualized as having the traits of a centaur. The frequency of these condensations and distortions in the drawings of schizophrenics is well known. A (non-deranged) autistic schizoid earlier had had a romantic attachment to a blonde named Lilian: henceforth blonde = Lilian. The validity of this principle would extend to primitive mentality (this is not the place to examine the validity of this hypothesis or the question of its relationship to the law of participation), and to *dreams*, another point of convergence with Freudianism. 'From the formal point of view all Freudian symbolism is based on the principle of von Domarus.'[24] The dream, being atemporal and in a sense spatializing and anti-

---

[21] This example can be interpreted as the manifestation of a particular form of de-dialecticization; a loss of the dialectic of the possible and the impossible, analogous to that noticed by Tosquelles (448). The transition is lost between 'John Doe, *possible* president of the United States' and 'John Doe, *real* president'. The schizophrenic does not understand the axiological privilege of existence in relation to non-existence (the 'partiality of existence' of which Le Senne talks), just as the hysteric does not understand the privilege of the true in relation to the false (the theme of pseudology).

[22] Arieti (14), p. 327.

[23] Arieti (11), p. 293.

[24] Arieti (14), p. 328. 'The same principle of von Domarus is applied in dreams. Freud has demonstrated that a person or object A, having a certain characteristic of B, may appear in the dream as being B or a composite of A and N. In the first case there is identification; in the second, composition. *The whole field of Freudian symbolism is based, from a formal point of view, on von Domarus's principle.*' (My italics.)

dialectical,[25] involves therefore a disengagement of *praxis*: 'To dream is to be disinterested', said Bergson. The preponderance of anti-dialectical identificatory logical structures thus enters into this context in a coherent way.[26]

Among profoundly regressed patients 'not only the ideas capable of being associated through similarity but also those associated through contiguity, are no longer associated but *paleologically identified*.[27] A hebephrenic on being asked about the person who was the first president of the United States, replied 'it is the White House'. In certain cases, with the development of the identificatory tendency, words come to represent increasingly wider contexts, to the point where impoverished language is reduced to a small number of stereotyped expressions. According to Sullivan, the verbal stereotype would be essentially 'a rather impractical concentration of meanings in a word'.[28]

This is therefore one aspect of the reification of language, an analogy of which is to be found in 'the language of politics' studied particularly by Laswell.[29]

These are the main points in S. Arieti's conception. He has demonstrated an anti-dialectical element in the logic of schizophrenics: egocentric identification. In fact, to base identification on the identity of predicates is to identify in an egocentric way. I have tried to demonstrate the same phenomenon in the logical structure of ideologies. In this sense it is permissible to say that in a general way ideology is dependent on a collective paleology.

---

[25] Mayer-Gross (quoted by Fischer) (158), p. 245, sees a law in this spatio-temporal balance.

[26] The analogies between schizophrenia and dream are classic. Jung (247) said that all that is required is to let a dreaming man walk as if he was awake to have a picture of *dementia praecox*. C. Schneider (422) sees analogies especially with the thought of a man in the process of dropping off to sleep or with 'tired thought' (*Müdigkeitsdenken*). Whatever it may be, it is obvious that these diverse theories are not contradictory with my interpretation of schizophrenia as anti-dialectical consciousness; rather they confirm it.

[27] Arieti (12), p. 260.

[28] H. St. Sullivan (438), quoted by Arieti.

[29] Cf. Lasswell (287); Stuart-Chase (101).

I

G. PANKOW'S CONCEPTION

G. Pankow's work[30] represents a synthesis of the phenomeno-logical and psychoanalytic points of view, a synthesis which in this form responds practically to the requirements of a 'dynamic phenomenology' such as Winkler defined it.[31] The therapeutic act consists essentially of a reconstruction of the concrete totality of the person, going hand in hand with the therapeutic temporaliza-tion of existence that is imprisoned by pure spatiality. This dynamic ensemble has as a corollary an awareness of sexuality; it is by entering into a structured, temporalized (dialectical) existence that these two patients really become women. The con-vergence with themes of sexual reification is obvious; for Caruso, sexual *pathology* is essentially reification; for Pankow, *normal* sexuality is dialectically both instrument and product of tempor-alizing dereification. This work (like that of Szondi before) reflects one aspect of the dialectical potentialities of analytical concep-tions. From this perspective the therapeutic act of the psycho-analyst appears as a real *disalienation* (dialecticization) in the Marxist sense of the term.

A patient 'spontaneously recognizes the spatializing character of his perception of the world'.[32] The essence of the analyst's effort consists of 'reunifying the dynamism of the body in such a way that the body perceives itself as desirable, and thus redis-covers its image and enters into the domain of time'.[33] Suzanne believes that her body is divided into two parts (left part com-munist, right part catholic); as there is only coexistence with no organic bond between these two parts, so, likewise, the patient's own world is divided into 'parts without a bond between them'.[34] From then on the treatment consists essentially of 'dialecticizing'

---

[30] Pankow (376).

[31] Cf. Winkler (471), p. 194, who describes as 'static phenomen-ology', 'phenomenology of fixed existence' (*Phänomenologie des Gewordenen*) the method of Jaspers, K. Schneider, Gruhle, and even Binswanger (ibid., p. 195); cf. also Lanteri-Laura (286).

[32] Pankow (376), p. 19.   [33] Pankow (376), p. 17.

[34] Pankow (376), p. 19.

(the term is mine) this fragmented world; therapeutic temporalization, contemporaneous with an awareness of sexuality seems to be dialectically both instrument and result of this effort. In fact, the structuration of the body itself, that is to say the recognition of the bonds of interaction between the parts that are originally spatially juxtaposed presupposes a relatively advanced degree of the formation of the notion of time. The reciprocal relationship of the parts is nothing more than 'the exchange of one concrete representation for another concrete representation, an exchange which is none other than time itself. As the patient is incapable of recognizing this reciprocal relationship between the parts, the notion of time can not be elaborated and the patient enters another stage of dissociation.'[35] After six months of analysis, Suzanne succeeded in 'locating her femininity in her historical time'; the introduction of time did not take long to complete 'the alienated Oedipean position in space in order to give her her real introduction into time'.[36]

All of this is typical. This is an example of a work which incorporates Minkowskian data[37] about the spatio-temporal structure of schizophrenic consciousness into a perspective of active psychotherapy, and this 'dynamic phenomenology' is of a kind that would satisfy Marxist requirements completely. I should add that Pankow refers to Matussek, as an author who is rather far removed from Freudianism,[38] but whose conception of deranged perception involves some reificational elements, as I shall show later.

DASEINSANALYSE AND MARXISM

It is not possible to summarize in a few pages a work of this importance, but I can try to pinpoint some of the essential elements for my subject.

[35] Pankow (376), p. 19. The analogy with Piaget's thought is striking.   [36] Pankow (376), p. 45.

[37] It is curious that in the French edition of this work, Minkowski's name is not mentioned.

[38] Cf. Matussek (324), published on the occasion of Freud's centenary.

(a) *Daseinsanalyse*[39] is often (more often than one would be tempted to believe) a *concrete analysis of the social conditions of mental illness.*

In S. Urban's case[40] the fact of being Jewish—*socially* and not *racially* Jewish—plays a concrete pathogenic role, particularly through its traditionalist conception of the family, which does not fit in with the otherwise modern style of life of this cultured woman. Another patient (J. Zünd)—under the influence of quite real social failures—wanted *to reverse the course of time,*[41] which ended in an actual reification of the *Dasein* and, in the event, of his being crushed by the world.[42] It is interesting to point out the paradoxical position of the *Daseinsanalyse*, which does not rely on historical materialism, but does commend concrete sociological explanations, in comparison with the Pavlovian

[39] To justify the preservation of the German term, I rely on the authority of Binswanger who is sceptical about different translations. For the same reason, I am keeping the word *Dasein*; the translation by 'presence' (J. Verdeaux) is very open to criticism. By contrast, it is impossible to avoid the translation of 'daseinsanalytisch' by *analytico-existential* as the only means of avoiding a paraphrase. Cf. Binswanger (57).

[40] Binswanger (62). Cf. my review in *Année Sociologique* (169 *bis*).

[41] Binswanger (60), p. 31; the same wish to reverse time (S. Urban (62), p. 31 French edition). For J. Zünd the reversal of the course of time possessed the significance of an existential reversal (*existentielle Umkehr*); a reversal of the direction (the French word 'sens' is more significant than 'Sinn') of life ('Verkehrung des Sinnes des Lebens" (ibid.). In his analytical interpretation of Lewis Carroll and his work, Schilder points out that time sometimes stops and sometimes begins to go in the opposite direction.

[42] The analysis of the social origins of the pathological temporalization of J. Zünd is only one of the many aspect of what we call the 'blatant sociologism' of existential analysis. In the 'Mary case' [(63) and later p. 199] the patient lives in two worlds with a different temporalization; these two worlds correspond to two different *social* existences that the patient has not succeeded in synchronizing. Cf. also the 'Erika case' of Boss (74) and page 133.

A dialectical position consistent with the problems has thus led existential analysis towards a sociologism that is very close to Marxism; inversely the anti-dialectical starting point of Pavlovism leads it to obscure the concrete social component of the psychopathological fact.

psychiatrists who appeal to Marxism, but for whom the sociological analysis of the involvement of the sick person in the world
practically never goes beyond the stage of generalities.

(b) *The category of totality* plays a primordial role in the
analysis of the Binswanger School. Binswanger himself emphasizes the similarities of his thought to those of Goldstein[43] and von
Weizsäcker; [44] for his part Conrad describes existential analysis
as *'Gestaltanalyse des Daseins'*.[45] In the first part of the present
study I emphasized the links which unite the dialectic of the
totality to Marxist sociologism which is called—rather inappropri-
ately—historical *materialism*. The structure of Binswangerian
thought confirms the existence of these links.

In the clinical analysis of the Binswanger School, we find as
common elements:

(c) The notion of a loss of the Subject-Object dialectic (Self-
World), otherwise known as praxis. The subject-object identification that is discussed by Roheim,[46] among others, is one aspect of
this loss; it is a technique to evade encounter: an attitude of
defeat and—like all anti-dialectical attitudes—a loss of liberty.[47]
Winkler, for his part, emphasizes the importance of what one
might describe as a crisis in the dialectic of Subject-Object
relationships.[48] The four defence mechanisms that he distinguishes: inversion, Subject-Object reversal,[49] mythization and
withdrawness of the Self, depend essentially on a reified psychology, and the phenomenon of withdrawness is the most important
of these. One is 'Self' (*Selbst*) only in a dialectical-axiological relationship with the *Mitwelt*; personality is a dialectical conquest.
'Circumstances must be humanly formed,' said Marx.

(d) *The description of phenomena of authentic reification,*

---

[43] Binswanger (64), p. 219.   [44] Cf. Binswanger (64), p. 218.
[45] Conrad (114), p. 505.   [46] Roheim (405), p. 210.
[47] Identification with the enemy is the worst form of depersonalization [cf. Thomson (446)]; it is the loss of freedom to be oneself.
[48] Winkler (472); the expression 'dialectic' is mine, but it has the
same meaning in Winkler.
[49] Cf. Winkler (472), pp. 199–200; this subject-object inversion
must, in Winkler's mind, be substituted for the notion of projection.
Cf. in Wyrsch (476), p. 30, a similar criticism of the notion of
projection.

corollaries of the loss of the Subject-Object dialectic. This reification involves—for Binswanger as in *Histoire et Conscience
de Classe*—two aspects: the loss of freedom with objectification of
the *Dasein*: this is the path of Jurg Zünd from the 'free Self to
the enslaved object' (*aus freiem Selbst zum unfreien Objekt*)[50] and
the crushing of the Dasein by a power alien to the Self;[51] the
'Dreadful' (*Das Schreckliche*) of Suzanne Urban. The Self sometimes reacts against this state of distress by means of actual
magical techniques[52] whose existence constitutes another point
of convergence with psychoanalysis.

(e) *Mundanization.* The translation of the term '*Verweltlichung*' poses certain problems. Binswanger gives several definitions which are not completely interchangeable: 'progressive
retreat from freedom of the Self and its crushing by intraworldly
necessities or processes';[53] 'the act of being sucked in by the
world'.[54] In the Suzanne Urban case, the generality of the phenomenon is emphasized in her relationship to a passionate logic:
'everywhere that the *Dasein* is alienated in an exclusive projection
of the world, even if it is in the form of an overwhelming
passion, which consequently involves a momentary limitation of
her liberty, we are witnessing her "unlimited mundanization"'.[55]

[50] Cf. (60), p. 22 and (61), p. 55; it is a question of 'Versteiner-
ung des Daseins' but these examples can be multiplied infinitely, for
Binswanger has a slight tendency to repeat himself.

[51] Cf. Binswanger (61), p. 74: 'This is possible because spatialization is here of a magical order, i.e. because it no longer depends
primarily on existence and comprehension but on a state of
abandonment and dependence [*Verfallenheit und Ausgeliefertsein*]
on a power alien to the *Dasein*.' The connection with Lukács is
obvious [cf. (309), p. 141], where Lukács uses the term 'fatalist necessity alien to man' (*menschenfremde und menschenferne fatalistische
Notwendigkeit*).   [52] The 'magical techniques' of Lola Voss.

[53] Cf. Binswanger, *Archives Suisses*, 1946, facs. 1, 2nd publication, p. 34.

[54] 'Aufgesogenheit der Existenz von der Welt'; ibid., Binswanger,
p. 55; 'Verweltlichung = Verausserlichung des Schicksals (exteriorization of destiny)'. This is still the Lukácsian theme; man no longer
dialectically forges his future, but passively submits to his fate
(unless he reacts *magically* like Lola Voss).

[55] 'Ueberall, wo das Dasein sich einem einzigen Weltentwurf
verschreibt, und sei es nur in der Form einer es überwältigenden

In short, the question of mundanization is, for Binswanger, related to that of the anthropological problem of life-order as Heidegger envisaged it on the philosophical level, and on the psychopathological level by Minkowski,[56] Zutt and Kulenkampff, and is one aspect, which I shall demonstrate later, of the Marxist-Lukácsian concept of alienation as a phenomenon of reification. Clinical facts such as the 'loss of the limits of the Self and the World' can be interpreted as attenuated forms of mundanization. The same applies to the *flight of ideas*, the real basic disturbance in schizophrenia for G. Schneider,[57] or the reciprocal phenomenon of the 'feeling of omnipotence' which, in translating the permeability of the *Dasein* through loss of the limits of the Self, is integrated into the general theory of a non-dialectical and non-historical involvement of existence in the world, which at the same time is an involvement in a position of defeat.[58]

Finally, phenomena of pathological *temporalization, spatialization* and *personalization* (*Zeitigung, Räumlichung und Selbstigung*). An overall view of these ideas, especially in their relationships with the structures described by Minkowski in 1927 will be outlined later. By linking the state of being crushed by the world to phenomena of sub-temporalization, sub-spatialization, and sub-personalization, *Daseinsanalyse* offers an actual pathogeny; in fact, the dialectical-axiological structure of existence constitutes

Leidenschaft, einer vorübergehenden Einschränkung seiner Freiheit also wohnen wir dem Schauspiel einer ins unendliche gehenden "Verweltlichung" des Daseins bei.' Binswanger (62), p. 94. Subsequently, it is a question of Jahweh, God of vengeance. It is, translated into existential language, a description of the spatialization of the world of false consciousness.

[56] Minkowski (337); Zutt (485); Kulenkampff (271).

[57] C. Schneider (422), p. 85 and *passim* considers the flight of ideas as the real basic disturbance in schizophrenia. But one can deduce the flight of ideas from spatialization and mundanization (disappearance of 'the axio-dialectical part' of the person: loss of limits), and consequently from the dialectical loss of being (reification) and, through the intervention of this latter, a link with morbid rationalism can be established.

[58] Cf. later the notion of 'loss of the upright position' (*Standverlust*) of Kulenkampff (268).

a barrier against the onset of derangement; 'what guarantees the healthy man against derangement or hallucination, is not his critical faculty, but the structure of his space', wrote Merleau-Ponty.[59]

The *Daseinsanalyse* is, all things considered, infinitely more close to open Marxism than its supporters imagine. In its essential themes, it is indirectly dependent on *Histoire et Conscience de Classe*.[60] It is not only the 'poetry of psychiatry' as J. J. Lopez-Ibor[61] said in an ambiguous compliment, but also a sociologism in which the notion of *Mitwelt* expresses the dialectical unity (concrete totality) of society and its members, that of *Dasein* corresponding more or less to the notion of social existence of man. There are other things in *Daseinsanalyse* and I do not claim to have summarized here its classic, most impressive cases. But there is one sociologizing-dialectical aspect of Binswanger's thought which I must discuss, for it confirms the point of view of this work, and also because it is generally misunderstood.

[59] Cf. Merleau-Ponty (330), p. 337: except that it is the presence of axiological and dialectical temporal elements which protect the *Dasein* against the irruption of the spatiality that carries possibilities of derangement. In social psychology, the temporalizing praxis protects class consciousness against the spatializing factor of *false consciousness*. Inversely, for reified consciousness, the irruption of the dialectic inherent in existence (temporal contamination of deranged spatialization) is experienced as *catastrophic* ('fantasies about the end of the World') in clinical terms. Cf. later, pp. 288 ff.

[60] Through the intervention of the influence that Lukács's work must have had on Heidegger; cf. in this connection Goldmann (199), appendix.

[61] Lopez-Ibor, quoted by Cabaleiro-Goas (82), p. 241.

JACOB WYRSCH'S CONCEPTION

By emphasizing the importance of the *objectivation of the psychotic experience*[62] among paranoids, J. Wyrsch places himself close to Lukács's thought as shown in the terminology used ('Vergegenständlichung' in Wyrsch, 'Verdinglichung' in Lukács). H. Ey emphasizes—not without reservation[63]—his similarities with the thought of Binswanger, Gebsattel and Strauss, but Wyrsch's work also evokes older resonances such as, for example, the work of D. Lagache on paranoid hallucinations[64] or that of C. Schneider and J. Berze, who talk not of *objectivation* but rather of *reification*. In the same realm of ideas, Hoskins spoke of *externalization of consciousness*.[65] In short, the element that is closest to the fundamental disturbance in the clinical picture of schizophrenia would be, first of all, the hallucinatory act; any schizophrenia would be more or less hallucinatory for Wyrsch, just as any schizophrenic would be catatonic for Perez-Villamil,[66] depersonalized for P. Balvet and deranged for H. Ey. It is in the same spirit that I believe that as an expression of reification of consciousness, all schizophrenia is *to a certain extent, morbid rationalism*. These theories of the type 'all schizophrenia is . . .' are significant, for they emphasize (beyond the intention of their authors perhaps) an objective convergence which suggests the view that—to borrow H. Müller-Suur's expression—'despite the existence of schizophrenias, one continues to talk about schizophrenia'.[67] Seen in the perspective of Wyrsch's conception the essential question is not to know why certain schizophrenics hallucinate, but to know how the 'hallucinatory mode of being' can, in certain cases, *not be accompanied* by sensory hallucinations.

[62] J. Wyrsch (476); H. Ey (146).
[63] H. Ey (146), p. 182.
[64] D. Lagache (279) (the notion of the *alienation* of the spoken word).
[65] Hoskins (233), p. 87.
[66] J. Perez-Villamil (384).
[67] Müller-Suur (363), p. 13.

I have just reviewed four theories of schizophrenia without counting Minkowski's, which it is not worth summarizing here. From the data deriving from individual psychological structures, data which inevitably have an effect on the respective theoretical expressions (and more so in therapeutic cases), it is clear that one element is common to all these conceptions, and this common denominator is the notion of reified consciousness. Arieti and the authors on whom he relies have outlined the epistemological side of reified existence (morbid epistemology based on a prevalence of the identificatory principle); the *Daseinanalyse* school particularly has seen the existential aspect, i.e. the particular structure of involvement in the world which, for Marxists, corresponds to a loss of 'praxis'. The concept of reification assures the unity of these different conceptions, a unity which would not otherwise be apparent. On the other hand, the brief analysis of G. Pankow's work (like that to be attempted later of M. A. Sechehaye's work) shows that there is a possible convergence between phenomenological psychiatry and psychoanalysis, and that reification is the nexus of this convergence.

Does such an observation possess any practical value whatsoever? I think so, for the same reason that the unity of schizophrenia (its very reality) can and has been effectively brought into doubt. A unificatory hypothesis tending to prove that the plurality of explanatory theories does not necessarily correspond to a nosological plurality, may constitute a certain progress. To the extent that it is possible to establish that the various symptoms of schizophrenia are aspects of non-dialectical existence in the world, it becomes useless and illogical to continue to speak of *schizophrenias*.

IDEOLOGICAL THOUGHT AND SCHIZOPHRENIC THOUGHT

Arieti notes that among schizophrenics the identity of predicates is sufficient to release the identificatory mechanisms, in other words, that the schizophrenic, who is quicker to identify than the normal, uses a less dialectical logic.

I made a similar observation almost at the same time as Arieti —without knowing his work—based on the analysis of an objective psychiatric document: the F. K. thesis.[68] My work was based on very different documentation from Arieti's, documentation mainly about the problem of derealist thought in ideologies. It seemed to me that the category of dialectical thought, a critical category of false consciousness in the hands of Marxist theorists of ideology, could be used in the critique of paranoid deranged thought, anti-dialectical thought *par excellence*, and therefore an individual homologue of false consciousness. In this perspective, it would not be so much a question of identification based on the identity of predicates, as Arieti postulates, as of the liberation of a subjacent identificatory-spatializing function following on the disappearance of the more recently acquired dialectical structures, all of which is very close to the conceptions of organo-dynamism. The difference between Arieti's hypothesis and mine is that the latter tends to be integrated into a general philosophy of structure of which the theory of alienation of Lukács, the philosopher of totality, is one aspect. The establishment of links with a psychopathology of axiogenic structures as, for example, that of A. Hesnard, proves to be easy. This methodological advantage is due to the *sociological* starting point of the present study.

However, this contrast has nothing absolute about it. In fact, identification based on the identity of predicates such as Arieti described it, is an egocentric identification, the choice of the special predicate being dependent on unpredictable subjective criteria. It is, furthermore, one aspect of the autistic nature of schizophrenic thought. I have described a similar phenomenon in political psychology: false identification which is an anti-dialectical, sociocentric identification. Sociocentrism dissociates concrete totalities and creates others, artificial ones, as a function of its pragmatic needs; furthermore, its dichotomizing tendency favours the anti-dialectical identification of the various elements

---

[68] Cf. (183), 1949 and (171), 1946. S. Arieti's first publications concerning the logical structure of schizophrenic thought date from 1949, but he certainly did not know my work (171) which appeared in Spanish.

of the *outgroup*. In its turn the presence of this element of anti-dialectical identification is one factor of spatialization of political duration; in this way, it is an agent of schizophrenization. Furthermore, Arieti, who is little interested in the sociological problem of false consciousness, nevertheless provides a significant example by emphasizing the *autistic* nature of racial prejudice.

DERANGED THOUGHT AND PALEOLOGICAL THOUGHT

We shall come later to the problem of deranged perceptions as considered by P. Matussek among others. Pankow refers particularly to Mattussek[69] who, for his part, is strongly influenced by *Daseinsanalyse*. I have been able to use Matussek's work in the analysis of an act of false consciousness: the deranged (reified) perception of the political adversary;[70] the fact that a work on the perception of paranoids can find a sociological application of this order is characteristic of the schizophrenic structure of political consciousness. I have not been able to draw on any direct interaction between Arieti and Matussek. Probably neither of the two authors knows the work of the other, but it is possible to reduce them to a common denominator; doing this, we should be able to provide a subsequent overall view of the theories of deranged perception.

Matussek maintains that the deranged perception of paranoids is characterized by the predominance of the perception of essential properties (*Wesenseigenschaften*) with dissociation of the significant totalities of perception. The result would be (Matussek emphasizes this expressly in his conclusions),[71] that at the basis of the identity of essential properties, two otherwise different elements can be identified through these patients, which particularly characterizes their symbolic experience.

Now, this notion of 'essential property' borrowed from Klages and Metzger is equivocal; I shall show later that this concerns elements of a reified perception based on the illegitimate identi-

[69] Pankow (376).   [70] Cf. (172).
[71] Matussek (322), p. 318.

fication of predicates chosen in an egocentric fashion, in other words, of perceptual structures located on the continuum provided by the law of von Domarus-Vigotsky. For further details, I shall return to my cited work as well as to later developments. Seen in this perspective, the essential difference between the conceptions of Matussek and Arieti resides in the fact that, for Matussek, illegitimate identification is a consequence, whilst for Arieti it is a cause. The schizophrenic, according to Arieti, does not identify because he has a particular sensitivity (*Feinfühligkeit*) for essences, rather it is because he identifies egocentrically that he elaborates artificial essences, products of a deranged abstraction. An 'idealist' element of the notion of *essential property* is thus eliminated and a bridge established between the anti-dialectical reificational structure of the logic of schizophrenics and their paranoid experience. I shall return to this question.[72]

REIFICATION IN EXPLANATORY
THEORIES OF SCHIZOPHRENIA[73]

In the preceding pages I have considered certain explanatory theories in rather an arbitrary manner. In actual fact, most publications on schizophrenia in general or individual cases include in one form or another the description of phenomena of objectivation or reification.

Dément (125) devotes one study to the problem of schizophrenics' dreams and establishes that they contain above all 'isolated, inanimated objects . . .' ('about half of chronic schizophrenics frequently reported dreams of isolated, inanimated objects apparently hanging in space with no overt action whatsoever').[74] What is most curious perhaps is that these are

---

[72] In short, for the role of identification in the experience of schizophrenics, Arieti's point of view (which is mine) is the result of a 'setting upright' (*Umstülpung*).

[73] The reading of this 'excursus' is not necessary for the comprehension of subsequent chapters.

[74] H. Faure (150).

secondary conclusions. H. Faure talks of an 'object derangement in relation to a patient who believed that little children are manufactured'. Mental illness, for H. Faure, is 'one of the most total attitudes of enslavement by objects'. H. Ey discusses 'the transformation of the living into an object'[75] and notes that in derangement 'man becomes more like a machine'.[76] The anti-dialectical nature of schizophrenic language—which implicitly underlies the research of Katan[77] and Roheim[78]—has recently been emphasized by J. Lacan.

In Minkowski's work, the reificational elements proper are more numerous in *Le Temps Vécu* and in his recent articles, whilst *Schizophrénie* is based mainly on the category of spatialization. This difference is certainly related to the evolution which brought Minkowski close to existential analysis.

The reifying function of the book possesses a well-known psychopathological dimension. Amongst the works dealing with this question I shall quote R. Held's article,[79] one by G. Tourney and D. J. Plazak[80] and, finally C. Kulenkampff's contribution, which has as its epigraph a quotation from *Huis-Clos*: 'Hell is other people.' The relationships between Sartre's ideas and reification—an obvious relationship, but discussion of it would take us outside the framework of this work—are more apparent in psycho-pathological applications than in the text; C. Kulenkampff's study is so characteristic that the translator can easily become complacent about the terminology. In fact, to translate

[75] H. Ey in *l'Encyclopédie* (37282 A.20, p. 10) where he discusses the question of 'links that are metamorphosized into objects and regression towards the "object" world.' This is pure reification but the word 'object' is used in the opposite sense; the question of connections between reification and the object relationship (similar to the connections between epistemological identification and analytic identification or between libido and value) is particularly complicated.

[76] Ey (148), *passim*; but when Ey compares the 'machinism' of surrealists and schizophrenics (p. 51) he forgets that this machinism *expresses* the reification of the world peculiar to schizophrenics whilst in surrealist production it essentially has the significance of a *protestation* against social reification.

[77] Katan (253). [78] Roheim (405).
[79] R. Held (218). [80] Tourney and Plazak (450).

'existentieller Erstarrungsprozess'[81] by *process of reification* would be permissible everywhere except in a thesis aiming to show the generality of the reificational element in the psychopathology of schizophrenia. The paranoid manifests a break in the *dialectic* between the 'seeing-reifying' and the 'seen-reified' mode of being-in-the-world (the use of the term reification is obviously mine), a dialectic which like all dialectics is a sign of freedom. It is, further-more, only one aspect of the Self-World (subject-object) dialectic or the Having-Being dialectic. The paranoid 'is seen by the other'; he is in the position of a Being that is seen or 'inhibited and solidified'. 'Being solidified as an object under the gaze of others', he is from then on unable to use his 'being for others' with a view to his own liberation as a project in the framework of his personal possibilities.[82] His mode of existence in the world is marked by a process typical of existential solidification due to the fixation of the patient in the position of a constantly observed being,[83] a situation which corresponds to the phenomenon of 'loss of the upright position'. The fundamental anthropological dis-turbance of the paranoid attack is that 'the world as a whole is transformed for the patient'; it assumes a pathological form of 'being for others', 'a morbid way of seeing things';[84] in this world, the patient is 'always looked at by someone, solidified (reified) in the position of a person under observation'.[85] It is easy to deduce from this the *syndrome of influence* which in this perspective appears as a phenomenon of reification.[86] In fact, loss of the

[81] (270), p. 6.
[82] 'So je von den anderen erblickt, ist er in seinem Erblicktsein gefesselt, estarrt, festgebannt. Als ein unter dem Blick der Anderen zum Gegenstand für die Anderen Erstarrter, vermag sich der Kranke nicht mehr wie der Gesunde aus seinem Für-Andere-Sein zum Entwerfen in eigene Möglichkeit zu befreien.' Kulenkampff (270), p. 6.
[83] Kulenkampff (270), p. 6.
[84] *Ein pathologischer Blickcharacter.*
[85] Kulenkampff (270), p. 8.
[86] Cf. Kulenkampff (270), p. 8: 'First of all one experiences the look of others as something which is watching us ... then it goes through walls which, for the normal person, signify protection against strangers. From this moment on, the look reaches the patient in his most private places. Finally, the world of thoughts is opened

upright position, loss of liberty, and reification are corollary phenomena;[87] it is in this sense that the psychopathology of sub-realist states (and not the whole of psychology) is a *pathology of freedom* (H. Ey). The sick person becomes the servant of others, a part of the other (*Der Andere für den ich Gegenstand bin ist meine Freiheit . . . Ich bin ein Teil von ihm*).[88] In the world of reification 'man becomes a part of the machine' (Marx).

Such a study opens up numerous avenues. In its origins it is attached to Binswanger and Zutt. The psychopathological importance of the 'life-order' (*Wohnordnung*) has been emphasized by Zutt[89] and Minkowski.[90] It converges with the ideas of Baeyer[91] who sees in the loss of the function of encounter (*Buytendijk*) the fundamental disturbance of the paranoid attack; 'there remains for the sick person only one single possibility for encounter, that which he realizes under the gaze of others as an object without freedom'.[92] An anthropological interpretation of

up to the look of others; they know at any moment what is going on in his head and this penetration of the look (*Blickpenetranz*) does not respect any barrier; it in fact prevents the patient from being a person, i.e. a being delimited in relation to the environment. In this existence 'where the patient is irremediably reified as a uni-lateral object of the other's gaze' [(270), p. 7] the latter sees himself in the situation of a persecuted person, his world is a universe of persecution which asserts itself as proximity and gaze (cf. Merleau-Ponty (330), p. 337: objects 'no longer keep their distance'). One sees therefore that Kulenkampff's idea is a good common denominator. But it is difficult to deduce *morbid rationalism*, Arieti's *paleology*, the prevalence of identification, or even the phenomenon of dissociation from it; now, my reificational hypothesis takes account of all of these. It is therefore closer to the real *fundamental disturbance.*

[87] Kulenkampff (270), p. 8.
[88] Kulenkampff (270), p. 8.
[89] J. Zutt (485).
[90] Minkowski (337). But I think that the description of the syndrome of the loss of 'the function of the Me–Here–Now' [(340), p. 93] is the real forefather of present-day German research on the phenomenology of the 'life-order'. (*Wohnordnung*.)
[91] V. Baeyer (24).
[92] Cf. also Baeyer (24): 'Der Paranoide existier, soweit sein Wahnsinn reicht, gar nicht eigentlich unter Mitmenschen sondern unter "Gegenüber-Menschen"' (an almost untranslatable passage

the Oedipus complex is interesting to consider: 'King Oedipus, crushed by the weight of enormous guilt, tore out both his eyes. Was this a sign that from that day on he did not want to look but only to be looked at? In the hopeless situation of the man that others look through with their gaze, he became neither paranoid, nor overwhelmed (*überwältigt*); he assumed his tragic fate by expecting divine judgement.'[93] The reificational nature of these phenomena cannot be contested. Thus a bridge is established between the phenomenon of sexual reification and, beyond Lukács, Marx's thought.

THE NOTION OF INTERNAL ATTITUDE AND ZUTT'S RESEARCH

J. Zutt introduced into psychopathology, rather a long time ago, the concept of *internal attitude (innere Haltung)*.[94] The internal attitude is a totality: when someone decides to imitate an angry person, he does not analytically imitate his gestures, which would kill the imitation; he tries to 'put himself into the skin of the person', he takes on the internal attitude; the details flow automatically from this. In this case, the Self is in an almost contemplative attitude in the face of the automatism of the internal attitude.[95] This is Zutt's hypothesis: the 'fundamental disturbance' which is the basis of the specific symptomatology of schizophrenia, consists in a change in the relationship between the Self and the internal attitude. In reality, most of the phenomena discussed by Zutt follow from an actual reification of the internal attitude. From this fundamental disturbance, Zutt tries to 'deduce' (consistent with a constant aim in trans-Rhenane

'human counter-existence replaces human coexistence'). But coexistence is valuing and therefore temporalizing and dialectical; 'counter-existence' is by contrast devaluing and spatializing (cf. Minkowski (337), p. 180: 'In space men collide') and what comes out of Kulenkampff' study is that it is also reifying. At the basis of phenomenological description, one again finds the dialectical structure of existence in the world and the loss of this dialectic.

[93] (270), 456.　　　　　　　　[94] Zutt (483).
[95] Zutt (483), p. 56.

psychopathology), the essential elements of the clinical picture; this is somewhat similar to what I would like to do. Some of Zutt's deductions are obviously dated; others have kept their value.[96] This forgotten study anticipates the work of Wyrsch more than Binswanger; the Wyrsch-Lukács relationship seems to me to be undeniable.

When there is a break between the Self and the 'internal attitude', it is not the emotion alone which is separated from the Self and becomes independent, but the whole internal attitude to which the significance of the gesture remains attached.[97] A schizophrenic kneels down as if to pray. He does not know the significance of this gesture, and he experiences the impression of being 'someone who prays', but his Self is not participating at all. Wernicke uses the characteristic term 'impotent spectator'.[98]

---

[96] Cf. his 'deduction' of waxlike flexibility (483), p. 349.

[97] Zutt (483), p. 342: 'Verselbständigung der inneren Haltung'. In this order of ideas and by building upon my conception of the basic aphasic disturbance as the opposite of the basic schizophrenic disturbance it is arguable that one might define aphasia-apraxia as the inability to *separate* the Self from the internal attitude.

[98] Wernicke, quoted by Zutt (483), p. 341. But the term 'contemplative attitude' keeps reappearing in Lukács's work and designates the situation of the worker caught in the web of reification; there is no need to add that this 'contemplative attitude' is not a restful one, quite the contrary. 'Diese Willenslosigkeit steigert sich noch dadurch dass mit zunehmender Rationalisierung und Mechanisierung des Arbeitsprocesses die Tätigkeit des Arbeiters immer stärker ihren Tätigkeitscharakter verliert und zu einer kontemplativen Haltung wird.' (This absence of will is only accentuated by the fact that rationalization and mechanization of the work processes take away from the worker's activity its creative nature; it becomes a contemplative attitude.) (*Histoire et Conscience de Classe*, pp. 100–1.) The problem of knowing whether these lines written in 1922, still correspond to the situation of the worker in 1961 faced with the process of production, and whether the introduction of automation confirms or weakens Lukácsian thought, is outside my subject. These developments are characteristic of schizophrenic reification and this is the essential point. Elsewhere (*Histoire et Conscience de Classe*, p. 101), Lukács says that personality 'becomes a spectator in a strange context'; this time, it is the same expression that Wernicke and Zutt use which reappears.

Starting with this initial hypothesis, the deduction of a clinical fact such as the 'syndrome of influence' becomes possible.[99]

Now it follows from Zutt's developments that the action of the Self on the internal attitude is essentially dialectical or rather dialecticizing, in a sense which is very close to Lukács, i.e. *structuring* and *historicizing*. Zutt speaks of the synthetic function of the Self. Schizophrenia consists essentially of an incapacity of the Self to structure the internal attitude.[100] In order to appreciate the value of this data it is worth remembering the date that this work appeared (1929); at that time, they were not looking for the fundamental disturbance in schizophrenia, but the specific organic lesion which might eventually characterize it.

This conception naturally offers numerous points of contact with Minkowski's ideas. The schizophrenic separation between the Self and the internal attitude necessarily involves the spatio-temporal co-ordinates of existence (of the *Dasein*, one would say today). In fact it is the act of submitting to the world and no longer acting on it which determines the importance of the 'now'; a link is thus established between the fundamental disturbance according to Zutt and a syndrome which occupies a central place for Minkowski. In *Histoire et Conscience de Classe*, the loss of the Subject-Object dialectic, with the crushing of man by the product of his own activity, is translated also through the spatialization of duration. Zutt disapproves of Minkowski for considering the loss of vital contact as a sort of fundamental disturbance;[101] he quotes the opinion of a French critic of Minkowski's book: 'one does not lose vital contact in the way that one loses a handkerchief'. I think that this present work in some measure provides an answer to this objection.[102]

---

[99] Zutt (483), p. 347.

[100] Zutt (483), p. 343: 'Unfähigkeit des Ich gestaltend auf die innere Haltung einzuwirken.'

[101] Zutt (483), p. 354.

[102] By showing that the dialectical-valuing-personalizing attitude on which, after all, vital contact depends, is the result of a permanent conquest, that any deterioration of personality—including deteriorations of organic origin—can jeopardize.

REIFICATION IN THE STUDIES
OF M. A. SECHEHAYE

If a space-time dialectic forms the framework of Pankow's work, then it is a reification-dereification dialectic[103] which seems to pave the way towards the cure of Sechehaye's patient. Renée 'wants to halt the passage of time', 'to fix eternity'.[104] Moreover she considers change as immoral. Her morals are reified, she appeals to what used to be known some years ago as objective morality, a completely external moral code;[105] constant reference is made to Piaget's thought.

EXISTENTIALISM AND SCHIZOPHRENIA

This raises a problem of philosophical interest. In an article that appeared a decade ago,[106] L. Duss made the same observation about the 'Renée case' that Gebsattel had made about a deranged melancholic.[107] The patient spontaneously used the vocabulary of existential philosophy; 'an interesting example of what psychology and psychiatry can bring to the understanding of a philosophical work'.[108] This opens the way to 'a psychiatric *critique* of existentialism'; this is indeed the title of the article.

A specific question arises here, the importance of which Duss does not seem to have considered. Is it a *critique* or a *justification* of existential philosophy?

[103] I emphasize once more that the use of Lukács's terminology is peculiar to me; the Swiss psychoanalyst does not talk about reification.

[104] M. A. Sechehaye (425), p. 169.

[105] Cf. (425), p. 157, which points out the 'moral reaction' of the patient in relation to child psychology (heteronomic morality); ibid., p. 75, with reference to Piaget; ibid., p. 77, etc. This 'moral realism' is in reality a reified morality. Cf. the case of B... described by me (177), pp. 468–9 who displays a rather similar type of 'objective morality'.   [106] L. Duss (139).

[107] Von Gebsattel (190), and above, pp. 187 ff.

[108] Durandin (137).

S. Follin[109] very pertinently describes Gebsattel's article as an 'attempt at justifying existentialism', but then one must make a choice, for it is difficult to understand why the use of an existentialist terminology by a schizophrenic should signify condemnation of this school whilst its presence in the case study of a deranged melancholic would be its justification. Duss notes the appearance of existentialist terminology in particular stages of the illness, but without wondering if this phenomenon is a sign of illness or improvement; in a case marked by ups and downs, this is a problem that cannot be neglected. Durandin wonders 'if existentialism as a philosophical system is not, to a certain extent, an attempt at *over-compensation* for a feeling of personal inexistence'.[110] The context seems to justify this exegesis. In Gebsattel's case, in fact, the appearance of existentialist terminology clearly signifies the cure; now in these two interpretations (Gebsattel and Duss), we must look for a common denominator, for it is illogical to admit that the same phenomenon in psychopathology might justify existentialism in one case and condemn it in another. Without wanting to settle this question hastily, I confess that Gebsattel's interpretation appeals to me more. The Renée case then appears not as a *critique*, but rather as a *justification* of existentialism. Seen from this perspective, the philosophy of existence is not a *romantic rebellion against reason*[111] but a *dialectical reaction* against the phenomenon

---

[109] S. Follin (162), p. 212, who talks very critically of an '*attempt at justifying* Heideggerian existentialism'. The salient fact is correct, but the justification of existentialism is written within the frameworks of a splendid *dialectical* analysis (an imperfect summary of it is given earlier, p. 190); it is this convergence which is significant.

[110] Durandin (137), p. 72.

[111] Cf. B. Callieri (84), p. 3: 'Una romantica ribellione contre la ragione' and L. Duss (139), p. 557: 'Existentialism therefore is revealed as a fundamentally anti-intellectualist reaction.' Duss is located in the line of a certain Marxist critique of existentialism (and also Freudianism!) which specifically indicted a certain anti-intellectualist tendency. Cf. Lukács (311), *passim*; H. Mougin (357); several articles and works of H. Lefebvre, etc. Now a rather more detailed account of M. A. Sechehaye's case (and a parallel with Gebsattel's case L.B...) shows that it is more a question of a *morbid*

of schizophrenic depersonalization, devaluation and de-dialecticization that false consciousness is; not an *anti-intellectualist* but a *morbid anti-rationalist* reaction. In fact Sechehaye's patient goes through reificational phases symptomatologically close to morbid rationalism and 'existentialist' phases.[112]

To admit that these latter represent an *improvement*, permits us not only to eliminate an ambiguity but also to integrate *validly* an exceptional clinical case into the debate surrounding one of the intellectual problems of the day.

CATEGORY OF TOTALITY AND SCHIZOPHRENIA

The question of the role of structures in schizophrenia has often been studied. It is sufficient, therefore, to refer here to well-known works such as those of Zucker, L. Bender, Ey, Conrad[113] or Hesnard. I do not want to go into the details of this problem here. But we must consider, however briefly, a few points, the sum of which provides a starting-point for any dialectical account of the problem of schizophrenia.

(1) The category of the concrete totality is a dialectical category; it is by emphasizing its primordial importance that *Histoire et Conscience de Classe* is classified as the *dialectical work par excellence* of contemporary Marxism. This is, also the real key to the book's disfavour and not the officially invoked 'idealist' deviation. Now is not the time to go into this question which I have discussed in several articles.[114]

(2) Between the category of the totality and the theory of *Gestalt* there can be (and there are) secondary differences, but the principle is the same. This is so obvious that all discussion would be superfluous if this evidence—about the dialectical value

anti-rationalist (anti-reificational) reaction than of rebellion against reason. This places the problem of existentialism in a completely different perspective.

[112] Cf. Duss (139), pp. 572–3, 582, etc.
[113] K. Conrad (114).
[114] Cf. (170) and (179).

of the Gestalt—was not disputed, and specifically from the Marxist side.[115]

There exists in official Marxism a certain malaise surrounding the question of totality (as around any philosophical problem bearing either slightly or closely on the problem of alienation or false consciousness); and Gestaltism is entirely rejected as being *idealist* without the dialectical quality of this theory being able to attenuate this verdict.

Now, the reasons for this rejection are, from the scientific point of view, rather weak; furthermore, no overall discussion has been carried out from the Marxist side, except for R. Garaudy's work that I just mentioned.

Garaudy observes that 'the Gestalt sees only one side of things; it separates synthesis from analysis. And from then on the synthesis becomes inexplicable . . .'[116] 'The Gestalt floats in the void.' This argument is without significance; a synthesis is perhaps unexplained at a given moment, but it is not therefore *inexplicable*; this is simple statement of fact. The observation that two gases can, by combining, give rise to a liquid might have constituted an inexplicable fact for the chemistry of a certain period; but it was as much a fact in Lavoisier's time as it is today. By eliminating as inexplicable what is simply unexplained, Garaudy makes an involuntary concession to idealism.[117]

[115] Cf. Garaudy (184), pp. 163–8, one of the rare coherent discussions of the problem, and several articles or parts of articles in the review *Raison*.

[116] Garaudy [(184), p. 165]. I would want to point out here that this confusion between the *unexplained* and the *inexplicable* translates the unformulated ahistoricism which underlies Garaudy's thought.

[117] Syntheses do exist; some of them are totally inexplicable in the state of knowledge in a given epoch. By neglecting them, one opens the door to 'idealist explanations'; it is in this way that facts of biological interaction that are perfectly explicable today gave rise to the influence of metaphysical ('idealist') explanatory entities such as the 'vital force'. An epistemological conception like Garaudy's leaves the ground free for irrationalism wherever experimental methods register a temporary failure. Garaudy is certainly an intransigent materialist thinker, but, in Marxism, dialectics and materialism make a whole (Marxism is also a *Gestalt*) and one cannot obscure such an important aspect of the dialectic as the category of the totality, without shaking its materialist foundations.

A passage from *Anti-Dühring* seems to shed light on this problem. During Bonaparte's Egyptian expedition, Engels said: 'two Mamelouks were absolutely superior to three French men; one hundred Mamelouks and one hundred French men were worth the same; three hundred French men were ordinarily better than three hundred Mamelouks; a thousand French men would always overthrow fifteen hundred Mamelouks'.[118] There is nothing mysterious about this; the Mamelouks were better equipped; the French more disciplined. For someone who did not know the explanation, related structural facts could constitute unexplained or even (subjectively) inexplicable data: the straightforward statement of these facts does not constitute an idealist step. Idealism would begin when one invoked the will of Allah who, for arbitrary reasons, would favour one or other of the groups present. In other words, the essential element in idealist conception is the intervention of the heteronomic factor, but in this case the principle of Gestalt is fundamentally anti-idealist; the acquisition of autonomy and a structured grasp of reality go hand in hand, as child psychology shows. (Likewise in *Histoire et Conscience de Classe*, autonomy of proletarian action and perception of the historical situation as a totality are corollaries.) Engels's example shows—more explicitly than does Lukács—the relationship between this category and the dialectical transformation of quantity into quality.[119] This provides the anticipated refutation of Garaudy's criticism; Engels poses the principle of *Gestalt* in terms that are both dialectical and materialist.

[118] Cf. Engels (143), p. 158.
[119] Cf. the rest of Engels's quotation: 'Just as for Marx a minimum quantity, specific rather than variable . . . of the exchange value was necessary to make possible its transformation into capital, so also for Napoleon, who required a specific minimum size of cavalry division to allow discipline in this force . . . to be shown' [(143), p. 158]. In short, any quantitative change involves a 'latent' qualitative change which, at a given moment creates an 'apparent' quality, and consequently a new structure. Likewise it is possible that three workers each having an 'A/3' strength may succeed at an insoluble task for two strong workers each having an 'A/4' strength. There is nothing mysterious about this; the possibility of dividing the same total strength into three parts instead of two allows for a structuration of effort that is adaptable to the concrete structure of the task.

The objection regarding the historical nature of the *Gestalt* is far more serious. This objection discussed by Garaudy,[120] in fact dates from Piaget, whose collaborators focused on its experimental basis: the experimental study of perceptual constancies.[121] An ontogeny of the structuring function is revealed that is incompatible with Gestaltism, which postulates, for its part, the invariance of the laws of organization in the course of individual evolution. This last statement should itself be treated with caution; the experimental basis of this criticism seems difficult to attack. But why should the theory of *Gestalt* be indissolubly linked to a sort of Platonism of structures? Such a liaison, even if it existed *in fact* among the majority of Gestaltists, would nevertheless be a contingent datum, just like the (relatively frequent) coexistence of the purely dialectical notion of the autonomy of the living with the idealist notion of an inexplicable vital force. There are idealist dialectics, but every dialectic is not necessarily idealist. It is hard to see why the fact that the problem of the whole and its parts, if raised dialectically, would force Gestaltism to raise the problem of the genesis of intelligence in an anti-dialectical way. The only question which is raised is that of deciding if a psychology of dialectical structures, based on the notion of a progressive integration of these structures in the course of individual evolution, still deserves the name of Gestaltism; this is solely a terminological problem.

(3) The category of concrete totality occupies a central place in the field of alienation in sociology; it is as the locus of a destructuration of totalities—the consequences of which are the prevalence of identificatory functions and spatialization of historical duration—that false consciousness is a form of consciousness of a schizophrenic structure.

The result is that the numerous psychopathological conceptions based on the principle of the totality of the structure or the *Gestalt* have, in theory, the same—positive—value for a dialectical psychopathology; the work of thinkers like Hesnard, Ey or Strauss is infinitely closer to Marxism than reflexology. A choice between these different doctrines can only depend on

---

[120] Garaudy (184), p. 166.
[121] Piaget (387), pp. 82 ff.

purely scientific considerations, to the exclusion of all judgements of 'dialectical value': to say that 'all that is dialectic is valid, all that is valid is dialectic' is the same as making an axiom of a dogmatism, therefore in fact rejecting the dialectic. *A priori* this seems infertile. To say that an author like Zucker who appeals to the Gestalt is oblivious to Marxism, but that the value of this application depends on the degree of its consistency with the facts, is a statement which runs the risk of making every non-Marxist and also some 'Marxists' smile. In reality, it is a little less simple and a little less sterile. In fact, if the notion of structure reappears in so many contexts and from so many different authors, it is because a fundamental dialectical fact underlies this convergence; likewise, behind the various forms of identification demonstrated by different authors there is the fact of identification which is a reificational act. On the other hand, false consciousness, being closer to 'essences' as a consequence of the partial elimination of the 'tertiary factor', reveals a logical link at the point where clinical investigation is limited to registering a coexistence, or even a coincidence. Defined as individual false consciousness—in other words as a clinical expression of anti-dialectical consciousness and existence—the concept of schizophrenia is closer to its disputed nosological unity; in terms of an attempt at purely theoretical thinking, this is a practical result. The unitary concept of schizophrenia is defined *dialectically* and —I might add—*sociologically*.

I have tried to show that this dialectical–sociological conception of schizophrenia could serve as a common denominator for theoretical conceptions of a different origin. The outline of a similar deduction with regard to a certain number of well-known symptoms constitutes the next stage. It is not my intention to provide an overall theory of such specific phenomena as, for example, fantasies about the end of the world. It is enough to show that it is possible to reinterpret such classical data in the light of this socio-pathological parallelism. In isolation, each of these 'deductions' seems to be like playing with possibilities, a game which *a priori* may seem sterile. It is at the point of intersection of these possibilities of interpretation that the claim to validity of my conception resides.

TIME, SPACE AND REIFICATION

'Time is the life of the mind' (Aeneid, III, 7).

'He is murdering time, off with his head' (L. Carroll).

Most of the research on schizophrenia is concerned with the problem of time and space. This is so not only with phenomenological work, but also experimental research (biological and psychotechnical) like that of Balken,[122] Wallace,[123] and Lhamon.[124] Inversely, philosophical or experimental research concerning the problem of time and space draw their examples from the realm of schizophrenia, such as the well-known work of P. Fraisse.[125] For older problems of philosophy, schizophrenia is still 'Nature's great experiment'.

A question is raised in connection with Minkowski's work: is it legitimate to contrast time and space radically? If I personally tend to contrast them with each other in a rather rigid way, it is because my earlier studies of political alienation seem to justify the value of such a contrast as a working hypothesis. In this sense my conception of ideology depends more on Minkowski's 1927 theory than his 1934 ideas. Between *La Schizophrénie* (1927) and *Le Temps Vécu* (1934) Minkowski's ideas seem to have evolved, perhaps under Binswanger's influence. In fact— we read in *Le Temps Vécu*—'. . . the contrast of time and space in its primary form can no longer be sufficient for us, for it cannot be said, *a priori*, that phenomena, in that they are living, are necessarily of a temporal rather than a spatial nature'.[126]

For his part, Binswanger[127] guards against a too absolute confidence in Bergsonian categories. The idea of a 'spatialized time', an attribute of the superficial Self, it seems to him should be treated with even more caution. Bergson arbitrarily identified a *form of space* (metric space) with the general idea of space and, without any valid reason, he moved from temporal structures to

---

[122] Balken (27).
[124] Lhamon (302).
[126] Minkowski (343), p. 367.

[123] Wallace (462).
[125] P. Fraisse (165).
[127] Binswanger (54), p. 599.

spatial structures, instead of deducing—as Heidegger does—the specific temporal form of the superficial Self from another temporal structure such as the *Zeitwirbel* which is the temporal expression of the inauthentic Self.

Let us try to see it clearly. To talk in psychology of space and (or) time is in any case an abstraction; no being exists in pure time or pure space, not even the most retarded of autistics as far as we know.[128] It is an abstraction, like talking in isolation of height and weight; and yet such abstractions can enter into valid scientific statements. To distinguish in the continuum which surrounds us a dynamic, irreversible element 'where one's place is not chosen' (conventionally called 'time') and a static element which does not know any special 'Here', and in which in theory all places are equivalent ('space'), is an abstraction, neither more nor less legitimate than the abstraction which distinguishes between the space of action and symbolic space (Gelb and Goldstein), mathematical space and representational space (Klages), clear space and dark space (Minkowski), or even one's own space and foreign space (Grünbaum and Schilder). If Lukács—probably influenced by Bergson—states that the concrete duration, which underlies the creative activity of the artisan, is degraded into spatialized time in the universe of the rationalization of the production line worker, this is no arbitrary step, whatever Binswanger may say, since the postulate of homogeneity has been chosen as an inevitable criterion of abstraction which isolates space from time; another criterion, that of proximity or distance, for example,[129] would have been just as arbitrary, and furthermore, inappropriate for describing the phenomenon in question. When I say—extra-

---

[128] The Argentinian psychoanalysts [Garma (187), Rascovsky (394)] postulate the existence of a bidimensional continuum *in utero*; this doubtless would be the extreme form of spatial existence, the third dimension—the dimension of the praxis—being already largely 'contaminated' by axiological and temporal elements. For my part, I have tried to establish [(171), 1946 and (181), 1949] that the aphasic existence, perhaps comes closest to a purely temporal existence. But these are obviously extreme cases.

[129] The notions of *Fernraum* and *Nahraum* (Binswanger (54), p. 602) should not be confused with *Fremdraum* and *Eigenraum*.

polating the concept of reification from economics to politics—
that the process of ideologization spatializes historical duration,
this means simply that the ideological conception of History
permits flashbacks, ex-post-facto manipulations incompatible
with the postulate of temporal irreversibility. One is tempted to
paraphrase a famous definition: space is the milieu which permits
such steps, time the one which prevents them. If it is permissible
to talk about a certain reification–spatialization in the child, it
is because his reaction at a given age to the tasks imposed by the
experimenters is such that the abstraction 'spatializing behaviour'
constitutes the most economical common denominator for
thought. It is in the same order of ideas that one can postulate
that time is axiogenic and space devaluing (the basis of the
conceptions of Ostwald, Köhler and Dupréel); but it is a
secondary problem to know whether it is time which creates
conditions of value or, on the contrary, whether it is the
presence of value which structures—and consequently temporalizes—the milieu; both possibilities may be true, according
to the chosen perspective, and in psychopathology, according
to the pathogenic mechanisms at issue. These are, therefore,
essentially working hypotheses, but the existence of a triple convergence (sub-axiology at the pre-temporal stage in the child,
the axiological void of the world of schizophrenics, with accompanying spatialization, and the axiological and personal crisis,
with accompanying spatialization, in the world of false consciousness) through their coherence brings to these hypotheses an
assumption of validity.

One can go further. It is reasonable to accept that heterogeneous space (the 'amathematical and ageometrical space' discussed by Minkowski)[130] is such, by reason of a sort of temporal
contamination; in fact, spatial heterogeneity is of an axiological
order, whilst values are located in time. If I were to have a picture
by Rembrandt at a distance of ten yards away on my left and
a picture of a beloved parent fifty yards away on my right, and
if my Self ceased to attribute value, these two values, however
different they might be, would remain interchangeable as would
the spatial sectors which contain them; we would be thrust

[130] Minkowski (343), p. 367.

into a mathematical space without a privileged 'Here' which is defined by this very characteristic of interchangeability. Furthermore, fifty yards and ten yards make a perceptible difference for *action*; for *inaction* it amounts to exactly the same thing; a milieu without perspective. I quoted earlier the curious experiment of H. L. Raush who demonstrates among other things that the world of schizophrenics is marked by a loss of perspective; the phenomenon of 'dark space' of Minkowski doubtless translates the same fact. According to Ostwald, axiological existence presupposes an irreversible milieu (conventionally called 'time'); now, *perspective*, an axiological dimension of space has at least this attribute of a temporal nature, that it is *irreversible*. We can therefore give this definition of perspective: it is the third spatial dimension of temporality. It is understood that certain forms of reified consciousness accentuate the disappearance of perspective: the space without depth that Tellenbach describes is, in reality, a super-space. Perspective, anyway, is a late acquisition, like higher values; it disappears in certain pathological states marked specifically by an axiological crisis.[131] Finally, let me say that if it is possible to distinguish (as does Binswanger and others) between *near space* and *distant space*, it is either because of the presence of axiological and therefore temporal elements, or (particularly for the space of habitation), because *near space* is the repository of elements of personal history.

The same applies to the distinction between *clear space* and *dark space*.[132] Clear space allows one to follow the temporal organization of the behaviour of others and to adapt to it dialectically; by taking Minkowski's conception to its extreme consequences, it seems that *dark space*, which most produces the elimination of axiogenic temporality (space without perspective, space without encounter) is in some way real space. It therefore seems legitimate to accept that the purest form of space is in fact metric space, as Bergson supposed, the different forms of 'living' space being dependent on temporal contamination for this

[131] I am thinking of melancholic states where the axiological crisis corresponds to the concept of 'mourning' introduced by the psychoanalysts [Freud, Lagache (281)].

[132] Minkowski (343), p. 392.

quality. The study of temporal structure, collective de-realist thought—false consciousness—shows the usefulness of a clear separation from the point of view of economy of thought. This separation therefore constitutes at least a good working hypothesis, the abandonment of which hardly facilitates the description of the phenomena.[133]

The number of works devoted to the spatio-temporal structure of schizophrenia is now considerable. Bächler[134] considers the works of Franz Fischer (a German psychiatrist who died in tragic circumstances) as the front-runners in this field. It seems that Minkowski's earliest publications (which do not appear in Bächler's bibliography) were a little earlier.

Minkowski's conception is well known. Recent research—particularly that of *Daseinsanalyse*—while going deeper into it, does not change it in essence and certain experimental studies (American for the most part, and often published in the *Journal of Abnormal and Social Psychology*) confirm it. I shall demonstrate on the other hand that a great number of symptoms may be reduced through the intermediary of the notion of reification of temporality to the 'anti-dialectical mode of being-in-the-world' postulated as a fundamental disturbance.

[133] I pointed out earlier that the recent work of G. Pankow (376) is in reality a synthesis of phenomenological data (in Minkowski's sense) and analytical data; the results of the two authors are thus mutually confirmed. On the question of spatio-temporal structure this convergence disappears if one adapts Binswanger's positions. Obviously the convergence with G. Pankow's work (or with any other research taken individually) is an appealing epistemological criterion but the existence of any valid research constitutes a *fact* of the same order as a clinical observation; the capacity for dialectical integration of other doctrines (its capacity for *Aufhebung*) is one of the dimensions of the value of a theory. We have shown elsewhere the concordance of the spatio-temporal structure of the reified universe with that described in *La Schizophrénie*; concordances with experimental studies will be pointed out later. A theoretical conception which abandons such concordances without substituting others, could not be described as progress. I am thinking here particularly of the description of the spatio-temporal structure of the *Dasein* of schizophrenics in Binswanger's contributions, compared with Minkowski's early ideas.

[134] Brennio O. Bächler (22 *bis*).

Thus, to say that hallucination is dependent on an anti-dialectical structure of the *Dasein* is, in this form, a statement devoid of meaning. But it is necessary to consider: (a) that a specific relationship exists between spatialization and hallucination[135] and that space is the non-dialectical element of our experience; (b) that the hallucinatory phenomenon presents structural similarities to the dream, an atemporal and therefore hyper-spatial phenomenon, like all manifestations of the unconscious;[136] and finally, (c) that the phenomenon of deranged perception can be interpreted as a reified perception with an identificatory, anti-dialectical, egocentric structure. Having accepted this, hallucination in fact takes on the appearance of a reificational phenomenon, capable of being understood as one aspect of anti-dialectical existence. Likewise, the famous 'mirror symptom' *can* be interpreted as a manifestation of the identificatory (therefore spatializing) tendency, either as a false '*Selbstigung*', or as an attempt at illusory transcendence of existence without perspective, or as an 'illusion of encounter'.

The first author who described the 'mirror symptom' as common—if not exclusive—to *dementia praecox* was certainly P. Abély [3 and 4]. Roheim ([405], p. 190) as early as 1919 pointed out the regressive nature of the mirror but resorted to folkloric rather than clinical material.

Rosenzweig and Shakow (408) in 1937 focused on an effective technique: observations of patients through a one-way mirror. The abnormal behaviour of one member of the observed group allowed the early diagnosis of schizophrenia, which emphasizes the clinical value of this symptom.[137]

According to Rosenzweig and Shakow, 'sometimes this phenomenon is based on the autism of the patient who thinks that he has found an interlocutor in the image in the mirror'. I am concerned throughout this study to demonstrate analogies between false consciousness and schizophrenia, convinced that, in isolation,

---

[135] Minkowski (343).

[136] Cf. in this connection Conrad's definition (112) and (113) 'The unconscious is non-structured.'

[137] This symptom is not elsewhere considered as pathognomonic of *dementia praecox*.

these analogies may seem to be capricious, but that, seen in a total context, they may contribute to the establishment of a general psychosociological theory of the conditions of dialectical thought.

Having said this, and with reservations, I can affirm that behaviour does exist on a societal level that is phenomenologically close to the psychiatrists' 'mirror symptom'. This is when a State—usually totalitarian—*chooses a fictitious interlocutor* in order to have an act of violence or a territorial conquest ratified in the form of a supposed negotiation. This is—just like the clinical phenomenon in question—an *illusion of encounter* with an artificial interlocutor; a behaviour of schizophrenic structure.

Obviously, like most data which characterizes false consciousness, this 'collective mirror symptom' falls between the domain of lucid decisions and that of structural changes in collective consciousness. It is *an act of false consciousness* only to the extent that it succeeds in finding an audience. Nevertheless—I repeat—such an *isolated* observation is hardly more than a caprice. But it assumes quite a different significance if it can be integrated into an overall theory of structural analogies between politicized consciousness and schizophrenic consciousness, a theory based on a phenomenological description of the underlying spatio-temporal structures.

This brief incursion into the realm of political psychology was necessary in order to place the 'mirror symptom' in the context of the various aspects of the anti-dialectical mode of being-in-the-world.

SPATIO-TEMPORAL STRUCTURE AND LIFE-ORDER

The idea of life-order,[138] introduced into psychopathology by J. Zutt, has often been exploited in the anthropological-existential interpretation of problems as different as poisoning madness, deranged perception, fantasies about the end of the world, and

[138] Cf. Zutt (485), etc. I translate 'Daseinordnungen' by 'coordanées de l'existence' (coordinates of existence) and 'Wohnordnung' by 'ordre d'habition' (life-order).

K

even catatonia.[139] It is therefore a fertile concept whose relationships with spatialization—and consequently with reification—do not need to be emphasized. Moreover, Minkowski's theory of the loss of the 'Me–Here–Now' function—which is more or less the equivalent of a loss of the faculty of living—again confers on him the rank of forerunner.

EXPERIMENTAL STUDIES: E. R. BALKEN'S RESEARCH

Certain studies of an experimental nature confirm the intuitions of the phenomenologists. Miss Balken studied schizophrenics with the aid of the Murray test: the experimental confirmation of certain themes of *Daseinsanalyse* is the most interesting part of this work. The prevalence of the 'present' tense or the 'present perfect' in the use of verbs is denoted by an absence of all reference to the future or the past.[140] The schizophrenic 'does not distinguish between past, present and future, any more than between reality and unreality; he is a victim of the inertia of the past'. The fears conjured up from the past have—for him—the same reality as imagined fears of the present environment. A tension arises between the possible and the real, and the patients attempt to resolve it 'by clinging (desperately) unconsciously to the present'.[141] The nature of the 'patient-examiner' relationship evokes the atmosphere of a tribunal (!) before which the patient must recount his life story.[142] The essential element in the picture is 'a disturbance in the subject-object relationship in the sense of alienation from reality'.[143] This is very close to the Marxist-Lukácsian concept of alienation; yet Balken refers explicitly to Minkowski. Balken considers that the fundamental disturbance of schizophrenia 'resides at the level of the psycho-

[139] In connection with the relationships between life order and catatonia, cf. Winkler (471), p. 181.

[140] Balken (27), p. 243.

[141] Balken (27), p. 256.

[142] Balken (27), p. 264. The theme of the *l'Univers morbide de la Faute* reappears here in an experimental context.

[143] Balken (27), p. 250; the expressions are typical.

logical relationship' or the awareness of distinction between subject and object, while formulae such as 'incapacity for categorization' or 'regression to the prelogical stage' represent only verbal solutions.[144]

Wallace[145] questioned schizophrenics on their future plans; the results, duly quantified, were evaluated in comparison with a control group. The problem of the past was deliberately left aside. The result of the experiment was that the control group was superior to the patients in the faculty for organizing the future logically and meaningfully.[146] The schizophrenic considers temporal periods that are less extended into the future,[147] and less well structured.[148] The interest of these two studies in my opinion lies in the fact that the rather old intuitions of phenomenological psychopathology here find experimental confirmation.

SPATIO-TEMPORAL STRUCTURES AND ORAL FRUSTRATION IN *ALICE IN WONDERLAND*

One is tempted to rank Schilder's article on *Alice in Wonderland* amongst experimental studies on the time of schizophrenics.[149] Lewis Caroll's work is admired by psychiatrists (Roheim among others), but less as a children's book than as a psychopathological document. The mathematics professor and Protestant minister, Charles Dodgson (Lewis Carroll in literature), was a

[144] Balken (27), p. 270. This criticism is directed against Goldstein as well as Arieti (through anticipation), but there is a common denominator between the subject-object crisis (Balken) and the law of von Domarus (Arieti): the notion of reified non-dialectical existence of which the first is the existential aspect and the second the logical aspect.

[145] Wallace (462).

[146] Wallace (462), p. 244.

[147] This disinterest in the future is also translated by a disinterest in descendants. Cf. Binswanger (62), p. 113.

[148] 'Both the length of the future time span and the organisation of its contents are significantly reduced.'

[149] Schilder (419).

schizoid personality, timid with adults, at ease only in the company of young girls. As a preacher, his favourite sermon was that devoted to *eternal damnation.* Alice's world (and that of his other story, *Through the Looking Glass*) is a strange, cruel world, filled with anguish. The story begins with a long *fall* (a theme of *Daseinsanalyse*). An atmosphere of constant anguish is related to variations in the body image. Alice feels that she is either too big or too small. Time sometimes stops or goes backwards (Jürg Zünd's fantasy!); space is without depth (King and Queen of cards!). Carroll himself one day wrote a letter beginning with the last word and finishing with the first. Schilder said that the born mathematician is perhaps characterized by the liberties that he can take with space and time.[150] Carroll also loved mirror writing. The whole story is marked by oral frustration and aggression and this aggression deforms the structure of experienced space.[151] Schilder was surprised at Carroll's success as a children's writer; I share his surprise, though the fate of Swift's work raises almost the same problem.[152] It is a surprising work in which analytical themes (oral frustration and aggression) and themes from *Daseinsanalyse* (transformation of the spatio-temporal structure) are intermingled.[153]

[150] Von Domarus points out the same phenomenon among hospitalized schizophrenics [(129) and (130), p. 645]. This is undeniably spatialization; time is irreversible by definition. The words spoken by Von Domarus's patients, like the letter written by L. Carroll, *do not live* in time; they are situated in pure spatiality. Inversely, aphasics are incapable of temporal reversal (do not spatialize sufficiently): a patient of Lhermitte *et al.* [(303), p. 589] is capable of reciting the months of the year, but incapable of reciting them backwards.

[151] Schilder develops this idea in his *Psychopathologie de l'espace* (418).

[152] Cf. Ben Karpmann (249) and my work (182).

[153] Cf. *Through the Looking Glass*, Chapter V (quoted by Roheim (405), p. 210): 'The queen explains that there is jam for yesterday and jam for tomorrow, but never jam for today.' Thus is the analytico-existential definition of the *inauthentic present* (cf. Binswanger (61), p. 58) seen from a psychoanalystic viewpoint (oral frustration and aggression).

SPATIO-TEMPORAL STRUCTURE AND *DASEINSANALYSE*. THE 'MARY CASE'

The interest of this short case study of L. Binswanger's is that it shows clearly the unstated sociologism of the *Daseinsanalyse* school; as in the most well-known case of Jürg Zünd, the origin of pathological temporalization, and therefore the deranged state, has concrete roots in the sick person's *social* mode of being. It is in such cases that the term 'deranged thought related to being' (*Seinsgebundenes Wahndenken* conceived according to Mannheim's model of *Seinsgebundenes Denken*) is fully justified. This English girl ('Mary') lived 'in two speeds'; two forms of temporalization[154] could not be synchronized. 'Slow time' was that of existence in the respectable society to which she belonged through her husband, an existence based on faithfulness to others and herself. The other time, a rapid one, was that of a rather matter of fact sensuality and passions from which her past was not exempt. This incapability of synchronizing the two times engendered a state of intolerable anguish.

For the patient herself, it was not so much a problem of the non-synchronization of two temporalities belonging to two different worlds, as a lack of synchronization of the *body* and *mind*. This naive formulation is not absurd: the extreme value of the temporal slow-down is in fact space, therefore an element of reification. One can, therefore, without forcing the interpretation of the case, talk about a beginning process of spatialization–reification in this patient; a suggestion of the 'end of the world syndrome' typically completes the picture. It is clear that behind what we see here as pathological fixation and dissociation hides

---

[154] The translation of 'Zeitigung' by 'temporalization' is unfortunate for the translation eliminates a part of the dialectical 'atmosphere' which surrounds this word; it would be better to say 'flow of temporality'. On the other hand, to translate 'Raumlichung' by *spatialization* is pejorative in French whereas for Binswanger it is the loss of spatialization which is bad. Having said this, I am nevertheless keeping these two expressions which are well established.

a fundamental problem of human existence; a problem of humanization (*Menschenwerdung*), a 'humanist' problem. This humanist problem is certainly the same as the one that we are concerned with: the problem of reification. On this subject we refer back to the 'Erika case' of Boss, analysed at length in passages devoted to the reification of sexuality; Binswanger's observation is strikingly similar to Boss's.

One specific question is raised. We have been able to show in the 'Mary' case that the pathological temporalization was of a reificational structure. Furthermore, we saw earlier that real reificational elements abound in Binswanger's descriptions (as in Boss's), accompanied, moreover, by a whole terminology homologous to that of the Marxist theory of false consciousness. Now, the reification of consciousness (in Lukács and in my analysis of political alienation) does not, let us remember, involve a loss of time and space; it involves a loss of the temporalizing function to *the benefit* of space: a process of de-dialecticization with concomitant spatialization. To rediscover the validity of these considerations in the area of deranged thought is the same as confirming the notion of morbid rationalism in its primary form. It is, in fact, permissible to wonder if it is legitimate to separate rigidly, or even to contrast, time and space. It certainly is permissible to contrast *dialectical perception* and *non-dialectical* (reified) *perception* of reality.

THE JÜRG ZÜND CASE

Let us take as an example the Jürg Zünd case. Nowhere in Binswanger's work does the sociologizing aspect of *Daseinsanalyse* manifest itself more clearly. J. Zünd lived in fear of *proletarianization*;[155] the *fall* that he fears—the familiar fall which plays such a major role in existential analysis—possesses, in this case at least, the very specific significance of a *social* fall. Having failed, he would like to begin again (in the same way that a child starts a new game when he has not won) or even force time to go back-

---

[155] Binswanger (60), p. 47.

wards;[156] the arrest of temporalization involves an arrest of personalization (*Selbstigung*). In a study by the psychoanalyst C. Thompson,[157] identification with the enemy is a factor of depersonalization, but this is more or less the same for all identification;[158] now, identification is a homogenizing and therefore a spatializing function (it is in this same perspective that it is possible to appreciate the philosophical value of P. Balvet's thesis).[159] Jürg Zünd's time is *time devoid of autism*. However, Binswanger tells us that we would be wrong to confuse it with the time of boredom; this also creeps along, but it creeps along while maintaining its structure, while autistic time is destructured; boredom possesses the structure of empty time, autism the non-structure of temporal emptiness.[160] (A cultured patient of Beringer and Mayer-Gross talks about 'bad eternity', using almost the same term as Hegel.) The emergence of the future (*Künftigung*) is blocked[161] and the present, which is caught between a de-realized past and future, is no longer any more than an inauthentic present.[162] The state of being crushed by the world is translated by a spatiality of *crushing proximity* (*erdrückende Nähe*) whose homologue is a temporality of *immediate urgency*.[163] The *Dasein* is, however, sometimes awakened in an effort which is soon exhausted; temporalization takes place therefore in fits

---

[156] Binswanger (60), p. 31.

[157] C. Thompson (446).

[158] Cf. Hesnard (221) and Hesnard (227); Lagache (283).

[159] Balvet (29) who sees depersonalization at the basis of all forms of schizophrenia.

[160] Binswanger (60), *J. Zünd*, p. 31: *Zeitgestalt der Leerheit . . . Ungestalt der leeren Zeit*. But one wonders if the difference is not purely of degree. A time that is entirely de-axiologized becomes, *ipso facto*, an '*Ungestalt*'; in other words: pure space. Some of these striking points involve only a play on words.

[161] Binswanger (60), p. 32; no emergence of the future; and no real present either.

[162] It is in this order of ideas that the clinician can offer experimental confirmation: if the undifferentiated succession of presents is hard to distinguish theoretically from homogeneous space, the maniacal disturbance (absolute present) is hard to differentiate *practically* (clinically) from the schizophrenic disturbance (spatialization).

[163] Binswanger (62), p. 85.

and starts before the fall into confirmed autism. Despite the gripping beauty of these descriptions the actual progress achieved in relation to Minkowski is not clear. An undifferentiated succession of presents in a non-structured and furthermore reversible continuum does not have a great deal in reality to differentiate it from space.[164] In vain one states that 'the arrest of time is also a mode of temporality';[165] it is merely a formal truth (rather as one might say to the unbeliever: 'atheism is your religion'). In reality, the loss of temporalization surrenders the *Dasein* to space, which attacks existence and crushes it with its *obsessive proximity*.

This problem—like any problem related to reification—has an axiological aspect. We have seen that structure (totality) was a corollary of value, either because value has a structural property (formal quality) (Lalo, Köhler), or because, and this amounts to the same thing, all structuration of our ambiance is necessarily of an axiological nature. On the other hand, the observation that the category of totality is central in dialectics has led us to another postulate; that of axio-dialectic equivalence: value is the subjective experience of the dialectical nature of reality. The dialectic of 'consistency' and 'precariousness' in Dupréel's axiology is one aspect of this more general dialectic: identification, and therefore space, is devaluing, for consistency here borders on precariousness.[166] But value is also dependent on another dialectic in other ways similar to Dupréel's: a dialectic of proximity and distance. A *concrete* value is both near and far: something which is too close is not yet a value; a value that is too far away ceases to be one. In the pure space which I am 'left' with after the arrest of temporalization there is neither perspective, nor structure, nor value; things are either in the infinite distance (The Castle), or in stifling proximity: axiological structures which 'keep the world at a distance' (the axiogenic obstacle or, to put it another way, the bulwark-value) disappear with the time that the Self ceases to secret.[167]

---

[164] See note 157 above.   [165] Binswanger (62), p. 85.
[166] The sacred is explained through itself: I am identical with myself, said Jahweh.
[167] Subjectively, distance is measured by the time needed to cover it; in an atemporal continuum, the displacement is immediate. Time

TEMPORALIZATION AND ENCOUNTER

Time is the milieu of the valuing encounter, just as space is the milieu of devaluing aggression. The Hebraic language—as Oppenchaim shows[168]—contains an implicit philosophy of the relationship between temporalization and encounter. The word 'Zman' signifies 'time designated for', in other words, valuing temporalization; it is also one of the ways of designating in Hebrew a *celebration (la fête)*.

The word which means encounter (*hizdamen*) is from the same root; it is—Oppenchaim tells us—a mutual temporalization.[169] But the encounter is at the same time an act of valuation and an expression of freedom: two groups of slaves may *cross each other*, but a duel is an armed *encounter* between two free people who have mutual respect. The word 'invitation' is also formed from the root of 'Zman'; the word *hazmanah* means 'directing time towards the projected encounter'.[170] Amongst the authors who have interpreted schizophrenia as a loss of the faculty for encounter (in Buytendijk's sense) the works of W. von Baeyer[171] and E. Strauss are certainly the most outstanding. The study of the relationship between temporalization and encounter allows us to link these ideas to Minkowski's and, through this intermediary, to my general notion of alienation.

THE PROBLEM OF THE LOSS
OF THE SENSE OF SPACE

The problem of space is raised in a different way from that of time. The loss of the sense of time in the process of mundanization confirms—as we have seen—Minkowski's (1927) ideas. Bins-

is the obstacle and, in this way, axiogenic; pure space, without an obstacle, is also devoid of values. The 'Leerform des Raumes' of which Scheler talks is therefore *very short space*; space is valued by being temporalized.

[168] Oppenchaim (372).   [169] Ibid., p. 69.
[170] Ibid.   [171] Von Baeyer (24).

wanger introduced a whole terminology to characterize the loss of the sense of lived space; now this terminology does not clarify the problem. From the dialectical and axiological point of view, pure space is already a product of deterioration in relation to time.

It is in fact clear that the loss of the sense of time (succession of 'present points' (*Jetzpunkte*) with the cessation of the emergence of the future (*Zeitigung*) entails a beginning of spatialization; the loss of space only *serves to emphasize its spatial nature*. To cut off time from its future dimension is the same as taking away an element of heterogeneity, and is therefore bringing it closer to space (likewise if one cuts the past from the present); from all the evidence, cutting off space from its dimension of depth does nothing but *accentuate its spatial nature* by depriving it of one dimension where the principle of equivalence of places and reversibility no longer operates and which, consequently, introduces a partially temporal structure. Language again provides some valuable indications; one says 'space of time' (in German too: *Zeitraum*) for a limited portion of duration; the opposite (designating a limited fraction of space by an allusion to time) would be inconceivable. One also says in German 'raumen', to empty. In a word, the limitation of a negative remains a negative. This reservation applies to most of Binswanger's points concerning the deterioration of the *Räumlichung* in his patients. When, in the 'Lola Voss case',[172] it is a question of friendly space versus hostile space, it is clear that an axiological—and therefore a temporal—element intervenes. When Ellen West[173] said, in an otherwise sublime metaphor, that 'the exits from the theatre of existence (*Lebensbühne*) are occupied by armed men', one cannot see how this limitation would modify the spatial character of space.

It follows that the process of existential loss in schizophrenia modifies the spatio-temporal equilibrium in favour of its spatial constituent; time is spatialized in its loss whilst the loss of lived space only emphasizes its 'spatiality'.

We have moved from phenomenology to social alienation—as we do systematically in the course of this study. The spatio-

[172] Binswanger (61), p. 75.   [173] Binswanger (56), p. 51.

temporal structure of false consciousness shows that the pre-valence of the spatial factor permits a convenient description of various manifestations of economic and political alienation as a working hypothesis. This is therefore the real fundamental dis-turbance of the de-realist (schizophrenic) nature of false con-sciousness.

This result, applied to the problem of the spatio-temporal structure of schizophrenia, allows a definite simplification of the problems. By accepting that, from the axiological and dialectical point of view, pure space is a product of the deterioration of the relationship to time, the notion of *spatialization* (in the pejorative meaning of the term) reassumes all its value. Through the con-siderable enrichment due to *Daseinsanalyse*, the conceptual framework of *La Schizophrénie* therefore remains almost intact.

PERMEABILITY OF THE *DASEIN* IN THE REIFIED WORLD: PARANOID POISONING MADNESS

Nothing justifies Minkowski's reservations about the ambiguity inherent in certain terminological elements better than the problem of *poisoning madness*. It is *a priori* perfectly conceivable that a normal man over-estimates his personal importance to the point of believing himself to be the object of poisoning attempts; in this case, this fear is integral to a normal intellectual mechan-ism. Certain epochs have had the custom of recognizing the social importance of a person by providing him with a 'food taster'. History has known periods of actual collective poisoning madness such as the Grand Siècle (the age of Louis XIV).[174] Now, the phenomena described by Lenôtre in one of his studies have no relationship to the mechanism of the paranoid disturbance; if one wants to look for a historical analogy for the latter, it could be found in the accusations of *well-poisoning* made against the Jews or the Tziganes. As far as the psychodynamic mechanism is concerned there is no common ground between the man who over-estimates his importance to such an extent that he believes

[174] Lenôtre: *Dossiers de police*, pp. 37–42.

himself to be the target of a poisoning attempt by a real or imaginary enemy, and the man who believes that a Tzigane, simply because he is different from the other inhabitants of the country, is a *poisoner*; both, however, have a poisoning madness. Cases of poisoning madness of a paranoid structure have been described. Only poisoning madness of a paranoid structure, of which the Strindberg case offers a famous example,[175] is interesting for our present argument. To say that the fear of being poisoned is, in certain cases, the expression of an anti-dialectical involvement in the world, constitutes once again a statement apparently devoid of meaning. But we can give it concrete content by using once again the works of the German phenomenological school. Affiliation can be demonstrated: poisoning madness is related to the anthropological problems of habitation which, for their part (at least this is my interpretation), are related to the spatialization of duration, a reificational phenomenon. It is not therefore necessary to go very far to be able to interpret paranoid poisoning madness as one possible expression of non-dialectical involvement in the world. In this order of ideas, poisoning madness is one of the forms that the 'World' adopts in order to crush the *Dasein*. It is therefore a form of mundanization. The vulnerability to poison is consequently only one aspect of the general vulnerability of the *Dasein* which is as if 'unprotected'[176] in a uniquely spatial and, consequently, anaxiological and non-structured world. In this perspective the madness appears from the subjective point of view as an aspect of depersonalization, and, from the objective point of view, as the translation of the devaluation (de-realization) of the morbid universe.[177]

[175] Jaspers (243), p. 119, and *passim*.

[176] 'Entbergung', cf. Kulenkampff (268).

[177] Or, if you like: the reificational devaluation of the Self and the World has a double effect: The Self without 'axiological bulwark' (the obstacle creates the value, but on the other hand, the value is an obstacle) is unprotected, vulnerable; the devaluation of the world appearing in the form of 'food' is experienced as poison. In a world which does not know the true encounter (of which the 'table' encounter is one of the most charming aspects) uni-laterally-acting poison (the poisoners of the Grand Siècle used knives poisoned on one side only) symbolizes the loss of the valuing encounter.

The question is raised as to why the theme of poisoning is so common in paranoid derangement, in preference to other means of destruction, electrocution being the exception. *Daseinsanalyse* responds that the act of eating together is an interhuman function of primordial anthropological importance. By recognizing the importance of the oral stage, psychoanalysis also emphasizes this fact, but, by linking it to the characterological factor of feeding, it has somewhat defocalized this idea. Existential analysis, which emphasizes the anthropological significance of the act of eating together (poisoning madness is the perversion of this) places it on a more dialectical level as in the problem of sexual reification. To invite someone to one's table is a sign of friendship as great and sometimes—rather paradoxically—greater than to invite someone into one's bed; in this order of ideas, any ownership of an apartment possesses in miniature this sovereign prerogative of states to naturalize or not to naturalize an outsider. Now—must it be emphasized?—we live historically: the different expressions which designate habitation are distinguished, among other things, by the degree of historicity which is inherent in them: the word 'abode' (*'demeure'*) contains more historicity than the word 'habitat'.[178] Historicity is not the only dialectical dimension of the act of living; the structure of the subject-object relationship is another; one transforms one's habitat (and one is transformed by it); it is possible to like one's personal disorder. 'This place is mine and I live here. I organize it and model it in my own way.'[179] The link between habitation and habit is emphasized both by the French ('habitation' and 'habitude') and German terminology (Wohnen, Gewohnheit) as well as the English. In short, habitation is not only, as Heidegger said, a 'primordial anthropological given', but also an act of dialectical valuation. The interior space of a habitat is saturated with axiogenic, subjective historicity: it is a landscape, therefore a state of mind.

It is paradoxical but true that one lives more in time than in space. It is quite significant to point out that states in which ideology is dominated by spatialism (national-socialist terminology is characteristic in this respect), are precisely those which do not

[178] Minkowski (337), p. 183.
[179] Ibid.

respect the private home. This is one aspect of totalitarian de-personalization.

If the foreigner is sometimes greeted with mistrust, it is to a large extent because he is the bearer of a misunderstood or not known historicity; he appears as a *Dasein* of pure spatiality.[180] It is curious to observe in this respect that an unknown past often antagonizes public opinion more than a known, even though notoriously unfavourable, past.

The food that one consumes 'at home' is food that one can eat without fear of poisoning; this fact has had a certain practical importance. To invite someone to one's table is a sign of confidence which proves that one no longer considers him as a stranger, i.e. as a potential poisoner. Inversely, certain categories (Jews, Tziganes) have often been accused in the past of poisoning the wells; sometimes Jews are still accused of being the poisoners of public spirit.

Among paranoids the 'coordinates of existence' (*Daseinsordnungen*) are deranged; the term 'derangement' (*dé-rangement*), a very typical one, signifies both destructuration and axiological deterioration. It is therefore a phenomenon of spatialization. In the works of Berze and others, one word reappears constantly: '*Nebeneinander*' = juxtaposed, i.e. non-organized and non-temporalized.[181] The paranoid is badly defended (*Entbergung*); he knows neither real distance nor real proximity;[182] for him there are neither real strangers nor real non-strangers. Earlier we mentioned the case of Pallis's agnosic who was incapable of identifying his wife from one visit to another; one of Kulenkampff's paranoids (a woman without roots like most of these patients)

---

[180] Cf. the case published by me where this internalized feeling of spatialization-alienation in a maladjusted emigré produced a curious form of sexual apragmatism (incapacity for cohabitation) (174 bis).

[181] For example Berze (51), pp. 40, 45 etc.

[182] One notices the same phenomenon amongst personalities of a slightly hypomaniac structure; they know neither true distance nor true proximity.
This analogy is doubtless related to the analogy of the spatio-temporal structure; the maniacal *Zeitwerbel* as destructured time that is 'made present' is phenomenologically similar to pure space.

reveals a *diametrically opposite* syndrome; she identifies the whole world.[183] The fact that many schizophrenics think they are spied on, or even maltreated, through walls, is essentially the consequence of a 'fundamental disturbance in communication', just like the hallucinatory act (Strauss) or—if you like—a 'disturbance in the meaning of living (habitation), a crisis of existential confidence'.[184] This world is characterized by an undialectical alternation between stifling proximity and hopeless distance; the impression of poisoning is the coenesthetic aspect of this experience of proximity, just as auditory hallucinations constitute its acoustic aspect, and deranged perceptions its visual aspect. The idea of *physiognomization* (introduced by Zutt) has always played a major role in the German interpretations of the schizophrenic world, yet not without some ambiguity: for certain people (Storch) there is an *excessive physiognomization*, for others (Matussek) an *absence of physiognomization*. Doubtless there is a misunderstanding: the world of the schizophrenic is both very physiognomized as a consequence of the menacing proximity of things ('the doors are eating me' said one of Storch's patients) and nonphysiognomized, because ahistorical. It is an immobile world seen through field-glasses.[185] From the viewpoint of reificational homogenization the inanimate comes to life at the same time as the living is reified, just as fetishism 'animates' the object—or considers partiality as totality which, from the dialectical point of view amounts to almost the same thing—while remaining incapable of 'encountering' the living partner as totality. The animation of the non-living is therefore complementary to the

[183] Kulenkampff (27), pp. 327–8. This enters into the frameworks of the contrast between 'the aphaso-apraxic's mode of being-in-the-world' and 'the schizophrenic's mode of being-in-the-world' which was the starting point for this study. For us, this is a manifestation of the 'compulsion for identification' (*Identitätszwang*)—with perhaps some intervention of the von Domarus-Vigotsky law—which does not contradict Kulenkampff's exegesis since the identificatory function is a spatializing function.

[184] Kulenkampff (271), p. 330: '... eine Störung des Wohnens und Vertrautseins'.

[185] Cf. the title of Lewis Carroll's novel: *Through the Looking Glass*.

reification of the living (a mechanism of compensation, or of defence in certain cases); it is by virtue of this same dialectic that one can speak both of *excessive physiognomization* and *non-physiognomization* in the schizophrenic.

To return to paranoid poisoning madness, the impression of toxicity in the world (cf. the important role of toxic gases) would thus translate three convergent facts of anti-dialectical involvement in the world: the feeling of being foreign surrounded by foreigners,[186] the impression of being 'unprotected' as a consequence of the disappearance of the axio-dialectical barrier protecting the person, and finally the incapacity to structure any foreign matter. This last aspect is the point of convergence with the theory of deranged perception. But it risks leading us too far astray. I simply want to show that it is possible to find a common denominator for phenomena as different in theory as morbid rationalism and paranoid poisoning madness, and that this common denominator may be the concept of reified existence. To say that the act of fearing being poisoned is anti-dialectical is —in this form—a vague generality, without interest. To say that the absence of real historicity and the disappearance of the personalizing and valuing praxis in the world of a *Dasein* deprives him of intimacy and precise limits, and that the experience of the vulnerability of this purely spatial—and consequently, anti-dialectical—existence may in *certain cases* be translated by the deranged fear of the presence of a poison in the atmosphere, even in food, is a concrete statement—correct or not is another question—which links poisoning madness to morbid rationalism, a pure form of reificational spatialism. Certainly any person wrongly believing himself to be the target for poisoning attempts, is not necessarily dependent on sub-realist mechanisms. The necessary differentiation between *false consciousness and false judge-*

---

[186] One theme reappears constantly in the literature: the bewildered servant in the service of foreign masters [cf. Kulenkampff (271) and Callieri (83)]. The fact that such a patient in his derangement claims to know everyone in no way contradicts this interpretation, for *to know everyone in the same way* is to know no one, just as the constant maniacal 'celebration' is in the last analysis, the same as an existence without 'celebration'.

ment is certainly one aspect of the difference between paranoid and paranoic madness.[187]

REIFICATION OF LANGUAGE
AMONG SCHIZOPHRENICS

Even normally, language involves a predominantly reificational element at its conceptual level (Head's *superior speech*); a certain degree of reification is the condition of interhuman communication. One cannot 'encounter the other' without going out of oneself; it is in this sense that we were earlier able to define the essence of aphasic disturbance as an *insufficient alienation* or as an insufficiency of the identificatory function, which, from an open Marxist point of view, amounts to the same thing. The essential identity of schizophrenic language and aphasic language has been postulated;[188] this hypothesis is a corollary of Goldstein's —the *over concrete* character of schizophrenics' thought—and are therefore jointly responsible for the weaknesses in this conception. Without going into the details of this problem, which is beyond my subject, let me quote a statement which is along the same lines: 'the schizophrenic submits to words; but words escape

---

[187] Paranoid people believe that they are spied on through walls. As they have a tendency to integrate technical progress into their madness, there are some, certainly, who suspect listening devices on their telephone. In this case, it is one aspect of mundanization, i.e. spatialization: a subrealist step. But I have known an important industrialist who, overestimating his otherwise real importance, also believed, rather absurdly, that his line was tapped. Now, this person was nothing of a Jürg Zünd. He was a strong dominating personality with remarkable success to his credit. For the one, an insufficiently structured logic and existence caused the intimacy of the Self which was unprotected by an axiological barrier to be isolated; for the other one sees rather an over-structured world surrounding an over-valued Self. In the first case, it is a matter of false consciousness, in the Marxist sense of the term, i.e. a dialectical and temporalizing incapacity; in the second, it is a question simply of *false judgement*.

[188] By Arieti among others [cf. (12), p. 420]. In opposition to this hypothesis the observation of Faure *et al.* provides a clinical argument of experimental value.

the aphasic'.[189] We can, in this order of ideas, speak of a certain 'mundanization' by man in relation to the word in schizophrenia; mundanization which is accompanied by an over-reification of language which is already reificational in its essence. 'Word becomes an object', said Katan, but this 'object' acquires an energetic content (hypercathexis) which makes it redoubtable. There is a definite continuity between the (undeniably reificational) structure of schizophrenic language and that of hallucination. It emphasizes the reificational nature of the hallucinatory phenomenon that Minkowski implicitly suggested in another context: that of the difference between *clear space* and *dark space*.

This reified-schizophrenic structure of the word is found in false consciousness. The elements of speech become independent of the consciousness which created them, and weigh it down; it is this phenomenon that Stuart Chase describes in his book *The Tyranny of Words*. The tyranny that the word exercises over politicized consciousness is, moreover, a corollary of the preponderance of identificatory functions, which comes back to Arieti's point, that they are certainly two facets of the same fundamental process of the de-dialecticization of consciousness.

The reified, magical nature of the language of schizophrenics is an old observation. In actual fact one ought to use the word 'hypermagical', for if normal language is reified, it is also 'normally magical' (Sullivan). With regard to the egocentric character of the vocabulary of schizophrenics, I have a striking documentary example: a paranoid man egocentrically adapted the Petit Larousse according to the needs of his own deranged theocratic system.[190] Racamier notes their 'administrative, depersonalized style, devoid of articles, laden with stereotyped statements, avoiding the concrete and the personal and preferring the abstract and the general';[191] furthermore, according to the same author, 'it is in the broad group of schizophrenias that the alienation of language assumes all its breath and interest'. G. Pankow talks about the 'materialization and spatialization of the word

[189] Racamier (392).
[190] I have published a page of this curious document in facsimile in *L'Evolution Psychiatrique*, April–June 1952, p. 323. (173.)
[191] Racamier (393), p. 5.

among schizophrenics'. In short, schizophrenic language is reified in two ways: (a) as mundanization (*Verweltlichung*) of the Self in relation to the word which, having become independent of consciousness, tends to extend beyond it (*überwaltigen*); hallucination, which is a process of alienation from the appropriate word (D. Lagache), is certainly the extreme degree of this mundanization, and (b) through the objectification of the word which, by placing itself in space (space, the sign of my power),[192] becomes the bearer of the schizophrenic's illusion of magical omnipotence. A third reificational element is perhaps the axiological-energetic movement between the Self and the 'alienated' word demonstrated by Freud.[193]

Amongst the authors of analytical orientation, Katan[194] and Roheim[195] have studied the language of schizophrenics. Their conclusions confirm the hypothesis of the reified character of the language of schizophrenics; this observation constitutes a new point of convergence between Marxism and psychoanalysis.

In Katan's observation, the castration factor stands out clearly. A man of twenty-eight comes under the (bad) influence of his elder brother; a naive way of swindling the insurance company through self-mutilation is carried out. This plan fails and the young man has a paranoid psychosis very much in the Hesnardian style. He accuses his brother of turning people against him to revenge himself for his physical inferiority. The brother who was very attracted to women, was still nevertheless a virgin at thirty because of a malformation which had only just been operated on. At the same time, fear of death and syphilis is expressed in typical

---

[192] Foucault (59), p. 89; but it links up with the following page: 'Space, the sign of my impotence.' In fact, illusory (magical) omnipotence and real impotence go together in pure spatiality. Only concrete duration permits the dialectical synthesis of the possible and the impossible which is the concrete praxis.

[193] According to one of Freud's hypotheses (1915) relating to schizophrenia, 'the patient, having become incapable of relationships with others, and thus forced to drop the substance for the shadow, transfers his interest to the inanimate substance of language'. P. C. Racamier (393), p. 6, Freud: *The Unconscious*, collected papers, vol. IV.

[194] Katan (253).

[195] Roheim (405).

puns.[196] Some discreet fantasies about the end of the world complete the picture. He accuses his brother of wanting to take over his identity in order to make everyone believe that it is he (the patient) who has a genital malformation. Their father had reproached this brother for incestuous tendencies towards the mother whose bed he had in fact shared until the age of nine.[197]

Katan believes—it is rather like the Freudian hypothesis—that, in the presence of instinctual danger, a double energetic movement takes place: on the one hand, a withdrawal of the libido from the world (Storch spoke of the 'world emptied of value'),[198] and then, libidinal restitution as an attempt at recovery of the lost world. The latter affects only words, which thus acquire a new importance and, in some way, an independent existence; they are substituted for objects by virtue of a familiar mechanism, common to hysteria and schizophrenia. Only the outlines of Katan's article are sketched here; the details, which are impossible to summarize briefly, are without importance in any case. For our problem, the essential fact is that an analytical mechanism is described here as a symptom of a reificational structure. If we are entitled to talk about reification here, it is not simply because of Katan's expression: 'the word . . . is no longer treated as a word but as an object' (a gratuitous remark proves nothing and, moreover, the word 'object' does not mean the same thing in Marxism and psychoanalysis), but because of the integration of this phenomenon into an overall context; egocentrization of the word (Woods) and its spatialization (Pankow).

Roheim emphasizes the importance of oral frustration in schizophrenia, 'it is the exaggerated role of the oral zone which explains the fact that schizophrenics tend to identify the *word* with the *object* or to use these latter magically'.[199] In *Alice in Wonder-*

---

[196] Katan (253), p. 364. Dr. van Kerkhof, a syphilis doctor = cemetery (Kerkhof–Kirchoff–cemetery); the actress Marga Graf = grave; Civilis (historical Batavian character) = syphilis, etc. Castrational anguish is clear.

[197] Katan (253), p. 354; the author's rather unclear explanation does not reveal very well where the deranged statements begin.

[198] Storch (435), p. 68.

[199] Roheim (405), p. 105.

land,[200] frustration, fear of castration, temporal destructuration and objectivation of the word typically go hand in hand. In short, if, for Roheim, individual oral frustration is responsible in certain cases for the beginning of subsequent schizophrenic evolution, then for historical materialists, the 'collective oral frustration' of humanity is the basis on which ideologies and, in the last analysis, false consciousness (collective schizophrenia), are built. This then is another point of dialectical convergence between Marxism and psychoanalysis.

HALLUCINATIONS AND DERANGED PERCEPTIONS

The hallucinatory act can be interpreted in several ways as the effect of a non-dialectical involvement in the world: as a corollary of the phenomenon of spatialization, either through preponderance of dark space over clear space (Minkowski), or through the 'formation of lines subordinate to the main line' (Berze),[201] or through the loss of the encounter discussed by Baeyer who expresses Strauss's notion but in other terms: the loss of the capacity for sympathetic communication (*sympathische Kommunikationsstörung*). Seen in this way, the hallucinatory act is a false consciousness of encounter (an 'illusion of encounter', which is one aspect of the illusion of totality) and is integrated into a general pathology of the encounter, a corollary of a psychopathology of dialectical thought, or in other words, a pathology of freedom (H. Ey).

It will be admitted that there exists a certain analogy between hallucinatory consciousness which, in its demand for homogeneity, is forced to alienate in a hallucinatory form the tendencies that it no longer manages to organize in a concrete totality, and, on the other hand, reified political consciousness which, in its postulate of political homegeneity—a postulate that the totalitarian state tries to put into practice—attributes to the *foreigner* (in the widest sense of the term, implying also political heterodoxy) facts for

[200] Schilder (419); Roheim (405), p. 204 and *passim.*
[201] Berze (51), p. 22.

which a simply dialectical consideration of reality would permit a rational explanation to be given.

The question of hallucinations is the oldest in mental pathology, while the question of deranged perceptions is the newest.[202] The problem of their relationship has not been studied very much. Deranged perceptions are mainly visual, paranoid hallucinations are essentially acoustic. Deranged perceptions constitute—especially since Matussek's research—a well-defined entity; the problem of hallucinations involves pluralist solutions, and not only on the level of the psychogenesis-organogenesis debate. The question of paranoic hallucinations has been discussed. Nocturnal fears in children[203] could be compared to hallucinations (?), in the same way as masturbatory fantasies. Last but not least, the problem of normal hallucinations should be raised: 'all our images', writes Dromard, 'have a tendency to be objectivized in reality; this is a fundamental property which belongs to them in their own right . . . to blend reality into a mental image, whatever it may be, is the path of least resistance'.[204] It is understood that in circumstances which may not go beyond the limits of the normal, the realist-dialectical (structuring-temporalizing) function which acts as a counterbalance, might appear to be lacking.[205] One can not therefore avoid the danger of wishing to base a nosological systematization on the presence or absence of hallucinations. Deranged perception is, by contrast, considered by different authors (Heidenberg, Kant, K. Schneider, Janzarik, Matussek) as literally pathognomonic of schizophrenia.

The problem of the relative rarity of visual hallucinations in schizophrenia has often preoccupied the theorists. Arieti[206] empha-

---

[202] Weinschenk (465) and Huber (235) approach the subject without reaching any formal conclusions.

[203] Mauco (325), p. 436.

[204] Dromard (134), p. 364.

[205] Cf. a typical observation of hallucination in a normal person, Arieti (12), p. 252.

[206] Arieti believes (12), p. 250, that when the patient hallucinates in the waking state, the visual centres are occupied by the perceptions emanating from the surrounding milieu and cannot participate in the hallucinatory activity. One could respond that the same applies to the auditory centres, but, in reality, they are much more

sizes in this connection that during sleep the most primitive senses come to the fore. The tactile and olfactory senses are certainly more primitive than the visual sense, but their role in the elaboration of symbolism is insignificant. Of the two main senses, vision is the most primitive, auditory images requiring a more developed elaboration, which is incompatible with the waking state. Furthermore, when one is sleeping, individual visual perceptions are eliminated and the centres which usually deal with them are free from any other activity. This is not the case in the hallucinatory state. Since the visual centres are then involved in a much more intense contribution than the auditory centres, the performance of the 'sensory' requirements of the deranged state would henceforth inhibit the latter. Schneider[207] has suggested a similar explanation. *Optical* hallucinations appear in schizophrenia involving extreme intellectual deterioration (Bumke). In fact, the realist structure of visual perceptions, compared to acoustic perceptions, enjoys a relative immunity due to a double mechanism: they are less intimately linked to the mental processes than acoustic perceptions; they also benefit from a greater constancy over time. The same degree of deterioration (de-dialecticization) of the cognitive possesses can thus be sufficient to produce real auditory hallucinations in certain cases, and deranged visual perceptions in clinical cases of limited seriousness. Schneider is also one of the first to insist on the similarities of schizophrenia, not so much with the dream, but with the state of falling asleep.[208]

The anti-dialectical structure common to the dream and the hallucinatory state, the result in both cases of the disinvolvement of the praxis, which is translated by the common validity of the

closely linked to intellectual activity (it is on this fact that C. Schneider bases his explanation (422), cf. further) and less sensitive to the stimuli coming from outside. During electro-encephalography, patients are asked to close their eyes, since the disturbing effect of visual stimuli is known; auditory stimuli are infinitely less disturbing.

[207] Cf. Schneider (422), pp. 85–6.

[208] In connection with this idea, I cannot resist the temptation to reproduce here, without comment, this quotation from André Gide: 'I am almost afraid to go to sleep. One is alone. Thought is projected as on to a black backcloth; future time appears in the darkness like a band of space' (*Les cahiers d'André Walter*, p. 18).

von Domarus-Vigotsky principle, thus finds, according to circumstances, either visual or auditory expression. It seems, therefore, that deranged perceptions in fact constitute the optical equivalent of paranoid auditory hallucinations with which they have precisely this anti-dialectical structure in common. Once again the concept of reification appears as a link, or rather as a common denominator. This is what I shall try to show in my critical examination of Matussek's ideas. If paranoid hallucinations are characterized by phenomena of over-spatialization,[209] perceptual disturbances seem to be dependent on the predominance of egocentric identificatory functions; in other words, they depend on the von Domarus-Vigotsky law which here operates at the perceptual level.

THE ANTI-DIALECTICAL STRUCTURE OF DERANGED PERCEPTIONS: A CRITICAL EXAMINATION OF P. MATUSSEK'S WORK

For traditional psychopathology, the concept of deranged perception makes little sense: if the physiological basis of the perceptual act is normal, perception must be so *ipso facto*; only the existence of a compulsion forcing the patient to bring what is perceived into symbolic relationships of a morbid structure marks the boundary between the pathological and the normal; Gruhle[210] summarized this point of view in a remarkably concise statement: 'In the sick person there is no disturbance in what might be called the elements of perceptual experience (colours, etc. . . .), nor in the structuration of these elements (a formation of definite structure), nor in the act of ascribing meaning (a table), nor in the more highly developed intellectual functions (a rococo table).

---

[209] Cf. Minkowski (342) and (343); dark space, cut off from irreversible axiogenic depth (perspective), is a space of accentuated homeogeneity: a 'super-space'. Naturally, my reasoning may seem, *a priori*, artificial, and so it is, *taken in isolation*; but I integrate it dialectically with an overall conception of the schizophrenic phenomenon, in which each of the elements constitutes the justification for the others.

[210] Gruhle, quoted by Matussek (322), p. 283.

The disturbance resides only in the act of symbolic compulsion.' This was the merit common to *Daseinsanalyse* and Gestaltism, that of having integrated the totality of the perceptual act not only in the organo-psychic totality of the perceiving subject, but in the total structure of his existence in the world. By adopting a Gestaltist position, Matussek therefore places himself on a dialectical plain; the importance of his work for an overall dialectical theory of schizophrenia resides in the fact that he extends into the realm of perception the validity of the anti-dialectical mechanisms of the cognitive schizophrenic act[211] such as they have been demonstrated by Arieti, among others. This is the essence of the study which exercised quite an influence on psychopathological thought in Germany and Italy.

P. MATUSSEK'S CONCEPTION

Matussek sees the essential nature of paranoid perception in the dissociation of significant totalities in perception,[212] parallel to a demonstration of the properties that, through a term borrowed from Klages and Metzger, the author describes as essentials (*Wesenseigenschaften*). The result would be a 'morbid tendency to be distracted by details in the perceptual field'; certain elements of perception are as though 'framed'. The 'newly formed intuitive relationships among certain deranged people'[213] tend to be based on non-objective properties of the external world: the establishment of relationships based on the identity of one essential property. 'The deranged phenomenon called "symbolic relationship" does not, in most cases, spring from a symbolic consciousness, but is based on the *identification of two different objects with the same essential properties.*'[214]

[211] I have used the term 'morbid epistemology' [Esprit (77/1951), p. 468].

[212] 'Lockerung der Wahrnehmungszusammenhänge'.

[213] 'Der sich neu entwickelnde anschauliche Zusammenhang bei manchen Wahnkranken' (Matussek (322), p. 318).

[214] Dem unter dem Namen Symbolzusammenhang gekennzeichneten Wahnphenomen liegt meistens kein Symbolbewusstsein zugrunde sondern es basiert auf die Identifikation zweier verschie-

I suggested earlier a possible rapprochement between this notion and Arieti's ideas and postulated that their common denominator was of a reificational nature. This is the place to go deeper into this question.

It is clear that the notion of essence is the stumbling block in Matussek's conception. He sought to establish a Husserl-Gestaltist synthesis, a legitimate ambition,[215] but he probably did not find the most suitable nexus for it. The concept of 'essence' means far too many things in philosophy,[216] and furthermore it lends itself too easily to egocentric distortion. It may therefore be dangerous to use it in the explanation of concrete psychological facts. Reference is made by the author both to female psychology and child psychology[217] which shows the weakness of his definitions.

In fact, at least one of the two references is false: the child is egocentric and tends—up to a certain age at least—to think spatially; woman is altero-centric and has a certain degree of spatial incapacity.[218] In other words, she *reifies less*, which is translated concretely into the relative rarity of fetishist perversion in women.

dener Gegenstände mit den gleichen Wesenseigenschaften (Matussek (322), p. 318). In two publications (171), 1946 (Madrid) and (181), 1948 (Lausanne), I developed the outline of a similar conception based on Meyerson's epistemology; the symbolic experience of schizophrenics is the manifestation of an abnormal prevalence of the identificatory function of epistemology; identificatory compulsion (*Identitätszwang*) and symbolism of identity.

[215] A legitimate ambition and even somewhat excessive six years after the *Phénoménologie de la Perception*.

[216] For Lukács 'the essence is endowed with a more profound existence than the phenomenon, which is only one of its constituent elements, whilst the essence is in fact the synthesis, the unity of these elements' [(311), p. 284]. In other words, the essence is the dialectical totality of partial determinations. Without going into a deeper discussion of this definition it should be recognized that it is *exactly the opposite* of the definition which underlies Matussek's work.

[217] [(322), p. 294.]

[218] Cf. Andrieux (10) for an experimental demonstration of the 'spatial incapacity' of women; A. Schoen-Levy (416) discusses the incapacity for structuration and hence the temporal incapacity in children, etc.

In his second publication, Matussek uses a formula which would have fascinated Berkeley: 'essentials are the non-objective properties (*ungegenständliche Eigenschaften*) of perceptual structures, for which, excluding arbitrary interpretation, there exist individual variations in the perceptual capacity'.[219] To ascribe as *essential* a property which depends on 'individual variations in the perceptual capacity' is not very logical. Does this concern the essence of the subject or the object?[220] Furthermore the clinical examples that the author gives do not even do justice to the reservation implied in the definition. It is clear that a patient who recognizes an amorous 'essence' in the doctor's gaze[221] is making a most arbitrary interpretation; the patient who equates his lame father with the devil afflicted by the same infirmity, and who also believes that his brother is in reality a detective 'because he watches him with the air of an inquisitor'[222] is not 'essentializing', but is thinking and perceiving in line with the von Domarus-Vigotsky principle. It is not therefore a question of essences, but of the products of a cognitive-perceptual step of a reified, anti-dialectical structure. Matussek implicitly confirms this interpretation by strongly emphasizing the destructuration of significant totalities,[223] a corollary of illegitimate identification based on 'essences', or rather, egocentrism.[224] These elements in

[219] Matussek (323), p. 209.

[220] P. Janet (239), p. 87, discusses the aggressiveness of perception. There is in fact in the perceptual act an aggressive, egocentric, spatializing element, in a word, a reifying element; it is certainly the exacerbation of this element which constitutes the essence of deranged perception. On this point the study of sociocentrism provides confirmation: sociocentric perception (represented among other things by a certain type of caricature) also picks out artificial essence by way of illegitimate identification.

[221] Matussek (322), p. 296.

[222] Matussek (322), p. 299.

[223] 'Where perceptual relationships [*Wahrnehmungszusammenhänge* = significant totalities of perception] are disturbed, isolated objects assume qualities different from those in a normal perceptual ensemble.' Matussek (322), p. 306.

[224] Matussek (322), p. 301; for example, a patient identifies the number '7' with a serpent (Matussek (323), p. 200, quoting Storch). It emerges under analysis that the identification involves an intermediary term which is the word 'penis'. An element of guilt

Matussek are rather 'upside down' as Marx would say, though it is not because he has a more essentialist vision than the one that the schizophrenic 'identifies'; it is because he identifies ego-centrically that, by way of obscuration, he tends to extract de-realist essences appropriate to his deranged needs. A simple change of viewpoint, but one which offers the common denominator necessary to link this theoretical conception—whose interest I am certainly not trying to minimize—to theories of spatialization (Minkowski), epistemological identification (Arieti) or psychoanalysis (Roheim and others) and, in the last analysis, to a general conception of paranoid derangement as de-realist, anti-dialectical thought.

This comes more clearly from a study by C. Kulenkampff[225] devoted to the relationship between deranged perception and the 'life order'. The relations existing between the deterioration of the *faculty for living* and spatialization do not need to be emphasized; by showing that the morbid rationalist does not know 'existentially' where he is (while knowing it cognitively: the loss of the Me–Here–Now function), Minkowski indicated, as early as 1927, the essence of the anthropological problem of *Wohnordnung* in psychopathology. To show the dependence of deranged perception on the loss of the faculty for living is to show implicitly its dependence on spatialization and through its intermediary, on the de-dialecticization of existence; this is exactly

obviously intervenes and the deranged perception does not express any essence but proceeds according to an identificatory step with an egocentric basis (guilt itself is reificational as an element of devaluation–de-dialecticization, cf. below). Another characteristic example is the following: a patient of Matussek's [(322), p. 301], an ex-prisoner in the USSR sees a countryside with primitive agricultural instruments. He says: This is like Russia, *I am in Russia.* He identifies the left side of the countryside (with the primitive instruments) with Russia; the right side with Germany. Obviously, the essence thus extracted is valid only from an egocentric viewpoint which is as primitive as the instruments in question; for the cultivated man (whatever his opinions may be) the *essence* of the USSR is something quite different (which emphasizes the often misunderstood importance of the prepsychotic personality). One could quote many more of these examples.

[225] C. Kulenkampff (271).

what is done by Kulenkampff, without doubt one of the most dialectical minds of the German anthropological school. His patient is again an alien—a theme which keeps on appearing as a *leit-motiv*—an underdeveloped young girl who was forced to leave the Sudetenland during the expulsion of the Germans from Czechoslovakia and found employment as a maid with some American officers in Germany. We have already mentioned this patient as the opposite of the Pallis case.[226] If the apraxic engineer living in an insufficiently spatialized duration is *incapable of identifying* (his wife on each of his visits seeming to be 'like new'), Kulenkampff's paranoid patient is the prisoner of a real identificatory compulsion (*Identitätszwang* in my terminology). She recognizes everybody; the day after her hospitalization, she wonders if a certain patient is not really her mother, someone else in reality her sister. Now, her mother does exist and sometimes comes to visit her. The result is a conflict with reality, a conflict that she resolves by believing in a world of universal falsity, where everybody wears masks.[227]

The beginnings of a poisoning madness characteristically complete the picture. Here the anti-dialectical structure of deranged perception is clearly in evidence; one should talk of *Erkennungswahn* rather than *Verkennungswahn*; a compulsion for identification in a person without roots whose own world tends towards spatialization.[228] The 'false judgement' is therefore not a primary disorder but—like the poisoning madness that is clearly exemplified by this patient—the manifestation of a pathological mode of being-in-the-world characterized by what Strauss calls the loss of the function of sympathetic communication, and which for me

[226] Cf. earlier, p. 170 and (375).

[227] Cf. in this connection, my earlier discussions about the spatializing function and the egocentric structure of the lie.

[228] This is exactly Bergson's mechanism of the '*déjà vu*', a morbid phenomenon of repetition and identification in a destructured and therefore de-dialecticized world. The analytical theory of repetition–compulsion is doubtless another aspect of the same reificational phenomenon [cf. the analysis of the Kierkegaard case and particularly of 'repetition', Lowtzky (308)]. My interpretation differs from Kulenkampff's in that I base mine on Bergson and Lukács and not on Heidegger, but this merely emphasizes the convergence of these different theories.

is nothing other than the deterioration of the dialectical and temporalizing 'praxis'; a case of real *alienation* in a person without roots. This patient, incapable of synchronizing her poor sense of personal historicity with that of her new milieu, lived in pure spatiality; the identificatory function, which is a reificational and spatializing function, was set in motion without any counter-balance.

THE DIALECTICAL NATURE OF THE REALITY OF EXISTENCE EXPERIENCED AS A CATASTROPHE: THE DERANGED EXPERIENCE OF THE END OF THE WORLD

For reified consciousness, history is doubly incomprehensible: as temporalization and as structuring valuation—or, if you like, as valuing structure—in other words, as dialectic. The result is that when the evidence of the historicity of existence forces itself on the misoneism of reified consciousness, it appears as an unexpected *catastrophe*, inexplicable and often attributed therefore to an external[229] action. This is the place to quote a fairly long passage from *Histoire et Conscience de Classe* which, by analyzing one aspect of social reification, implicitly poses an important problem for the psychopathology of schizophrenia.

'The main historians of the 19th century'—wrote Lukács—'.... could not fail to notice the modification of structures (*Strukturformen*) which, as elements of mediation between man and his environment, determine the objective forms (*Gegenständ-*

---

[229] Cf. 'the policing conception of history' [Sperber (431)], a general phenomenon, and one which provides a real analogy with the *syndrome of external action* in psychiatry. For sociocentrism the privileged system being perfect, any change (particularly any unfavourable change) is the work of external maleficent powers. For the misoneism of the schizophrenic who is present as an 'impotent spectator' of his own attitudes and gestures (cf. Zutt (483), and earlier, p. 243), these acts or gestures not being attributable to the will or the self are attributed to an external action—much more easily than in the case of the self deprived of the axiological bulwark —and this is confused with the surroundings.

lichkeit) of his internal and external life. But this is possible only to the extent that the individuality . . . of a given period or historical figure, which is grounded in the particularity of these structures, can be demonstrated through them. Nevertheless neither the people who experience it nor the historian has direct access to immediate reality in these structural forms. It is first necessary to search for them and to find them, and the road to their discovery is the road to a knowledge of the historical process as totality. At first sight—and anyone who insists upon immediacy may never go beyond this "first sight"—it seems that this transcendence (of the immediate) implies a purely intellectual exercise, a mere process of abstraction. But this is an illusion which is itself a consequence of the habits (intellectual and emotional) of pure immediacy which tend to consider the immediate objective forms (*die unmittelbar gegebenen Dingformen*) of things, the fact of their existing here and now and in this particular way (*Dasein* and *Sosein*) as something primordial, real or objective, whilst their interrelationships seem to be secondary and subjective. *For anyone who sees things in such immediacy, all effective change must consequently appear incomprehensible. The indisputable fact of change is reflected in the awareness of immediacy as a catastrophe, in other words, it appears in the form of a sudden change coming from outside and excluding all mediations.*[230] And later: 'As consciousness goes further away from pure immediacy and develops a greater network of "interrelationships", integrating "objects" into their context, so the change is denied its mysterious character and its illusion of catastrophe; it becomes comprehensible.'

We accept as a working hypothesis that the phenomenon described, probably for the first time, by Freud[231] and known as

---

[230] *Histoire et Conscience de Classe*, p. 169. Lukács quotes as a concrete example the theory of crises and the origins of law. It is clear, writes Lukács, that if historiography misunderstands the category of totality, the great turning points of History—the migration of peoples, the German decline after the Renaissance—seem to be 'sinnlose Katastrophen'. Let me add that the historical sensitivity of Marxian orthodoxy immediately after the war was dominated by another schizophrenic category: that of repetition. Cf. my work (179).   [231] Freud (167).

the *deranged experience of the end of the world* (*Weltuntergangs-erlebniss* or *WUE* by German authors)[232] is the psychopatho-logical homologue of this phenomenon of false consciousness: the passage quoted from Lukács is almost a pathogeny. Personally I have never had the opportunity of studying this phenomenon in a schizophrenic,[233] but on this point, the literature offers sub-stantial compensation; the descriptions of WUE in literary works are common and often masterly, which is not surprising since these descriptions benefit from the rare convergence of self-observation and literary talent. The description in *Aurelia* is characterized by the clarity of the deranged perceptions which accompany it; in Strindberg, the WUE goes along with a very typical form of poisoning madness and with a feeling of being crushed by the world.[234] The work of the Austrian poet, G. Trakl, is also typical. A remarkable description, very much in the paranoid *Wahnstimmung*, is in a story by Maupassant[235] who,

[232] Certain Italian authors [Callieri (83)] keep the abbreviation of German origin: WUE = *Weltuntergangserlebniss*. For reasons of convenience I follow this usage in places.

[233] I observed it once in a deranged maniac similar to the case of Tosquelles (448), but the question of the relationship with the WUE is debatable. G. de Nerval, whose literary works contain at least one splendid description of WUE (*Aurelia*, pp. 72 ff.), could have been a manic-depressive psychotic, according to J. Delay (121), but B. Callieri [(83), p. 395, note] believed him to be schizo-phrenic; the number of deranged perceptions in *Aurelia* supports the second hypothesis.

[234] Cf. Jaspers (243), p. 155. Strindberg talks about the 'unmerci-ful judgement pronounced against Sodom' and wonders if this is not the 'Middle Ages beginning again'. If Kafka's work is a sort of self-analysis, Strindberg's can be described almost as *existential self-analysis*, since the themes of *Daseinsanalyse* are so plentiful in it: a feeling of being crushed by the world (Jaspers (243), p. 143) the impression of being 'laid bare' (Jaspers (243), p. 162), (cf. the mechanisms of denudation discussed by Minkowski [(339), p. 76] and especially Strindberg's poisoning madness, analysed in a masterly way by Jaspers [(243), pp. 118–19]). Strindberg found that the air was heavy, as if poisoned: he could work only with the windows open.

[235] *La Nuit* in the 'Clair de Lune' collection. The description is masterly. But perhaps Maupaussant merely wished to imitate Nerval?

as we know, was not at all schizophrenic; this constitutes a useful caution against the *uncritical* use of literary documents.

The diagnosis of the Schreber case remains doubtful. Freud, who hesitated between paranoia and paraphrenia, explains the pathogenesis of end of the world fantasies as a process of libidinal retreat from the world followed by a deranged reconstruction. This mechanism is the same as that discussed by Katan for the formation of the verbal apparatus of schizophrenics (though the patient does have a trace of WUE). This is, therefore, essentially the projection of an internal catastrophe: Hoskins,[236] who discusses the experience of dissociation proper, experienced through cosmic identification as a world catastrophe, is basically not saying anything different. Arieti, on the other hand, considers this phenomenon as a subjective experience of progressive de-socialization.[237]

Callieri shows that in the end of the world fantasies, the 'essential properties' of the objects of perception are emphasized or changed in a more general way, 'which emphasizes their relationship with deranged perceptions'.[238] The passages quoted from *Aurelia* later are, in this respect, perfectly characteristic. Callieri interprets this syndrome as the 'wrecking of the sick person's mode of being-in-the-world, as the cessation for him of the validity of our categories and formal laws of thought',[239] which is the translation in analytico-existential language of Arieti's sociologizing thesis. In this form, it is nothing more than

---

[236] Hoskins (233), p. 86.

[237] Cf. Arieti (12), p. 304. This is also Kunz's opinion (274) who considers 'a radical retreat, or at least a partial retreat, from the common world into a private universe' a probable explanation. This interpretation does not explain the dramatic nature of the phenomenon. The essential fact is not therefore a progressive retreat into a private world but, on the contrary, the irruption of the 'eventful' character of reality (i.e. its moving, structured and valued character) into the anaxiological, ahistorical and destructured world of reified consciousness. Cf. the observation of Kretschmer Jr. [(267), pp. 209–10] where fantasies of the end of the world are seen as an expression of the struggle of Good and Evil. (*Le Diable*.)

[238] Callieri (83), p. 396.

[239] Callieri (83), p. 402.

a generality which needs to be given concrete content. Callieri establishes elsewhere a remarkable rapprochement between end of the world fantasies and J. Zutt's *esthetic syndromes.*

The dialectical interpretation of the phenomenon offers one advantage, that of linking two apparently unconnected clinical data into a coherent whole: the syndrome of external action and the deranged experience of the end of the world. In the spatialized universe, the event, as we have seen, is doubly proscribed: as act of temporalization and as creation of value.[240] Consequently, when the event forces itself into reified consciousness, the latter makes this evident through a double technique of partial obscuration: from the point of view of causal explanation it interprets it as the act of an external power; on the level of lived experience, it experiences it either as a catastrophe or, on the contrary, as a sudden significant (and always heteronomic) irruption into the axiological void of the world itself: a *divine mission.* In short, like a manic crisis, the WUE is an axiological crisis, a sort of storm of values on the boundaries of two atmospheres of different axiological-dialectical density.[241] If one takes as a starting point the postulate of axio-dialectical equivalence (axiogenic function of the category of concrete totality) and the axiological nature of the libido, one sees that an interpretation, Marxist in its origins, can without difficulty link up with Freudian conceptions; furthermore, it provides a common (reificational) denominator for the phenomenon of deranged perception—interpreted earlier as anti-dialectical perception—and the WUE, which it thus organically

---

[240] In the case of Storch-Kulenkampff [(436), p. 103], the patient (a young peasant) said in characteristic fashion: 'Growth has ceased: so has human creation' (*das Wachstum hat aufgehört und das Schaffen der Menschen*) and later (p. 105) it concerns the 'solidification of the world as a result of the deterioration of the future' (*aus dem Werdensverlust entspringende Welterstarrung*), etc. Cf. a detailed analysis of the case later, p. 293.

[241] In Binswanger's 'Mary case', the dialectical aspect of the difference between the 'two worlds' is clearer: the 'low gear' world of refined existence and fidelity; and the rapid world of inferior pleasures; in short, opposition beteen the sexual-dialectical and the reified-social worlds.

integrates into the general phenomenological structure of derangement.

Thus a connection is created between morbid rationalism and the phenomenon of the end of the world experience.[242] It is as one aspect of the anti-dialectical mode of being-in-the-world that one can place the WUE in the same ambit as deranged perceptions, hallucinations and other elements of sub-realist experience.

Storch and Kulenkampff provide us with a case of paranoid psychosis with grandiose WUE in the style of *Crépuscule des Dieux*, where the interpretation is of a specifically dialectical inspiration (though saturated with existentialist terminology), and constitutes a valuable confirmation of my point of view. For this reason it is permissible for me to summarize it in a little more detail.

A young Swiss peasant had already had an attack of schizophrenia in 1945. In 1947 he happened to witness an aeroplane *crash*; this event was interpreted by him as the sign of the imminence of the end of the world. Furthermore he considered himself and his father to be jointly responsible for it;[243] the theme

---

[242] A connection which implicitly contains a Freudian interpretation (167); the universe devalued by libidinal withdrawal becomes homogeneous, and therefore of a spatial structure. A crisis of temporalization (similar to that described by Binswanger) exists in the Schreberian world but, in Freud's description, it passes to the second level (cf. (167), p. 59 where it is *a chasm of temporal oblivion in the history of humanity*; p. 58 Schreber believes that he has been at Professor Flechsig's sanatorium for 212 years etc.).

To direct research towards this element of sub-temporalization is the same as simply changing the perspective, without any modification of the facts at issue, from psychoanalysis to *Daseinsanalyse*.

[243] The word 'responsibility' is used with reservation, for it is a question of 'guilt' which, in a sense, is just the opposite; cf. my remarks about L. Duss's interpretation of the 'Renée case'; it is by confusing 'responsibility', an act of dialectical-axiogenic structuration, with 'guilt', a reificational act, that L. Duss manages to describe schizophrenia as an 'existentialist crisis', when it is a sub-realist crisis. The flight from guilt towards responsibility (from reification to the dialectic or, if you wish, from dissociation towards totality) is one of the implications of *The Trial* by Kafka (the judge's inquiry).

L*

of the *morbid universe of guilt* is present, which is one aspect of the reificational devaluation of the universe of the schizophrenic. In fact, his father had 'uprooted' an oak tree; the misfortunes of the Universe date from this mistake. From the hole, water had spread over the whole surface of the earth.[244] Another 'mistake' responsible for the catastrophe was the transformation of a main gateway, repainted in black and modified: this is the reificational misoneism of schizophrenic consciousness. Since the sun's rays were not able to get through this door, the sun had to remain in a different spot.[245] All growth was arrested and all creation stopped (!). The atmosphere itself became unbreathable.

All of this is integrated into a familiar context: the theme of uprooting; and it was the *uprooting* of a tree which was the beginning of events. The deeper reason for the whole of this catastrophe is that the people were no longer at home. He said 'I no longer find myself in the *proper place*.'[246] Furthermore his closest friends turned their backs on him. On examining more closely the changes in this patient's world, we can see the reified structure of the phenomenon described. Manifestations of the patient's view of the world, such as, for example, the fact that the earth had become flatter, the mountains had levelled (*eingeebnet*), the oceans had disappeared, reveal a loss of the variety of forms, a general *levelling*.[247] In this universe without

---

[244] Cf. in *Aurelia*: 'The water rose in the neighbouring streets; I ran down the rue Saint-Victor and with the idea of stopping what I believed to be a universal flood I threw the ring that I had bought at Saint-Eustache into the deepest part. At the same moment, the storm abated and a ray of sunlight began to shine' (Nerval, *Aurelia*, p. 76). A splendid picture: an end of the world fantasy, magical action, and a feeling of omnipotence, not to mention the deranged perceptions which abound in this book.

[245] In the Schreber case, the cause of the catastrophe is 'a withdrawal of the sun, which would freeze the earth' [(167), p. 56]; there are other analogies with the case of the Swiss peasant, such as the fact of being the only real survivor of the catastrophe. All these arguments favour Schreber's hypothesis of schizophrenia.

[246] Storch-Kulenkampff (436), p. 103.

[247] Storch-Kulenkampff (436), p. 104. Cf. the need for homogeneity in Goldstein's example [(250), p. 25], in which Goldstein sees—wrongly without any doubt—signs of over-concretized

frontiers (*Entgrenzung*), the *Dasein* is 'unprotected' (*Entbergung*); without a reference point, orientation becomes problematical; the *Dasein* no longer occupies a privileged position;[248] unprotected, vulnerable, it lives in an atmosphere of mistrust. The notion of poisoning concretizes this world of mistrust: poisoning madness quite logically completes the picture,[249] in the most typical way: unbreathable air, *blue gas*.

The rootless person without firm ground under his feet, feels the earth becoming hollow: people tend to fall (cf. Ellen West),[250] the hollow sucks him in. A 'loss of becoming' or more exactly a general decline in becoming translates this manner of being 'abyssal' in the world.[251] Thus, we have in a coherent picture all the elements for a dialectical interpretation of this syndrome: the theme of the *illegitimate* event[252] which, being unable to be

thought, when it is in fact a need for reificational-spatializing homogeneity, as clearly emerges from the example above. Cf. my criticism of this idea, earlier, pp. 161 ff.

[248] The question arises as to whether there is not a contradiction between the loss of the privileged position of the Self in space (which is translated through the loss of the Me–Here–Now function) and egocentrism. This would be no more contradictory than the fact that the child is egocentric while ignoring the 'I' and designating himself by a third person. In reality (and this is an idea close to Maine De Biran's, who was one of the founders of the philosophy of existence) it is by acting on the 'Non-Me' that one fixes one's real place in the world: the deterioration of the praxis makes the patient believe himself to be the centre of the world (Mme. Sechehaye's Renée thinks that the moon is following her) while not knowing the place of the real *Dasein*.

[249] The word '*crédence*' (*Kredenz* in German: *kredencz* in Hungarian) used to mean a small cupboard next to the table which *inspired confidence* (*credere: croire*), i.e. something which was not supposed to contain poison. (Cf. Kulenkampff (269), p. 5, note.)

[250] The term 'abgründige Entgründung [(436), p. 105] is easier to reproduce than to translate.

[251] '... privation des Werdens ... umfassende Werdensverlust ... ein Ausdruck dieser abgründigen Seinsweise' [(406), p. 105]. The translation of *abgründig* by *abyssal* is dubious but I cannot see anything better. This terminology is strictly analytico-existential, without any relationship to psychoanalytic terminology.

[252] In this case the uprooting of the tree, and the changes made to the door.

integrated into a dialectical causal chain, appears as a catastrophe and starts in motion, through a sort of chain reaction,
a cosmic catastrophe; the theme of uprooting symbolized by the
uprooting of the old oak tree, the theme of spatialization ('general
levelling') of the world, and finally the de-dialecticization of
experience. Now we can understand what the destruction of the
tree might signify to the patient. It was the sign of cosmic
upheaval. The whole cosmic future was profoundly disturbed by
it, it 'jumped its rails in order to yield to its downfall'.[253] In
effect this tree symbolizes *life*. Man also lives uprooted from the
soil and breathes the invigorating air above. For the person who
is a *stranger to existence*[254] the root of life becomes 'space for dead
men' and the 'invigorating air' is transformed into noxious gas.

This chapter had a limited goal. Starting with the hypothesis that
schizophrenia is the form *par excellence* of anti-dialectical existence in the world, I have tried to show that this idea—which is a
unitary idea as a consequence of the mediation of the category
of false consciousness—could be considered as the common denominator for a certain number of theories and as the fundamental disorder for a certain number of symptoms. It would be
possible to pursue this demonstration but at the risk of losing in
clarity what might have been gained in extension. We have
deliberately, on the other hand, avoided the problem of catatonia
which, in this order of ideas, might have led to conclusions of a
suspect nature. To explain the fact of deranged perception in
terms of a dissolution of significant totalities with a demonstration

[253] [(436), p. 105.]
[254] In his interpretation of the significance of Kafka's work, K. H.
Volkmann-Schluck (459) introduced the idea of 'permission to
stay in existence'; the agent K. . . (in the *Trial*) is guilty because he
does not have this permission. In a study devoted to 'Kafka, the
the novelist of alienation' (175), I tried to show that the world of
Kafka's novels is the same as the world of reification in Lukács,
described with the novelist's modes of expression.
  The young peasant in the Storch-Kulenkampff case is *alienated*
in this specific sense of the term; it is a guilt derangement in an
adialectical (reified) universe. The climate of this case is reminiscent
of Kafka.

of anti-dialectical structures, is a statement of a scientific nature, which constitutes progress to the extent that it satisfies the requirements of logic and corresponds to the facts. The same applies to my interpretation of the phenomenon of fantasies about the end of the world as the lived experience of a dialectical reality through the distortion of a reified consciousness; an interpretation of this order may be correct or it may not be; one can only comment that this says very little. To say of a patient who does not move that he is *behaving anti-dialectically*, seems at first sight to be a terrible commonplace; it is not false as such nor even necessarily devoid of value, but it becomes a *scientific statement* only in the context of a confirmed theory about the generally anti-dialectical involvement of the *Dasein* in the world. It is this context that I have tried to define in this last chapter.

To base a theoretical hypothesis on others' observations may seem to invite criticism. Obviously, this is not, properly speaking, a clinical method, but neither is its negation, since every theoretical conception is, in the last resort, a crystallization of clinical observations. It is permissible to invoke the example of Freud and others[255] for support. In other respects, the exclusive use of personal observations is not completely free from danger. Beyond the risk of ideological interference,[256] scientific work carried out on personally observed material tends in fact—if not necessarily—to underestimate the point of view of other authors, thus falling into the trap of a kind of scientific autism. It is rather tempting when one has arrived at an interesting conclusion through the study of a personal case to consider research that has a different

[255] Several of Freud's discoveries are due to work on other people's clinical material. Freud devoted a study to the question of aphasia (a remarkable study in that it is perhaps the first to do justice to Jackson). In connection with this study, I may quote the opinion of Walter Riese [(404), p. 6]: 'One of the most remarkable and distinctive characteristics of this book is that it was written by an author who, as he confesses himself in the very beginning, had no personal observations to offer. This makes the book a rare and brilliant piece of medical thought.' Some remarkable interpretations are due to non-medical thinkers, such as Klages' theory of hysteria or Cassirer's interpretation of aphasia.

[256] Cf. for this question, W. Baranger (30).

conclusion as negligible and to respond to objections with Goya's profound words: 'Yo lo vi!' Consequently, it is permissible to wonder if arguments about the observations of others are not, from the epistemological point of view, the surest source of information, because of the same mechanism of decentration which often makes it preferable to have an examiner who does not personally know the candidate, or which requires two different signatures on certain documents.

To illustrate this thesis, I may again quote the well-known work of K. Goldstein on the *over-concretized* character of the thought of schizophrenics, a work that has already been examined critically in a different context. I have shown the criticisms to which this idea might be exposed and tried to establish that the notion of *reified thought* advantageously eliminates the ambiguity inherent in the polyvalent use of terms such as 'abstract' or 'concrete'. This ambiguity is prevalent in the Kasanin anthology and even in the otherwise coherent thinking of S. Arieti. Arieti in fact admits, on the one hand, the validity of Goldstein's hypothesis and, on the other, the von Domarus-Vigotsky principle. Now, to equate the basic with the secondary—as this law stipulates—is equivalent to obscuring the essential, which would not be a solid step forward. But without going into these details considered elsewhere, one fact is certain: the *abstract* (and not concrete) character of schizophrenic thought has been clearly emphasized by many authors, including Binswanger; now such a doctrinal divergence *itself* constitutes a fact which must be interpreted. Inversely, the statement of doctrinal convergence between two independent researchers or schools is just as legitimate a source of scientific progress as the careful analysis of personal observations.

It is possible to distinguish three types of convergence:

(1) *Convergence of symptoms:* certain coexistences are typical such as, for example, that of poisoning madness with the phenomenon of WUE in paranoid derangement; the relationship between deranged perception and anthropological problems of habitation which, for their part, are linked to the phenomenon of the spatialization of duration; structural analogies between

end of the world fantasies and deranged perceptions, etc.[257] In this case, the hypothesis of the non-dialectical structure of existence and thought postulated as a fundamental disorder, offers to these coexistences a theoretical base which allows us to go dialectically beyond the stage of purely empirical observations.

(2) *Convergence of doctrines:* such as, for example, those pointed out between existential and psychoanalytic analysis, between these two schools and (open) Marxism, between Minkowski's ideas and certain psychoanalytic works (G. Pankow— and to a lesser degree—M. A. Sechehaye), and finally:

(3) *Convergence between individual and collective anti-dialectical structures:* in other words, the schizophrenic character of false consciousness.

The anthropological interpretation that Kulenkampff gives to the *Oedipus complex*, is one example of these convergences. Oedipus, guilty of incest, puts himself into the position of a person *who is seen, without himself seeing*; this artificial paranoid situation allows him to avoid the 'morbid universe of guilt' in the form of a real paranoid attack.[258] But the breakdown of the 'seeing'–'being seen' dialectic, one of the facets of the fundamental disorder of the paranoid attack, as we have seen, has a reificational, and consequently a *spatializing* dimension.

Now, the analytical doctrine of the Oedipus complex and its transcendence entails an axiological and dialectical aspect; it is, to a certain extent, the metapsychological expression of the process of transcending a pre-dialectical stage, a reificational stage in a sense. The publications of A. Hesnard are particularly significant as a theory of the transcendence of the Oedipus complex as a stage in the process of dialectical personalization.[259] As an example we can use the case of Sören Kierkegaard as F. Lowtzky did.[260] F. Lowtzky observes in the author of *Répétition* a violent

[257] Callieri (83), p. 396 (a change in the so-called essential properties of objects in deranged perception and in WUE).

[258] Kulenkampff (270), p. 7.

[259] Cf. Hesnard (224, 225, and 226), *passim*, and (27), pp. 60, 69 etc.

[260] F. Lowtzky (308). But it is only as an example of possible psychodynamics that I use this article, given the extreme complexity of the case of the Danish thinker. F. Lowtzky makes the diagnosis of

Oedipus complex involving identification with the father and desire for *repetition* of the primitive scene, a desire being reified in the form of the homogenization (and consequently, spatialization) of duration. D. Lagache, for his part, points out the possibility of 'an intimate liaison between certain identifications and the attitude of the subject in relation to time'.[261] The nature of this 'intimate liaison' could be conceived only in one way that is satisfying to the mind; the preponderance of identificatory functions in their various forms (identification with one or the other parent, with the enemy, etc. . . .), is crystallized in the form of a *general identificatory attitude*, as logical expression, the von Domarus-Vigotsky principle, the pre-eminence of which spatializes time.[262] It is therefore, possible to establish a convergence

melancholia; Hellveg (219) of circulatory psychosis. Schizophrenia was diagnosed by Boström and by the non-medical specialist in German studies, A. Closs (109), p. 288: 'The suppression of desires in K. is certainly not characteristic of the creative genius in general, but only of the schizophrenia of this author.' A. Tosquelles published the case of a maniac with Kierkegaardian themes (448); I have been able to observe (without publishing it) the case of a schizophrenic with religious mania recalling the same themes. The case is therefore complex. What is certain is that the temporality of the *Répétition* is that of morbid rationalism.

Personally, I believe that K. was suffering from an affliction of the schizophrenic type with 'existentialist' and 'morbid rationalist' oscillations (phases of reification and de-reification), similar to the Renée case of Sechehaye. For this neurotic genius the 'existentialist phase' is simply . . . existentialism. But it is impossible to develop a definitive idea about Kierkegaard without knowing him. It is for this reason that I am quoting F. Lowtzky's ideas without committing myself.

[261] D. Lagache, *L'Evolution Psychiatrique*, July–September 1955, p. 580.

[262] The specific question of the relationship between epistemological identification (Meyerson) and psychoanalytic identification (sometimes depersonalizing or alienating) 'with other people, or even surrounding objects' (Roheim (405), p. 117) does not seem to have been raised, not even in Hesnard's important work (227), devoted entirely to the problem. I do not claim to have resolved it. But I am one of the first to point out that schizophrenia, a reificational syndrome, tends to confuse these two aspects (cf. my work in 1951 (177), p. 481). Here again, schizophrenia is 'Nature's great experiment'.

between the analytical and anthropological interpretations of the Oedipus complex and this convergence, which is integrated into the overall psychopathology of dialectical thought, is oriented towards the concept of the spatialization of duration, in other words, towards morbid rationalism.

It is in this same order of ideas that one can join G. Pankow in talking of the 'Oedipus situation alienated in space'.[263] (Daim speaks of '*dialektische Akzentverlagerung*' of the Oedipean situation which amounts to the same thing.)[264] So we find the same constituent elements in each of these interpretations: identification, spatialization with sub-temporalization, and regression to a pre-dialectical stage. But the respective place of this data in the causal nexus varies depending on the perspective of the therapeutic approach and also the individual case.

A similar convergence can be established between the interpretation of paranoid poisoning madness and the deranged end-of-the-world experience. Poisoning madness comes from an anti-dialectical structure of the involvement of man in the world in the way considered earlier; the Self-World dialectic (the 'praxis') creates values; it heterogenizes and therefore temporalizes the spatio-temporal structure of the world itself. By contrast, the loss of this dialectic involves a process of homogenization (spatialization) of the environment and in the homogeneous (reified) atmosphere the *Dasein*, without a defensive, axiological barrier, is 'unprotected' and it experiences all alimentary contributions— and even the atmosphere—as 'poison'. Let me say, in a rather simplistic way, that the dialectic is structuration and, consequently, valuation; the alimentary act is similar in its own way; the *Dasein*, which no longer structures, finds itself, *vis-à-vis* the alimentary act, somewhat in the position of an organically sick person who is incapable of assimilating food and for whom all food is *effectively poison*.

We again find the same element in different analytical interpretations, though integrated into a different causal arrangement. The pathogenic role of *oral frustration* has been emphasized most strongly (to my knowledge) by Roheim and Schilder,[265] and the

---

[263] Pankow (376), p. 45.
[264] Daim (120), p. 249.   [265] Cf. (419).

importance of identification by Roheim, who also insisted on the analogies between schizophrenia and magic. They are probably various aspects of the same fundamental anti-dialectical structure: the relationship between the oral stage and identification are well known; as are those between orality and magic.[266] Whether these magical techniques postulate a symbolism of total identity and *a pars pro toto* with an illusion of totality analogous to fetishism,[267] they are facts which do not need to be considered here. As for the spatio-temporal structures of magical action, here is a quote from Schilder: 'Magical action is a form of action which influences the body image, irrespective of actual distance of space.'[268] It is clear that in the spatio-temporal continuum, the 'time' factor constitutes the *axiogenic obstacle* and that, consequently, in a pure spatiality with atemporal displacement (spatiality of the 'magic carpet') the distance to be travelled no longer counts. Magic, an identificatory and schizophrenic technique, thus appears at the same time as a spatializing technique based on an illusion of praxis or[269]—if you like—a sort of cheating of the natural dialectic.[270]

According to Roheim, the future schizophrenic does not succeed in overcoming the energy crisis of separation from the mother.[271] The category of totality reappears in this context: 'the schizophrenic is incapable of considering himself as a whole without the mother'; he reacts to it by a strong identificatory

[266] Roheim (405), p. 118.

[267] In this order of ideas, fetishism, a schizoid, reificational sexual technique, is also a *magical sexuality*.

[268] Schilder (418), p. 277.

[269] Magical activity claims to command nature *without* obeying it.

[270] Magic postulates a false Self-World dialectic where the resistance to reality, represented among other things by the 'distance to be travelled', is obscured in a more or less voluntary manner depending on the particular case.

[271] An energy crisis which has a thermal aspect: 'the separation from the maternal body involves an enormous loss of temperature' (Bak (26 *bis*), p. 69). The subsequent difficulties of homeostasis (Gottlieb and Linder (203 *bis*), p. 785) date from this. Bak's patient who identified with the sun was compensating for this 'thermal' birth trauma. Cf. also the role of the sun in the Schreber case, Freud (167), p. 44.

tendency, which allows him to resist acceptance of reality by restoring the 'original child-mother or subject-object unity[272] in fantasy. All the elements of *false consciousness* are present: the destructuration of totality (de-dialecticization, in other words, a reificational tendency), the illusion of totality, the loss of the subject-object dialectic, and a superimposed identificatory tendency, which, from the analytical viewpoint, all arise out of the *primum movens* of the oral trauma. But it is a short step from the notion of oral trauma to poisoning derangement. Westerman Holstijn[273] maintains that separation, the 'primary castration' (Stärcke), produces a chronic state of buccal excitation with buccal aggression against the mother or one's own body. The subsequent impression of *being poisoned* is derived from it, and is of libidinal origin; the word *venenum* comes from Venus. Without going into details, we can see once again that this analytico-existential coverage leads towards a common denominator, dialectical in its positive aspect, and reificational in its negative aspect.[274]

The problem of the *deranged experience of the end of the world* was earlier the object of an interpretation along the lines of an axiological crisis through the interference of two climates with different axio-dialectical density, in other words, like an explosion of temporal dialectics into the spatialized world.[275] In his interpretation of the 'Schreber case', Freud sees it as the withdrawal of the libido from the world, a 'libidinal de-investment

---

[272] Roheim (405), p. 222. Another aspect of the Marxism-psychoanalysis convergence: the analogy between the child-parent dialectic and the subject-object dialectic.

[273] Westerman-Holstijn (467), p. 174.

[274] For anthropological psychiatry, the act of believing oneself to be poisoned is due to a too purely 'geometric' existence where the person is 'unprotected'. For the psychoanalytic authors I have quoted, separation does not end in the formation of a new, autonomous totality, so the child seeks refuge in compensatory anti-dialectical identification. On the other hand, oral frustration (unsuccessful separation) materializes (is reified) in the form of poisoning derangement. One can see that my conception: derangement = non-dialectical thought = individual false consciousness is the equation for both of them.

[275] Cf. the 'two speeds', in reality 'two universes', in the 'Mary case', where Binswanger effectively establishes the presence of WUE.

from objects' the subjective experience of which would be the WUE. Freud formulated his theory on the basis of someone else's observation, a diagnosis which, in other ways, was doubtful: the hypothesis of a schizophrenic state has a sufficient number of arguments in its favour for it not to be thrust aside immediately. From the viewpoint of *Daseinsanalyse* the nostalgia for feminine sexual behaviour can be understood as a sexualized form of the attitude of being overwhelmed by the world, which is one of the basic concepts of anthropological analysis and is perhaps best expressed—and in any case most graphically—by C. Kulen-kampff's 'loss of the upright position' (*Standverlust*). One can then postulate that the sterility of Schreber's marriage partially reified his lived experience of duration by cutting it off from the valuing dimension of the future; in this case, the fantasy about the end of the world would be due to the intervention of the spatialized universe of masculine sterility and the nostalgia for the axiological event that feminine fantasy expresses.[276] There is no contradiction between this interpretation and the one based on a dialectic of the libido: in his analysis of the Schreber case, Freud in fact carried out a *Daseinsanalyse*. If the anthropological inter-pretation of the Oedipus complex raises the problem of relation-ships between epistemological identification and analysis of poisoning derangement, the problem of the relationship of the dialectical category of totality and oral frustration, then it is the particular question of the relationship between the libido and the general philosophical concept of value which is raised in the Schreber case, and the general question of the phenomenology of the deranged experience of the end of the world.

The critical demonstration of these dialectical convergences could be an interesting task for an overt Marxist pyschopathology; it is

---

[276] Cf. the patient of Storch-Kulenkampff (436) who complained of the cessation of the future of all creation. As for the question of the relationship between temporality and the fantasy of being a woman, cf. again the experimental research of C. Andrieux (10), which, by demonstrating the spatial incapacity of women, implicitly reveals their superiority with regard to the experience of lived duration. Cf. my contribution (170).

also the one most deliberately neglected by orthodox Marxism. The reasons for this are gnoseo-sociological; it is one aspect of the dialectical malaise of orthodoxy. It is a malaise which is seen particularly clearly in questions concerning the *Umstülpung* of idealist dialectics. Elsewhere[277] I have defined scholastic Marxism as the Marxism which accepts Hegel's *Umstülpung* through Marx but without continuing this line. The global rejection of 'idealist' dialectics (like Bergonism) is one of the characteristic traits of scholastic Marxism; it is also the actual viewpoint of Marxist critics of psychoanalysis. The attitude towards non-official dialectics is one of the touch-stones of the open or closed nature of a Marxist system. Open Marxism welcomes the dialectical aspects of non-Marxist (and particularly idealist) dialectics as supplementary proof of the validity of the dialectical principle; scholastic Marxism would see it as the 'illegal exercise of the dialectic', to paraphrase a well-known juridical term. It is difficult to say whether Marx was a scholastic Marxist or not: on the specific issue of the integration of idealist dialectics, his personal attitude was clearly that of *open Marxism*. If he had anticipated some of today's criticism, Marx might not have committed the act of extreme intellectual confusion (a dialectical synthesis of the doctrines of a well-known idealist with that of a materialist), which was the act of *giving birth* to Marxist doctrine.

In psychopathology, non-dialectical Marxism occupies a special place; real dialectical effort is developed on an idealist plane. In fact the gnoseo-sociological position of psychiatry is rather special. Its sociological—and even its political—implications make it particularly sensitive to social reification which it mirrors; on the other hand, the existence of analogies between deranged thought and false consciousness risks starting a dialectical psychopathology critical of *all* ideologies. Marxist psychiatry has thus become the appropriate domain for mechanistic materialism, and the inevitably dialectical evolution of science has taken place outside the Marxist arena. Now, nowhere perhaps are the chances for *Umstülpung* better than in the area of psychopathology: the whole school of anthropological and phenomenological psychiatry in the widest sense of the term (including not only Binswanger

[277] Cf. my contribution (170).

and his followers but thinkers such as Minkowski, Gebsattel and Caruso) practises pure dialectics which simply need to be integrated.

The nature of this *Umstülpung* is certainly different from case to case. We have seen this in the criticism of Matussek's theory of deranged perception: the inversion of the fundamental step in this theory (i.e. a structuration singularly different from its elements) allows us to eliminate an ambiguous notion, that of *essential property*, and by the same token allows us to see a link between the theory of deranged perception and data that is as well defined as the notion of the preponderance of the identificatory function, and which can be extended to analytical psychopathology (Roheim) and also to the theory of ideology. In the case of Minkowski's research this step consists essentially of a sociologization of the biological bases of the doctrine: the notion of loss of *praxis* is thus substituted for the notion of loss of vital contact. This permits us to use the notion of *morbid rationalism* in the area of ideological criticism by adding a historicist dimension to it. Furthermore a link is thus established with child psychology and—through the intermediary of the concept of identification—psychoanalysis. Binswanger's 'Contributions', where the concept of the praxis is constantly used in its Marxist sense, from this point of view already constitutes a sociologization of Minkowski's ideas. In certain cases the '*Umstülpung*' consists mainly in the elimination of a parasitic terminology which only serves to make an otherwise valid description unnecessarily complicated.

The possibility of a Marxist integration of certain theories more or less directly inspired by Heidegger, implicitly raises the question of the relationship between existentialism and Marxism. I have, on several occasions, referred to L. Goldmann's hypothesis about Lukács's relationship with Heidegger's thought.[278] I

---

[278] Cf. L. Goldmann (199), pp. 245–6. I have considered this whole problem (the relationship between the sociology of knowledge and *Daseinsanalyse*) in my critical account of Binswanger's 'Susan Urban case' (169 *bis*).

am not here considering a problem of philosophical erudition that is beyond the frameworks of this work. From a purely psycho-pathological point of view, the results of my study contribute two elements in favour of this hypothesis. On the one hand, the balance-sheet of clinical cases who have an 'existential crisis' (Sechehaye, Duss, Gebsattel) shows that this crisis appears as a *reaction* against the reificational structure of the derangement; it is therefore permissible to suppose, by extrapolation, that the thinking of the existentialist school as a whole represents a reaction against the anti-dialectical schizophrenization of collective consciousness, or, in other words, a reaction against false consciousness. On the other hand, I have established that the psychopathological theories that depend on the *Daseinsanalyse* are generally of a dialectical inspiration and can, through a straightforward materialist re-evaluation be integrated into a general Marxist psychopathology. The essential elements of this re-evaluation were reviewed in earlier chapters. Richer clinical material would have been required for the establishment of a complete Marxist theory of schizophrenia. However, I am convinced that the direction of this theory lies in the analysis of the subject-object dialectic on the clinical level, and in the materialist integration of theories of existential anthropology.

The question of knowing wheher Marxism is truly a materialism has often been raised. Let me point out, without any claim to originality, that the term 'materialism' is used by the Marxists with two different meanings in ontology and sociology. In discussions of this kind, it is useful to refer to the original texts, however well known they may be. 'In the social production of their existence'—writes Marx—'men enter into definite relationships, that are indispensable and independent of their will; these relationships of production correspond to a degree of development determined by their material powers of production. These relationships of production constitute the economic structure of society, the concrete base on which a juridical and political superstructure is built and to which definite forms of social consciousness correspond. The mode of production of material life conditions the process of social, political and intellectual life in general. It is not the consciousness of men that determines their existence, but on the contrary their social existence which determines their consciousness.'[279] The links between this Marxian conception and the hypothesis of the ontological primacy of matter, are in reality of a psychological rather than an objective nature; it is not impossible, nor even inconsequential that a Platonist should believe that the objects of this world are the reification of external ideas, while believing that on the social level, our belonging to a group fashions our thinking. By using the common term of 'materialism' for these two different intellectual attitudes, Marx and Engels introduced—in the name of the necessities of the political struggle—an actual *identificatory expression.* It would be interesting to follow its progress through the process of ideologization of Marxism. In its origins historical materialism is in fact closer to a sociologism with a more economic slant than Durkheimian sociologism; its links with *ontological* primacy of matter are, on the contrary, contingent, not to mention arbitrary. Let me add that the dialectic—particularly in the Lukácsian meaning of the term—is such a specific concept that I have been able to define a nosological entity as its opposite, whilst the concept of materialism, which is much less specific in its origins (Berkeley described as a *materialist* any thinker admitting that only matter exists), has practically been emptied of all meaning by the sociocentric dichotomization of orthodoxy. This dichotomization probably influenced non-Marxist philosophical thought to a larger extent than is believed.

Now, this dialectical sociologism, arbitrarily described as 'materialism', is so little at odds with the general spirit of existential analysis that it could have been formulated almost *expressis verbis* by the founder of this latter school. Things do not 'happen' writes Binswanger—'as if an abstract Self was placed in an abstract World, and this Self later endowed with definite needs, desires and instincts. Nor does this happen within the frameworks of a world endowed "as an afterthought" with a certain physiognomy and a certain expressive content. On the contrary, Self and World constitute a dialectical unity in which each pole gives significance to the other, or, more exactly, in

[279] Cf. (321).

which all meaning is a result of their interaction.'[280] Marx would have agreed with such a statement. As for the differences which might exist between 'World' and 'Society', they remain mysterious, even (and especially) after reading Binswanger's *Contributions*. For Binswanger, as for Marx, man and environment form a concrete dialectical totality; man is personalized by transforming his environment. Whether sick or healthy in mind, the individual is *concretely integrated* (and not simply 'placed') in his social environment. In talking of *Seinsgebundenes Denken*, Mannheim did not abandon the materialist conception of history; he merely gave it a specific formulation. The result is that if there are only vague links between *historical materialism* and *ontological materialism* there are very specific (and almost obligatory) ones between historical materialism and a dialectic of totality: a subsequent sociologism can be nothing other than dialectic. In psychopathology the research of the existential anthropological school is an example of this; it shows how a dialectical point of view at the beginning, leads—as if by immanent logic—towards a concrete scientific consideration of the data from the social context. Pavlovism illustrates this thesis *a contrario*.[281]

I would like to avoid one misunderstanding: I am not *criticizing* Pavlovism here; such a criticism would have to be experimental in order even to begin to have any validity. I am not casting doubts on the scientific value of Pavlovism, but rather its quality as a dialectical doctrine; this is not the same thing. From the point of view of dialectical epistemology it is important not to confuse the judgement about the scientific value of a doctrine with the judgement about its dialectical nature (which is not a value judgement). The confusion of the two comes from a dogmatic notion of truth. A scientific truth offered at a given historical moment, necessarily involves a non-dialectical dimension (a legitimate abstraction) without which its existence would postulate an absolute truth appearing in a superhuman, or, at least, extra-social intelligence. When Marx talks about capitalism

---

[280] Binswanger (54), p. 622.
[281] Since the writing of this passage, Pavlovian dominance over Marxist psychiatry has considerably diminished.

in general, without concerning himself overmuch with national differences, when he deliberately neglects the economic incidence of colonialism, he is not proceeding dialectically but is practising a legitimate anti-dialectical abstraction for his time. A non-dialectical conception may be very scientific if it comes from a legitimate abstraction; a conception with dialectical pretensions is anti-scientific if it postulates non-existent totalities or is based on totalities with insufficient content.

Now it is clear that, for Pavlovism, the dialectical interaction between man and the social environment is reduced to a single formula: this explains the relative facility with which the Pavlovians transpose the results of animal experimentation to man. One thus arrives at an inevitable paradox if one persists in seeing Pavlovism as Marxist psychiatry *par excellence*: the normal consciousness of man is determined by his social existence; morbid consciousness is, by contrast, extra-social and dependent on the action of essentially biological factors.[282] Against Pavlovism as pure scientific theory, this argument is without significance. Against Pavlovism as *Marxist theory*, it is almost without an answer. It is only to the extent that it remains possible to analyse, as the existential anthropologist does, the 'person in the world', i.e. for us the individual dialectic of social integration —the structure of the 'praxis'—that the Marxian thesis of *consciousness determined by existence* maintains its chances of validity.

In the *Daseinsanalyse* school, Boss and Binswanger (and C. Kulenkampff, who is less well known outside Germany) are the closest to positions of open Marxism. Binswanger's thought provides unexpected points of convergence with the latter. He is closer to open Marxism than Heidegger is to Lukács; for the practitioner the contact of clinical reality is for him the only factor of *Umstülpung*. When Binswanger talks about the dialec-

[282] Obviously, this is partly the thesis of '*La Conscience Morbide*', but it is not so easy to avoid the contradiction, since orthodox Marxism objects to Durkheimianism in general and the Blondelian work in particular. When we discover the biological mechanism for the latest mental disorder, then we must recognize the limited validity of Marx's statement: 'Consciousness is determined by existence.'

tical unity of the Self and the World,[283] when he discusses 'the close functional correlativity of the "Gnosie" and the "Praxie" '[284] or emphasizes in a general way the importance of the *praxis*,[285] it is difficult to see what separates him from an open form of Marxism.[286]

Among the French authors, the evolution of A. Hesnard is no less interesting. E. Steck recently pointed out a certain inflexibility in Hesnardian thought about *Daseinsanalyse*;[287] this inflexibility goes hand in hand with an accentuation of his encounter with the themes of open Marxism. With Minkowski's *La Schizophrénie*, the *Univers morbide de la Faute* is certainly the psychiatric work that is closest to the Lukácsian climate—though Hungarian philosophical works have not been quoted here. Two major themes predominate in the later writings of A. Hesnard, themes whose correlativity is proved both by the phenomenology of false consciousness and the schizophrenic attack. These themes are: the role of axiogenic structures (concrete totalities) in the *Univers morbide de le Faute* and the role of anti-dialectical, depersonalizing identification in the *Psychanalyse du lien interhumain*. The 'morbid universe of guilt' is that of reificational devaluation: an inauthentic universe of guilt which is also a universe of inauthentic guilt.[288]

A Marxist theory of deranged thought is not therefore an external application of Marxism to a scientific problem: as a critique of false consciousness, Marxism is essentially a critical theory of a form of deranged thought, a theory infinitely advanced in relation

---

[283] Binswanger (54), p. 624.

[284] Binswanger (54), p. 604.

[285] Cf. (61), pp. 46, 62 etc. Elsewhere (60), p. 33, the usefulness of ergotheraphy is interpreted as an 'artificial factor of temporalization' (*Zeitigungsersatz*). It would be impossible to be more 'sociologizing'.

[286] Cf. earlier, pp. 263 ff. The influence of the patient's *social* mode of being-in-the-world on the spatio-temporal structure of his own universe. This latter acts in its turn as a defensive barrier—more or less efficiently—against the onset of derangement.

[287] In his report to the congress of Paris (1950).

[288] Analogous to the universe of *political responsibility*. Cf. earlier, pp. 111 ff.

to the psychopathology of its time. But Marxism does not only have its requirements or priority claims to contribute to this problem; it also contributes to the quest for solutions through the coherence of its structures, and its terminology that has been sharpened by its semi-secular application to ideological criticism. To the extent that it is possible to 'deduce' from the postulate of a fundamentally anti-dialectical structure of existence and, consequently, of consciousness, the symptomatology of schizophrenia (the present study does not claim to be anything other than an outline of this task), the unity of schizophrenia emerges, reinforced, and this dialectically achieved unity is organized round the nosological concept of morbid rationalism of a *schizophrenic type*. The integration of this concept into a Marxist context provides a dialectical dimension of individual historicity and, because of this, a possible common denominator with analytical interpretations. For its part, the notion of the dialectic itself emerges strengthened by a socio-psychiatric confrontation; the very fact that the negation of the dialectic has a natural (or, in this case, clinical) reality proves its value *a contrario* not only on the level of knowledge but also on the level of Existence.

Conclusions

The concept of *morbid rationalism* has appeared throughout this study, as the essential element of a global theory of alienation: the common denominator of its individual and social forms. In fact, the preponderance of the spatializing-reificational aspect of the perception of reality—over its temporalizing-historical aspect—is the common denominator of the various forms of economic and political alienation, including voluntary mystification. Furthermore, morbid rationalism, the expression *par excellence* of non-dialectical, reified, anaxiological consciousness, appears as the *schizophrenia type*, i.e. as the closest clinical form to a hypothetical 'fundamental disorder'. It is the dialectical structure of his involvement in the world which protects man (individual or social) against derangement. The mechanisms of ideologization and the mechanisms of deranged neostructuration should thus be mutually illuminating.

Thus, no one can ignore the important role played by the problem of subject–object relationships in discussions about the problem of alienation. In 1923, Lukács defended the theory of the identicalness of the historical subject and object; he subsequently revised this opinion. Undeniably, the word 'identical' has a connotation that is not very dialectic; its presence in this context perhaps simply proves the impossibility of a consistent dialectical position within the framework of idealist thought.[1] But this observation ought not to put Marxist thought in an insoluble dilemma. Between the theory of the 'identicalness' of the subject and object and that of 'reflection'—in other words between

---

[1] Schizophrenic thought is both anti-dialectical in its logic, and idealist in its perceptual functions; it therefore proves empirically the correlativity of these philosophical notions.

idealism and mechanistic Marxism—it is necessary to seek, and there is a hope of finding dialectically, a 'third way'.

The phenomenology of the schizophrenic attack specifically indicates this third way. We have seen that the work of a major group of theorists of schizophrenia is oriented precisely towards the problem of the subject-object dialectic.[2] Now in this research, it is the deterioration of the subject–object *dialectical unity* which governs the process of disinvolvement from reality; on the other hand, anti-dialectical identification and spatialization appear as techniques of compensation, or even as means of counter-balancing dialectical failure. On the clinical level, the equating of subject–object does not therefore appear as a dialectical transcendence of this reification, but as the expression of this reification. This is a contribution from the phenomenology of clinical alienation to the general problem of alienation, a contribution which deserves to be taken into account.

J. J. Lopez-Ibor writes in a similar vein to Jaspers—that a biological reaction is *explicable*, a psychological reaction is *comprehensible*, an intermediary reaction is both explicable and comprehensible but can not be completely one or the other.[3] My work has been mainly directed towards the second aspect of the question; it is not an *explanation*, but a Marxist *interpretation* of the schizophrenic phenomenon that I have outlined. *Explanation* here means pathogenia; in psychiatry one explains only individual cases, whilst an overall phenomenon can be interpreted.[4] An explanation presupposes, among other things, the espousal of a position in the organogenesis–psychogenesis debate,

---

[2] Cf. the works of Roheim, Balken, Winkler, etc., and particularly Zutt whose 1929 article was the forerunner of this research. I have emphasized elsewhere the role of the *contemplative attitude* in Zutt and Lukács. Elsewhere, in the same article, Zutt points out that the schizophrenic self is in a position of pure recording *vis-à-vis* the world, without an 'internal attitude'. (Winkler talks of the 'withdrawnness of the self'.)

[3] Lopez-Ibor, quoted by Cabaleira-Goas (82), p. 206.

[4] This is certainly one of the difficulties of nosologism in psychiatry, but it will be noted that in the analysis of the de-realist structures of political psychology, explanation and interpretation may coincide, which, in its turn, justifies the explanatory use of the socio-pathological parallelism.

which would be marginal to this study. The only thing that might be said here is that socio-pathological parallelism, in the way that I have considered it, constitutes an assumption—and nothing more than an *assumption*—in favour of psychogenesis akin to the statistical demonstration of the pathogenic role of certain familial structures or the success of certain analytical cures. Other facts might support the opposite view.[5] Any organic, psychic or even social factor, capable of preventing the dialectical perception of reality may become an agent of reification in individual consciousness. Since dialectical thought is a 'costly' technique, it is quite permissible to admit that a deterioration of organic origin may, in certain cases at least, start a regression towards pre-dialectical intellectual techniques that respond to new needs for economy. In this sense, one can say that neither existential analysis, phenomenological psychopathology, nor psychoanalysis are incompatible with *a certain form* of organogenesis.

There exist in effect two possible ways[6] of conceiving the organogenesis of a mental disturbance: explanation by anatomical lesion or specific functional loss, and explanation by organic deterioration of a general nature. There are some apartments whose doors cannot be closed because the keys have been lost and there are others that cannot be closed because in a 'generally deteriorating' building the doors fit badly. This statement shows that along with many other terms in a scientific vocabulary the word 'organogenesis' involves at least two meanings that are incompatible in theory.

Now, concerning the mechanism of the first model (organogenesis, 'general paralysis' type), it is worth noting that the work of researchers has shown itself to be rather sterile up to this point. Too many possible mechanisms have been demonstrated and each of the results therefore constitutes the experimental

---

[5] For example, the aphasia–schizophrenia opposition (table, p. 157) which implies an assumption in favour of organogenesis.

[6] The ideas that refer to a deterioration in the homeostatic functions (N. Rozensweig (407), etc.) are half-way between the two notions. But I can only schematically raise the philosophical problem of the organogenesis–psychogenesis debate to which I intend to devote a later work.

refutation of all the others.[7] Taken in isolation, each result[8] represents progress from the pharmaco-dynamic or physiological point of view, but it could provide a foundation for a truly explanatory theory only if the individual researcher systematically neglected the knowledge acquired from the work of others. Organogenesis thus understood gives up trying to *interpret* schizophrenia but still does not succeed in *explaining* it.

There remains the second type of mechanism (general organic loss); it is not incompatible with any other interpretation, not even with a Marxist interpretation, as we have just seen.[9] Under the title 'multifactor psychosomatic theory of schizophrenia', L. Bellak[10] formulates a theoretical conception which expressly aims to create the conditions for a synthesis of different viewpoints. For Bellak, schizophrenia is not a *disease entity* but the symptomatic expression of severe Ego disturbance, a possible consequence of the action of a large number of somatic or psychic factors. Schizophrenia would be placed at one extremity of a continuum going from the viewpoint of the 'Ego strength' of normality to schizophrenia, passing through the neuroses and the

[7] The article by Garcia Badaracco in *L'Encyclopédie*, and the studies of Azima (22) contain a complete picture of the various aspects of organogenetic work. Because of its relevance to my subject, I would add the work of Helbig (218) who observes a real morbid rationalism (loss of the 'Me–Here–Now' function) in amanitine intoxication.

[8] Kasanin *et al.* (250) raise the notion of *'maternal overprotection'* as a pathogenic factor; they admit besides, that this maternal attitude is often started by a discreet organic inferiority felt rather than diagnosed by the mother. The constant pressure and, at the same time, the extreme variety of 'organic disorders' among schizophrenics is thus explained in a satisfying way, but is it organogenesis or psychogenesis?

[9] L. Bellak (41) and (42), who has a critical overall view of different organic explanations of schizophrenia between 1935 and 1945.

[10] L. Bellak (43), p. 65. The question of the pathogenic role of familial structures has been studied statistically, particularly in the U.S. (cf. Kasanin *et al.* (250), etc.). These studies, which are generally positive about the role of the nature of parent–child relationships, at the same time support psychogenesis, but Bellak's article shows that this verdict has nothing absolute about it.

manic-depressive state. An early and non-diagnosed trauma in the cerebral tissues or an early deterioration of the mother–child relationship could, by the same token, be responsible for a subsequent schizophrenic development. A theoretical conception of this order has the advantage of taking account of the existence of various forms of symptomatic schizophrenias;[11] but on the other hand it sacrifices their unity. One of the goals of my research was to show specifically that the concept of 'reified consciousness' and the socio-pathological parallelism that its use implies, permits us to rediscover a form *sui generis* of nosological unity, a form appropriate to the particular nature of the mental illness, that is, independent of the need for pathogenic unity. By postulating that psychiatric nosology must be necessarily based on the same criteria as medical nosology, this unity makes a discrete—and unjustified—concession to organogenesis.

Although the concept of *false consciousness* is dependent on various social psychological mechanisms, it nevertheless retains a specific character as 'framework' for different aspects and forms of a sub-dialectical and historical (reified) perception of reality. An analogous development may legitimately assure the unity of schizophrenia beyond the organogenesis–psychogenesis dualism, and even beyond the pluralism of explanatory theories. My chapter devoted to the *dialectical drama of alienation* is only an initial attempt at unification. I think, however, that I have succeeded in showing that its rational integration into a general theory of human alienation illuminates the schizophrenic phenomenon in general, and morbid rationalism in particular, in a way that clinical considerations that are quite separate from sociologism cannot.

[11] For example, syndromes of a schizophrenic type as a conseqence of meningitis [cf. M. Schachter (412)] or those appearing during certain treatment (impaludism).

Appendix

(Response to Robert Vander Gucht, *Revue philosophique de Louvain*, 1964)

In the February 1964 issue Robert Vander Gucht published a critical review of my book *La fausse conscience*.[1] Obviously expressions such as: 'excellent review', or 'quite remarkable summary' can appear to be empty statements of politeness, even as *captatio benevolentiae*. I will therefore restrict myself to saying that I prefer to be criticized at this level than to be praised at a lower level. This is why I think that a discussion might prove fertile by giving me the opportunity to elucidate some epistemological problems that have been dealt with only marginally in my book.

I read in Vander Gucht's critique: 'sometimes . . . de-dialecticization, or reification, is presented to us as "the deterioration of the subject–object *dialectical unity* which governs the process of disinvolvement from reality" (p. 314), therefore as a fall into the pathological; sometimes, on the other hand, reification is seen to assume a role that is to a certain point positive. "A certain degree of reification constitutes normality", we read with some surprise on p. 143. The fully dialectical perception of reality, in this second perspective, ceases to be an ideal to be attained and becomes an extreme to be avoided: "one comes to the point of theoretically conceiving two forms of pathological existence in the world: through lack of and excess of reification" (p. 143). There is morbid rationalism, but also "morbid realism" (p. 157). Schizophrenia is the counterpart of aphasia, "the aphasic's mode of

[1] Paris, Editions de Minuit, 1962: this work was presented as a doctoral thesis (Paris, 1962) under the title: *La Réification*.

being-in-the-world" (p. 143). The word would in fact be "already reificational in its essence" (p. 99); "every word depends on an anti-dialectical *false identification*" (p. 99). The perfect dialectician from this perspective is Cratylus, the philosopher, a disciple of Heraclitus, who came to believe that it was not necessary to say anything and who contented himself—if we can believe Aristotle —with moving his finger. . . . But if the dialectic does not indicate normal relationships between the person and the world or other people, his natural involvement in reality, if it is an intuition about various things that no process of identification manages to keep in equilibrium, then questions arise: at what point does reification become pathological? where can we draw a boundary between science and ideology?' (pp. 250–1.)

These are important questions. I like very much the expression 'fall into the pathological'; a condition of health makes me think of a car that is advancing at a decreasing speed towards a goal, and is threatened with 'falling' over a precipice on the way. It seems to me, however, that this road is bordered by precipices *on both sides*; the 'fall' into the pathological may take place on the right or the left. In most of its concrete manifestations, a condition of health, therefore, appears as an *ethical virtue* in the sense of 'L'Ethique à Nicomaque'; thinness is often a sign of illness and obesity is far from being symptomatic of an excess of health. There is hyperthermia and hypothermia; hyperthyroidism and hypothyroidism, etc. This is the criticism that I made of Charles Blondel's classical work: that of having developed a *unipolar theory* of morbid consciousness. Now, once the notion of 'dialectical thought' is introduced into psychology, there is nothing paradoxical about a 'median' function being assigned to it: involvement in the world must be *dialectical*, but not too *dialectical*; man's socialized thought must *include* reified categories, without being *overwhelmed* by them. This is no more paradoxical than saying that a picture must be seen from an optimum distance: not too close and not too far away.

In fact the involvement of man in his world (*In-der-Welt-Sein*) is both an adaptation to changing 'dialectical' *Nature*, and to *society* whose institutions *normally* include a reified sector. Certainly one does not drown in the same river twice, but certainly one is sometimes forced to apply the same law twice, to go over the same course twice. Consequently, there is nothing paradoxical in supposing that an over-developed adaptation of man to Nature, to the detriment of his adaptation to society, might end in a loss of the *instrument* of social communication: language. This is the significance of my interpretation of aphasic disturbance as *morbid realism*, an interpretation based on the work of a certain number of specialists of this disorder, particularly Klaus Conrad. The aphasic disturbance would be the expression of a form of over-dialectical, over-authentic, insufficiently reified consciousness, that is incapable of dissociating the concrete totalities of experience, even incapable of legitimate identification; Conrad talks characteristically about *Gestaltungsprozesse . . . die nicht gezügelt werden können*. It is therefore, an over-totalizing consciousness.

In this order of ideas, Cratylus' sponsorship does not frighten me, since *he confirms my interpretation*. Cratylus, a disciple of the founder of dialectics, accuses his master of inconsistency for, by using a conceptual language, he 'goes into the same river several times'. In order to remain a consistent dialectician, Cratylus therefore condemned himself to a kind of controlled aphasia. The various interpretations of aphasia that I have used do not say anything else in essence. We therefore find ourselves in agreement with one of the many admirable pre-scientific intuitions of Greek thought.

Having raised this, there remain two other points to be discussed:

(1) What is the precise point at which reification becomes pathological?

(2) How to differentiate *false identification*, a component of ideological thought, from *legitimate identification*, an instrument of scientific research?

The first question does not call for a specific response. It is no more possible to indicate the 'precise point' which separates normal reification from pathological reification than to precisely fix the point at which 'tension' becomes 'hypertension', 'temperature' becomes 'fever' or 'corpulence' becomes 'obesity'. Numerous factors, subjective or objective, intervene to make all claims to be able to determine an exact frontier illusory. A picture—I would say—must be considered from the optimum distance. But this 'optimum distance' depends on the spectator and the picture (the 'subject' and the 'object'); it is not the same for a short-sighted person and a long-sighted person, no more than it is the same for a Bosch, a Vermeer, a Turner or a Rembrandt. Everybody agrees in thinking that a man weighing 130 kgs (260 lbs) is obese and with blood pressure of 25–18 has hypertension; it is when one has to 'classify' a weight of 75 kgs (150 lbs) or a blood pressure of 17–12 that the difficulty arises. The social factor intervenes to complicate everything: a reified, 'schizoid' mind, prone to abstraction and combined with lack of feeling, constitutes less of a vital handicap in a cashier than in a teacher or a spiritual leader. A *certain degree* of false consciousness is inseparable from collective existence; one thinks of those 'conventional lies' to which Max Nordau devoted a work, which has now unjustly fallen into oblivion.[2] Going further, I would say that, false or not, the stereotyped vision of the enemy, the result of a Manichean perception of the world, may prove to be *useful* in a period of tension or war, particularly in cementing unusual, but necessary, coalitions. Let me say in summary that a certain degree of reification and false consciousness is necessary for individual or collective existence. Beyond a certain limit, quantity is transformed into quality, and the pathological makes its appearance. But the precise point of this transformation depends on the interaction of a great number of factors; it cannot therefore be the object of an objective determination.[3] It depends on the specific case.

[2] Max Nordau, *Die Konventionelle Lügen der Kulturmenschheit.*
[3] This transformation of quantity into quality is—since *Anti-Dühring*—one of the great philosophical themes of orthodox Marxism, particularly Soviet Marxism. It is considered as an 'objective property' of natural reality and the classical example of Engels is used: boiling water. But no! The temperature of boiling water depends on a certain number of factors at least one of which is essential: atmospheric pressure. It does not therefore have an absolute value. The same applies and *a fortiori* in the human sciences, particularly on the question of reification and false consciousness.

The last question raised by Vander Gucht remains: that of relationships existing between *ideology* and *science*. This is a question that is all the more legitimate since both are dependent on 'the human spirit's appetite for identity' that P. Calvez refers to. To talk about 'false identification' in ideological discourse and 'legitimate identification' in science is merely a verbal solution, for the problem consists in finding as precise a criterion as possible for the legitimacy and falsity.

I tried in my book (p. 93) to extract some of these criteria. Scientific identification is conscious of its limits; ideological identification is seemingly fascinated by itself, and takes itself too seriously. The same applies to the deranged identification of schizophrenics.

Scientific identification simplifies complicated realities in order to put them within reach of science; ideological identification 'over-simplifies' sometimes simple realities in order to gain, in exchange for the intellectual comfort offered, mass support. Scientific identification is in theory *autonomous* for it does not pursue goals that are outside the sphere of science; ideological identification is always *heteronomous*, for its goal is not to establish a law, but to compromise an adversary. Identification, according to Emile Meyerson, aims at making something known by comparing it with *something that is already known*; identification of ideologies aims at making something detested by comparing it with *something that is already detested* (comparison of Trotskyism with Nazism, etc.). This is not the same thing.

Having said this, let us recognize:

(1) that the limits are far from being precise, and
(2) that there can be forms of transition, and mixed forms. The really distinctive criterion certainly lies in the use of common sense that is as difficult to codify in the abstract as it is often obvious in the concrete.

Serious historians speak about Macedonian or Roman *imperialism* (and also Ancient *capitalism*). This is an anti-dialectical, ahistorical identification since the economic structures which underlie Macedonian and Roman expansion are not the same, and, moreover, the word 'imperialism' originated in the nineteenth century and designates a phenomenon *sui generis*. We are, however, faced with a legitimate scientific identification—in the meaning that Emile Meyerson gives it—for his aim is in no way to compromise Scipion Emilien by putting him in the same category as Lord Kitchener (or vice versa), but to analyse a psycho-sociological residue which makes man always want to extend the limits of his possessions. The term 'imperialism' refers here to a scientifically useful 'ideal type' for it serves not only for studying the similarities of different historical forms of the 'imperialist phenomenon', but also to demonstrate the differences; it is in this way that Weberians understand the methodological use of ideal types. A concept like 'Hitlero-Trotskyism' is by contrast without scientific value for its aim is not to study objectively the 'Trotskyist phenomenon' but to channel the feeling of the masses against Nazism against Trotskyism. The sectarian spirit is as if hypnotized by the supposed identity of the terms and *a priori* objects to their differences. Its development is therefore purely ideological without usefulness for the historian.

Finally, there are 'mixed cases': in certain cases an absolute identification that was more or less one of passion in the beginning, contributes to disclosing the existence of partial identities, possessing an objective value *as such*. The concept of 'racism' covers the two main contemporary forms of this aberration: Nazism and Southern racism in the United States. It sets forward an 'illegitimate' (ideological) identification in as much as it is a matter of 'proving' the essential identity of post-war American politics and the politics of Nazi Germany.[4] By contrast, it is a legitimate scientific identification to the extent that it restricts itself to observing the existence of a core common to different aspects of racism, based on the stereotyped (reified) perception of the so-called 'inferior' race.

The diagnosis of the illegitimacy of an identification is very often a *postfestum* diagnosis, an 'autopsy'. The ideological or

---

[4] One remembers that this was one of the great themes of the external propaganda of Stalinism. Cf. the work by Yves Farge, *La guerre d'Hitler continue* (Paris, about 1948), who merely summarizes the *leit-motiv* of all this propaganda.

utopian nature of a form of consciousness directly constitutes an objective dimension. The evidence for this 'objective character' often appears only in a historical perspective. We are justified today in speaking of a *chiliastic utopia* for we know the sequence of events; at the time of his crusade, Thomas Munzer did not believe himself to be utopian. The same often applies to the ideological nature of a form of consciousness and, consequently, of the legitimacy of the 'identifications' which underlie it.

The word 'Judo-Bolshevism' was one of the *leit-motivs* of Nazi propaganda. The identification which it crystallizes is certainly illegitimate. We must accept, however, that after the First World War, the idea of a conspiracy between Judaism as a whole and Communism could appear plausible, even to unprejudiced minds, given the importance of the Jewish participation in the communist governments at the time (75 per cent in Hungary in the Garbai-Bela Kun government) as well as the pro-communist sympathies of a large section of the Jewish intelligentsia. New facts have emerged since, the most important of which is certainly the appearance of anti-semitism in the communist camp. These new facts constitute a *retrospective* contradiction of the concept of 'Judo-Bolshevism' which never possessed a scrap of sociological content and which would have been from the beginning a 'false identification'. In any case this became evident only in the light of subsequent events. There exist illnesses that are diagnosed only at the autopsy; nevertheless they exist before the autopsy.

In summary, it seems to me that the essential criterion for the scientific or ideological character of an 'identification' is above all the *autonomous* nature of scientific identification and the *heteronomic* character of ideological identification. Scientific identification does not pursue goals that are external to science and, for it alone, this fact shelters it from absurdity. Yet there are 'identifications' which belong both to ideology and science, and, on the other hand, the ideological character of certain identifications is often revealed only by means of subsequent events.

Vander Gucht criticizes my study for lacking an epistemological foundation. This criticism is partially justified. My aim was limited: to separate out the psychopathological dimension from a theory seen by Marxism from an essentially economic angle and developed by Lukács in a more philosophical direction. This work is only outlined in my book: the *psychoanalytic* aspect of the problem of reification has been neglected for it could be studied validly only by an experienced psychoanalyst, familiar with the data of dialectical philosophy. By introducing epistemological considerations I would have complicated still further a discussion whose major quality is not simplicity; furthermore I would have gone beyond the limits of my competence.

However, it does contain the *outline* of an epistemology, but it is an elementary epistemology, an epistemology for psychiatrists and not for the use of philosophers. The epistemological and logical analysis of derangement is in fact still in its infancy. My effort is, therefore, limited to clearing the ground by eliminating a certain number of tenacious misunderstandings inherited from traditional Marxism. These misunderstandings have kept the Marxist theory of alienation in an impasse, making any psycho-pathological application and the development of any coherent theory of false consciousness illusory. I applied myself in the first place to showing that—contrary to the conceptions of popular Marxism—the dialectical quality of a doctrine and its scientific values (its 'degree of validity') are two different things: a dialectical theory is not *ipso facto* a valid theory, and a valid theory is not necessarily a dialectical theory. The result is that, as de-dialecticizing neo-structuration of the perception of the world, false consciousness is not synonymous with *tenacious collective error*.[5] This statement is necessary for understanding

[5] This 'cognitive-Manichean' interpretation (the expression is mine) of false consciousness has been defended by Lucien Gold-mann in various writings and particularly in his paper to the Stresa Congress of Sociology. Cf. L. Goldmann, *Conscience réelle et conscience possible; conscience adéquate et fausse conscience*, in *Actes du Quatrième Congrès de Sociologie*, September 1959, vol. 4.

For Goldmann, the general category of false consciousness is inappropriateness, in other words, error. Now, the notions of 'truth' or 'error' are relative ideas and their scientific use inevitably involves an 'absolutization' (in German *Hypostasierung*) from the appropriate point of view. A theory of false consciousness based on the

how identification, an eminently anti-dialectical step, can simultaneously play the role of a legitimate element of the scientific 'train of thought' and a constituent of ideologized thought. This leads us to a thinker (cited earlier) whose work constitutes the real epistemological basis of my attempt: Emile Meyerson. Everything that the author of *Identité et Realité* tells us about the role of identification in the processes of knowledge and on the limits, nay the dangers, of its abuse[6] enter into the frameworks of this *epistemology of reification* that Vander Gucht protests against. But the work of a thinker who died in 1933 naturally could only provide a starting point in 1964.

Paris, November 1964

concept of *collective error* could not, therefore, be defended in any other way than in the frameworks of an authoritarian context which arbitrarily determines its truth.

The introduction of the *dialectical criterion of false consciousness* freed from the hypothesis of a search for appropriateness or inappropriateness aims at providing an objective basis for the theory of alienation. In fact one can define objectively what the dialectic is. The notion of congruence with reality could not be defined in any other way than as a function of a dogma, or at least in a privileged sociological perspective (*Standort*).

[6] Cf. this passage: 'Total identification ... not only seems placed in an infinite distance, but also appears as unreal and in some way absurd, since by identifying the whole, *one would make entire reality disappear and one would deny sensation itself.* Consequently, the mind, as if by a sort of modesty in the face of this paradox, is happy to stop on its way, contenting itself with partial satisfactions.' (*Le Cheminement de la Pensée*, p. 58, my italics.) This cause-effect relationship between the hypertrophy of the identificatory function and the loss of contact with reality contains in germ a whole epistemology of reified consciousness that I have tried to apply—for the first time—to the *individual* reification of consciousness, known by the name of *morbid rationalism*. (Cf. my article in the November 1946 issue of *Actas Españalos de Neurologia y Psiquiatria: Contribución al problema filosófico planteado por la patologia del simbolismo.*)

Bibliography

1 Mauricio ABADI, Consideraciones psicoanaliticas acerca de algunos aspectos de una psicosis con amaurosis congenita, *Revista de Psicoanalisis*, Buenos Aires, 1956.

2 Mauricio ABADI, El autorreproche melancolico, *Revista de Psiconalisis* (Buenos Aires), 1956.

3 Paul ABELY, Etat schizophrénique et tendances homosexuelles, *Annales Médico-Psychologiques*, 1927.

4 Paul ABELY, Le signe du miroir dans les psychoses et plus spécialement dans la démence précoce, *Annales Médico-Psychologiques*, 1930.

5 G. ADLER, Bedeutung der Illusionen für Politik und soziales Leben, 1904.

6 T. W. ADORNO, Uber den Fetisch-Karakter in der Musik und die Regression des Hörens, *Zeitschrift für Sozialforschung*, Paris, 1938.

7 T. W. ADORNO, *et al.*, The Authoritarian Personality, New York, 1950.

8 ALEXANDER, Buddhistic training as an artificial catatonia, *Psychoanal. Review*, 1931.

9 Ferdinand ALQUIÉ, Humanisme existentialiste et humanisme surréaliste, *Cahiers du Collège Philosophique*, 1948.

10 Cécile ANDRIEUX, Différence entre les sexes dans la perception spatiale, *l'Année Psychologique*, 1955.

11 Silvano ARIETI, Autistic thought; its formal mechanisms and its relationship to schizophrenia, *The Journal of Nervous and Mental Disease*, 1950.

12 Silvano ARIETI, Interpretation of Schizophrenia, New York, 1955.

13 Silvano ARIETI, Primitive habits and perceptual

alterations in the terminal stage of schizophrenia, *Archives of Neurology and Psychiatry*, 1945.

14 Silvano ARIETI, Special Logic of Schizophrenic and other forms of autistic thought, *Archives of Neurology and Psychiatry*, 1948.

15 Silvano ARIETI, The placing into mouth and coprophagic habits studied from a point of view of comparative developmental psychology, *The Journal of Nervous and Mental Disease*, 1944.

16 Ramond ARON, La sociologie allemande contemporaine, Paris, 1936.

17 Raymond ARON, La Sociologie de Pareto, *Zeitschrift für Sozialforschung*, Paris, 1937.

18 Raymond ARON, L'Idéologie, *Recherches Philosophiques*, 1936–7.

19 Raymond ARON, Conférence à «Preuves», 14 May 1957.

20 Henri ARVON, Le Marxisme, Paris, 1955.

21 H. AUBIN, L'Homme et la Magie, Paris, 1952.

22a H. AZIMA, Fundamentals of neo-jacksonian conception of psychiatry and neurology; Henry Ey's organodynamism, *Arquivos do Neuro-Psiquiatria*, 1953, Sao-Paulo.

22b B. O. BAECHLER, Psychopathologie der Zeit, *Fortschritte der Neurologie, Psychiatrie u. ihrer Grenzgebiete*, 1955.

23 Alcyon BAER-BAHIA, El contenido y la defensa en la creacion artistica, *Revista de Psicoanalisis*, Buenos Aires, 1952.

24 Walter v. BAEYER, Der Begriff der Begegnung in der Psychiatrie, *Der Nervenarzt*, 1955.

25 Percival BAILEY, Janet and Freud, *Archives of Neurology and Psychiatry*, 1956.

26a Read BAIN, Our schizoid culture, *Sociology and Social Research*, 1935.

26b Robert BAK, Regression of Ego-Orientation and Libido in Schizophrenia, *Int. Journ. of Psycho-Analysis*, 1939.

27 Eva Ruth BALKEN, A delineation of schizophrenic language and thought in a test of imagination, *The Journal of Psychology*, 1943.

28 Gustave BALLY, Zur Anthropologie der Kriegszeit, *Schweizer Archiv für Neurologie und Psychiatrie*, 1948.

29 Paul BALVET, Le sentiment de dépersonnalisation dans les délires de structure paranoïde, Thèse, Lyon, 1936.

30 Willy BARANGER, Interpretacion y Ideologia, *Revista de Psicoanalisis*, Buenos Aires, 1957.

31 Roland BARTHES, Mythologies, Paris, 1950.

32 Henri BARUK, Précis de Psychiatrie, Paris, 1950.

33 Henri BARUK, La Psychiatrie sociale, Paris, 1955.

34 Roger BASTIDE, Sociologie et Psychanalyse, Paris, 1950.

35 André BAZIN, Le Drame, c'est qu'ils y croyaient, *France-Observateur*, An 7, 5 July 1956.

36 François BAYLE, Psychologie et Ethique du National-Socialisme, Paris, 1956.

37 Simone de BEAUVOIR, Pour une morale de l'ambiguïté, Paris, 1947.

38 Samuel BECKETT, En attendant Godot, Paris, 1952.

39 Albert BEGUIN, Faiblesse de l'Allemagne, Paris, 1945.

40 Louis BEIRNAERT, Marxisme et Psychiatrie, *Etudes*, June 1954.

41 Leopold BELLAK, A multiple factor psychosomatic theory of schizophrenia: an attempt at a consistent conceptualisation, *The Psychiatric Quarterly*, 1949.

42 Leopold BELLAK, The Etiology of Dementia Praecox, *The Journal of Nervous and Mental Disease*, 1947.

43 Leopold BELLAK, Towards a unified concept of schizophrenia: an elaboration of the multiple factor psychosomatic theory of schizophrenia, *The Journal of Nervous and Mental Disease*, 1955.

44 G. BENEDETTI, Die Alkoholhalluzinosen, Stuttgart, 1952.

45 G. BENEDETTI, H. KIND and F. MIELKE, Forschungen zur Schizophrenielehre, 1951 bis 1955, *Fortschritte der Neurologie Psychiatrie u. ihrer Grenzgebiete*, 1957.

46 Nicolas BERDIAEFF, La transformation du marxisme en Russie, *Esprit*, August 1948.

47 Nicholas BERDIAEFF, Sources et sens du communisme russe, Paris, 1938.

48 Nicholas BERDIAEFF, Un nouveau Moyen Age; Réflexions sur les destinées de la Russie et de l'Europe, Paris, 1927.

49 Peter L. BERGER, The Sociological Study of Sectarianism, *Social Research*, 1954.

50 Edmund BERGLER and Géza ROHEIM, Psychology of time perception, *Psychoanalytic Quarterly*, 1946.

51 Josef BERZE, Psychologie der Schizophrenie, Berlin, 1929.

52 Rudolf BILZ, Das Belagerungserlebnis in den Alkoholhalluzinosen, *Der Nervenarzt*, 1956.

53 Hans BINDER, Das anonyme Briefschreiben, *Schweizer Archiv für Neurologie und Psychiatrie*, 1948.

54 Ludwig BINSWANGER, Das Raumproblem in der Psychopathologie, *Zeitschrift für die gesamte Neurologie und Psychiatrie*, 1948.

55 Ludwig BINSWANGER, Introduccion a la psicoanalisis medica, *Actas Luso-Espanolas de Neurologia y Psiquiatria*, 1957.

56 Ludwig BINSWANGER, Der Fall Ellen West. Eine anthropologisch-klinische Studie, *Schweizer Archiv für Neurologie und Psychiatrie*, 1944–5.

57 Ludwig BINSWANGER, La «Daseinanalyse» en psychiatrie, *L'Encéphale*, 1951.

58 Ludwig BINSWANGER, La fuite des idées, translation summarized by Henri Ey, Paris, 1952 (cyclostyled).

59 Ludwig BINSWANGER, Le Rêve et l'Existence, Introduction de Michel Foucault, Paris, 1954.

60 Ludwig BINSWANGER, Studien zum Schizophrenieproblem, Der Fall Jürg Zünd, *Schweizer Archiv für Neurologie und Psychiatrie*, 1947.

61 Ludwig BINSWANGER, Studien zum Schizophrenieproblem, Der Fall Lola Voss, *Schweizer Archiv für Neurologie und Psychiatrie*, 1949.

62 Ludwig BINSWANGER, Studien zum Schizophrenieproblem, Der Fall Susanne Urban, *Schweizer Archiv für Neurologie und Psychiatrie*, 1952 et 1953. (French translation, Paris, Desclée de Brouwer, 1957).

63 Ludwig BINSWANGER, Symptom und Zeit, *Schweizerische Medizinische Wochenschrift*, June 1951.

64 Ludwig BINSWANGER, Uber die Daseinsanalytische Forschungsrichtung in der Psychiatrie, *Schweizer Archiv für Neurologie und Psychiatrie*, 1946.

65a Maurice BLANCHOT, La grande tromperie, *La Nouvelle Revue Française*, 1957.

65b M. BLEULER, Endocrinologia y esquizofrenia, *Actas Luso-Espanolas de Neurologia y Psiquiatria*, 1956.

66 Charles BLONDEL, La Conscience Morbide, Paris, 1914.

67 Marcel BOLL, La logique et sa caricature dans les questions actuelles, Paris, 1935.

68 Marie BONAPARTE, Time and the unconscious, *International Journal of Psychoanalysis*, 1940.

69 L. BONNAFÉ, Interprétation du fait psychiatrique selon la méthode historique de Marx et Engels, *L'Evolution Psychiatrique*, 1948.

70 L. BONNAFÉ, CHAURAND, TOSQUELLES, CLÉMENT, Gestalt theorie et structures en psychiatrie; la dialectique fond-figure dans la nosologie et la séméiologie, *Annales Médico-Psychiatriques*, 1945.

71 L. BONNAFÉ *et al.*, Valeur de la théorie de la forme en psychiatrie; la dialectique du moi et du monde et de l'événement morbide, ibid., p. 279.

72 S. BOREL, MAISONNY, R. DIATKINE, R. NARLIAN and P. C. RACAMIER, Troubles du langage, *Encyclopédie Médico-chirurgicale* (Psychiatrie), t. I, pp. 37–130 A sq.

73 M. BORNSZTAJN, Le processus de schizophrénisation, *L'Evolution Psychiatrique*, 1947.

74 Medard BOSS, Sinn und Gehalt der sexuellen Perversionan, Berne et Stuttgart, 1952 (2nd edn.).

75 P. BOUR, Schizophrénie et dissociation familiale, *L'Evolution Psychiatrique*, 1958.

76 Jean BOURJADE, L'Intelligence et la pensée de l'enfant, Paris, 1942.

77 G. H. BOUSQUET, Vilfredo Pareto, sa vie et son œuvre, Paris, 1928.

78 David BRAYBROOKE, Diagnosis and remedy in Marx's doctrine of alienation, *Social Research*, New York, 1958.

79 Léon BRUNSCHWICG, Les Ages de l'Intelligence, Paris 1934.

80 Léon BRUNSCHWICG, Progrès de la conscience dans la philosophie occidentale, Paris, 1928.

81 J. BURSTIN, Schizophrénie et mentalité primitive, Etude comparative, Thèse, Paris, 1935.

82 M. CABALEIRO-GOAS, Problemas actuales de las psicosis esquizofrenicas, Madrid, 1954.

83 Bruno CALLIERI, Contributo allo studio psicopatologico dell' esperienza schizofrenica di fine del mondo, *Archivio di Psicologia Neurologia e Psichiatria*, 1955.

84a Bruno CALLIERI, Psicopatologia ed esistenzialismo, *Rassegna di Studi Psichiatrici*, 1952.

84b B. CALLIERI and A. TARANTINI, Sui cosidetto «delirio mistico» (Contributo psicopatologico e clinico), *Rassegna di Studi Psichiatrici*, 1954.

85 Jean-Yves CALVEZ, La pensée de Karl Marx, Paris, 1956.

86 Albert CAMUS, Le Socialisme des potences, *Demain*, no. 63, 21–7, February 1956.

87 Albert CAMUS, L'Etranger, Paris, 1942.

88 Igor A. CARUSO, Das Ich, die Vergegenständlichung und die Angst, *Sitzungsberichte des «Wiener Arbeitskreises f. Tiefenpsychologie»*, Cahier III, 1956–7.

89 Igor A. CARUSO, Das Symbol in der Tiefenpsychologie, *Studium Generale*, 6th year, fasc. 5, 1953.

90 Igor A. CARUSO, Excerpta Anthropologica, *Jahrb. f. Psychologie u. Psychotherapie*, 6th year, fasc. 1–3, 1958.

91 Igor A. CARUSO, Notes sur la réification de la sexualité, *Psyché*, Paris, December 1952.

92 Igor A. CARUSO, Psicoterapia y religion, *Rev. Psicol. Gen. Apl.*, vol. 4, 1949.

93 Igor A. CARUSO, Psychanalyse ouverte et psychanalyse fermée, *Bulletin de Psychologie*, 1956.

94 Igor A. CARUSO, Psychologische Methoden u. Einheit der Psychologie, *Archivio di Psicologia, Neurologia e Psiquiatria*, 1953.

95 Igor A. CARUSO, Symbol und Welterfassung, *Revista de Psicologia Normal e Patologia*, no. 1, 1955.

96 Igor A. CARUSO, Viktor E. Frh. v. Gebsattel zum 78. Geburtstag, *Jahrbuch f. Psychologie n. Psychotherapie*, 1st year, fasc. 2, 1952–3.

97 Igor A. CARUSO, Zum Problem des Gewissens, *Jahrbuch für Psychologie und Psychotherapie*, 1st year, fasc. 2, 1952–3.

98 Ernst CASSIRER, Contribution à la pathologie de la pensée symbolique, *Journal de Psychologie*, 1929.

99 José Carlos CAVALCANTI-BORGES, Primeiros ensaios com o Bender-gestalt-test, resultados em squizofrenicos, *Neurobiologia*, t. 18, June 1955.

100 Henri CHAMBRE, Le marxisme en Union soviétique, Paris, 1955.

101 Stuart CHASE, The Tyranny of Words, New York, 1938.

102 Marise CHOISY, Toute-puissance de la pensée et péché d'intention, *Psyché*, Paris, 1955.

103 Paul CITROME, Conclusion d'une enquête sur le suicide dans les camps de concentration, *Cahiers Internationaux de Sociologie*, 1952. Vol. XII.

104 Henri CLAUDE, Mécanisme des hallucinations; syndrome d'action extérieure, *L'Encéphale*, May 1930.

105 Henri CLAUDE, Rapports de l'hystérie avec la schizophrénie, *Annales médico-psychologiques*, 1937.

106 H. CLAUDE, A. BOREL and G. ROBIN, Considérations sur la constitution schizoïde et la constitution paranoiaque; genèse des idées délirantes, *L'Encéphale*, 1923, no. 8.

107 H. CLAUDE and M. MONTASSUT, Délimitation de la paranoia légitime, *L'Encéphale*, 1926.

108 H. CLAUDE, L. VIDART and Y. LONGUET, Journal d'un schizoïde, *L'Encéphale*, no. 2, 1940.

109 A. CLOSS, Gœthe und Kirkegaard: gleichgewichtige Mitte und Entweder-Oder, *Etudes Germaniques*, Paris, 1949.

110 Bertram D. COHEN, Motivation and Performance in Schizophrenia, *Journal of Abnormal and Social Psychology*, no. 2, March 1956.

111 M. COLLEVILLE, Georg. Trakl, *Etudes Germaniques*, 1952.

112 Klaus CONRAD, Das Problem der gestörten Wortfindung in gestalttheoretischer Betrachtung, *Schweizer Archiv für Neurologie und Psychiatrie*, 1949.

113 Klaus CONRAD, Das Unbewusste als phenomenologisches Problem, *Fortschritte der Neurologie, Psychiatrie u. ihrer Grenzgebiete*, fasc. 1, 1957.

114 Klaus CONRAD, Die Gestaltanalyse in der Psychiatrie, *Studium Generale*, fasc. 8, September 1952.

115 Auguste CORNU, L'idée d'aliénation chez Hegel, Feuerbach et Karl Marx, *La Pensée*, March–April 1948.

116 Benedetto CROCE, Essai d'interprétation et de critique de quelques concepts du marxisme, Paris, 1898.

117 R. H. S. CROSSMAN, Bertrand de JOUVENEL, Hans KOHN and A. KOESTLER, Gibt es politische Neurosen? *Der Monat*, Berlin, fasc. 68, May 1954.

118 Armand CUVILLIER, Durkheim et Marx, *Cahiers Internationaux de Sociologie*, 1948.

119 Armand CUVILLIER, Sociologie de connaissance et idéologie économique, *Cahiers Internationaux de Sociologie*, 1951.

120 Wilfried DAIM, Umwertung der Psychoanalyse, Wien, 1951.

121 Jean DELAY, Autour d'Aurélia, *Les Nouvelles Littéraires*, 29 May 1958, no. 1 604.

122 J. DELAY, P. PICHOT and J. PERSE, Méthodes psychométriques en clinique; tests mentaux et interprétation, Paris, 1955.

123 Honorio DELGADO, Anormalidades de la conciencia del tiempo, *Revista de Psiquiatria y Psicologia Medica de Europa y America Latina*, no. 1, 1953.

124 Honorio DELGADO, Définition de l'hystérie, *L'Encéphale*, no. 4, 1952.

125 William DEMENT, Dream recall and eye movements during sleep in schizophrenics and normals, *The Journal of Nervous and Mental Disease*, no. 3, 1955.

126 Isaac DEUTSCHER, La Russie après Staline, Paris, Editions du Seuil, 1954.

127 R. DIATKINE, La notion de régression, *L'Evolution Psychiatrique*, July–September 1957.

128 Maurice DIDE, L'Hystérie et l'Evolution humaine, Paris, 1925.

129 E. von DOMARUS, The specific laws of logic in Schizophrenia, in «Language and Thought in Schizophrenia», Berkeley and Los Angeles, 1951.

130 E. von DOMARUS, Uber die Beziehung des normalen zum schizophrenen Denken, *Archiv f. Psychiatrie u. Nervenkrankheiten*, 1925.

131 J. M. DOMENACH, La propagande politique, Paris, 1950.

132 J. M. DOMENACH, Le Mensonge politique, *Esprit*, February 1952.

133 J. DOMARCHI, Matérialisme dialectique et conscience de classe, *Esprit*, May–June 1948.

134 Gabriel DROMARD, L'Interprétation délirante, *Journal de Psychologie normale et pathologique*, 1910.

135 Georges DUMAS, Le surnaturel et les dieux d'après les maladies mentales; essai de théogenie pathologique, Paris, 1946.

136 Eugène DUPRÉEL, Esquisse d'une philosophie des valeurs, Paris, 1939.

137 Guy DURANDIN, Journal d'un schizophrène (compte rendu d'ouvrage), *Revue Philosophique*, January–March 1955.

138 Guy DURANDIN, A propos du mensonge à soi-même, *Société française de psychologie sociale*, Communication of 6 December 1956.

139 L. DUSS, Critique psychiatrique de l'existentialisme; expérience existentialiste chez un schizophrène, *Annales médico-psychologiques*, December 1948.

140 Maurice DUVERGER, La Schizophrénie politique, *Le Monde*, 14 February 1957.

141 Mircea ELIADE, Le mythe de l'éternel retour, archétypes et répétition, Paris, 1949.

142 Mircea ELIADE, Symbolisme indien de l'abolition du temps, *Journal de Psychologie*, October–December 1952.

143 Fr. ENGELS, Philosophie, Economie politique, Socialisme (contre Eugène Dühring), Paris, 1911.

144 G. EWALD, Zur Theorie der Schizophrenie, *Deutsche Medizinische Wochenschrift*, no. 49, December 1954.

145 H. EY, A propos du «Délire» de Kurt Schneider (réflexions sur le caractère primitif du délire), *L'Evolution Psychiatrique*, October–December 1955.

146 H. EY, A propos de la personne du schizophrène, de J. Wyrsch (réflexions sur l'état actuel de la psychopathologie de la schizophrénie), *L'Evolution Psychiatrique*, fasc. 1, 1951.

147 H. EY, Groupe des psychoses schizophréniques et des délirants chroniques (les organisations vésaniques de la personnalité), *Encyclopédie*, T. 1.

148 H. EY, La psychiatrie devant le surréalisme, *L'Evolution Psychiatrique*, 1948.

149 H. EY, Contribution à l'étude des relations des crises de mélancolie et des crises de dépression névrotique, *L'Evolution Psychiatrique*, fasc. 3, 1955.

150 Henri FAURE, L'investissement délirant des objets; *Entretiens de Psychiatrie* (Cercle H. Ey), 1953.

151 H. FAURE, C. IGERT and Ph. RAPPARD, Aphasie et alternances cyclothymiques chez une grande délirante, *Cahiers de Psychiatrie*, Strasbourg, June 1955.

152 Otto FENICHEL, La théorie psychanalytique des névroses, Paris, 1953.

153 Gaston FERDIÈRE, Le dessinateur schizophrène (présentation d'un créateur), *L'Evolution Psychiatrique*, 1951 (no. 2).

154 S. FERENCZI, The phenomena of hysterical materialization, In «Further contributions to the theory and technique of psycho-analysis», London, 1950.

155 Enrico FERRI, Socialisme et science positive, Paris, 1896.

156 FILOZOFIAI ÉVKÖNYV (Annales de Philosophie) (in Hungarian), Budapest, 1952.

157 Fr. FISCHER, Zeitsruktur u. Schizophrenie, *Zeitschrift für die gesamte Neurologie u. Psychiatrie*, 1929.

158 Fr. FISCHER, Raum, -Zeit-Struktur und Denkstörung in der Schizophrénie, *ibid.*, 1930.

159 Bela (Adalbert) FOGARASI, Bevezetés a marxi filozofiâba (Introduction to Marxist philosophy), Vienna, 1922.

160 Bela (Adalbert) FOGARASI, Marxizmus és Logika (Marxism and Logic), Budapest, 1946.

161 S. FOLLIN, Contribution à la discussion sur les fondements théoriques de la psychologie, *La Raison*, no. 9–10, 1954.

162 Sven FOLLIN, Les processus de dépersonnalisation, Premier Congrès Mondial de Psychiatrie, Paris, 1950.

163 Sven FOLLIN, Rationalisme moderne et psychiatrie, *L'Evolution Psychiatrique*, 1948, fasc. 4.

164 Michel FOUCAULT, Maladie mentale et personnalité, Paris, 1954.

165 Paul FRAISSE, Psychologie du Temps, Paris, P.U.F., 1957.

166 S. FREUD, Psychologie collective et analyse du Moi, In «Essais de Psychanalyse», Paris, 1951.

167 S. FREUD, Remarques psychanalytiques sur l'autobiographie d'un cas de paranoia (dementia paranoïdes), *Revue française de Psychanalyse*, no. 1, 1932.

168 G. FRIEDMANN, La crise du Progrès, Paris, 1936.

169a J. FUSSWERK, Affaiblissement du pouvoir formel chez quelques malades mentaux, *Congrès des aliénistes et neurologistes de langue française*, Rennes, 1951.

169b J. GABEL, Analyse existentielle et marxisme en psychiatrie, *L'Année Sociologique*, 1960.

170 J. GABEL, Communisme et dialectique, *Lettres nouvelles*, April–May 1958.

171 J. GABEL, Contribucion al problema filosofico planteado por la patologia del simbolismo, *Actas Espanolas de Neurologia y Psiquiatria*, April 1946 (no. 2).

172 J. GABEL, Contribution au problème de la psychiatrie sociale, *L'Année Sociologique*, 1955–6, Paris, 1957.

173 J. GABEL, Délire politique chez un paranoïde, *L'Evolution Psychiatrique*, no. 2, 1952.

174a J. GABEL, Die Verdinglichung in Camus «L'Etranger», *Jbuch f. Psychologie u. Psychotherapie* (5), fasc. 1–2, 1957.

174b J. GABEL, Espace et Sexualité. A propos d'un cas de réification sexuelle, *Annales Médico-Psychologiques*, June 1960.

175 J. GABEL, Kafka, romancier de l'aliénation, *Critique*, November 1953.

176 J. GABEL (L. Martin), L'âme néo-stalinienne (Esquisse d'une psychopathologie), *Masses*, December 1947, January 1948.

177 J. GABEL, La Réification, essai d'une psychopathologie de la pensée dialectique, *Esprit*, October 1951.

178 J. GABEL (L. Martin), Les fondements pseudo-scientifiques de la doctrine nationale-socialiste, *Masses*, March 1939.

179a J. GABEL (L. Martin), Psychologie de la pensée communiste, *Revue Socialiste*, 1949.

179b J. GABEL, Psychopathologie de Kafka, *Entretiens Psychiatriques* (Cercle H. Ey), 1953.

180 J. GABEL (L. Martin), Signification du maccarthysme, *La Revue Socialiste*, December 1954.

181 J. GABEL, Symbolisme et schizophrénie, *Revue Suisse de Psychologie et de Psychologie appliquée*, 1948.

182 J. GABEL, Swift et la Schizophrénie, *Psyché*, Paris, 1949.

183 J. GABEL, Un ejemplo clinico de racionalismo morboso, *Actas Luso-Espanolas de Neurologia y Psiquiatria*, April 1949.

184 R. GARAUDY, La théorie matérialiste de la connaissance, Paris, P.U.F., 1953.

185 R. GARAUDY, G. COGNIOT, M. CAVEING, J. T. DESANTI, J. KANAPA, V. LEDUC and H. LEFEBVRE (avec une lettre de G. Lukács), Mésaventures de l'anti-marxisme, Paris, 1956.

186 J. Garcia BADARACCO and H. AZIMA, Pathogénie des psychoses schizophréniques, *Encyclopédie Médico-Chirurgicale* (Psychiatrie), t. 1.

187 Angel GARMA, Interpretaciones en suenos del psiquismo prenatal, *Revista de Psicoanalisis*, January–June 1957.

188 C. O. de la GARZA and Ph. WORCHEL, Time and space orientation in schizophrenics, *The Journal of Abnormal and Social Psychology*, March 1956.

189 GAUPP, Zur Lehre von der Paranoia, *Der Nervenarzt*, 1947.

190 V. GEBSATTEL, Zur Frage der Depersonnalisation (Ein Beitrag zur Theorie der Melancholie), *Der Nervenarzt*, April 1957.

191 GEBSATTEL, Ueber Fetischismus, *Der Nervenarzt*, 1929.

192 V. GEBSATTEL, Zeitbezogenes Zwangsdenken in der Melancholie, *Der Nervenarzt*, 1928.

193 G. M. GILBERT, Psychologie de la dictature; Frank, Keitel, Hess, *Les Temps Modernes*, November 1954.

194 Gilbert ROBIN, La guérison des defauts et des vices de l'enfant, Paris, 1948.

195 William GOLDFARB, Receptor preferences in schizophrenic children, *Archives of Neurology and Psychiatry*, December 1956.

196 Lucien GOLDMANN, Le Dieu Caché, Paris, 1955.

197 Lucien GOLDMANN, Les Hommes et l'Univers (L'épistémologie de Jean Piaget), *Synthèse*, Bruxelles, 1952.

198 Lucien GOLDMANN, Marxisme et Psychologie, *Critique*, June–July 1947.

199a Lucien GOLDMANN, Mensch, Gesellschaft und Welt in der Philosophie Emmanuel Kants (Studien zur Geschichte der Dialektik), Zurich, 1945.

199b L. GOLDMANN, Recherches dialectiques, Paris, 1959.

200 Lucien GOLDMANN, La Réification, *Les Temps Modernes*, 1959.

201 Lucien GOLDMANN, Sciences Humaines et Philosophie, Paris, 1952.

202 Kurt GOLDSTEIN, Methodological Approach to the Study of schizophrenic thought disorder, in «Language and Thought in Schizophrenia», Berkeley and Los Angeles, 1951.

203a Kurt GOLDSTEIN, The signification of psychological research in schizophrenia, *Journal of Nervous and Mental Disease*, 1943.

203b J. S. GOTTLIEB and F. E. LINDER, Body temperature of persons with schizophrenia and of normal subjects, *Arch. Neurology and Psychiatry*, 1935.

204 H. GOUHIER, Vision rétrospective et invention historique, *Archivo de filosofia*, no. 1, 1954.

205 Ernst GRÜNWALD, Das Problem der Soziologie des Wissens, Wien-Leipzig, 1934.

206 Paul GUILLAUME, Psychologie de la Forme, Paris, 1948.

207 Paul GUILLAUME, L'intelligence et la perception d'après les travaux récents de Jean Piaget, *Journal de Psychologie*, April–June 1949.

208 L. GUMPLOVICZ, La lutte des races, Paris, 1893 (Fr. trans. Ch. Baye).

209 GUMPLOVICZ, Ratzenhofer szociologiája (The sociology of Ratzenhofer), *Huszadik Szàzad*, Budapest, 1907.

210 G. GURVITCH, Le problème de la sociologie de la connaissance, *Revue Philosophique*, 1958.

211 G. GURVITCH, Structure et Sociologie, Colloque sur le Concept de «Structure», Paris, January 1958.

212 HALBWACHS, Origines du sentiment religieux, Paris, 1925.

213 J. HANN, Symptomatische Psychose schizophrener Prägung nach Blitzschlagverletzung, *Der Nervenarzt*, March 1957.

214 Heinz HARTMANN, On rational and irrational action, *Psychoanalysis and the social sciences*, Vol. 1, 1947.

215 F. M. HAVERMANS, Uber Pseudologia Phantastica, *Wiener Archiv für Psychologie, Psychiatrie und Neurologie*, T. 5, December 1955.

216 H. HECAEN, J. de AJURIAGUERRA, C. MAGIS and R. ANGELERGUES, Le problème de l'agnosie des physiognomies, *L'Encéphale*, 1952.

217 H. HECAEN, M. B. DELL, and A. ROGER, L'aphasie de conduction (Leitungsaphasie), *L'Encéphale*, 1955.

218 Hans HELBIG, Beitrag zur Psychopathologie Knollenblätterpilzvergiftung, *Der Nervenarzt*, 1956.

219 R. HELD, Psychopathologie du regard, *L'Evolution Psychiatrique*, 1952.

220 Hjalmar HELWEG, Søren Kirkegard en psykiatrikpsykologisk studie, Copenhagen, 1933.

221 Lucien HENRY, Les origines de la religion, Paris, 1937.

222 Jeanne HERSCH, Les expériences communistes et l'optimisme éclairé, Conférence au Collège Philosophique, December 1958.

223 Pierre HERVÉ, La Révolution et les Fétiches, Paris, 1956.

224 A. HESNARD, Méconnaissance du complexe d'Œdipe comme fondement structurel de la personne, Congrès des Aliénistes et Neurologistes de langue française, Paris, 1951.

225 A. HESNARD, Une notion psycho-pathologique nouvelle: l'altération du lien interhumain, *Le Sud Médical et Chirurgical*, June 1955.

226 A. HESNARD, Néo-structuration du monde psycho-pathique, *L'Evolution Psychiatrique*, October–December 1955.

227 A. HESNARD, Psychanalyse du lien interhumain, Paris, P.U.F., 1957.

228 A. HESNARD, L'Univers morbide de la faute, Paris, P.U.F., 1949.

229 G. HEUYER, S. LEBOVICI and N. ANGOULVENT, Le test de Lauretta Bender, *Enfance*, September–October 1949.

230 Lawrence E. HINKLE Jr. and Harold G. WOLFF, Communist interrogation and indoctrination of «Enemies of the State»; *Archives of Neurology and Psychiatry*, August 1956.

231 Edouard HITSCHMANN and Edmond BERGLER, La Frigidité de la femme, *Revue française de Psychanalyse*, 1935.

232 Stefan HOLLOS, Ueber das Zeitgefühl, *Intern. Ztschr. f. Psychoanalyse*, 1922.

233 R. G. HOSKINS, The Biology of Schizophrenia, New York, 1946.

234 Georgina D. HOTCHKISS, Lisa CARMEN, Anne OGILBY and SHIRLEY WIESENFELD, Mothers of young male single schizophrenic patients as visitors in a mental hospital, *The Journal of Nervous and Mental Disease*, no. 5, 1955.

235 Gerd HUBER, Das Wahnproblem, *Fortschritte der*

Neurologie, Psychiatrie und ihrer Grenzgebiete, January–February 1955.

236 Jean HYPPOLITE, Phénoménologie de Hegel et Psychanalyse, *La Psychanalyse*, no. 3.

237 Jean HYPPOLITE, Aliénation et objectivation, *Etudes germaniques*, April–June 1951.

238 Franz JAKUBOWSKI, Der idéelogische Ueberbau in der materialistischen Geschichtauffassung, Dantzig, 1936 (Doctoral Thesis, Basle.)

239 P. JANET, L'hallucination dans le délire de persécution, *Revue Philosophique*, 1932.

240 Vl. JANKÉLÉVITCH, Bergson, Paris, 1931.

241 Vl. JANKÉLÉVITCH, Du mensonge, Saint-Amand, 1942.

242 Werner JANZARIK, Der Wahn schizophrener Praegung in der psychotischen Episoden der Epileptiker und die schizophrene Wahnwahrnehmung, *Fortschritte der Neurologie und Psychiatrie und ihrer Grenzgebiete*, 1955.

243 K. JASPERS, Strindberg et Van Gogh; Hölderlin et Swedenborg (preface by M. Blanchot), Paris, 1953.

244 W. Stanley JEVONS, Commercial crises and sun-spots, *Nature*, 1878.

245 W. Stanley JEVONS, Sun spots and commercial crises, *Nature*, 1879.

246 André JOUSSAIN, Bergsonisme et marxisme, *Ecrits de Paris*, April 1956.

247 C. G. JUNG, The Psychology of dementia praecox, New York, *Nervous and Mental Diseases Monographs*, no. 3, 1936.

248 O. KAISER, Beitrage zur Differentialdiagnose der Hysterie und Katatonie, *Allgemeine Zeitschrift für Psychiatrie*, 1902.

249 Ben KARPMAN, Neurotic traits of Jonathan Swift as revealed by Gulliver's travels, *The Psychoanalytic Review*, 1942.

250 Jacob KASANIN, Elisabeth KNIGHT and Priscilla SAGE, Parent-child relationship in schizophrenia, *Journal of Nervous and Mental Disease*, 1934.

251 Jacob KASANIN (ed.), Language and thought in schizo-phrenia, University of California Press, Berkeley and Los Angeles, 1951.

252 Jacob KASANIN (ed.), The disturbance of conceptual thinking in schizophrenia, 1951.

253 M. KATAN, A contribution to the understanding of schi-zophrenic speech. *The International Journal of Psycho-analysis*, 1939.

254 R. KAUFMAN, Religious delusion in schizophrenia, *The International Journal of Psychoanalysis*, 1939.

255 Paul KECSKEMETI, Ideology and Class Consciousness, *Modern Review*, January 1950.

256 Hans KELSEN, Allgemeine Rechtslehre im Lichte materia-tistischer Geschichtsauffassung, *Archiv für Sozialwissen-schaft, und Sozialpolitik*, 1931.

257 Stetson KENNEDY, Introduction à l'Amérique raciste (Collection *Les Temps Modernes*), Paris, 1955.

258 L. KLAGES, Les principes de la caractérologie (trans. W. Real), Paris, 1930.

259 O. KLINEBERG, Social Psychology, New York, 1940.

260 Philippe KŒCHLIN, A propos du symbolisme schizophré-nique, *Entretiens psychiatriques* (Cercle H. Ey), 1955.

261 W. KOHLER, The place of value in a world of facts, New York, 1938.

262 A. KŒSTLER, Petit guide de névroses politiques, *Preuves*, 1954.

263 Gilberto KOOLHAAS, El tiempo de la dissociacion, de la repression, de la reparacion, *Revista Uruguaya de Psico-analisis*, 1957.

264 Karl KORSCH, Marxismus und Philosophie, 2nd edn., completed 1930.

265 Albert KRANOLD, Uber den ethischen Gehalt der sozialis-tischen Idee (Und das Verhältnis des Marxismus zur Ethik), Breslau, 1930.

266 Ernst KRETSCHMER, Die mehrdimensionale Struktur der Schizophrenien mit Bezug auf Ihre Therapie, *Zeit-schrift für Psychotherapie und medizinische Psychologie*, September 1957.

267   Lawrence S. KUBIE, A critical analysis of the concept of repetition compulsion, *The International Journal of Psychoanalysis*, 1939.

268   C. KULENKAMPFF, Entbergung, Entgrenzung, Uberwältigung als Weisen des Standverlustes (Zur Anthropologie Paranoiden Psychosen), *Der Nervenarzt*, March 1955.

269   C. KULENKAMPFF, Uber den Vergiftungswahn, *Der Nervenarzt*, January 1956, fasc. 1.

270   C. KULENKAMPFF, Erblicken und Erblickt-Werden, Das für Andere-Sein (J.-P. Sartre) in seiner Bedeutung für die Anthropologie der paranoiden Psychosen, *Der Nervenarzt*, January 1956, fasc. 2.

271   C. KULENKAMPFF, Uber Wahnwahrnehmungen. Ihre Interpretation als Störung der Wohnordnung, *Der Nervenarzt*, August 1953.

272   H. KUNZ, Die Grenze der psychopathologischen Wahninterpretation, *Zeitschrift für Neurologie*, 1930.

273   Wolfram KURTH, Ueber Entstehungsursache von Sektierertum und Konventikelbildung zugleich eine differentialdiagnostische Erörterung des Paranoia-Schizophrenieproblems, *Zeitschrift für die gesamte Neurologie und Psychiatrie*, 1943.

274   Jacques LACAN, La psychose paranoiaque dans ses rapports avec la personnalité, Paris, 1932.

275   Jacques LACAN, Fonction et champ de la parole et du langage en psychanalyse (Rapport au Congrès de Rome), 1953.

276   Victor LAFITTE, Former humainement les circonstances, *La Raison*, no. 1.

277   René LAFORGUE, A propos de la frigidité de la femme, *Revue française de Psychanalyse*, 1935.

278   Daniel LAGACHE, Deuil maniaque, La Semaine des Hôpitaux de Paris, January 1958.

279   Daniel LAGACHE, Les hallucinations verbales et la parole, Paris, Alcan, 1934.

280   Daniel LAGACHE, Intervention au symposium sur les états dépressifs, *L'Evolution Psychiatrique*, July–September 1955.

281 Daniel LAGACHE, Le travail du deuil (Ethnologie et Psychanalyse), *Revue française de Psychanalyse*, no. 1, 1938.

282 Daniel LAGACHE, Psychanalyse et psychologie, *L'Evolution Psychiatrique*, 1956, fasc. 1.

284 Daniel LAGACHE, Structure et psychologie (colloquium on the concept of «structure»), January 1958.

285 Charles LALO, l'Art et la Morale, Paris, 1934.

286 Georges LANTERI-LAURA, Philosophie phénoménologique to psychatrie, *L'Evolution Psychiatrique*, October–December 1957.

287 H. LASSWELL, N. LEITES, *et al.*, Language of politics, New York, 1949.

288 Harold D. LASSWELL, Psychopathology and politics, in «The political writings of H. D. Lasswell», 1951, The *Free Press*, Glencoe.

289 Owen LATTIMORE, Ordeal by Slander, Boston, 1950.

290 Gustave LE BON, Psychologie des foules, Paris, 1947.

291 Gustave LE BON, La vie des vérités, Paris, 1914.

292 S. LEBOVICI, Approche psycho-dynamique, et psychothérapique dans la schizophrénie infantile, *Revue de Neuropsychiatrie infantile et d'hygiène mentale de l'enfance*, November–December 1956.

293 Maurice LECONTE, L'agonie des maladies mentales entitées: feu la psychasténie, *La Semaine des Hôpitaux*, May 1955.

294 Henri LEFEBVRE, La notion de totalité, *Cahiers internationaux de Sociologie*, 1955.

295 Henri LEFEBVRE, Le matérialisme dialectique, Paris, 1939.

296 Henri LEFEBVRE, La philosophie de G. Lukács, Conférence à l'Institut hongrois de Paris, 8 June 1955.

297 Henri LEFEBVRE, Les problèmes actuels du marxisme, Paris, 1958.

298 Henri LEFEBVRE, Une discussion philosophique en U.R.S.S.: logique formelle ou logique dialectique, *La Pensée*, January–February 1955.

299 Henri LEFEBVRE, Critique de la vie quotidienne, Paris, 1947.

300 Claude LEFORT, L'aliénation comme concept sociologique, *Cahiers internationaux de Sociologie*, Vol. 18, 1955.

301 Ernst LEWALTER, Wissenssoziologie und Marxismus, *Archiv f. Sozialwissenschaft u. Sozialpolitik*, 1934 (60).

302 William T. LHAMOND and Sanford GOLDSTONE, The time sense (estimation of one second duration by schizophrenic patients), *Archives of Neurology and Psychiatry*, Vol. 76, December 1956.

303 Jean LHERMITTE, Gabrielle LÉVY et N. KYRIAKE, Les perturbations de la représentation spatiale chez les apraxiques: à propos de deux cas cliniques d'apraxie, *Revue neurologique*, 1925.

304 David LIBERMAN, Acerca de la percepcion del tiempo, *Revista de Psicoanalisis* (Argentine), July–September 1955.

305 Paul LIGETI, Der Weg aus dem Chaos (Eine Deutung des Weltgeschehens aus dem Rythmus der Kunstentwicklung), Munich, 1931.

306 Rodolphe LOEWENSTEIN, Psychanalyse de l'antisémitisme, Paris, 1952.

307 A. LORIA, La sociologia, il suo compito, le sue scuole, i sui recenti progressi, Verona, 1901.

308 Fanny LOWTZKY, Kierkegaard, Etude psychanalytique, *Revue française de Psychanalyse*, Tome IX, no. 2, 1935.

309 Georges LUKÁCS, Geschichte und Klassenbewusstsein, Berlin, 1923. (French translation by K. Axelos and J. Bois, Paris, Editions de Minuit, 1960.)

310 Georges LUKÁCS, Die Zerstörung der Vernunft, Berlin, 1955.

311 Georges LUKÁCS, Existentialisme ou marxisme, 1948.

312 J. MALLET, Hystérie de conversion, *Encyclopédie Médico-chirurgicale* (Psychiatrie), t. 2.

313 Karl MANNHEIM, Essays on sociology and social psychology, London, 1953.

314 Karl MANNHEIM, Historismus, *Archiv f. Sozialwissenschaft u. Sozialpolitik*, 1924.

315 Karl MANNHEIM, Ideologie u. Utopie (German edn.), Bonn, 1929.

316 Karl MANNHEIM, Ideologie and Utopia, English trans. by Wirth & Shils, London, 1936.

317 Jacques MAQUET, Sociologie de la connaissance, sa structure et ses rapports avec la philosophie de la connaissance. Etude critique des systèmes de Karl Mannheim et de Pitirim A. Sorokin (Louvain, 1949).

318 Gabriel MARCEL, Etre et Avoir, Paris, 1935.

319 Gabriel MARCEL, Les hommes contre l'humain, Paris, 1951.

320 K. MARX, Misère de la Philosophie, Paris, Editions Sociales, 1947.

321 K. MARX and Friedrich ENGELS, Etudes Philosophiques, Paris, 1951.

322 Paul MATUSSEK, Untersuchungen über die Wahnwahrnehmung. 1. Veränderungen der Wahrnehmungswelt bei beginnendem, primären Wahn, *Archiv für Psychiatrie und Nervenkrankheiten vereinigt mit Zeitschrift für die gesamte Neurologie und Psychiatrie*, T. 189, fasc. 4, 1952.

323 Paul MATUSSEK, Untersuchungen über die Wahnwahrnehmung. 2. Die auf einem abnormen Vorrang von Wesenseigenschaften beruhenden Eigentümlichkeiten der Wahnwahrnehmung, *Schweizer Archiv für Neurologie und Psychiatrie*, T. 71, fasc. 1–2, 1953.

324 Paul MATUSSEK, Freud und die gegenwärtige Psychiatrie, *Fortschritte der Neurologie, Psychiatrie und ihrer Grenzgebiete*, 24, fasc. 10, 1956.

325 G. MAUCO, La psychologie de l'enfant dans ses rapports avec la psychologie de l'inconscient (d'après les travaux de Freud et de Piaget), *Revue français de Psychanalyse*, 1935.

326 Robert MEIGNIEZ, L'univers de la culpabilité (Réflexions sur les bases du stalinisme intellectuel en Europe), *Psyché*, Paris, April 1952.

327 Frederic MEINERTZ, Was ist inadäquat bei der Schizophrenie? *Der Nervenarzt*, June 1955.

328 M. MERLEAU-PONTY, Les aventures de la dialectique, Paris, 1955.

329 M. MERLEAU-PONTY, Humanisme et Terreur, Paris, 1947.

330 M. MERLEAU-PONTY, La phénoménologie de la perception, Paris, 1945.

331 E. MEYERSON, Du cheminement de la pensée, Paris, 1931.

332 I. MEYERSON and M. DAMBUYANT, Un type de raisonnement de justification, *Journal de Psychologie*, October–December 1946.

333 H. MIGNOT et J. GABEL, Contribution à la question de la validité du test de Szondi, *Revue de Psychologie Appliquée*, January 1952.

334 F. MINKOWSKA, A la recherche du monde des formes: de Van Gogh à Seurat et aux dessins d'enfant, Paris, 1949.

335 E. MINKOWSKI, A propos de la réalisation. Problèmes de l'existence et hygiène mentale, *Revue Suisse d'Hygiène*, 1946.

336 E. MINKOWSKI, Bergson's conceptions as applied to psychopathology, *Journal of Nervous and Mental Disease*, 1926.

337 E. MINKOWSKI, Espace, Intimité, Habitat, in *Situation*. (Contributions à la psychologie et à la psychopathologie phénoménologiques), Utrecht-Antwerpen (Spectrum), 1954.

338 E. MINKOWSKI, L'anesthésie affective, *Annales Médico-Psychologiques*, 1946.

339 E. MINKOWSKI, La réalité et les fonctions de l'irréel (Le troisième monde), *Evolution Psychiatrique*, 1950, no. 1.

340 E. MINKOWSKI, La Schizophrénie, Paris, Payot, 1927, Desclée de Brouwer, 1955.

341 E. MINKOWSKI, L'atteinte schizophrénique, *Giornale di Psichiatria e di Neuropatologia*, 1953.

342 E. MINKOWSKI, Le problème des hallucinations et le problème de l'espace, *Evolution Psychiatrique*, 1952 (reproduced in «Le Temps Vécu»).

343 E. MINKOWSKI, Le Temps Vécu (Etudes phénoménologiques et psychopathologiques), Paris, 1933.

344 E. MINKOWSKI, Les conséquences psychopathologiques de la guerre et du nazisme, *Archives suisses neuro-psychiatriques*, 1948.

345 E. MINKOWSKI, Les notions bleulériennes. Voies d'accès aux analyses phénoménologiques et existentielles, *Annales Médico-Psychologiques*, 1957.

346 E. MINKOWSKI, Névroses animales et psychiatrie humaine, *L'Encéphale*, 1957.

347 E. MINKOWSKI, Phénoménologie et analyse existentielle en psychopathologie, *L'Evolution Psychiatrique*, 1948.

348 E. MINKOWSKI, Psychopathologie et Philosophie, Milan, 1952 (Extract from «Archivio di Filosofia»).

349 E. MINKOWSKI and P. CITROME, Schizophrénie? (clinical observation), *Annales Médico-Psychologiques*, December 1953.

350 E. MINKOWSKI and E. TISON, Considérations sur la psychopathologie comparée des schizophrènes et des paralytiques généraux, *Journal de Psychologie*, October 1924.

351 Arnold H. MODELL, Some recent psychoanalytical theories of schizophrenia, *The Psychoanalytic Review*, April 1956.

352 John MOFFATT-MECKLIN, Le Ku-Klux-Klan, Paris Payot, 1934.

353 Jules MONNEROT, Sociologie du Communisme, Paris, 1949.

354 Marcel MONTASSUT, La constitution paranoïaque, Thèse, Paris, 1924.

355 E. MORIN, L'heure zéro des intellectuels du parti communiste français, *France-Observateur* (7), no. 337, October 1956, pp. 18–20.

356 S. MOSCOVICI, Logique et langage dans la propagande: quelques résultats, *Bulletin de Psychologie*, April 1955, Paris.

357 Henri MOUGIN, La sainte famille existentialiste, Paris, 1947.

358 E. MOUNIER, On demande un psychiatre, *Esprit*, January 1950.

359 E. MOUNIER, Qu'est-ce que le personnalisme? Paris, 1946.

360 Christian MULLER, Der Ubergang von Zwangsneurose

in Schizophrenic im Lichte der Katamnese, *Schweizer Archiv für Neurologie und Psychiatrie* (72), 1953.

361 C. MULLER, M. BURNER et J. L. VILLA, Hystérie ou schizophrénie, contribution au diagnostic différentiel, *L'Encéphale*, no. 3, 1956.

362 S. MULLER, Uber die Beziehungen der Pseudologia phantastica zu den schizophrenen Psychosen, Basel, 1942 (Thesis).

363 H. MULLER-SUUR, Der Psychopathologische Aspekt des Schizophrenieproblems, *Archiv f. Psychiatrie u. Nervenkrankheiten vereinigt mit Zeitschrift. f. die gesamte Neurologie u. Psychiatrie* (193), 1955.

364 Maurice NADEAU, Histoire du Surréalisme, Paris, 1945.

365 Georges NADOR, Napjaink, szofisztikaja. Az imperialiste korszak hamis burzsoa gondolkodàsànak logikai elemzéséhez (La sophistique contemporaine. Contribution à l'analyse logique de la fausse pensée de la bourgeoisie), *Filozofiai Evkönyv* (Annales de la Philosophie (1)), Budapest, 1952.

366 André NEMETH, Kafka ou le mystère juif, Paris, 1947.

367 Gérard de NERVAL, Aurélia, Paris, 1942.

368 C. P. OBERNDORF, Time, its relation to reality and purpose, *Psychoanal. Review*, 1941.

369 André OMBREDANE, L'aphasie et l'élaboration de la pensée explicite, Paris, 1951.

370 André OMBREDANE, Le problème de l'aphasie (Conférences de l'Institut linguistique de l'Université de Paris), 1939.

371 Marvin E. OPLER, Culture, Psychiatry and Human Values, Springfield, 1956.

372 M. OPPENCHAIM, Aspects hébreux de la psychologie du Temps, *Revue d'Histoire de la Médecine Hébraïque*, July 1937.

373 Franz OPPENHEIMER, Der Staat, Frankfurt, 1907.

374 R. OTTO, Le Sacré, Paris, 1949.

375 C. A. PALLIS, Impaired identification of faces and places with agnosia for colours, *Journal of Neurology, Neurosurgery and Psychiatry*, Vol. 18, 1955.

376 Gisèle PANKOW, Structuration dynamique dans la schizophrénie, *Revue suisse de Psychologie*, suppl. no. 27, Berne, 1956.

377 G. PARCHEMINEY, Critique de la notion d'hystérie de conversion, *L'Evolution Psychiatrique*, January–March 1949.

378 G. PARCHEMINEY, Le problème de l'histérie, *Revue française de Psychanalyse*, 1935.

379 Ernst PARELL, Was ist Klassenbewusstsein, *Politisch-psychologische Schriftenreihe*, no. 1, Copenhagen, 1934.

380 V. PARETO, Traité de sociologie générale, Paris, 1917–1919.

381 PARODI, Les bases psychologiques de la vie morale, Paris, 1928.

382 Jean PAULHAN, Entretiens sur des faits divers, Paris, 1945.

383 A. PERELMANN, Zur Frage der Verwandschaft zwischen Hysterie und Schizophrenie, *Zeitschrift für die gesamte Neurologie und Psychiatrie* (100), 1926.

384 J. Perez VILLAMIL, La piretoterapie no malarica en diversas formas de esquizofrenia y estudio de las reacciones de la microglia a variados agentes piretoterapicos (Thesis for the doctorate in Medicine), Santiago, 1931.

385 Jean PIAGET, Le développement de la notion du temps chez l'enfant, Paris, 1946.

386 Jean PIAGET, Le jugement moral chez l'enfant, Paris, 1957.

387 Jean PIAGET, La psychologie de l'intelligence, Paris, 1947.

388 Jean PIAGET, Pensée égocentrique et pensée sociocentrique, *Cahiers internationaux de Sociologie*, 1951.

389 G. Plechanow, Beiträge zur Geschichte des Materialismus, Holbach, Helvetius, Marx, Stuttgart, 1900.

390 Raymond POLIN, La création des valeurs, Paris, P.U.F., 1944.

391 R. QUENEAU, Saint Glinglin, Paris, 1948.

392 P. C. RACAMIER, Hystérie et Théâtre, *Entretiens Psychiatriques* (Cercle Henri Ey), Paris, 1952.

393 P. C. RACAMIER, Troubles de la sémantique (Aliénation du langage), *Encyclopédie Médico-Chirurgicale*, Psychiatrie, t. 1.

394 A. RASCOVSKY, *et al.*, Integracion de la interpretacion en los niveles perorales, *Revista de psicoanalisis*, Buenos Aires (14), no. 1-2, January–June 1957.

395 G. RATTRAY TAYLOR, Une interprétation sexuelle de l'histoire, Paris, 1954.

396 Harold L. RAUSCH, Object constancy in schizophrenia; the enhancement of symbolic objects and conceptual stability, *The Journal of Abnormal and Social Psychology*, March 1956.

397 Fritz REDL, The Psychoanalytic Study of Child, Vol. 1, London, 1945.

398 William REICH, La crise sexuelle, suivi de «Matérialisme dialectique et psychanalyse», Editions Sociales Internationales, Paris, 1934, collection «Problèmes».

399 William REICH, Mass-Psychology of Fascism, New York, 1946.

400 Suzanne REICHARD and Paul TILLMAN, Patterns of parent-child relationship in schizophrenia, *Psychiatry*, 1950.

401a Salomon RESNIK, Sindrome de Cotard y depersonalización, *Revista de Psicoanalisis*, Buenos Aires (t. 12), no. 1, January–March 1955.

401b M. J. M. REYNEAU, Démence précoce et hystérie, Thesis, Bordeaux, 1905.

402 Paul RICŒUR, Vérité et Mensonge, *Esprit*, December 1951.

403 Paul RICŒUR, Histoire et Vérité, Paris, 1955.

404 Walter RIESE, Hughlings Jackson's Doctrine of Aphasia and its significance today, *The Journal of Nervous and Mental Disease* (122), July 1955.

405 Geza ROHEIM, Magic and Schizophrenia, New York, 1955.

406 H. ROSENFELD, Uber Partialdefekte bei Katatonie, *Monatsblatt für Psychiatrie u. Neurologie*, 1905.

407 Norman ROZENZWEIG, A mechanism in Schizophrenia, *Archives of Neurology and Psychiatry*, November 1955.

408 S. ROSENZWEIG and D. SHAKOW, Mirror Behaviour in schizophrenic and normal individuals, *Journal of Nervous and Mental Disease*, 1937.

409 R. RUYER, La philosophie des valeurs, Paris, 1952.

410 Gottfried SALOMON, Historischer materialismus und Ideologienlehre, *Jahrbuch f. Soziologie*, T. II, Karlsruhe, 1926.

411 D. de SAUGY, La tension internationale étudiée par les psychiatres, *La Semaine médicale professionnelle et médico-sociale*, 22 April 1956.

412 M. SCHACHTER, Trastornos de comportamiento de orden esquizofreniforme consecutivos a una meningitis tuberculose curada, *Revista Espanola de Pediatria*, September 1953.

413 David S. SCHECTER, M. SYMONDS and I. BERNSTEIN, Development of concept of time in children, *The Journal of Nervous and Mental Disease* (121), April 1955.

414 Max SCHELER, Die Wissensformen und die Gesellschaft, Leipzig, 1926.

415 Alexander von SCHELTING, Der Streit um die Wissenssoziologie, *Archiv f. Sozialwissenschaft u. Sozialpolitik*, 1929.

416 Ariane SCHOEN, Psychogenèse du ton affectif, *Recherches Sociologiques*, June 1955.

417 Jordan M. SCHER, Perceptions; Equivalence, Avoidance and Intrusion in Schizophrenia, *Archives of Neurology and Psychiatry* (77), February 1957.

418 P. SCHILDER, Psychoanalysis of space, *The International Journal of Psycho-Analysis*, 1935.

419 P. SCHILDER, Psychoanalytic remarks on Alice in Wonderland and Lewis Carroll, *Journal of Nervous and Mental Disease* (87), 1938.

420 Rudolf SCHLESINGER, Soviet legal theory, London, 1945.

421 B. SCHMITZ and A. GREEN, Le deuil maniaque (à propos d'un cas), *L'Evolution Psychiatrique*, January–March 1958.

422 C. SCHNEIDER, Beiträge zur Lehre von der Schizo-

phrenie I. Die Analyse der Störungen des inneren Erlebens Schizophrener, *Archiv f. Psychiatrie u. Nervenkrankheiten*, 1926 (73).

423 Camille SCHUVER, Kierkegaard et la répétition, *Volontés*, September–October 1938.

424 L. H. SEBILLOTTE, Notes sur Kafka, *L'Evolution Psychiatrique*, 1956.

425 M. A. SECHEHAYE, Introduction à une psychothérapie des schizophrènes, Paris, P.U.F., 1954.

426 M. A. SECHEHAYE, Journal d'un schizophrène, Paris, 1950.

427 Philibert SECRÉTAN, La destruction de la Raison, *Esprit*, April 1957.

428 Ignazio SILONE, Invitation à un examen de conscience, *l'Express*, 7 December 1956, suppl. to no. 285.

429 G. SIMMEL, Die Philosophie des Geldes, Leipzig, 1900.

430 P. SIVADON, Psychothérapie collective des mères de schizophrènes, *Annales Médico-Psychologiques* (113), no. 5, December 1955.

431 Manes SPERBER, La conception policière de l'Histoire, *Preuves*, February 1954.

432 H. STECK, La mentalité primitive des schizophrènes, *Premier Congrès mondial de Psychiatrie*, Paris, 1950.

433 Alfred STERN, La philosophie des valeurs, Regard sur les tendances actuelles en Allemagne, Paris, 1936.

434 Helmuth STOLZE, Das Obere Kreuz, Munchen, 1953.

435 Alfred STORCH, Das archaisch-primitive Erleben und Denken der Schizophrenen, Berlin, 1922.

436 Alfred STORCH and Gaspar KULENKAMPFF, Zum Verständnis des Weltuntergangs bei den Schizophrenen, *Der Nervenarzt*, March 1950.

437 E. STRAUSS, Vom Sinn der Sinne (Ein Beitrag zur Grundlegung der Psychologie), 2nd edn., Berlin-Göttingen-Heidelberg, 1956.

438 H. SULLIVAN, The language of schizophrenia, in «Language and Thought in Schizophrenia», 1951.

439 P. SZENDE, Verhüllung u. Enthüllung, Der Kampf der Ideologien in der Geschichte, Leipzig, 1922.

440 P. SZENDE, Soziologische Theorie der Abstraktion, *Archiv f. Sozialwissenschaft u. Sozialpolitik*, April 1923.

441 Jacob TAUBES, Theology and Political Theory, *Social Research*, no. 1, 1955.

442 Hubert TELLENBACH, Die Räumlichkeit der Melancholischen; über Veränderungen des Raumerlebens in der endogenen Melancholie, *Der Nervenarzt*, July 1956.

443 Hubert TELLENBACH, Zum Verständnis von Bewegungsweisen Melancholischer, *Der Nervenarzt*, January 1956.

444 A. THALHEIMER, Einführung in den dialektischen Materialismus, Wien-Berlin, 1928.

446 Clara THOMSON, Identification with the enemy and loss of the sense of self, *The Psychoanalytic Quarterly*, 1940.

447 Trude TIETZE, A study of mothers of schizophrenic patients, *Psychiatry*, 1949.

448 Fr. TOSQUELLES, Analyse d'une psychose aiguë, *L'Evolution Psychiatrique*, 1955.

449 Ferdinand TÖNNIES, Gesellschaft und Gemeinschaft, Leipzig, 1935.

450 Garfield TOURNEY and Jean J. PLAZAK, Evil eye in myth and schizophrenia, *The Psychiatry Quarterly*, July 1954.

451 Tristan TZARA, Le Surréalisme et l'après-guerre, Paris, 1947.

452 Roger VAILLAND, Le Surréalisme contre la révolution, Paris, 1948.

453 J. P. VALABREGA, Aux sources de la Psychanalyse, *Critique*, Paris, May 1956.

454 J. P. VALABREGA, Hypothèses concernant les rapports du malade et du médecin, *Psyche*, Paris, June–July 1952.

455 J. P. VALABREGA, Les théories psychosomatiques, Paris, 1954.

456 L. van der HORST, Psiquiatria y antropologia, *Actas Luso-Espanolas de Neurologia y Psiquiatria*, January 1956.

457 Georges VEDEL, Rôle des croyances économiques dans la vie politique, *Revue française de Science politique*, January–June 1951.

458 Jean VINCHON, Un schizophrène conscient, *Journal de Psychologie normale et pathologie*, 1923.

459 K. H. VOLKMANN-SCHLUCK, Bewusstsein und Dasein in Kafkas «Prozess», *Neue Rundschau*, fasc. 1, 1951.

460 A. de WAELHENS, La philosophie de Martin Heidegger, Louvain, 1942.

461 Jean WAHL, Les philosophies de l'existence, Paris, 1954.

462 Melwin WALLACE, Future time perspective in schizophrenia, *The Journal of Abnormal and Social Psychology*, March 1956.

463 J. WALLON, Mentalité primitive et psychologie de l'enfant, *Revue philosophique*, Paris, 1928.

464 Wellman W. WARNER, Sociology and Psychiatry, *The British Journal of Sociology*, September 1954.

465 Curt WEINSCHENK, Illusionen, Halluzinationen u. Wahnwahrnehmungen, *Archiv f. Psychiatrie u. Nervenkrankheiten vereinigt mit Zeitschrift f. die gesamte Neurologie u. Psychiatrie*, 1952.

466 Hans Jorg WEITBRECHT, Der Frage der Specifität psychopathologischer Symptome, *Fortschritte der Neurologie, Psychiatrie u. ihrer Grenzgebiete*, fasc. January 1957.

467 A. J. WESTERMAN-HOLSTIJN, Oral erotism in paraphrenia, *International Journal of Psycho-Analysis*, 1934, no. 15.

468 Hans E. WIECK, Zur allgemeinen Psychopathologie, *Fortschritte der Neurologie, Psychiatrie u. ihrer Grenzgebiete*, Year 25, January 1957.

469 E. WILLEMS, As dimensôes do tempo e espaco no desenvolvimento da sociologia, *Sociologia*, Sao Paulo, March 1954.

470 P. WILLEN, Le rire de l'autoritarisme, *Problèmes du communisme*, July–August 1955.

471 W. Th. WINKLER, Bericht uber den Verlauf einer psychotherapeutischen Behandlung bei einer an Katatonie leidenden Patientin, *Acta Psychotherapeutica Psychosomatica et Orthopaedagogica*, Bâle, 1957 (Vol. V, fasc. 2–4).

472 W. Th. WINKLER, Dynamische Phenomenologie der

Schizophrenien als Weg zur gezielten Psychotherapie, *Ztschr. f. Psychoth. und med. Psych.*, 1955, fasc. 5.

473 Richard WOLF, Das Raum und Zeiterleben unter abnormen Bedingungen besonders im Meskalinrausch, *Deutsche Medizinische Wochenschrift* (77), no. 6, February 1952.

474 Joseph WORTIS, Soviet Psychiatry, Baltimore, 1950.

475 Jacob WYRSCH, Los limites de la esquizofrenia, *Actas Luso-Espanolas de Neurologia y Psiquiatria*, May 1952.

476 Jacob WYRSCH, Die Person des Schizophrenen, Berne, 1949.

477 Heinz O. ZIEGLER, Ideologienlehre, *Archiv für Sozialwissenschaft und Sozialpolitik*, 1927.

478 Victor ZOLTOWSKI, La fonction sociale du Temps et de l'Espace; contribution à une théorie expérimentale de la connaissance, *Revue d'Histoire Economique et Sociale*, Vol. 26, Year 2, 1947.

479 V. ZOLTOWSKI, Les cycles de la création intellectuelle et artistique, *L'Année Sociologique*, 1952, Paris.

480 K. ZUCKER, Funktionsanalyse in der Schizophrenie, *Archiv f. Psychiatrie*, 1939.

481 Jurg ZUTT, Der aesthetische Erlebnissbereich und seine krankhaften Abwandlungen, *Der Nervenarzt* (23), 1952.

482 Jurg ZUTT, Der Lebensweg als Bild der Geschichtlichkeit. Ueber Krisen auf dem Lebensweg, *Der Nervenarzt* (25), 1954.

483 Jurg ZUTT, Die innere Haltung, Eine psychopatologische Untersuchung und ihre Bedeutung für die Psychopathologie insbesondere im Bereich schizophrener Erkrankungen, *Monatsschrift für Psychiatrie* (73–74), 1929.

484 Jurg ZUTT, Gedanken über die menschliche Bewegung als mögliche Grundlage für das Verständnis der Bewegungsstörungen bei Geisteskranken, *Der Nervenarzt* (28), January 1957.

485 Jurg ZUTT, Uber Daseinsordnungen, Ihre Bedeutung für die Psychiatrie, *Der Nervenarzt*, Year 24, fasc. 5, May 1953.

486 K. AXELOS, Marx penseur de la technique, Paris, Editions de Minuit (Collection «Arguments»), Paris, 1961.

487 I. A. CARUSO, Die Verdinglichung, Gedanken zu «La

Fausse Conscience: Essai sur la Réification». *Jahrbuch fur Psychologie Psychoterapie und medizinische Anthropologie*, Year 9, 1962, pp. 319–26.

488 I. A. CARUSO, Note sur la nécessité et l'ambivalence de l'aliénation, *Bulletin de Psychologie*, 5 November 1960, pp. 29–32.

489 I. A. CARUSO, Psychanalyse et synthèse personnelle (Desclée de Brouwer), Paris, 1959.

490 I. A. CARUSO, Psychanalyse pour la personne (Seuil), Paris, 1962.

491 I. A. CARUSO, Soziale Aspekte der Psychoanalyse (Ernst Klett Verlag), Stuttgart, 1962.

492 Fr. FEJTO, Qu'est-ce que le révisionnisme moderne? *France-Forum*, November 1960.

493 Fr. GANTHERET, L'Image du Corps. Thèse de Doctorat en Psychologie, Paris, 1962. (In manuscript.)

494 L. GOLDMANN, Conscience réelle et conscience possible; conscience adéquate et fausse conscience, *Actes du Quatrième Congrès de Sociologie* (Milan-Stresa), September 1959, Vol. 4.

495 G. GURVITCH, Sociologie et dialectique (Flammarion), Paris, 1962.

496 Jean LACROIX, La Fausse Conscience, *Le Monde*, 9 April 1963, p. 11.

497 G. LAPASSADE, L'Entrée dans la Vie, Editions de Minuit (Collection «Arguments»), Paris, 1963.

498 H. LEFEBVRE and N. GUTERMAN, La Conscience mystifiée, N.R.F. (Coll. «Les Essais»), Paris, 1936.

499 E. MORIN, L'Esprit du Temps. Essai sur la culture de masse (Bernard Grasset), Paris, 1962.

500 K. PAPAIOANNOU, Marx et la critique de l'idéologie, *Preuves*, February 1963, pp. 24–35.

501 R. PARIS, Aujourd'hui comme hier: que vaut la fausse conscience comme concept opératoire? *Annales E.S.C.*, no. 3, 1963.

502 R. PARIS, Histoire due fascisme en Italie. I. Des origines à la prise du pouvoir, Maspero (Les «Cahiers Libres», nos. 37–38), Paris, 1962.